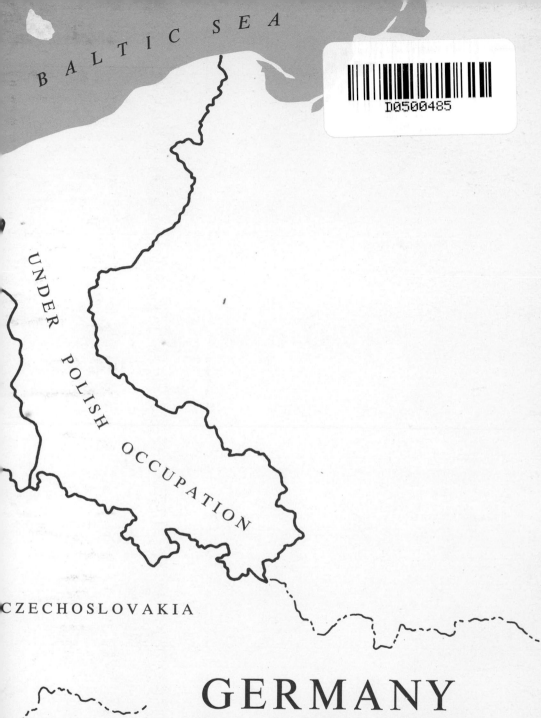

BALTIC SEA

UNDER POLISH OCCUPATION

CZECHOSLOVAKIA

USTRIA

GERMANY
Zones of Occupation
1946

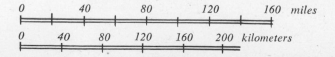

| 0 | 40 | 80 | 120 | 160 miles |

| 0 | 40 | 80 | 120 | 160 | 200 kilometers |

THE FOURTH
AND RICHEST
REICH

THE FOURTH AND RICHEST REICH

EDWIN HARTRICH

MACMILLAN PUBLISHING CO., INC.
New York

COLLIER MACMILLAN PUBLISHERS
London

Macmillan Publishing Co., Inc.
866 Third Avenue, New York, N.Y. 10022
Collier Macmillan Canada, Ltd.

———————

Library of Congress Cataloging in Publication Data
Hartrich, Edwin.
The Fourth and richest Reich.
Includes bibliographical references and index.
1. Germany, West—Politics and government.
2. Germany, West—Economic conditions. 3. Germany—
History—Allied occupation, 1945–   I. Title.
DD259.4.H35   943.087   79-26058
ISBN 0-02-548480-X

———————

FIRST PRINTING 1980

Designed by Jack Meserole

Printed in the United States of America

To "Red" with love

Contents

Contents

Foreword

I have seen many different faces of contemporary Germany. The variety and sharp contrasts of these images of the restless, energetic, and sometimes schizophrenic nation which has dominated European history in modern times fascinated me and led ultimately to the writing of this book.

As a young American visitor I witnessed the last chaotic days of the Weimar Republic in the autumn and winter of 1932–33, just prior to Hitler's takeover of the German Republic and the beginning of the "thousand-year Reich" that was to last for only twelve years. This was a time when thousands of jobless workers went hungry and hopeless in the cruel pinch of the Great Depression and savage street fighting took place between the Nazi storm troopers and the *Rotfront* bullyboys of the Communist party for political control of the great seaport of Hamburg; I was left with vivid memories of my first encounter with Germany and its people.

My next memory of Germany in action was also tinged with violence. While working as a U.S. journalist, I was pinned down in the tulip fields of Holland when a German parachute battalion dropped from the skies in a surprise attack on The Hague, capital of the Netherlands. It was early in the morning of May 10, 1940 during the opening phase of Hitler's unprovoked *Blitzkrieg* of the Low Countries.

After the five-day conquest of Holland I moved to Berlin. I remained there during the summer when Nazi armies planted Nazi flags from the Atlantic coast to the Bug River in eastern Poland. From a room in the Adlon Hotel overlooking the cheering crowds on the Unter den Linden, I saw the first and only victory parade ever staged in Berlin by the Third Reich. The last time German troops had marched in triumph through the Brandenburg Gate was in 1871, returning from another victorious war against France. After that festive July 18, 1940, the tide began to turn against Nazi Germany, but so imperceptibly that the war was to continue unabated for another four years.

Later I saw at firsthand the face of Germany in combat, this time as a soldier in the U.S. Army. I learned to respect and to fear the fighting expertise of the German soldier when my 44th Infantry Division and the 17th SS Panzer Grenadier Division confronted each other in 144 days of consecutive action. However, once the Rhine was crossed, the fighting gradually petered out.

My next view was the face of Germany in surrender, a sharp contrast

ix

to the memories of 1940. As my division advanced through the lovely springtime landscapes of Swabia and Bavaria, the towns and villages signaled their capitulation by displaying white flags from every house and shop. The war was finally over for them.

Then came military occupation and rule by the victorious Allied forces, with defeated Germany lying broken and prostrate at their feet. I returned to Germany again as a journalist for the *New York Herald Tribune*. In company with other observers, we concentrated our professional attention on the plans and operations of the Allied military governments. We paid scant attention to the surviving Germans, who, in our estimation, had no place in the postwar world except as citizens of a third- or fourth-rate power stripped of virtually all military, political, and economic powers and assets.

In those early days after World War II, Germany was a pariah in the community of nations. The defeated enemy was to be punished for the casualties and damages inflicted on the victims of Hitler's aggressive warmaking; it was to be "reformed" as the price for its continued survival, but at a very reduced standard of living. The Allied plans for defeated Germany were harsh and draconian; the first three years after the war were, in the words of the *Economist* of London, "utter economic hell." This period was probably the lowest point for the German people since the Thirty Years War of the seventeenth century.

The swift and widespread repair and reconstruction that followed the currency reform in June 1948, therefore, came as a dramatic surprise to all of us who had been living in Germany since the shooting stopped. We had underestimated the resiliency of the German and his capacity to survive and to rebuild his shattered life on the ruins of his former existence. Sixty million surviving Germans, substantially assisted by a fortuituous combination of time, circumstances, and personalities, plus the unexpected advent of the cold war, were able to climb out of the abyss of defeat and devastation and, in the short span of a generation, transform their country into the economic superpower of postwar Europe.

I have lived with this development from the time of its inception and through the successive stages that led to West Germany's emergence as the strongest and most viable power of the European community—fully sovereign, politically independent, and the military ally of the United States of America. But this all resulted from the West German economic comeback as "the machine shop" of not only Europe, but also of the world at large.

Today the Germans have finally achieved the *Lebensraum* for their restless energies, ambitions, and talents, which they failed to conquer in the aggressive Second and Third Reichs. Today the West Germans have a new *Lebensraum* in the expanding global markets for their modern goods and services; they have become the number two trading nation of the world, affluent beyond any dreams and expectations of those of us who had known the other Germanies of the twentieth century.

Initially as an American journalist and later as an independent industrial consultant to many German firms, including Friedrich Krupp of Essen, Friedrich Flick K. G., and Willy H. Schlieker, the original of the *Wirtschaftswunderkinder,* I have enjoyed a small degree of participation in the creation of this new postwar Germany. In this book I have tried to explain how it all came about.

EDWIN HARTRICH

Orland Park, Illinois
February, 1980

THE FOURTH
AND RICHEST
REICH

Prologue

The German Reich has been built more truly on coal and iron than on blood and iron.

—JOHN MAYNARD KEYNES

Today economic power holds the place that infantry divisions held under the Kaiser.

—FRANZ JOSEF STRAUSS,
Finance Minister, 1966 to 1969

"WIRTSCHAFT ÜBER ALLES!"

One morning in July 1948 two men faced each other across the broad expanse of a large mahogany desk in the office of the former chairman of I. G. Farben. In a curious fashion, both men were intruders. The former occupant of this impressive executive suite, Karl Krauch, the last chief executive of the great German chemical trust, was at that time behind bars in Landsberg prison as a convicted Nazi war criminal. His chair and office were now occupied by America's proconsul in Germany, Gen. Lucius D. Clay, military governor of the U.S. occupation zone. The giant I. G. Farben building on the northern outskirts of Frankfurt had been requisitioned to serve as the headquarters for the U.S. armed forces in Europe. It was better known in army circles as the "European Pentagon."

The two men conferring in Herr Krauch's spacious and luxuriously furnished office could hardly have been more dissimilar. General Clay was lean, crisp, and authoritarian. He spoke briefly and to the point, sitting ramrod-straight in his leather-backed chair, occasionally making a note on a yellow scratch pad, chain-smoking Chesterfield cigarettes. He was the embodiment of a top-ranking staff officer of the U.S. Army.

Opposite the general sat a pink-complexioned, cherubic-faced, blond German, smoking a black cigar in a paper holder. His baggy suit was rumpled and his tie slightly askew, but he was concerned with matters of greater substance than his appearance. He was Prof. Ludwig Erhard, chairman of the Economic Council of Bizonia, the embryonic government of the emerging West German state. Gesturing with his cigar, Professor Erhard spoke earnestly in the soft accents of his native Franconia.

Professor Erhard, the ranking German official in the bizonal administration of the British and American occupation zones, had been summoned to this meeting by General Clay to answer for an action he had taken on his own initiative. Professor Erhard had just abolished the rationing of food and other essentials and had wiped out all wage and price controls. In effect, he was legitimatizing the law of supply and demand that governed the widespread and flourishing black market in every West German city and town. This action appeared to undermine the whole economy of West Germany at a time when the cold war was a continuing threat to its political existence.

General Clay quickly came to the heart of the matter. He addressed the German official opposite him: "Herr Erhard, my advisers tell me that what you have done is a terrible mistake. What do you say to that?"

The German reply came swiftly and without hesitation: "Herr General, pay no attention to them! My own advisers tell me the same thing."

With this exchange, Professor Erhard launched into a persuasive sales pitch for his economic program to revive the defeated and bankrupt West Germany. He identified it as the *Soziale Marktwirtschaft,* translatable as a "socially responsive free-market economy"; in other words, "capitalism with a conscience." In this meeting the arguments of the Bavarian professor won over the West Point engineer; he came away with the stamp of approval of the U.S. military governor for the abrupt termination of all rationing and wage and price controls.

This Clay-Erhard conference was undoubtedly the most fateful event in the history of postwar Germany. It set the character and form of the Federal Republic of Germany that was shortly to be launched on the European scene. Twenty-five years later, marking the anniversary of this history-making encounter, the national daily newspaper, *Die Welt,* editorialized:

This dramatic discussion in Frankfurt in the early summer of 1948 marked the hour of·birth of the free market economy in this country, and therefore the actual beginning of what has been described as the *Wirtschaftswunder*—the "economic miracle."

From this moment on, West Germany began to climb out of the abyss into which it had fallen at the end of World War II. It seems like an accident of history that, in the face of widespread doubts and opposition, Professor Erhard almost single-handedly grafted his economic philosophy on the fledgling West German state; this hybrid took root, blossomed, and bore fruit—a veritable cornucopia beyond compare. In the following quarter-century, *Soziale Marktwirtschaft* transformed the infant West German republic into the third-ranking economic power in the world, after the U.S. and the Soviet Union, as well as making it the richest state in terms of billions of reserves in gold and dollars.* Professor Erhard's formula for capitalism with a conscience, which involves giving a larger slice of the national pie to the masses than is the case in most capitalist economies, has proven to be the greatest producer of wealth, modern technology, and womb-to-tomb social security of any ideology or political system practiced since the start in Europe of the Industrial Revolution of the nineteenth century. It has produced capitalism's "finest hour" and inflicted the decisive defeat of Marxian socialism in the land of its birth; it is the biggest success story of the twentieth century.

In 1961, *Fortune* magazine described the Federal (West) German Republic, which had been a sovereign nation for more than a decade, as "an economy which had not yet become a full-fledged state." As late as 1975, *The New York Times* repeated the often-published simile that West Germany was "economically a giant, but politically a dwarf." This image-making by very reputable international publications has left an impression on the world that this comparatively new and young state has made its debut on the international scene as some sort of a mongoloid body politic by its sudden transformation into an economic colossus. However, this is a distorted reflection of something quite different. Instead of being a misshapen country lacking the balance and other attributes of a modern nation, we find a unique creation formed and conditioned by its time and the circumstances of its birth: the first modern *eco-political* state of the twentieth century.* It is another important result of the Clay–Erhard meeting in Frankfurt, in July 1948.

If, in the light of modern European history, postwar West Germany seems to be somewhat lopsided in its physical makeup and character, that is due to the fact that it operates according to a different set of values and goals than the other continental nations. This eco-political West Germany is governed by the basic principle that its economic strength and resources, not its military muscle, are the true measure of its power and influence on the world scene today. In practice, economic considerations generally take precedence over political affairs at home and abroad, not the reverse, as is the case with most modern industrial states. Confirmation of this unusual policy line is repeatedly found in the words and actions of the chancellors of the Federal Republic, conservative or Social Democrat alike. For example, in a interview in February 1975 in the Swiss journal *Finanz und Wirtschaft,* Chancellor Helmut Schmidt put it simply and explicitly. He said: "For some years now our economic policy has simultaneously been our *foreign policy.*" (*"Unsere ökonomische Politik ist schon seit Jahren zugleich Aussenpolitik gewesen."*)

Note the specific commitment: Bonn's foreign economic policy has not been the basis of its foreign policy, but is the foreign policy itself.

Out of this eco-political rationale, West Germany has capitalized on its ability to be the machine shop of Europe, pouring out high-quality industrial goods and technology which can successfully compete in all the market places around the world. By becoming once again the number one industrial nation in Europe, West Germany's economic strength and resources serve to promote and to protect its legitimate self-interests more assuredly than the possession of a fleet of bombers or a stockpile of atomic weapons.

In the stormy decades before World War II, Germany sought to achieve its all-consuming ambition to be the dominant power on the European continent through the harsh imperatives of Bismarck's "blood and iron" foreign policy, Kaiser Wilhelm II's demand for a "place in the sun," and for Hitler's aggressive drive for more *Lebensraum* (living space). The Wilhelmstrasse, particularly in Hitler's time, was deeply influenced by the seductive appeals of geo-politics; this theory lays down the fundamental principle that the basic politics of a country are determined by its geographical location and features. Germany straddles Central Europe and its hegemony of the European continent could only become a reality through massive land-grabbing aggression, which assured its *Autarkie*—or economic self-sufficiency in the vital raw materials for industrial production and oil for its fuel and energy requirements. Hitler's "Operation Barbarossa"—the massive, three-pronged invasion of the Soviet Union in 1941— was aimed at capturing the Russian grain belt, the oil fields of the Caucasus, and ore deposits of the Donetz basin, and to be held and exploited solely for Nazi Germany's benefit. Therefore, geo-politics dictated that Germany's security could only be maintained by subduing or docilizing its neighbors to the east and west through military conquests or by political tactics.

However, in the short span of a generation, this new postwar Germany finds that it has unlimited *Lebensraum* in which to expand, as it marches to a different drummer. With its millions of Volkswagens, machine tools, locomotives, heavy-duty engineering equipment, machinery, motors, and other exports, it has established business bridgeheads in countries around the world more secure and more lasting than ever established by Hitler's millions of soldiers in their unsuccessful military conquests in Europe, Russia, and Africa.

This West Germany of today, a far larger and more complex industrially developed country than was Hitler's Third Reich, has also solved its problem of *Autarkie:* West Germany has easy and continued access to the raw materials and oil it needs to survive, because it can produce and supply the wide range of industrial and consumer goods and services that the countries with the raw materials and oil must have for their own economic development. In short, the German businessman has given proof of the validity of Emerson's maxim: "If you build a better mousetrap, the world will beat a path to your door."

Alone of the major industrial powers, West Germany consistently enjoys a favorable trade balance with the oil-producing states of the Middle East. Even though it is dependent on oil from the Persian Gulf for 75 percent of its daily fuel and energy consumption, West Germany has lifted this economic millstone from off its shoulders by earning more dollars for its exports to the OPEC bloc than it has to pay out for the river of oil that it imports from the Middle East.

This favorable trade situation can be maintained under the present circumstances because West Germany has the world's most modern and technologically advanced industrial capacity, which gives it a decisive competitive advantage over its European competitors in that market. Today West Germany has become the number two trading nation in the world, and is close on the heels of number one, the U.S. It has also become the dominant—even if it is not the dominating—power on the Continent by virtue of its superior economic capabilities and resources. Hence it is quite evident that eco-politics has succeeded in achieving for the Germans in this postwar era what geo-politics failed to accomplish in the days of Wilhelm II's *Kaiserreich* and Adolf Hitler's *Dritte Reich*.

Revolution is often preceded by a lost war. The Germany of Kaiser Wilhelm II and the Second Reich created by Bismarck lost World War I. The Armistice of November 11, 1918, was immediately followed by a bungled revolution which led to the establishment of the short-lived Weimar Republic. However, as history painfully teaches us, a revolution does not always generate the long-range social and political reforms that a nation needs—the lack of which probably contributed to the nation's defeat in the first place. In the turbulent fifteen years of the Weimar Republic, its harassed governments had to spend their time and energies fighting for survival and for their right to govern against *putsches,* armed rebellions, and other threats from both the militant right and left wings of the political spectrum.

The Republic succumbed to the intrigues of Adolf Hitler and his Nazi cohorts, who took power and began what was proclaimed to be the "thouand-year Reich." Within six years World War II had begun; it lasted for five years and ended with death tolls in the tens of millions of victims and a Europe devastated and pillaged from the Atlantic to the Volga.

Thus a lost war was followed by an aborted revolution, which in turn led to a second world war that also ended in defeat. But the ground was made fertile to germinate the seeds of major social, political, and economic changes and reforms. The Germans had suffered millions of casualties, as well as the loss of incalculable amounts of real and personal wealth and property, not to mention the damage to the moral and social character of their nation. They paid and will continue to pay a stiff price in the future to erase the shame of the Hitler years. However, the very magnitude of their losses of wealth and property surprisingly paid off in the dividends of reeducation and reform for the Federal Republic of Germany.

Instead of facing a revolution after being defeated in World War II— there was nobody to revolt against except the armed forces of the victorious Allies which would have snuffed out any spark of rebellion in a minute—a broken and divided Germany collapsed into a cataleptic state of suspended animation. The picture presented was discouraging. Surviving

Germans seemed to be existing in their ruined cities and towns in a trance, drained of all normal emotions. Apathy replaced anger; resignation replaced desire for revenge. The spirit of the people seemed on the verge of sputtering out like a dying candle. Was there any hope of recovery and rehabilitation for this pariah in the family of nations? The future was indeed bleak and foreboding.

After the collapse of the Third Reich at the end of World War II, the surviving Germans were collectively in a state of shock. They could not grasp all the reasons and causes to explain the violent and disastrous changes in their lives and fortunes. However, this they did know—viscerally, if not intellectually—that waging war is a very costly way of trying to make a living and to justify their existence as Germans. Losing two world wars only a quarter of a century apart brutally awakened their minds to new standards and values. The mystique of *Deutschland über Alles* vanished in the swirling dust and rubble of their war-gutted cities and towns; in the crowded hospitals where no pain-killing drugs were available for the hundreds of thousands of wounded and disabled; in the long queues of women in black waiting for their share of the dwindling rations; in the lack of coal to provide warmth against the bitter frost; in the lack of privacy as hundreds of thousands had to live jammed together in crowded rooms and air-raid shelters; in the loss of savings and pensions, now redeemable only in inflated and worthless *reichsmarks;* in the loss of work and income for the able-bodied, as the economic life slowed to a halt; and finally in having to face the bleak prospect that life would continue at this substandard level for months and years to come. These were the ugly realities that men and women tried to escape from with a few hours of sleep. But each morning they had to awaken to another day of coping with the same problems and same realities. But such bitter fare seemed to be the only recipe for the mass reeducation and reform of a nation that had been led down the garden path to disaster.

Yet we did not know or realize at the time that this was the gestation period for a new eco-political state which was soon to be born. The American and British military governors served in the roles of unwitting midwives to the *accouchement*. The infant *Bundesrepublik* learned to walk and talk; it also began to reveal characteristics of a mutant. Going through a relatively short adolescence in the eyes of foreign observers, it grew into an "economic giant," while paradoxically it remained a "political dwarf." However, with today's longer perspective, we see something quite unexpected; the new eco-political West Germany had made a clean break with its turbulent and Teutonic past, its traditions, characteristics, and outlook.

In evaluating its postwar standards of values and priorities, postwar West Germany, with its capital in the old university town of Bonn along the green banks of the Rhine, is light-years removed from the Germanies of Potsdam and Berlin. The Germans of today have rejected the "blood and iron" *Weltanschauung* of Bismarck and the *Lebensraum* muscle flexing

of Adolf Hitler's Third Reich in favor of a more prosaic, but more re-
warding, economic body-building of the *Soziale Marktwirtschaft,* as evan-
gelized by Adam Smith's twentieth-century disciple, Prof. Ludwig Erhard.

During World War II, as Hitler's Third Reich consolidated its military control of Europe—except for Switzerland, Sweden, Spain, and Portugal—anti-Nazi resistance movements began to flicker into life in response to
the harsh occupation rule of the dreaded SS organization. These underground factions were essentially political in character and objectives: they
labored ceaselessly to sabotage the Nazi occupation of their respective
countries and to hasten the day of complete military defeat of the Third
Reich.

However, there was one underground resistance group that was unique;
it was in Germany and it was essentially economic and not political in its
objectives. A small company of intellectuals and economists, centered in the
faculty of the University of Freiburg in Württemberg—a southwest corner
of Germany that is very un-Prussian in character—worked to restore a free-
market capitalism system that would replace the *Autarkie* and national
socialism of the Third Reich when it was brought down in ruins. This
capitalist cell inside the totalitarian economy of the Third Reich was led by
Prof. Walter Eucken and Prof. Wilhelm Röpke,* who introduced Professor
Erhard, then an economist, to the works and ideas of Adam Smith. Out
of this secret collaboration came the *Soziale Marktwirtschaft,* the "socially-
responsive free-market economy," which Professor Erhard was later to
impose on the embryonic West German state with the assistance of General Clay.

According to reliable press reports, Professor Erhard had established
a close personal contact with Karl Goerdler, mayor of Leipzig and one of
the key organizers of the July 20 plot to assassinate Hitler.* At Goerdler's
request, Erhard had drafted his recommendations for a postwar economic
policy for a Nazi-free Germany. Erhard had mailed the draft to Goerdler's
house in Leipzig, not knowing that the mayor was being hunted down by
the Gestapo. A naïve or kindly postman failed to deliver the incriminating
document to the Goerdler apartment, where the Gestapo sat waiting, and
returned it to Erhard with the notation: "Addressee moved." It was a nar-
row escape.

This economic philosophy can trace its origin directly back to Adam
Smith of Kirkcaldy, Scotland. It was Smith's historic study, *The Wealth of
Nations,* first published in 1776, that laid the foundations of modern
capitalism. The Scotsman's doctrine was to have a profound effect on German thinking in the nineteenth century, when the Reich began to emerge
from its pastoral adolescence to become the industrial giant of the European
continent at the turn of the twentieth century.

By the mid-nineteenth century, Karl Marx was publishing his anticapitalist *Communist Manifesto* in Cologne and Germany's industrialists and merchants were avidly reading Smith's *Wealth of Nations,* absorbing its doctrine of free-enterprise capitalism. They even had a name for this economic system, *Smithianissmus,* and widely accepted its tenets as the correct and workable formula for economic growth and prosperity.

After Napoleon's defeat at Waterloo, the influence of England on German thinking was strong and pervasive. As Britain's leading diplomatic historian, G. P. Gooch reported that "the doctrines of Adam Smith had steadily filtered into Germany" with the result that:

The rapid transformation of Germany from a geographical expression into the strongest military power of the world was scarcely more remarkable than the simultaneous change from homespun to purple and fine linen. Prosperity came to her, as power had come, with a rush. The nineteenth century dawned on a poor country and closed on a rich one. . . . The rapid accumulation of wealth in turn fortified the power of the state by promoting the industrial, commercial and colonial activities, from which modern nations in large measure derive their strength and prestige. . . . The founders of Germany's greatness were not statesmen and warriors alone, but were *chemists and bankers, inventors and shipowners, the lords of iron and the kings of coal.** [Italics added.]

At the close of the Napoleonic wars, Germany was a patchwork quilt of middle-sized and small kingdoms, smaller principalities, duchies, and minuscule fiefs of the lesser nobility. Each sought to function as if it were a sovereign state in its own right. Each supported itself in piecemeal fashion by what local taxes it could impose and collect from its middle classes and peasants, and on the tariffs levied on goods crossing its frontiers. For example, in 1818 in Prussia, the biggest kingdom, there were sixty-seven different tariff schedules. This profusion of customs barriers also existed in the other German states and resulted in an economic swamp and a stagnant commercial existence.

Then came Friedrich von Motz, the man who was to take the lead in achieving the economic unification of this political Noah's Ark. Von Motz, Prussia's finance minister, was among the first of the aristocratic elite to grasp the full implications of what England's Industrial Revolution (1760–1840) meant for Germany's future. He was no hidebound Junker type, but one of the few liberals in high government circles who was also an ardent advocate of Adam Smith's doctrines of free trade and of competitive enterprise. The finance minister could envisage the business-making potentials of the middle classes if they were given the freedom and the incentives to involve themselves in commerce and industry and the increased tax revenues from such activities that would flow into his treasury.

In 1829, von Motz set forth his proposal for a *Zollverein,* a customs union, between Prussia and the German states to the south. He argued persuasively that the elimination of the tangled skein of trade and tariff barriers could lead to a "truly united . . . and free Germany under the protection of Prussia." Five years later eighteen German states agreed to a customs union, and by 1850 virtually all the German states and principalities were members of the free trade pact and Europe's first "common market."

Next it was the turn of Friedrich List, the American consul in Leipzig, to make the major contribution to the economic unification of this embryonic German nation. List was born in Reutlingen, a small industrial town in Württemberg. He first attracted attention by organizing industrialists into associations in order to press for abolition of tariff barriers and other economic reforms. But the Württemberg government sent him into exile for his liberal views. List came to the U.S. in 1825, where he quickly took root by becoming a citizen, serving as an editor of a newspaper in Reading, Pennsylvania, and acquiring a fortune through his mining investments. He also made detailed surveys of America's expanding transportation system of railroads and canals, and built and operated a 21-mile railroad line in the Blue Ridge Mountains. In 1833 he returned to Germany as U.S. consul in Leipzig, bursting with energy and with economic plans and reforms "for the crippled child . . . that is my fatherland."

He saw that Germany must have an adequate and integrated transportation system if its commerce and industry were to develop their full potentials. He produced a master plan for a national railway network. As a result of List's unremitting efforts, by 1850 Germany had 5,800 kilometers (3,480 miles) of operational railway lines. By 1860 this trackage had doubled to 11,000 kilometers (6,600 miles). Railway development continued unabated until 1911 when expansion had reached the saturation point of 40,000 kilometers (24,000 miles). The railroads later merged into a national railway network, transforming Germany into an economic entity. The main lines tied the country together, but more importantly, they stimulated the growth of industry by facilitating the shipments of raw materials to the factories and their finished products to near and distant markets. Historian Gooch observed:

The immediate effect on national life was even more invigorating than in England and France. . . . List's program of the systematic exploitation of national resources was carried out with a resolution and skill in no way inferior to the simultaneous development of the United States.

England, which was more industrially advanced than Germany, was flooding the continent with its exports. German manufacturers were placed at a disadvantage and finally prevailed upon Bismarck to bring an end to free trade in 1879. The chancellor reinstated a protective tariff system. From that time on, Germany's industrial growth accelerated rapidly, so that in 1914, on the eve of World War I, it was out in front as the greatest industrial power on the Continent and swiftly overtook Great Britain as a supplier to the world's markets. Germany's GNP was increasing by 21.6 percent every decade, compared to Britain's 12.5 percent for the same period.* These formative years laid the groundwork for Germany's economic power, which was resilient enough to survive two destructive world conflicts. During the period from 1879 to 1914, to paraphrase the words of the late President Calvin Coolidge, "the business of Germany was business."

The influence of Adam Smith on postwar Germany is readily discernible. For example, the Kirkcaldy scholar reasoned that a free and untrammeled commerce and industry would best serve the interests of the nation and its citizenry because such a system would be based on a self-perpetuating and fundamental economic fact of life: man's own acquisitive instincts to seek after material gain for himself and his family. As Adam Smith said: ". . . by pursuing his own interests, the individual frequently promotes the interests of society more effectively than when he really intends to promote it."

Professor Erhard's admonition to the postwar Germans to "turn the money and the people loose and they will make the nation strong," was not so pedantic as Smith's dictum, but it carried the same message: only freedom and incentives can produce solid and continuing economic growth. The Bavarian economist was a pragmatic man in his approach to the problems of postwar Germany. He directed his efforts to harnessing together two of man's most basic instincts: self-survival, cost what it may; and man's insatiable appetite for personal gain in terms of money, property, and so on. With these two forces pulling in tandem, he was able to move his country out of the abyss of defeat and national bankruptcy onto the high and sunny plateau of world acceptability and prosperity.

Professor Erhard often described himself as an economic liberal. In speech after speech he was critical of *Dirigissmus*—his personal contribution to the postwar vocabulary—which meant heavy-handed government control and direction of the national economy, as in Hitler's time. In the early days of Bizonia and after the establishment of the Bonn government, Professor Erhard preached and fought for his free-market system—no controls whatsoever—with a messianic fervor. At the outset his economic remedies, so simple in their outlines as to seem ineffective, had a Utopian character. The effect of the Erhard doctrine on the daily economic life of West Germany, in the days and months after currency reform, tended to be obscured by the decisive impact of the new deutschemark on the marketplace, where the cost and quality of daily living could be easily measured. Much credit for Germany's amazing and swift recovery has been attributed to the currency reform of June 20, 1948, just a few days before Professor Erhard's proclamation that ended all rationing and price controls. However, to achieve any measure of economic recovery, these two measures had to be coordinated. Each by itself could not have accomplished much. Currency reform had come first, imposed arbitrarily on the West Germans by the Allied authorities by *force majeure*. But the new deutschemark, which was a fiat currency that did not have an ounce of gold or silver behind it, could not have ushered in a new and brighter day, if Professor Erhard had not decreed an end to all rationing and price controls. The two measures together restored the market place to its normal functions. The new deutschemark brought goods out of hoarding and back onto the store shelves. The end of rationing and price controls permitted the normal laws of supply and demand to operate, thus allowing the seller to adjust his prices according to the scarcity and value of the goods for sale. Finally, the fact that the new currency was accepted by the merchants in payment for goods gave the deutschemark its needed credibility and acceptance by the public.

Professor Erhard had also supplied the vital common denominator, in the incentive for gain, which immediately encouraged every able-bodied German to start repairing and reconstructing, to begin producing and profiting from his labors. Erhard had swept away virtually all the barriers. Now the individual German could sell his labor or his product at its true market value, not at what government bureaucrats said it was worth. Storekeepers stocked their shelves; manufacturers and workers were given incentive: the more time and energy the German citizen put into his labor, the greater were his rewards.

There were many American and British military government officials as well as German bureaucrats who predicted that Professor Erhard's free-market economy would bring chaos and food riots in the marketplace. On the first days after his proclamation, Erhard was beset by angry officials. One U.S. Army colonel demanded: "How dare you relax our rationing system, when there is a widespread food shortage?"

The German economic director of "Bizonia" replied: "But, Herr Oberst, I have not relaxed rationing; I have abolished it! Henceforth, the only rationing ticket the people will need will be the deutschemark. And they will work hard to get these deutschemarks, just wait and see."

This economic approach seemed too simple to be credible. Many Allied as well as German officials contended that what money and materials were available for repair or reconstruction should be rationed and allocated only for projects that appeared to benefit the greatest number of people. For example, this logic dictated that rebuilding a bombed railway bridge was more important than rebuilding a small shop. Professor Erhard argued that if a man wanted to spend his money, time, and energy to open up a barber shop or *Bierstube* (local pub), he should be free to do so. If these projects provided jobs for the unemployed, profits for the entrepreneur, and goods and services for which others would spend their money, then such projects were proportionately and collectively as important to the revival of the national economy as the rebuilding of a railway bridge or a power plant. Professor Erhard's objective was to encourage everybody to get back into business again; the more the merrier. Let everyone produce, buy, or sell as much as he could.

Professor Erhard's gospel of *Soziale Marktwirtschaft* did not meet with instant understanding or acceptance by the German politicians or the public. The postwar economic liberalism almost foundered in its early stages when the scarcity of consumer goods caused prices to rise too sharply and aroused a storm of protest and renewed demands for stabilization measures to control prices. But Professor Erhard, who had more of the mentality of a gambler in his outlook than of a rule-abiding government official, won the approval of the Allied authorities for a reduction in tariffs, thus increasing the imports of foods and consumer goods from Germany's neighbors in the west. In addition, he organized the *"Jedermann"* (every man) crash program of manufacturing a line of cheap clothing, shoes, and other necessities that were in short supply. By spring 1949 prices began to decline and the deutschemark began to "harden" on the foreign exchanges. Heinz Nordoff, the managing director of Volkswagen, which produced and sold millions of the ubiquitous "Beetles" that restored life and vitality to the postwar automotive industry, commented succinctly about Erhard's management of Germany's economy during that crucial stage: "From then on, things went."

The popular expression *Wirtschaftswunder* (economic miracle) grew increasingly distasteful to the great majority of West German businessmen who participated in the amazing postwar recovery of their country. They resent the implication that only a miracle can explain what seems to be an impossible achievement in the early years following the war: West Germany's comeback from total defeat and collapse after Hitler's catastrophic *Totalerkrieg*. But the full recovery of a bankrupt and crippled country calls to mind the mythical phoenix, which rises from its own ashes to fly off, restored to youth and vigor. It was the foreign observers in West Germany who described Germany's totally unforeseen revival as an "economic miracle," and the label stuck. The German industrialists and bankers who masterminded the repair and reconstruction of their country saw it as the result of the hard work of their compatriots, plus intelligent planning and management, that enabled the Federal Republic of Germany to rejoin the front ranks of the major industrial powers of the world. Yet what really happened was not quite that simple and fundamental; nor is it accurate to ascribe the rebirth of this new postwar Germany as the *Wirtschaftswunder*. In reality it can be put down to a fortuitous concurrence of circumstances; the time, the place, and the outside factors were beyond the control of the Germans themselves.

One must bear in mind that Germany's defeat in World War II resulted in a major development: the old social order was swept clean off the board. After World War I the hierarchy of the Prussian nobility, the officer corps of the *Reichswehr,* and the civil service of the government had emerged unscathed; they survived to sabotage the ill-fated Weimar Republic and to pave the way for Hitler. However, after Nazi Germany's complete defeat in World War II the old social hierarchy was both dispossessed and discredited. The old social order was *kaputt.*

The Prussian aristocracy, which for decades had been collectively the most powerful segment of German society before Hitler came to power, was fatally injured in the disintegration of the Third Reich. Prussia, a kingdom under Frederick the Great, Bismarck, and Kaiser Wilhelm II and a state under the Weimar Republic, had always been the fountainhead of German expansionism.* For centuries past Prussia had been governed by the Junker nobility, firmly based on their great landed estates east of the Elbe. They had a virtual monopoly in providing the officers for the *Reichswehr* until the mass levies of Nazi *Führer* loosened the Junker grip on Germany's armed forces. The second and third sons of the Junker nobles usually went into the civil service, the judiciary, and other administrative offices of the government.

The elimination of the Junker aristocracy as a powerful force in Germany was accelerated by the heavy casualties it suffered in World War II. The decline was further hastened by the abortive July 20 plot to assassinate Hitler, which was organized by a cadre of high-ranking Prussian officers and generals. They paid dearly at the hands of Himmler's sadistic execution squads for conspiring against the Nazi Führer. After the war was over, the Communist governments in Poland and East Germany proceeded to raze the castles and expropriate the great Junker estates. All vestiges of the centuries-long dominance and presence of the Junker nobility in the lands bordering on the southern shores of the Baltic were swept away.* One of the first acts of the four-power Allied Control Council in Berlin was to officially wipe out the state of Prussia from the postwar map of Germany. Surviving Prussian aristocrats who sought refuge in West Germany were bereft of their homeland and left impoverished and powerless as a social entity. They had hopped onto the Nazi bandwagon expecting it to serve their own purposes; it was an error with fatal consequences.

A few surviving Junker officials did not lose their appetite for political power and sought to keep alive the Junker mystique. An example is Gen. Hasso von Manteuffel, scion of an ancient East Prussian family whose great-great grandfather, General von Manteuffel, was the head of the Prussian military cabinet and was one of the creators of the German General Staff system in the 1850s. Gen. Hasso von Manteuffel was one of the few Prussian generals trusted by Hitler and had been given command of the Ardennes offensive in December 1944. After the war and his release as an Allied prisoner, General von Manteuffel settled in Neuss, a suburb of Düsseldorf, where he became export manager of a firm manufacturing screws, nuts, and bolts. He later managed to win a seat in the federal Parliament as a representative of the Free Democratic party (centrist liberal). While not many of his fellow generals were able to get back into governmental circles most of the surviving Junker officers did find employment in industrial firms.*

After the war the giant corporations of German industry, finance, and commerce were paralyzed and virtually helpless to defend themselves or to resume normal business operations. In addition to the severe physical damage done to their plants and equipment in the closing months of Allied bombing and ground fighting, these firms were literally decapitated. As the Allied military governments took the control and direction of defeated Germany, their first priority was to round up and imprison all the owners, directors, and leading executives of the major German companies. These men were hauled out of their homes and offices and taken to large POW camps, where they were to be held until the degree of their support for the Nazi regime or their connection with any war crimes could be determined. The industrial baronies in West Germany such as Krupp of Essen, the number one arms producer; I. G. Farben, the world's largest chemical firm; Vereingte Stahlwerke, the major steel producer; as well as the Big Six banks, which dominated the German financial world, were all placed under trustees who were appointed by the Allied military governors. Several years were to elapse before the owners or stockholders could exercise even limited proprietary rights.

At the bottom of the social ladder, the masses of workers and their families were also immobilized by the national defeat and collapse, politically as well as economically. When Hitler had come to power, he had smashed the old social democratic trade unions and substituted the Nazi Labor Front in their place. In turn, this *ersatz* trade union was outlawed by the Allied occupation authorities, leaving the millions of workers with no agency or organization to speak or act for them. Not until October 1949 did the first legitimate postwar trade union federation, the *Deutscher Gewerkschaftsbund* (DGB), begin to function.

Meanwhile, immediately following the war, the widespread destruction of plant and equipment and the breakdown, for all practical purposes, of the national economy resulted in large-scale unemployment. Those workers who had jobs were paid in old reichsmarks, a currency that was becoming increasingly devaluated with every passing day. As a result, the working masses had neither the means nor the leverage to improve their sad state of affairs. The strike weapon remained in its sheath because striking against the almost-bankrupt owner of a war-damaged factory was nonsensical.

In the absence of any postwar revolution involving violence and disorder, the middle class came to power when Chancellor Konrad Adenauer organized the first sovereign government of the new West German state. This was not so much an acquisition as an inheritance of power by default. The middle class had not been organized, politically or economically, to take any specific line of action; nor as a distinct social group had it any plans or programs for the new Bonn government. Power was thrust upon the middle class because the old ruling forces had disappeared from the postwar corridors of power. The aristocracy, the officer corps of the *Reichswehr,* and the civil service were disbanded; millions of workers were unable, as well as unwilling, to mobilize their collective strength in any power struggle. They had personal problems enough, of feeding, housing, and making a livable existence for themselves and their families. Political activity was a luxury they could not afford.

The middle class had little left to distinguish it from the rest of the Germans during those immediate and hungry years after the shooting stopped; they were as poor as everybody else. But they were resolutely middle class in their thinking and outlook, in their aspirations and ambitions. So they imprinted their own tone and character on the new Bonn government, as we shall see in greater detail in succeeding chapters.

The emergence of the middle class was largely triggered off by the mass internment of thousands of Germans as "active Nazis and ardent Nazi sympathizers," in addition to the millions of *Wehrmacht* soldiers and officers held in POW camps. As the Supreme Allied Commander, Gen. Dwight D. Eisenhower, in outlining the objectives of military-government rule for West Germany, specifically ordered the "elimination of Nazism, Fascism, German militarism, the Nazi hierarchy and their collaborators."

With this blanket authority, the Americans, British, and French in West Germany skimmed off the top levels of German society and officialdom— with the noteworthy exception of Protestant and Catholic churchmen— and locked them behind barbed-wire fences. It took months and years for these internees to gain their freedom and return to their private lives and families.

As a result of the mass internment of thousands of "active Nazis and ardent Nazi sympathizers," as the Allied Military Government *Handbook* described them, a new generation of managers, directors, officeholders, civil servants, and such took over the desks of their interned predecessors. These replacements had several things in common: they had not been identified to the same degree as Nazi activists and they were aware that involvement in political affairs can be detrimental to one's own career. Hence they were motivated to be cautious and to hew to a middle-of-the-road line in their decision making. They avoided any involvement or commitment, especially in political matters. Whether this new generation of managers and administrators was in private industry or in state or local government, all had more than enough to occupy their time and thinking in the arduous task of repairing and reconstructing their war-battered country.

The Americans, especially Gen. Clay, had also been devoting much thought to the future of this defeated and ravaged nation. This divided land could not be allowed to remain an economic slum populated by a hungry and despairing people who were deprived of any vision or hope of a return to a normal living. General Clay was the first to see the essential dichotomy of American policy vis-à-vis defeated Germany.

At the end of the war Americans settled down to occupy their part of Germany, with the twin but somewhat conflicting objectives: to punish the Germans for their war crimes and reform them from their predisposition to totalitarian or Caesarian rule to something resembling a modern democratic society.

The U.S. policy-makers seemed to have opted primarily for a punitive policy, to the exclusion of other considerations. For example, the official military-government *Handbook* listed the following guidelines for the Allied occupation of Germany after its unconditional surrender:

1. No steps looking toward the *economic rehabilitation* of Germany are to be undertaken, except as may be immediately necessary in support of military operations.
2. Germany will always be treated as a *defeated country,* and not as a *liberated country* . . .* [Italics added.]

However, after the intensification of the cold war, with its implied threat of a Soviet advance through West Germany to the Rhine River, the Americans began to question the validity of their initial policy line. If carried out to its logical conclusion, the results might push or persuade the Germans of the three Allied zones of the merits of communism as a substitute for the democracy of the western powers. General Clay felt strongly that the only way to halt the spread of communism—that is, the expansion of Soviet power and influence—was to reverse U.S. policy and carry out the forbidden economic rehabilitation of defeated and bankrupt Germany. Economic recovery in his eyes was of first priority. He reasoned that, like Napoleon's army, democracy "marches best on a full stomach." Democracy blooms only in a country that is economically sound and healthy. If West Germany was to be immunized against the virus of communism, its economic life must be revived and invigorated. General Clay further rationalized his own brand of *Realpolitik:* the Russians had more troops, guns, tanks, and other weaponry poised for action on their side of the Iron Curtain; but the Americans could call upon a new weapon, dollars— literally billions of Marshall Plan dollars—to prime the pump of the moribund West German economy, and that of western Europe, too.

So, to the surprise of his own political and economic advisers, as well as the German politicians, in that history-making conference in July 1948 the U.S. military governor gave his approval to Professor Erhard's action of wiping out the rationing and price controls of the managed economy of occupied West Germany. This was the necessary prelude to the introduction of the new and untested *Soziale Marktwirtschaft,* or the system of "capitalism with a conscience" that was to transform West Germany into the number three economic power of the world in the next fifteen years and to decisively block the westward advance of communism.

After its debut on the European scene in September 1949, the infant West German republic was blessed with more than its share of good luck in having its political and economic affairs in the hands of two men whose talents and energies were fully equal to the opportunities that faced them. Adenauer, seventy-three years old when he took office as Germany's first postwar head of government, was a superpolitician to his fingertips. He was probably the most subtle and supple leader that modern Germany has had since Otto von Bismarck. But Adenauer was also imbued with a cause—to restore Germany's good name and reputation in the light of the odious history of Hitler and his murderous Third Reich. The second pillar of the new regime, Erhard and his *Soziale Marktwirtschaft,* was a man of competence, also with a cause—to rebuild his war-shattered country and to bring back economic stability and security to the forty-five million surviving Germans.

The Adenauer–Erhard combination gave the new *Bundesrepublik* a quality of intelligent and effective leadership that soon won strong support from the German population and kept the team functioning in office for the next fourteen years without change. The two men differed greatly in character and outlook, but each complemented the other. Adenauer cared only for politics and international affairs; Erhard was concerned only with economic affairs and had little talent or taste for the rough and tumble of the political arena. Each man provided a special service that, when taken together, largely accounted for Germany's amazing recovery.

Adenauer was interested in economic developments only insofar as they affected the political strength of his government and his Christian Democratic Union (CDU). He reserved for himself the overriding supervision and control of domestic political affairs and West Germany's foreign relations. The tall, austere Rhinelander was a devout Catholic and family man. With his moral sensitivities he was acutely aware that the road back for the Germans would be long and painful. As chancellor of a country that was considered a pariah in the family of nations, he conceived it to be his duty and responsibility to prove to the Western democracies that a new Germany could be created, one that was a clean and decisive breakaway from the militaristic, aggressive, and stridently nationalistic *Kaiserreich* and *Dritte Reich*. His first step was to demonstrate that their new leader could be a "good European" in word and deed, so he would lead his compatriots down the path of atonement and reparations for the war crimes of nazism. In sharp contrast to the aggressive and nationalistic prewar Germanies, Adenauer's new Germany would be peace loving, nonmilitaristic, and internationally minded. The new convert "would be more Catholic than the pope."

With these objectives firmly in his sights, Adenauer was to keep occupied for years to come with what amounted to his master international public-relations program: to win back for postwar Germany some measure of goodwill and friendship of the transatlantic community of nations. The chancellor was fully convinced that West Germany must bind her future to the West and, in particular, achieve a special relationship with France, Germany's neighbor and traditional foe. Feeling confident that West Germany's economic affairs were in the good hands of Erhard and his associates, Adenauer left himself free to concentrate on Germany's international problems.

What most observers found hard to understand was Adenauer's complete delegation of authority and responsibility for economic affairs to Erhard. Terence Prittie, veteran foreign correspondent of the *Manchester Guardian,* reported on the chancellor's official relations with his economic minister as follows:

Ludwig Erhard was given a complete free hand in the economic field. According to Erhard (in a private conversation with the author), Adenaeur did not merely take next to no interest in economics, he did not even want to know about such matters.*

The great strength and staying power of the Adenauer–Erhard combination was due to the fact that they understood what the great majority of Germans wanted from life. The two men had discovered the "security syndrome"—the almost paranoid fixation of most adult Germans for a sense of security in their lives. World War II was punishing and disastrous and Germany's defeat dropped everybody's standard of living deep into the cellar. The essentials of daily living—a roof over one's head, food on the table, a fire in the stove, a steady job, an income in a currency that had a solid purchasing power—were considered important. *Sicherheit!* Security! It governed all emotions, thought processes, choices, careers, marriages; every aspect of daily life in occupied Germany was influenced by the deep-seated, almost instinctive yearning for protection against any repetition of what had happened after world wars I and II.

When times got better, the memories of that substandard existence stayed and influenced German political attitudes for years to come. The great majority of Germans voted *Magenpolitik,* "stomach politics." Political ideologies and slogans left them benumbed and indifferent; the programs and panaceas of democracy, socialism, or communism evoked little positive response among the adults. They were in no mood for adventures or experiments that would take them out of familiar surroundings; but they were prepared to work hard and to save, eat, sleep, get up and work, and save another day. They wanted protection for their savings and pensions and other rewards for hard work which would not be depreciated by inflation such as had destroyed the reichsmark twice before.

This is the essence of the discovery that Adenauer and Erhard made,

which guided and controlled their policies and practices during their administration of the Republic. It shaped the character and structure of the
new West German state in those early formative years so decisively that
even later, when the Socialists came to power, they could not change the
economic pattern and had to adjust their Marxian ideology to the *Soziale
Marktwirtschaft*.

This postwar security syndrome of the German adults was not understood by the military-government authorities or by the world press.

However, what is much harder to understand was the apparent inability
or unwillingness of the Socialist party (SPD)—the party of the working
classes—to read the handwriting on the wall and be guided by it. Kurt
Schumacher was the leader of the party from 1945 to 1952. He was a
crippled but dedicated Marxian Socialist who had spent twelve years in
Hitler's concentration camps. An embittered fanatic, he was determined to
impose his political and economic programs on postwar Germany. A man
of integrity, honest and incorruptible, Schumacher was such a powerful
personality as leader of the SPD that he was able to command unquestioning obedience of his followers until his death in 1952. But he never knew
what motivated the hearts and minds of the workers or of the middle class.
Schumacher was never to be found in a local *bierstube* having a glass or
two with the working stiffs, and getting to know what it was they wanted
out of life and what was on their minds. Instead he acted the role of
father-knows-best, leading a docile flock of unquestioning colleagues.

Schumacher's great lack of perception may be due to the fact that he
was a sick and crippled man. He had lost an arm and carried seventeen
pieces of steel shrapnel in his body as a result of his combat service in
World War I. After twelve years in Hitler's concentration camps he was so
physically debilitated that he had to have a gangrenous leg amputated.
Hence he had little time and less energy to seek out the wants and aspirations of the working classes.

Schumacher made speeches, built party platforms, demanded political
and economic reforms and changes, all of which had little if any direct
relationship to the daily problems and cares of the Ruhr steelworker or
coal miner. He politicked for nationalization of heavy industry and for a
strong and centralist Socialist government; he railed against the Marshall
Plan, collaboration with West Europe, the development of Bizonia, and
so on. He was ever conscious of the mistakes the Socialists had made in
prewar times, of being "too internationalist" in the eyes of the Germans.
Hence he held the SPD to a strong nationalist line—which itself was distasteful to the apathetic and disillusioned German masses in the postwar
period. According to press reports at that time, Schumacher told an American diplomat that "never again will the Social Democrats be less nationalistic than the parties to the right." This in itself represented a 180-degree
turn from Social Democratic policy of pre-Hitler times.

Schumacher was ignorant of the real bread-and-butter issues of *Magen-*

politik and he was bitterly surprised when Adenauer came to power after the first federal election in 1949. When Schumacher died in 1952 he was spared the agony of seeing the conservative CDU reelected to office in 1953, 1957, and 1961. In the third election of 1957, the Christian Democrats, for the first time, obtained an absolute majority. The CDU's winning slogan in this election was: "At Peace, Our Daily Bread." Unemployment was nil and six million new work places had been created in the wholesale repair and reconstruction. Economic recovery was in full swing and Germany on its way to *Wirtschaftswunder*. Four-and-a-half million new homes had been built, whole new cities were rising on the ruins of the old. The D-mark (deutschemark) was Europe's strongest currency, except for the Swiss franc. Germany's standard of living was approaching that of Denmark and Sweden. Voters were appreciative; over 50 percent of the total 88 percent of eligible voters cast their ballots for the Adenauer–Erhard ticket. For the first time in the industrial *Ruhrgebiet,* large blocs of workers deserted the SPD to vote for Adenauer's administration. This third and decisive defeat shook the SPD leadership right down to their ideological bootstraps and led to a major restructuring of West Germany's politics and economics.

In this new eco-political Germany, economic rather than political considerations dominated the planning and decision-making of the federal government's day-to-day operations. The measurement of national progress at home and abroad was in terms of economic growth. If asked to pinpoint the approximate time and place when this burgeoning West German republic became eco-political in fact if not in theory, the answer would be the special conference of the Socialist party in Bad Godesberg in November 1959.

Party leaders finally faced up to the problem that if they ever wanted to win power they must change their public image and their political ideology, so as to increase their voter appeal to the millions of the German middle class. At this historic conference the SPD dumped Marxian dogma overboard and put in its place a policy doctrine that the press quickly labeled "consumer socialism." A party declaration stated:

The consumer's freedom of choice and the worker's freedom to choose his job are fundamentals of a socialist economic policy, while free enterprise and free competition are important features of it.

The SPD jettisoned its age-old identification as the party of the working classes and its basic commitment to nationalize heavy industry; also much more of the Marxist baggage of this 100-year-old political party was discarded. In short, by their ideological housecleaning, the Socialists acknowledged that they must abandon their basic credo that politics must control economics and not the reverse. The party leadership shifted from the left wing to a more central position on the political spectrum, so as to appeal to the middle-class voters, who long had been considered to be the property of the CDU. To guide them on their journey into the land of the *Bürgerlicheleute,* the SPD established a Secretariat for the Middle Class, as a sort of political Baedeker. However, the seriousness of this quest for a new image and ideology can be noted in the oft-repeated emphasis by Chancellor Willy Brandt and his successor, Helmut Schmidt, that, ". . . our party must not abandon the 'new center' because without that center, we cannot muster the power to govern."

Karl Marx must have twirled in his grave in London's Highgate Cemetery where he was buried, when the Social Democrats opted for "consumer socialism" as the only way to attract sufficient votes to win a national election.

That was undoubtedly capitalism's finest hour in its long struggle with socialism and other ideologies. It also marked the coming of age of this vigorous new eco-political state.

BOOK I

THE ALLIED
OCCUPATION

I

In the beginning was chaos; for the beginning has to be the ghastly years between 1945 and 1948. . . . Germany paid for its sins with three years of utter economic hell.

—From the Economist *in a survey of postwar Germany, October 15, 1966*

The Germans have no liking for the game of revolution, and have usually behaved clumsily under lawless conditions.

—GOLO MANN *in* History of Germany Since 1789.

THE DARKEST HOUR

AFTER the unconditional surrender of the German armed forces, on May 9, 1945, the *Oberkommando der Wehrmacht* (German High Command) issued its last communiqué of World War II, describing this moment as "the darkest hour in German history." By comparison with the blustering rhetoric of other communiqués, this May 9 valedictory had the bleak and chilling ring of truth.

Hitler had threatened that if his armies could not achieve final victory, he would pull the German people down with him into the abyss of defeat. That was one promise the Nazi *Führer* fulfilled to the last jot and tittle. Not since the Thirty Years War, which devastated feudal Germany and killed off one-third of its population in the savage religious conflicts of the seventeenth century, had the Germans suffered such losses of life and property, such destruction of cities and towns, coupled with the disintegration of the whole social structure by which man lives and earns his daily bread.*

In West Germany, about forty-five million Germans survived; they were joined shortly by ten million East Germans who were fleeing the Russians. These refugees brought nothing with them but their poverty and problems. Their sudden influx added to the already savage competition for the growing scarcities of food, housing, and other necessities. However, in the coming years these refugees were to prove to be a sterling asset. Their skilled labor would be a vital contribution to West Germany's industrial recovery.

For these surviving Germans, the world ended "not with a bang but a whimper." As the "thousand-year Reich" shattered into fragments, in the

27

twelfth year of its short life, the Germans fought to save themselves from being buried in the collapse of the nation and its gangster *kultur*. Survival at any price was the new and overriding law of the land.

When the shooting stopped there was no political revolution or social upheaval such as the Kaiser's Germany had gone through after defeat in World War I. Nor were there any street demonstrations, demanding the heads of Nazi leaders who were responsible for this *Götterdämmerrung:* for the series of climaxing defeats from Stalingrad, El Alamein, to the last battle of the Ardennes, which brought down a nation that to friend and foe alike had seemed invincible.

First, there were no streets in which to have revolutionary demonstrations, just crooked lanes between piles of broken bricks and stone in the ghostly ruins of the once bustling cities. As for scapegoats, all the surviving Germans, with few exceptions, had raised their arms in stiff salutes to their Nazi choreographers and shouted "Sieg Heil!" as Hitler's aggression progressed from one conquered nation to another. However, few Germans would admit to any share in the collective guilt of the nation; they closed their minds to this unpleasant truth. At this stage the Germans who survived World War II broke off connections with their past. For the postwar Germans, hunkered down in their squalor and misery, the past was all failure. The past had robbed them of their present and their future— so it seemed to the millions of hungry, homeless, and jobless men and women.

In the eyes of these Germans, Hitler had become a nonperson, virtually wiped out of their daily consciousness because he had failed to achieve final and conclusive victory. As historian Golo Mann, son of novelist Thomas Mann, pointed out:

It was not what Adolf Hitler had done to other nations that was held against him; people might have gotten over that. It was the situation into which he had led his own people which condemned him forever. Those who could do so rapidly disowned his heritage; as did others who, on closer inspection could not do so.*

What was surprising and almost unbelievable in the early days of the military occupation was the complete collapse of the Nazi movement or ideology. The Allied armies were expecting to encounter some resistance on the homefront from the remnants of *Führertreu* Nazis. In Bavaria the U.S. forces remained on the alert for any sabotage or guerrilla activity of the youthful *Werewolves*. But when the guns stopped firing, so did any resistance, open or covert, from Nazis.

During the first years of the occupation the U.S. and British military governments attempted to search for die-hard Nazis buried in the woodwork. They conducted postmidnight raids in the Bavarian countryside, triggered by reports from informants that certain small villages were the hideouts of a Nazi underground organization. Counterintelligence units went through farmhouses, from hay lofts to pigpens, without even finding a dog-eared copy of Hitler's *Mein Kampf*.

The initial reaction was: "We have missed them!" For it was virtually impossible in those early days after the war to even consider the possibility that there were no secret Nazi groups in action, engaged in clandestine political activity to keep alive the myth of the "thousand-year Reich." It was soon obvious that many high-ranking Nazis, especially members of Himmler's dreaded Gestapo, the SS, and S-D organizations, had disappeared; they were hiding behind false identification papers until such time as they could escape to South America or some other receptive asylum for ex-Nazis. They were avoiding political activity in any form which might call the attention of the Allied authorities to their existence and reveal their identities as wanted war criminals.

However, above ground, so to speak, were literally hundreds of thousands of ex-Nazis trying desperately to cover up their political pasts, so as to avoid being brought before the denazification tribunals to answer for their past activities on behalf of *Der Führer*.

Also notably absent in the immediate aftermath of World War II was any mood or atmosphere receptive to the fetid growth of another *Dolchstosslegende,* the fiction of the "stab-in-the-back" first voiced by Field Marshal von Hindenburg to explain away Germany's military defeat in World War I. This time there was no ready or facile alibi that could salvage Germany's wounded pride and dull some of the pain of losing everything in the total defeat of World War II. Gen. Alfred Jodl and Admiral Hans von Friedeburg, on behalf of the German High Command signed the articles of unconditional surrender in England on May 7, 1945, to the Allied commanders represented by Gen. Bedell Smith and his Russian, British, and French colleagues. After the capitulation ceremony, General Jodl asked permission to say a few words: "With this signature, the German people and the German armed forces are, for better or for worse, delivered into the hands of the victors. . . . In this hour I can only express the hope that the victor will treat them with generosity."

There were no comments from the other side of the surrender table. The time had come for the German people to break decisively with their turbulent past. There was to be no carry-over of nazism into the postwar period. Swastikas and other artifacts of the Hitlerian Reich disappeared in surreptitious bonfires. The pernicious Nazi ideology that the Germans were a race of *Übermenschen* destined to be masters of Europe's weaker and less warlike tribes—by virtue of superior Teutonic genetics— died with Hitler's suicide in the closing hours of the war.

After the Armistice of World War I, the German troops, still in possession of their arms, had marched home to be received by a joyous civilian population, as if they were returning victorious from the field of battle. In Berlin the German troops were accorded the honors of a victory parade, marching through the Brandenburger Tor and down the Unter den

Linden. But in World War II, after the capitulation ceremony at Rheims, some 2.5 million Germans soldiers were herded into prisoner-of-war camps to await their fate.

The Russians and the French regarded the German POWs in their hands as a form of reparations to be employed as slave labor for as long as it was profitable to do so. The French and Russians had been dragooned by the Nazis into forced-labor battalions during the war and now it was their turn to pay back the *Boche* in kind.*

The Americans processed and released their German prisoners as expeditiously as possible but, together with the British and the Russians, held onto the high-ranking officers and specialists in the fields of science, intelligence, rocketry, weaponry, and such. At Oberursel in the Taunus hills northwest of Frankfurt, the American army established its own think tank of German generals. The objective of this establishment was to "brain drain" these high-ranking officers of their collective and personal knowledge and experience concerning all aspects of their wartime operations against the Russians. The cold war had started and every scintilla of information the Americans could extract from the German generals about the military strengths and weaknesses of the Soviet armed forces was like finding money on the sidewalk.

The individual German generals were treated as VIPs, but it was made clear to them that their release and return to their homes and families depended on the degree of their cooperation and the information they provided. The Oberursel think tank proved to be one of the most productive intelligence-gathering operations of the World War II period. Out of this came the *Gehlenorganisation,* the postwar German intelligence service founded and financed by the CIA, until taken over by the *Bundesrepublik* years later.*

Piled on top of the casualties, the loss of property and wealth, the lack of housing, and scarcity of food and other necessities, insult was added to injury by the conquerors. The Germans were to be treated as pariahs, social outcasts, unfit for the company of men. As Supreme Commander of the Allied forces in the West, General Eisenhower issued a "no fraternization" order to all troops, prohibiting any social contact between the soldiers and the defeated civilian population. This was later shown to be completely unworkable, as the soldier traded his cigarettes and chocolate for the favors of the frauleins, blithely disregarding the attempt to constrain his off-duty social life.

The U.S. Army newspaper, *Stars and Stripes,* mounted an editorial campaign against any fraternization with the distaff side of the enemy population—German men were not of particular importance or interest to the Allied soldier. The feature of this campaign was a series of cartoons about the antics of a buxomy Teutonic slattern named Veronika Dankeschon, or VD for short. The message, carried with sledge-hammer bluntness, was that German females were likely carriers of venereal disease. In the eyes of their occupation masters, the Germans had become something akin to the *Untermenschen* (subhumans)—a descriptive term that the Nazis had applied to the Jews and Slavs living in Russia.

In the closing weeks of the war, the *Wehrmacht*'s chief of staff, Gen. Heinz Guderian, tried to convince the *Führer* that it was futile to continue to fight when all hope of victory had vanished. By suing for peace while Germany still possessed some fighting forces in the field, something might be saved on which the German people might rebuild a new postwar existence. But Hitler was adamant: if he lost his war, the German people would go down with him. To make sure of this, on March 19, 1945, as the American and British armies in the west and the Russians in the east were pouring over the borders of the Reich, Hitler issued the first of several general orders of first priority. These called for the destruction of all military and industrial installations, and all communication and transportation systems, as well as stocks of foods and other supplies that might help or support the advancing enemy forces.

This would be a scorched-earth policy without compare since Atilla and his Huns rode out of Asia to ravage and set medieval Europe to the torch. Hitler planned to leave what was once Europe's greatest and most powerful industrial nation a gutted wasteland and to deprive those who survived of the means of sustaining themselves when the Third Reich finally crashed down in total defeat.

Albert Speer, who was one of Hitler's few personal intimates and who was then minister for armaments and war production, had the courage to protest in a long memorandum to *Der Führer*. But Hitler refused to swerve from his demonic rush to destruction. He told Speer that:

If the war is lost, the nation will also perish. This fate is inevitable. There is no necessity to take into consideration the basis which the people will need to continue a most primitive existence. On the contrary, it will be better to destroy these things ourselves because the nation will have been proved to be the weaker one and the future will belong to the stronger eastern nation. Besides those who remain after the battle are only the inferior ones, the good ones have been killed.*

Speer later listed for his Allied interrogators the details of Hitler's scorched-earth directives, which involved the destruction of "all industrial plants, all important electrical facilities, water works, gas works, all stocks of food and clothing, all bridges, all railways and communications installations, all waterways, all shipping, inland as well as oceanic, all freight cars and all locomotives."*

The Nazi armaments minister did not carry out the program of wholesale destruction demanded by Hitler. He didn't have to; the Allies advancing from the west and Russians from the east effectively "scorched" the

German landscape with the overwhelming firepower of their ground and air forces. By continuing the war until the collapse of the last decimated Nazi combat unit—Hitler himself did not commit suicide until the Russian assault forces were within mortar range of his underground bunker—the *Führer* assured that a maximum of devastation and carnage would be inflicted on Germany's cities and towns, on its homes and factories, on its railroads, power plants, communications systems, and the whole infrastructure of a modern industrial society.

Speer was one of the few perceptive intellects who had entrée to Hitler's immediate circle of aides and military advisers. He was also one of the first to learn that the war was irretrievably lost because of the heavy and continuing Allied air raids on Germany's industrial concentrations and transportation and communication systems. Each morning Speer received a special casualty list: the names and locations of the industrial plants producing the armaments and other essentials for the Nazi armed forces in combat which had been bombed out of action in the previous twenty-four hours. He read from these daily reports of the inexorable pulverization of the Reich's industrial power, as the Allied "Jabos" and Flying Fortresses ranged at will in the skies over Germany, bombing with little or no deterring interference from the *Lüftwaffe*'s air and ground defenses.*

When the bombing and shelling stopped and time permitted a study of the effects of the war on the German scene, what met the eye seemed unbelievable, so enormous and widespread were the chaos and destruction. It was incalculable, immeasurable at first glance. The urban populated centers of Germany were reduced to piles of rubble, skylines of broken walls, and shattered buildings whose fallen bricks and stones had blotted out the patterns of streets and highways.*

The most striking picture of what it means to fight and to lose a total war was to be found in the Ruhr. About fifty miles long and twenty miles wide at its middle, this oval shaped and densely populated congestion of cities and towns, dominated by coal mines and steel mills, had been the machine shop of Europe for generations. Now for the first time in man's memory, the skies above the Ruhr were clean and blue, replacing the dense pall of smoke that had formerly belched upward from thousands of tall chimneys that towered over the conglomeration of steel mills, coal mines, power plants, and related industrial installations. What few chimneys had survived the air raids intact no longer emitted plumes of thick smoke. From their heights the vista was the same in every direction—the ruins of Europe's greatest concentration of industrial power.

According to early surveys, it was estimated that between 30 and 40 percent of all industrial plants had been put out of action as a result of war damages.* This was largely due to the round-the-clock air raids of the British and American air forces. In the closing weeks of the war, the

"Jabos" (*Jagdbomber,* hunter-bomber)—the nickname used by the Germans for the Allied fighter-bombers, which attacked any likely target that came within their gunsights—roamed the skies above Germany unchallenged by the *Lüftwaffe.* As a result, the damage to Germany's industrial installations was heaviest in the west, in such densely concentrated areas as the Ruhr. Further to the east in *Mitteldeutschland,* where the industrial sites were fewer and more desegregated, less damage was inflicted. Hence the overall percentage of destruction of plants and factories was higher in the Ruhr than the national average of 30–40 percent, but lower for the more remote industrial areas of Bavaria, Württemburg-Baden, and so on.

In July 1945 the U.S. military government made a quick on-the-spot survey of all industrial installations in the American zone of occupation. They found only 10 percent of approximately twelve thousand factories and plants were in limited production. The others had been bombed out of business.

Later when the rubble was cleared away, it was found that much of the industrial machinery was reparable and usable. But first the factories had to be rebuilt, with new walls and roofs. However, the salvage operations in most cases proved to be pointless. If the machinery was operational, it was subject to be dismantled for reparations. Hence there was no incentive for the owner to clean up his factory premises and get the wheels of production turning again. He would only risk the loss of his capital assets by having them requisitioned for reparations and shipment out of the country.

It was impossible to get the raw materials, as the whole system for production and distribution had broken down. Finally, the fuel and energy needed to power the industrial machines was in short supply. Electrical power plants had been heavily damaged and these had to be repaired. Coal to fuel these plants first had to be mined and then transported. The railways, essential to the distribution of Ruhr coal, were heavily bombed in the closing phases of the war. For example, in the British and U.S. zones of occupation, it was found that 2,341 railway bridges had been destroyed, including all the bridges spanning the Rhine, Wesel, and Main rivers. These three inland waterways, now closed to shipping, had accounted for almost one-fifth of all inland goods transport. The railways handled over 75 percent of the total volume of transportation, and at the close of the war over 50 percent of the locomotives and 30 percent of the freight cars had been knocked out of action by war damage. Automotive transport ran a poor third to the railways and inland waterways in handling goods and freight and most of the trucks had been put to service with the *Wehrmacht.* At the war's end, what few were left were taken over by the occupation forces.

The surviving German civilian population faced an acute housing shortage which was to remain a serious social and political problem until economic recovery took its first hesitant steps with the currency reform in June 1948. The destruction of homes and multifamily housing units roughly paralleled and equaled the heavy destruction meted out to the neighboring industrial installations. The blanket pattern of mass bombings by the American and British air forces did not make any distinction between civilian homes and the factories nearby. The German lost both his job and the roof over his head if he lived in any of the industrial-congested Rhine and Ruhr areas.

For example, the city of Essen, which was built around the great munitions complex of Friedrich Krupp, suffered a loss of 87 percent of its prewar housing. In fact Essen was virtually a dead city at the war's end, due to the heavy and incessant Allied air attacks on the Krupp works. By contrast, the whole of Bavaria, supported largely by its agricultural economy, lost only 14.8 percent of its prewar housing though major cities such as Munich, Nuremberg, Ulm, Augsburg, and others suffered heavily from Allied air raids directed at their inner sections. Generally speaking, those who lived on the farms or in the suburbs sustained proportionately less combat damage. At the end of the war, farm communities were compelled to provide shelter and living space to the hundreds of thousands who had lost their homes and had borne the brunt of air raids and property losses.

This problem was further aggravated by three other competitors for what little functional housing that remained. First came the millions of American, British, French, and other Allied troops in the West; while several million Red Army troops settled down to occupy East Germany. The American army had over three million troops in Europe at the end of the war and most of them were in Germany.

Quite naturally the officers were allotted living quarters according to their rank in the undamaged houses in the better residential areas.* All available hotels and inns of every description were also requisitioned, as well as schools and other public buildings, to house the troops. While every large city has impressive German army barracks, most of them had been bombed or shelled and left only partially habitable, so thousands of soldiers had to be quartered elsewhere in apartments. In addition, theaters, restaurants, and cafés were taken over and transformed into clubs and other entertainment or social facilities for the occupation forces.

Second priority for housing was allocated by the occupation authorities to care of the displaced persons—the ubiquitous DPs who had been transported to Germany to work as forced labor by the Nazis. At the end of the war there were 6.5 million of them in Germany. Of this total about 2 million refused to be repatriated to their homelands in the Baltic countries, which had been forcibly taken over by the Soviet Union, and in the Ukraine of the USSR. While they faced an uncertain future in occupied Germany, to return to the Soviet Union meant more forced labor in one of Stalin's many prison camps in Siberia. Meanwhile the DPs became the wards of UNRRA (United Nations Relief and Rehabilitation Administration), which was largely supported by the U.S. Treasury, and they occupied living quarters requisitioned from the Germans.

Then the remaining 45 million civilians had to cope with a flow of German refugees and expellees from the east totaling 7.8 million for the British and American zones of occupation, an influx that increased the German population by 23.6 percent. Thus on bottom of the housing priority list was this influx of the homeless and propertyless. Virtually all they possessed were the clothes on their backs and what could be carried in their handbags and they had to be fitted into the straitened and declining lifestyle of the resident population of West Germany. The refugees, of course, competed for the diminishing food supplies. The word "housing," used in connection with postwar Germany, is a misnomer, for it connotes a dwelling place with four solid walls, a roof, and windows, and heating, cooking, and toilet facilities. Instead, shelters against the elements were improvised, cannibalized from the wreckage of buildings. This is, perhaps, a more accurate description of what ensued.

The homeless and the refugees moved into sheds and shacks of every size and shape; they burrowed like moles into the cellars and interstices of bombed-out buildings. They used bricks, wood, cardboard, and sheets of metal to shield themselves against the rain and snow, the wind and the cold. A piece of stovepipe projecting from a basement or a bricked-up wall marked the rabbit warren of the human flotsam and jetsam of World War II.

The war had reduced German cities to dusty heaps of broken stone and brick rubble, desolate façades of gutted buildings: roofless, windowless, and without floors. Even thinking about the task of clearing away the debris and rebuilding was a hopeless, mind-boggling exercise at best. As the remaining cadre of German officials surveyed the ugly scene of urban devastation, they could only measure the time required for reconstruction of these population centers in decades.

For example, with typical Teutonic thoroughness, the officials of Kassel, population 181,000 and once the capital of the Napoleonic kingdom of Westphalia, estimated that there were 51.5 cubic meters of debris piled up for every one of the city's population. Using manpower and earth-moving equipment, if it were available, they calculated it would take twenty-two years to remove the 9,321,500 cubic meters of rubble. In a report to the House of Commons, the British Labor government estimated that even if 1,000 tons of debris a day could be removed, it would still take thirty years to clean up Berlin.

The ancient cathedral city of Cologne was so severely mauled that at first it was written off as a total loss by the city fathers. The town council seriously considered whether or not to just abandon the ruins of Cologne and to build an entirely new city some miles north of it along the banks of the Rhine. But the tug of history and tradition was to prove too strong—

the city was founded by the Romans as a military outpost and was later the first Christian bishopric—plus the fact that the cathedral, though heavily damaged, was still standing. Its twin spires, 515-feet high, towered above the flat Rhine landscape.

The shortage of food, coupled with the almost complete collapse of industrial production in West Germany, began to assume crisis proportions by 1946. The Germans, who had been accustomed to a prewar daily intake of 3,000 calories, were now reduced to 1,550 calories according to the official ration. The food supplies continued to drop rapidly, due to the swelling refugee population and also because of declining farm production. The lack of fertilizer—German agriculture has been dependent on nitrogen and phosphates for generations—was the main stumbling block. This postwar deficiency could not be corrected because of the severe war damage to Germany's great chemical plants. Hence the growing food shortage caused a further cut in daily rations to 1,015 calories in the Ruhr and 1,100 in the U.S. zone. But on many days of the month those who stood for hours in the long queues for bread and other rations went back to their burrows empty-handed; there was not enough to meet all ration cards. During the very severe winter of 1946–47—the coldest winter in a century—the rations in the industrial *Ruhrgebiet* dropped to 600–700 calories per day, which for most adult Germans was ambulatory starvation. According to the League of Nations in 1936, 2,400 calories per day were necessary to keep an adult healthy and functioning.

The Ruhr's coal production had dropped from a prewar norm of over 400,000 tons per day to less than 110,000 tons, of which 25 percent was diverted to export reparations to other European countries also deficient in fuel and energy supplies. The bitterly cold winter coupled with the lack of coal for home heating made the daily existence of the German civilian almost unbearable. The plight of the average German caused Josef Cardinal Frings of Cologne, the senior Catholic prelate in West Germany, to formally announce that it was no longer a sin to steal coal anywhere it was available. However, the freezing citizenry needed no clerical dispensation from the seventh commandment to pillage fuel with a clear conscience. For example, any time a coal train stopped in a populated area, it was set upon by gangs of adults and children who pilfered the coal like locusts stripping a field of grain.

The decline in food quickly revealed its serious effects on the population, and particularly among children and infants. Hamburg reported 10,000 cases of hunger edema. In the British zone, 260,000 new cases of tuberculosis were found, and the death rate had risen by 50 percent. Malnutrition was especially harmful to the young. In the cities and towns of Hesse, 90 percent of the children developed rickets. The mortality rates for infants and young children reached 15.4 percent in the Ruhr and 16 percent in Berlin—almost a one-third increase for the urbanized areas of West Germany.

Meanwhile the food situation was further aggravated in West Germany when the Russians began cutting off shipments of potatoes and grain from East Germany, which was formerly called the "bread basket" for the once-united Reich. This was in reprisal for failure to get large reparations in the form of industrial equipment, especially from the Ruhr. This development paved the way for the rapid growth of the *Zigaretten Wirtschaft,* or the cigarette economy.

With hunger stalking the land and industry paralyzed because there was no incentive to produce merely to acquire more worthless reichsmarks, the Germans were forced to sell their personal possessions piece by piece. The currency was virtually without value because it could not entice what remained of the stocks of consumer goods back onto the store shelves. No storekeeper wanted to deplete his slim inventory of goods for reichsmarks, which would not replenish his reserves. So to live and to get enough food to survive, the German had to sell what he had been able to salvage from the war: jewelry, silverware, china, furniture, clothing, household appliances, tools—virtually everything had a value on the black market, because such items were not for sale in the few remaining stores that kept open.*

Every day there would be an exodus from the crowded cities into the countryside. Each German would be laden with his *Aktentasche* (briefcase), or bags, suitcases, and assorted parcels containing personal possessions to be bartered for food from the farmers. In the evening they would return; the lucky ones would have filled their briefcases and bags with a few kilos of potatoes, eggs, butter, meat, or other food items.

The farmers were becoming the new rich. Except for areas where the Allies had engaged in combat operations, the land and buildings of the farmers had suffered little if any war damage. As a social group they emerged from the war with fewer property losses, proportionately, than any other sector of German people. And in the immediate postwar period they alone had sufficient food for themselves. Now their excess food supplies found a ready market at high prices. They didn't have to move off their farms to boost their standards of living; the black market trudged out to their doorsteps. Soon their produce enabled them to cover their floors with Persian rugs; decorate their kitchen tables with fine china and silver; and fill their bedroom *Schranken* (wardrobes) with furs and warm clothing.

However, the flourishing black market quickly established itself in all the big cities, usually in the immediate area of the main railway stations. In its own disorganized and unplanned fashion, it marked the beginning of the economic recovery of postwar Germany; it was being financed indirectly and unwittingly, by the American government to the tune of about $500 million and by the British treasury in the amount of $300 million.

The complete story of this curious aspect of postwar finance in conquered Germany has been shielded behind "top secret" classification, but the ensuing developments were too open and widespread to hide the broad outlines of the $800 million currency swindle by the Soviets of their western Allies.

Out of a wartime London conference came an agreement that the Americans, British, and Russians—the French were included later—would issue a common occupation currency in their respective zones in Germany. Each occupation mark would be equal in parity to a reichsmark and must be accepted as valid money by the German civilians. The U.S. Treasury arranged to print the new occupation currency, which was to be distributed to the Allies in amounts sufficient for their needs, such as paying for their soldiers and for other services. For some as yet unexplained reason, Henry Morgenthau, Jr., the U.S. secretary of the treasury, gave the Soviet authorities a full set of the new printing plates for the occupation currency, as the Russians said they wanted to print their own marks. This would prove to be a disastrous error, because the Russians were given a potent instrument with which to play havoc with the already inflated reichsmark and to inflict immeasurable political and economic damage in West Germany, if they saw fit to do so.

Meanwhile, the Western powers tied their own hands regarding the use of this occupation currency. For example, in the U.S. zone the occupation mark had a real value of ten cents each, as they were redeemable in U.S. dollars. The three million American soldiers in Germany at the end of the war would receive their monthly pay in occupation marks but could transfer them into dollar-denominated U.S. postal money orders or in dollar savings accounts with army finance. There were no limits placed on the amounts of occupation marks that could be redeemed for dollars.

Simultaneously, in East Germany millions of Russian combat troops were paid off in the same currency. The great majority of the Russian soldiers and officers had not received any pay for months and years of combat service. However, with the end of the war in Europe, the Russian troops received their back pay in wads of occupation marks. These marks were not redeemable in Russian rubles and had no exchange value in the Soviet Union. Hence they had to be spent in occupied Germany. The result was not long in coming; the occupation mark had a dubious and short-term value to Ivan, the Russian soldier, but a quick-dollar value to the American G.I. It could also be exchanged for pounds sterling by the British troops in Germany.

The Russian soldiers were in the black market for anything of value that could be carried away with them to the Soviet Union. The "Ivans" would pay fantastic prices for consumer goods, especially items from the U.S. Army's PX stores. For example, a cheap PX wristwatch, costing $15 or $20, would sell for as high as 5,000 Russian-printed occupation marks, which in turn could be redeemed by the American seller for a $500 postal money order. In addition, the G.I.'s found that they could unload $1.00 cartons of American cigarettes in the Berlin market (the price was lower in West Germany) for 1,200 to 1,500 marks each, or $120 to $150 when cashed in at the army finance or postal offices.

By the end of July 1945 it began to dawn on the financial wizards of the U.S. Treasury that they were subsidizing a large part of the Soviet military occupation cost by redeeming billions of the Russian-printed marks at the rate of ten cents each. Fortunately these Soviet marks were distinguishable from the occupation currency of the American and British zones by a small dash in front of the serial number. Hence, without any advance warning, at the end of July 1945 it was announced that the Russian marks were invalid in western Germany and could not be redeemed at any American or British finance or postal office for dollars or pounds sterling. However, before the barn door was locked, the Americans had been fleeced out of $500 million and the British out of $300 million by the Communist financiers.

Further and equally unsuccessful attempts were made by the U.S. Army high command in Frankfurt to curb the widespread participation of the G.I.'s in the German black market. In December 1946 the occupation mark, which had been legal tender in any transactions between the German civilians and the American army personnel, was replaced by a military script. This currency was only acceptable at army installations such as the PX, clubs, canteens, and so on; it was without value to any German.

However, this abortive currency reform had its own unforeseen backlash. It established the American cigarette as the new medium of exchange in place of the occupation mark for all transactions between the G.I.'s and the German population. In effect, this gave the booming cigarette economy a solid foundation and established it as an integral part of daily commercial life. The cigarette became the yardstick of value and prices were quoted in packs and *Stangen* (cartons), which also served to further eliminate the inflated and virtually worthless reichsmark as a viable currency. The occupational "federal reserve system" which pumped the ersatz money into the daily commerce and supported the ubiquitous pack of Lucky Strikes as the universally acceptable medium of exchange was the U.S. Army's PX network.*

The army PX system soon had to ration cigarettes, but each soldier received a generous allowance and there never seemed to be a shortage for black-market purposes. It was a seller's market for the American G.I. He paid $1.00 for a carton of cigarettes which retailed on the black market for 1,000 reichsmarks or its equivalent value in merchandise. By comparison, the weekly take-home pay of a semi-skilled German worker was about 80 RMs. So tobacco was, in truth, worth its weight in gold.

The Germans soon became so conditioned to the cigarette economy that they began pricing goods and services in terms of cigarettes. Cigarettes were too valuable to smoke; though somewhat bulky, they served as an easily negotiable ersatz money. For example, in 1947 the *New York Herald Tribune* contemplated rehabilitating a bombed-out office building in Frankfurt for its news and circulation bureaus. A local contractor submitted a cost estimate of 155 cartons of cigarettes for the bricks, cement, other materials, and labor for the reconstruction work. The New York business manager angrily rejected this cost estimate as something of a bad joke; he could not justify this sort of a transaction to the auditors.

The cigarette economy also served to revive intellectual life. Willy Cornides, one of the young thinkers began publishing a small monthly journal, *Europa-Archiv,* to educate his generation to the contemporary history that had long been hidden from them by Nazi propaganda. He appealed to me for ten cartons of cigarettes, explaining that with this capital investment he could continue publishing through the long winter months ahead. *Europa-Archiv* survived that winter on the *Herald Tribune* largesse, and at last reports it was still being published.

The black market was the only area of vigorous trade and commerce in the whole of the economic stagnation of defeated and bankrupt Germany. It was a subeconomy, as an American military government survey explained for the education of the policy-makers in Washington. Its illegal price structure ignored the prices set on rationed goods by the government authorities; but it did not ignore the laws of supply and demand. The report stated:

For black market wages the worker will exert himself. For black market prices which really buy goods, the businessman and the farmer will take risks, produce and part with their goods. These free though illegal prices perform their historical function of stimulating production and the exchange of goods, and supply goods that cannot be found on the counters left bare by *"Schachtism."**

As the Allied military occupation in Germany settled down to a semi-permanent state of affairs, the black market flourished when the Allied military personnel became personally and profitably involved. The occupation soldiers found a ready market for a wide variety of goods and items that would have cost the German stiff prices in his own stores. Coffee, chocolate, soap, cooking fats, fountain pens, cigarette lighters, and flints were in high demand and were on sale at the PXs until it became apparent that these goods were moving into the black market in very substantial quantities. Soon all PX items that had sales potential on the black market were rationed. But this did not stop the enterprising businessmen in the G.I. olive-drab uniform.

They were also quick to discover that the U.S. and army postal systems could be put to profitable use. There were virtually no restrictions on the number of packages that could be mailed from the U.S. to the soldiers serving in Germany and elsewhere in Europe. Soon the APOs (army post offices) were inundated with thousands upon thousands of bulk shipments of cartons of cigarettes, the most negotiable item on the black market.

The volume of cigarettes imported into Germany by the soldiers became so great that they almost paralyzed the army postal system; further shipments of tobacco were completely banned. But this was only a temporary break in the black market's trading. The imports quickly changed over to bulk shipments of other negotiable goods such as canned coffee, tinned foods, soap, and so on, all destined for the German black market.

The soldiers traded their bulk goods for jewelry, sets of silver and Meissen porcelain china, antiques, rugs, furs, and cameras, as well as for the social arts of wine, women, and song.

Finally it began to dawn on the Army High Command that trying to eliminate the black market, or at least American participation in this illegal commerce, was impossible. The law of supply and demand was not amenable to U.S. army policy. So the army fell back on the time-tested political maxim: "If you can't beat 'em, join 'em." Two official "Barter Marts" were set up in Berlin and Frankfurt under the direct supervision and control of the U.S. Army. The objective was twofold: to regularize and channel the black marketeering of the American personnel; and to establish an equitable trading system, so that the German civilian received fair value for the personal possessions that he exchanged for American cigarettes, coffee, and other consumer goods imported from the U.S. The American High Command was acutely aware that "plunder and spoilation" of a defeated nation by its conqueror had been adjudged a war crime by the Nuremberg tribunals. The black marketing of one-dollar cartons of cigarettes for goods of much greater intrinsic value had the smell of "plunder and spoilation" by the victor over the vanquished enemy.

In Frankfurt the Barter Mart was located in a large empty store in the main shopping street. This Kaiserstrasse trading center soon became the busiest commercial enterprise in West Germany. The Frankfurt Barter Mart attracted Germans from all over the American and British zones of occupation. Prior to Christmas 1947, the *Bundesbahn* had to add special trains to its Düsseldorf–Frankfurt line to handle the thousands of Germans from the Ruhr who traveled to Frankfurt to obtain some delicacies for the Christmas season.

In a series of connecting rooms upstairs, a team of German experts would appraise the articles brought in to be bartered by a German. A value was set in barter points which could be spent downstairs for items brought in by the Americans. The Americans also exchanged their coffee, cigarettes, canned foods, and such for barter points which would be used to purchase items exchanged by the Germans. The main floor of the Barter

Mart resembled a vast general store, a sort of supermarket crossed with an antique shop. An astonishing variety of merchandise was on sale. Everything from an etching by Albrecht Dürer to a can of Crisco. The turnover of the Barter Mart, ranging from 50 percent to 85 percent each day, would make Bloomingdale's green with envy.

The U.S. Army inadvertently strengthened American involvement in the black market by permitting the wives and families of officers and soldiers to join their men in Germany. For many occupation housewives, life became an adventure of shopping in the ruins of Frankfurt, Berlin, and other cities in the U.S. zone. It was bargain day and their avarice was stimulated by the possibilities of acquiring a grand piano for fifty cartons of cigarettes, a new mink coat for two hundred cartons, a Leica camera for twenty, a set of Meissen china for ten, and a set of sterling silver for fifty.

Here again the U.S. postal system aided and abetted the acquisitive Americans. There were no restrictions on the number or size of boxes or packages that could be sent by parcel post to America at no cost to the sender because the American army personnel enjoyed free mailing privileges. If the colonel's lady found the APO could not mail a grand piano home, the army would transport it when the family received its travel orders to return to America.

Despite its sordid and degrading characteristics, this period of the cigarette economy will no doubt be identified by future historians as the crucible that forged the new and affluent eco-political West Germany. Their energies and their efforts were concentrated on one simple and basic objective, self-survival: obtaining food for the next meal, a place to live, and a job to assure a small income in a dubious and inflated currency. For most Germans existence was clinging desperately to the rim of an abyss, hoping for the strength to avoid falling into it.

In those years of economic hell the German was like a starving man. His mind was occupied with mouth-watering visions of plates piled high with savory meats and potatoes, of strudel buried under thick mounds of whipped cream to fill his aching stomach. All his waking hours were spent meeting his physical needs; there was little incentive for introspective thought and analysis, of what went wrong and what must be done to avoid a repetition of another defeat and its aftermath.

In fact, like shutting off a flow of water, the Germans closed the faucet on the past. This was noticeable in ordinary conversation and in the press. Meaningful and tradition-evoking words such as *Reich* and *deutschtum* disappeared from the German vocabulary. The past lost its meaning and its power to awaken patriotic emotions.* What remained of the German government was a shambles, handing out ration cards instead of rifles, suffering a loss in public respect and authority.

The lesson to those who navigated this traumatic passage through the immediate postwar years of defeat and devastation was simple and clear: economic security was the supreme prize in life. But at this juncture of German history there seemed scant possibility that any of the surviving civilian population would enjoy economic security again in their lifetimes.

2

PROCLAMATION NO. 1

To the People of Germany:

I, General Dwight D. Eisenhower, Supreme Commander of the Allied Expeditionary Force, do hereby proclaim as follows:

The Allied Forces serving under my command have now entered Germany. *We come as conquerors* [italics added], but not as oppressors. In the area of Germany occupied by the forces under my command, we shall obliterate Nazism and German militarism. We shall overthrow the Nazi rule, dissolve the Nazi party and abolish the cruel, oppressive and discriminatory laws and institutions which the party has created. . . .

—Issued, March 1945

"WE COME AS CONQUERORS"

A T the height of Hitler's military power, his swastika flags waved over a conquest area stretching from the Bay of Biscay in the west to the banks of the Volga River in the heart of Russia; from Norway's North Cape above the Arctic Circle to the burning deserts of Libya and Egypt. Then with defeat in a two-front war, the "thousand-year Reich" collapsed like a punctured balloon. The victorious Allies redrew the map of Europe to their own designs and specifications. Germany was stripped of all its military and political conquests and was reduced to about two-thirds its prewar area.

The state of Prussia, the wellspring of Pan-Germanic expansionism and the spawning ground of generations of general staff officers, was simply wiped off the maps as a geographical and political entity in one of the few unanimous decisions of the Allied Control Council. Prussia, formerly a kingdom under the Hohenzollerns, over the years had expanded to occupy almost two-thirds of the German state at the start of World War II. It extended from the frontiers of France, Belgium, and Holland in the west over seven hundred miles to Lithuania and Poland in the east.

What remained of the Third Reich was Balkanized by the victorious powers, who divided it into four separate occupation zones. The Russians took over East Germany, with approximately seventeen million people, the traditional breadbasket of the Reich. The Americans settled down in Bavaria, which was primarily agricultural and alpine, they also held the states of Hesse and Württenburg-Baden, which had some industrial concentrations. The British moved into North Germany and into the Ruhr, an area that had been the industrial heart of Europe for decades with its hundreds of steel mills, coal mines, and heavy-duty manufacturing plants. The French were given the southwest corner of Germany and the Rhine-Palatinate with its Moselle vineyards, some of the finest wine-producing areas of Europe. These western zones which were later to coalesce and become the Federal Republic of (West) Germany (*Bundesrepublik Deutschland*) had a population of about 45 million, not counting the millions of refugees who had settled here after fleeing eastern Europe.

Each zone of occupation was a facsimile of a small state; it had its own guarded frontiers and rigid border controls imposed on the movement of Germans and their goods between the zones. Travel outside occupied Germany was virtually impossible for the ordinary German.

Each zone had its own chief of state, the military governor heading the Allied occupation force assigned to the zone. His orders and decrees took precedence over any German law and could not be challenged by any German. The zonal military governor was answerable for his actions only to his superiors, either in Washington, Moscow, London, or Paris.

A wartime agreement reached in London provided that the supreme governing authority of defeated Germany would be vested in an Allied Control Council (ACC) established by the victorious powers in Berlin. The respective military governors of the four zones of occupation would constitute the ACC, whose work would be carried out by an administration composed of representatives of the four powers. On paper the ACC would provide for common political and economic policies and administration, covering all aspects of the daily existence of the vanquished Germans.

However, this four-power administration soon proved to be unworkable. Each of the Allied powers had its own basic objectives and programs vis-à-vis the defeated enemy state, and there were too many points of conflicts developing to achieve any unanimous decisions on major problems. The ACC suffered a growing paralysis from which it never recovered. The blossoming cold war between Washington and Moscow led, inexorably, to the division of Germany by the Iron Curtain.

Under the command of General Eisenhower, the Americans and British came into Germany armed with a common policy and program for the control and administration of Germany. However, the passage of time and changing circumstances began to disclose the differences in the philosophies and objectives between Washington and London on how to deal with the vanquished Germans.

At the outset, the coordinated policies and guidelines for British–American military government were set forth in an official *Handbook*. Its opening pages reflected a stern, no-nonsense approach toward the defeated enemy; it listed the following basic principles that would guide military-government personnel:

1. No steps looking toward economic rehabilitation of Germany are to be undertaken except as may be immediately necessary in support of military operations.
2. No relief supplies are to be imported or distributed for the German population, or for the displaced enemy, or ex-enemy nationals beyond the minimum necessary to prevent disease and disorder, as might endanger or impede military operations.
3. Under no circumstances shall active Nazis or ardent sympathizers be retained in office for the purpose of administrative convenience or expediency.
4. Although the Nazi party and all subsidiary organizations will be dissolved, administrative machinery of certain dissolved organizations may be used when necessary to provide essential functions, such as relief, health and sanitation, with non-Nazi personnel and facilities.
5. Germany will always be treated as a defeated country and not as a liberated country.

Within the British and American occupation zones, virtually every facet of human existence and activity was subject to the supervision and direction of the military government forces: food, housing, public health and welfare, education and religious affairs, public utilities, transportation, communications, newspapers, radio and every other medium of information, telephone and postal services, public and private finance, banking, property controls, labor and management, as well as every agency of government still extant.

The official military government *Handbook* listed over 1,250 separate and distinct areas of Allied supervision and control of German civilian life, as well as the basic rules and regulations to be enforced. This 300-page *Handbook,* with its copious appendices, would delight the heart and mind of any professional bureaucrat and desk warrior.

It is a document unique in the annals of warfare. Never before had a nation at war prepared such detailed plans and programs for the treatment of its enemy once the latter is defeated and forced to surrender, and followed that up with more to make sure he stays submissive to the victor's demands.*

The *Handbook* instructed military-government units on how to grasp the levers of power in every German community and how to maintain their controls with the assistance of local German officials whose collaboration could be counted on. The *Handbook* also detailed the broad and comprehensive military policy powers of the occupation forces, involving the suspension of all civil rights of the enemy population, unlimited search and seizure, wiretapping, inspection of civilian mail, income tax audits, as well as psychological and propaganda measures designed to stimulate German acceptance of military-government rule and its objectives.

Of the four occupying powers, the Americans were unique in their approach and in their policy toward the defeated enemy. The Americans carried in their knapsacks a tailor-made revolution to be imposed on the surviving Germans. Ostensibly it was dressed up as "reform and rehabilitation" and was encapsulated in the "Four-D" program. This seemed to have been created by a Madison Avenue advertising agency, as it had all the surface glibness and curative promises of a television commercial. The program of the Four-Ds seemed to possess the virtues of clarity, conciseness, and comprehension—or so it seemed at first glance. In successive stages it provided for the demilitarization, denazification, deindustrialization, and democratization of what was left of the defeated and devastated Third Reich. On paper this seemed to be a logical and feasible way to deal with an ex-enemy state; it coupled punishment with reform, and ultimately prepared the Germans for their conversion to the political ideology of their conquerors and new masters.

In contrast to the American plan to undertake the wholesale reform and rehabilitation of defeated Germany, the British, Russians, and French settled down for an extended stay, each seeking to carry out more pragmatic and limited objectives than the complete transformation of the German people. Having a more cynical turn of mind, as well as a longer and more personal relationship with their neighbor on the other side of the Rhine, the French never budged from their conviction that one can't reform a German; therefore he must be thoroughly subjugated. Germany must be kept divided, rendered powerless, and made subservient to Paris. Hence the French wasted little time and effort making their military rule palatable: they set out to strip their occupation zone of as much loot as the traffic could bear, in the name of reparations. To keep a resentful populace in line, the French employed the most intelligent and able ex-Nazi officials to serve as their front men and collaborators; this same policy applied to the French-controlled newspapers and radio. The main qualifications demanded of ex-Nazis were professional competence and loyalty to the French military government.

As for the Russians, they viewed Germany as a lauching pad for Western attacks on the Soviet Union, so the defeated enemy state must become a political and economic satellite under the iron-fisted control of the Kremlin. Stalin operated on the principle that the Germans must become a nation of helots to serve the objectives of Communist empire building.

The Kremlin had a long-range policy, but it employed decidedly short-range occupational practices that were to prove self-defeating in the years to come. In the initial stages of the occupation of East Germany, the Russians operated similarly to the French. They plundered their zone of virtually everything that could be unscrewed and transported back to the Soviet Union, from toilet bowls to complete factories. They installed German Communists who had come out of political exile in Moscow with the Red armies to head up various local governments and administrative agencies. To enforce obedience, the new Red regime drafted a police force of war-hardened men with slumbering consciences, strong appetites, and a lust for power. The Russians recruited their cadres of watchdogs and bloodhounds from the ranks of ex-Gestapo and SS-men. In return for loyal and unquestioning service to their new KGB overlords, the ex-Nazis and SS-men escaped punishment for their war crimes against the Allies and fellow Germans. This shift in allegiance from Hitler's dictatorship to Communist totalitarianism was made easy for the eager recruits. They merely exchanged the Nazi swastika for the Communist red star; in return they were assured food, lodging, and other perks of their police status, while hundreds of thousands of their fellow Germans remained hungry, homeless, and with little prospect of gainful employment.

The British—slow to anger but much slower to forgive, as Terence Prittie, veteran correspondent of the *Manchester Guardian* has pointed out —had a long account to settle with the Germans. Germany had twice upset the delicate European balance of power so carefully nurtured by Whitehall. Germany had started two world wars, each of which bled Britain of the manpower and wealth which had been piled up after decades of empire building. Since Bismarck's time, Germany had been Britain's most formidable industrial competitor in European and world markets. Germany's complete defeat, culminating in the unconditional surrender, was a long-awaited opportunity for Britain to get recompense for past losses, to reduce the enemy to the political status of a third- or fourth-rate power on the European scene, and to emasculate Germany as a trade competitor. With the direct control of the industrial Ruhr in its hands Britain was in a position to achieve these objectives.

As Robert Burns reminded us, . . . "the best-laid schemes o' mice and men / Gang aft a-gley." And so it was with the grandiose plans of the Americans and British as they were faced with unforeseen developments for which no contingency plans had been made.

The first rude notice to the U.S. Army High Command that winning the war did not necessarily mean achieving widely heralded victory came in the late autumn of 1945. In Manila, twelve thousand American G.I.'s staged a protest demonstration against the slow redeployment of troops to the U.S. With the speed of a chain reaction, the protest movement spread around the world wherever there were large concentrations of U.S. forces. This was to have decisive effects in rearranging the postwar political alignments on a global scale.

In November and December of the same year Paris and Frankfurt were the scenes of other GI demonstrations demanding their immediate release from the armed forces. The war was over for the rank-and-file soldiers. They had served their time in combat and had completed the task of "liberating" Europe. They had given up years of their own lives and they wanted out; let the army use enlisted men to serve in the occupation forces in Germany and Japan. Their demonstrations were so spontaneous and apparently so reflective of the feelings of the majority of the three million American soldiers in the European theater that they could not be lightly dismissed or ignored. In a detailed survey of this surprisingly strong "Let's-go-home" development, the *New York Herald Tribune* reported:

Both the GIs and the commanding officers of the United States Army have been amazed and confused by the discovery of the great source of power that was unleashed by the soldier demonstrations, precipitated in many parts of the world as a result of the re-deployment slowdown.

Angry soldiers began to write to their congressmen, who in turn put pressure on the Pentagon. The U.S. Army reacted by mobilizing all its resources to transport these soldiers back to America. They were shipped home faster in peace time than they had even been shipped to Europe under the urgency of war. A point system governed the discharge priorities of individual soldiers; points were allocated for overseas duty. Those with the most points were pulled out of their units, regardless of the consequences to the unit's military roster or its combat effectiveness, and ordered to the "zone of the interior," the army's designation for the U.S.

The stripping down of the U.S. Army in Germany of its excessive manpower of almost three million men was inevitable. As an occupation army it was too big and unwieldy; its soldiers had little to do to occupy their time and energies. But the redeployment of troops under the point system began to hurt when trained military-government officers and personnel, also included in the point system, were returned to the States.

Early in the war when the army began to form and train cadres of military-government officers and troops, it was understood that their term of service would be longer than that of the conscripted troops. The work of the milgov men would begin after the shooting stopped. They were specialists, and were to administer and control a defeated nation. In their ranks were found lawyers, doctors, economists, sociologists, educators, policemen, and government officials on leave from their jobs, as well as men trained in the mechanics of society such as the operation of public utilities, transportation, police, public health and welfare, and other service fields.

A large number of these officers had followed the U.S. forces from the North African beaches through Italy and France to the banks of the Elbe. Under the point system, many of them readily qualified for honorable discharge along with the most experienced combat troops. Unfortunately, no incentive system had been devised to persuade the milgov personnel to

stay on the job for the years necessary to give continuity and substance to
the U.S. occupation policies vis-à-vis the Germans.

By the second year of the occupation, there were large gaps in the
table of organization of military government in the U.S. zone. When the
majority of able and experienced men had been shipped out of Germany,
the army was left with men who wanted to, or had to, stay in Germany for
personal reasons. Some of these were regular U.S. Army personnel, assigned to fill the military-government jobs vacated by the point system.
They were untrained for the specialized work of administering and influencing the German civilian population. Others remained in Germany because life there was agreeable; their standard of living, due to the black-
market value of cigarettes, was much higher than they could hope to attain
in America. Others could not find stateside employment comparable to
what they had in Germany. All in all, the quality and effectiveness of the
U.S. military government suffered a marked decline. This soon became so
obvious that Gen. Joseph T. McNarney, the first U.S. military governor,
appealed to Washington for help. But the military pay scale did not
attract many men of the desired character and ability.

The Russians also had military-government problems in large proportions. First, only a small number of Red Army officers had ever
been outside of the Soviet Union before the war. Hence there was a severe
shortage of military-government personnel who had a working acquaint-
ance with a capitalistic European society and a knowledge of how it was
put together and functioned. The Russian High Command also had a
fear, bordering on paranoia, that their soldiers would be politically contaminated by their contact with the outside, non-Communist world through
uncontrolled and free contacts with the German civilian population. Hence,
when the occupation settled down, the Red Army kept its soldiers confined
to their barracks areas as far as circumstances permitted. As a result the
political commissars pulling the strings in East Germany had to work in
large measure through members of the German Communist party in organizing their own military government administration and controls. Most
of these Communist leaders had been out of touch with contemporary
Germany, either due to wartime exile in Russia or time spent as prisoners
in Nazi concentration camps; their political and economic know-how was
of dubious value.

However, the caliber and effectiveness of the French and British milgov
personnel were noticeably superior to their Russian and Americans counterparts. The French, for example, had thousands of German-speaking
Alsatians and Lorrainers to draw upon. These people had lived across the
Rhine from Germany for generations and for some of these periods had
been Germans themselves. For many, German was their mother tongue,
Müttersprache; they understood the German character and way of life.
More importantly the Alsatians and Lorrainers had the enlightening experience of having lived under the occupation rule of the Nazis. They knew

all the tricks of underground opposition and how to thwart the controls of their military masters. So after 1945 the French felt they were sufficiently armed with knowledge and experience to maintain full control over the Germans and to achieve their immediate objectives without arousing any serious opposition.

The life of French military-government personnel in occupied Germany was far better than in postwar France, which was suffering severe shortages. On the east side of the Rhine there was plenty of food and drink for the French officers, excellent housing, servants, transportation, and all the amenities of the good life. Consequently among the French there was much competition for military-government assignments in Germany.

The British also had recruited a large cadre of civilians who had a good working knowledge of Germany and its language to staff their military-government organization. England and Germany had long been doing business together. The British had a solid background of industrial and commercial relations with Germany which enabled them to mobilize sufficient numbers of businessmen who were well informed concerning the German economy and how it operated. As a result, these military-government officials had little trouble taking over effective control of the *Ruhrgebiet,* the core of Germany's industrial machine, after the unconditional surrender. Also many of the senior British army officers had participated in the occupation of Germany after World War I. Lastly, the British avoided the mistake of the Americans; they held on to their military-government personnel by giving them specific long-term commitments or service contracts, good pay, and excellent living and recreational facilities. The British milgov officer could plan on spending a number of years in Germany, living and growing in experience in his job. It contributed to intelligent decision-making in the long run.

While the cadre of trained and professional military-government officers was being shipped back to the States under the army's crash redeployment program, what remained of the Nazi government was being dismantled in the American and British zones. Acting under military decrees signed by General Eisenhower, "all active Nazis and ardent Nazi sympathizers" were to be removed from all public service posts at every level of government. At the same time German officials were told to remain at their posts, pending a decision on their retention or dismissal by the local military-government team. However, these orders were in conflict because virtually every German government official had been an active Nazi party member, a necessary condition to keeping or obtaining a national, state, or local government job in Hitler's Reich. Hence military-government teams had to search out Germans with anti-Nazi backgrounds and install them in public office with scant regard for their administrative qualifications; there were very few anti-Nazis available.

The purging of government officials was most drastic in the U.S. zone. In practice it meant outlawing the German government, or at least what remained of it after the unconditional surrender. The main effect, however, was to place a great burden of the control, supervision, and administration on the U.S. military government. American officers became directly and heavily involved in the direction and management of political and economic affairs, as well as German social and cultural life. Even with the best will in the world, plus experience and talent for this sort of thing, the direction and administration of a modern industrial state of alien culture, language, and tradition is an impossible task for an occupation army. Defeated Germany resembled an iceberg, seven-eighths of which was submerged. It was only the one-eighth of the ice peak which floated above the water that the military-government teams actually controlled and directed. From that point on the margin of Allied power and influence decreased.

As a quasi-political instrument of the Pentagon and State Department, the American army of occupation in Germany was called on to handle military occupation of a large European state, a task that with each passing day became more complex and difficult. Career army officers—and by the second year of the occupation most of the officers who had supplanted the civilian soldiers were "regulars"—are essentially nonpolitical men, rigid and doctrinaire. Their lives and their attitudes are governed by "SOP"—"Standard Order of Procedure." Meanwhile the caliber of the soldiers assigned to the army to carry out its tasks in Germany suffered a sharp decline by the end of the first year of occupation. Most of the combat soldiers had departed from the scene of their victories. They were replaced by postwar draftees, whose average age was nineteen, and of this group few, if any, had ever before stepped outside the continental U.S.

The Army High Command was faced with the serious problem of replacing the combat troops that had been redeployed, in order to meet the continuing U.S. military commitment in Europe. There ensued a hasty sweeping of army training camps in America for almost anybody able to walk and to breathe. On the average, these postwar draftees had only been in the army from six to eight weeks before being shipped overseas. Few of these men had ever fired a gun; their military indoctrination and training had been ragged and superficial. Almost 50 percent of them were officially categorized as Class Four or Class Five soldiers, which meant that they possessed an intelligence rating below 90, the passing grade, to the low 50s. At that time a Class Five soldier with a rating below 75 was considered little better than a moron in uniform, fit only for simple labor such as trench-digging. As a result the discipline and behavior of the occupation army deteriorated; these soldiers were continuously embroiled in incidents with German civilians.

As the *New York Herald Tribune* correspondent in Germany at that time, I was assigned to cover the U.S. forces in Germany, as well as the development of the military occupation and its relationship with the German civilian population. I toured the near and distant outposts of the U.S. Army and witnessed personally the sad decline in morale and character of the U.S. forces resulting from the influx of untrained, undisciplined, and unmotivated soldiery of below-average intelligence. I well remember one evening in the ancient university city of Marburg on the Lahn, which had become a processing center for incoming draftees. In the company of two combat veteran sergeants, we visited "Duffy's Tavern," a G.I. nightclub, situated only steps away from the historic cathedral where Martin Luther had preached his first sermon after breaking with Rome. The NCO in charge of Duffy's Tavern, a noisy and raucous place filled with drunken draftees, whose beery beligerency required the constant presence of two military policemen to keep some semblance of order, commented scornfully one evening: "These punks get a skinful of this fifteen-percent beer, and then they go around the town imagining they are the 'conquerors' that Eisenhower talked about, and think they won the war."

Dr. E. Y. Hartshorne of Harvard University, one of the few trained military-government officers who elected to continue serving as supervisor of Marburg University, had repeatedly appealed to the Army High Command to close down the Marburg processing depot, but to no avail; he later said that the ugly behavior of the draftees and their frequent beatings of German students and civilians was creating a brushfire of opposition to the American occupation. Dr. Hartshorne, a noted educator in his own right, explained that the incoming young draftees felt the psychological need to assert themselves as soon as they arrived in Germany because they had not experienced combat action and hence suffered from an inferiority complex.

In Garmisch-Partenkirchen, Germany's leading winter-sports resort and recreation center for the American occupation troops, on five successive nights in April 1946 I saw bands of drunken G.I.'s chasing civilians, particularly German girls. They knocked off pedestrians' hats and shouted "Goddamned Krauts, we'll show 'em who won the war!" Similar outrageous, reprehensible conduct was suffered by the inhabitants of Bamberg, Hof, Augsburg, Regensburg, and other cities in Bavaria.

The U.S. High Command in Frankfurt admitted privately that it had been a big mistake to react so precipitously to the G.I. demands to be sent home after the war ended. The growing misconduct of the replacement draftees had created a major political problem. Their lack of discipline and their unsoldierly conduct in a country where the military uniform had been respected above all else was seriously harming American prestige and influence. The American occupation forces had become flabby and their combat value, if any hostilities resumed in Europe, was quite dubious. What was needed was a small but highly-trained and disciplined occupation force of professional soldiers. Out of this need came the U.S. constabulary, a motorized and mobile armored force, approximately the strength of two divisions. Its purpose was twofold: to quell any overt opposition to the U.S. military government and to guard the eastern frontiers against infiltration by Communist agents from the other side of the Iron Curtain. The constabulary, however, never had to fire a shot in anger against any person or group posing a threat to the U.S. military rule in Germany; it was gradually phased out.

3

In looking back, I think if we had then realized the confusion and chaos which existed, we would indeed have thought ours was a hopeless task.
—GEN. LUCIUS D. CLAY, *U.S. military governor in postwar Germany.*

A man may build himself a throne of bayonets, but he cannot sit on it.
—DEAN W. R. INGE, *Canterbury Cathedral*

THE DE-TEUTONIZATION OF DEUTSCHLAND

THE AMERICANS approached the problem of a defeated Germany as if a great moral question was involved in dealing with its surviving population. General Eisenhower's first proclamation to the German people catches this note of righteous indignation, joined with a firm resolve to cleanse the Augean stables of the filth and abominations of nazism. To the American decision-makers in Washington and in the field, Nazi Germany was an outlaw, a pariah in the family of nations. As they viewed it, Germany must be purged of the sins of nazism and put on the road to moral redemption. This required the surviving Germans to submit to the rigors of the Four-Ds: to be demilitarized, denazified, deindustrialized, and finally to be democratized. This attempted purging of an entire nation was a questionable gamble to say the least. History has provided few, if any, examples in which a conqueror successfully reformed a conquered people; even the more successful at this trade—Attila the Hun, Alexander the Great, and Napoleon Bonaparte—could not achieve this goal.

The City Council of Essen has ruled that street car conductors can wear the
shoulder straps similar to those formerly worn by German Army lieutenants.
The conductors have had difficulty in controlling the conduct of passengers in
over-crowded street cars. A touch of military insignia might help to restore
good order and public discipline, it was explained.

—*From a report in the* Frankfurter
Rundschau, *August 1947*

1] The Demilitarization of Germany

The postwar memoirs of the German generals all agree that Hitler had
a simple and inflexible military objective in World War II which he repeatedly demanded of his field commanders in every battle: *Die Vernichtung des Feindes,* the annihilation of the enemy. No halfway measures of
combat were acceptable. As the war continued to be fought with ever-
increasing ferocity and as the slaughter and destruction grew apace, it was
not surprising that the Allies would also settle for nothing less than
Deutschlands Vernichtung, culminating in the unconditional surrender of
all armed forces.

Thus, at the end of the war, the demilitarization of Germany was, for
all practical purposes, a *fait accompli.** There was little more to be done
to complete the destruction of what had been the most powerful and
cohesive military force ever mounted by one nation, except to tidy things
up a bit and make an inventory of the prizes of war.

The armies of the Nazi Reich had disintegrated: about 2.5 million
German soldiers were behind the barbed-wire fences of prisoner-of-war
camps; some 2.1 million were known to have fallen in battle and another
2.9 million were missing in action and presumed to be dead. Hitler's
vaunted *Stuka* dive bombers, the giant Tiger tanks, the deadly all-purpose
88-mm guns, and all the other weapons of war were now in Allied hands.
The airfields throughout the Reich were strewn with the burnt-out planes
of the once-feared *Lüftwaffe.* The harbors and naval bases were plugged
up with the wreckage of Nazi submarines and warships. The *Siegfried*
line was reduced to broken chunks of concrete blockhouses, littering the
green and forested landscapes of the western frontier. The massive air
raid shelters in every German city and town were now housing hundreds of
thousands of the local population and refugees made homeless by the war.

The hospitals were filled with the human debris of war: the sightless,
armless, legless; the scarred, burned, and mutilated soldiers, the still-living
human sacrifices to Hitler's war making. The streets and shop queues were

crowded with millions of war widows dressed in black. Few of these women could ever visit the burial places of their soldier dead who were interred in unmarked, unlisted, and unhonored graves, scattered from the rubble of Stalingrad to Cherbourg, from Narvik to the Qattara Depression.

Germany's will to fight on, or to offer any resistance to the conquerors' rule, was broken. Germany had truly been "demilitarized," physically, mentally, and spiritually.

Three years after the war's end, Clay cabled his superiors in Washington on July 19, 1948 that: ". . . the world is now facing the most vital issue that has developed since Hitler placed his political aggression. . . . Only we have the strength to halt this aggressive policy here and now. It may be too late the next time."

The occasion for this clarion call to action was the beginning of the Berlin blockade by the Russians. West Berlin, with its 2.5 million civilians and thousands of American, British, and French troops, was isolated from West Germany. Barricades were erected by the Red Army on all roads and rail lines connecting western Germany with Berlin to force a showdown, a confrontation with the Americans and their Allies that the Russians were confident they would win.

This was the high point of the cold war, which had suddenly and menacingly blossomed across divided and defeated Germany. The master geo-politician, Stalin wished to dominate all of Germany, because Germany had always presented the most dangerous military threat to Russia. With Germany in his control, Stalin could call the tune which the western European nations must dance to. Only the United States stood in his way, so it was imperative to force the Americans to leave Europe and to abandon any defense commitments toward its old allies.

In formulating this strategy Stalin appears to have committed a major blunder. He had been encouraged to believe, on the basis of the hurried redeployment of U.S. combat forces from the Continent, brought on by the "we-want-to-go-home" demonstrations of thousands of G.I.'s, that the Americans were washing their hands of Europe. From this premise it seemed logical to conclude that the Americans had neither the will nor the stomach to fight a second war with the Russians for the political control of Europe. Hence the Kremlin's immediate postwar strategy was simple and blunt: force the Americans and their British and French allies to make a humiliating evacuation from blockaded Berlin under Soviet pressure tactics. This would demonstrate to all Europeans that the U.S. government had become—in the words of Mao Tse-Tung—"a paper tiger" unwilling and unable to defend its allies.

Stalin's second mistake was to underestimate his opponents, particularly the U.S. military governor, whose courage and determination to stay on in besieged Berlin rallied his troops and the flagging Western Allies to hold their ground against the Russian cold-war aggression. Clay clearly understood the master strategy of the Kremlin in Germany and what it portended for the West. On April 2, 1948 he had cabled the Pentagon:

We have lost Czechoslovakia. Norway is threatened . . . When Berlin falls, Western Germany will be next. If we mean to hold Europe against communism we must not budge. . . . If we withdraw, our position in Europe is threatened. If America does not understand this now, does not know that the issue is cast, then it never will and communism will run rampant. I believe the future of democracy requires us to stay . . . This is not a heroic pose, because there will be nothing heroic in having to take humiliation without retaliation.*

On June 24, 1948 the Russians blockaded all road, rail, and water-ways between western Germany and Berlin. Clay's riposte was to organize an aerial supply line between the beleaguered city and the outside world. The Allied airlift—the German description of it as the *Lüftbrücke,* or air bridge, is more evocative of what became a superb melding of men and planes to feed and support a city of 2.5 million people entirely by air trans-port—was to be a resounding success. When it began the Americans calcu-lated that a bare-bones minimum of 4,000 tons of cargo, principally coal for the city's power plants and food, would have to be airlifted into Berlin every twenty-four hours, regardless of the weather. The U.S. Air Force could only mobilize one hundred aging, twin-motored Dakotas, each with a cargo capacity of only two and a half tons. Later, as the airlift became better organized, 160 C–54s were employed, each with a cargo lift of ten tons. In the final months of the blockade, Berlin was receiving daily ship-ments of over twelve thousand tons, more than enough to keep the city functioning with a cushion to spare. In the latter stages of this stark con-frontation, the Russians began to feel the backlash of world opinion con-cerning their cruel and ineffective political extortion. Their ground barri-cades began to look ridiculous, as they were flown over by the unceasing stream of huge transport planes of the American and Royal air forces. On May 11, 1949, the Russians lowered their barricades on all roads, rail lines, and waterways to Berlin from the West. The blockade was over.

However, the success of the airlift in beating back a Russian squeeze play on West Berlin did not obscure the lesson that this political con-frontation had made plain. Western Europe must now have an active and viable defense system against the constant threat of Russian aggression. Equally important in the eyes of the Pentagon and the U.S. High Com-mand in Frankfurt was the necessity of West Germany becoming an in-tegral part of this defense system. This meant an end to the demilitariza-tion of the Germans and the first steps in re-creating a postwar German army, navy, and air force.

The French balked at this proposal; the British also dug in their heels to a lesser degree. Both these longtime allies of the U.S. were in no mood to once again face the specter of German militarism so soon after the end of World War II. However, the balance of power had changed decisively in the postwar years. The U.S. was the acknowledged leader of the western nations, by virtue of its atomic arsenal and its superior naval and air power. America was also the strongest and richest industrial nation; Uncle Sam would underwrite the military defenses of Europe from its vast stores of weaponry. Finally, Marshall Plan aid would rebuild and modernize the economies of western Europe. Therefore, *ipso facto,* America would have a major role in postwar European development.

However, executing a reversal of the demilitarization policy of Germany was a difficult and frustrating task. There is a certain momentum and stability built into a fixed government policy line that resists changes of direction and movement. For example, on May 8, 1950, the fifth anniversary of the unconditional surrender of the *Wehrmacht,* the three Allied high commissioners* in Bonn promulgated a law, designed to prevent German rearmament and to insure that West German heavy industry remained demilitarized. This action was carried out at a time when the Pentagon in Washington was actively planning the creation of a new West German defense force as part of the North Atlantic Treaty Organization (NATO). The following September Secretary of State Dean Acheson lifted the curtain a bit on Washington's plans with his proposal that West Germany should organize a ten-division army to be incorporated into NATO. To Europeans, the U.S. government seemed to be suffering from a touch of schizophrenia, with one part seeking to demilitarize Germany indefinitely, while another part was planning an early remilitarization of the ex-enemy state.

A scant eight months later, General Eisenhower, supreme commander of NATO, made a highly publicized journey to Frankfurt. During this visit he "extended the right hand of friendship to the Germans and offered them a chance to join in building up the military strength counted on to bring security to Western Europe."*

The New York Times further described General Eisenhower's mission as a ". . . bold and clever move to win greater German cooperation on defense by the man, whose name more than any other signifies the defeat of the Third Reich . . . (he) told the German people . . . 'For my part, let bygones be bygones.' "

On the following day, the NATO commander had a meeting with the new chancellor of the *Bundesrepublik,* Adenauer, and other leading German officials, in which he stated that the ordinary German soldier "did not lose his honor" in World War II because of Nazi atrocities.

The degree to which General Eisenhower and his military colleagues had changed their political opinions about the Germans can be judged by the sharp contrast to the views he had expressed two years earlier in his memoirs, *Crusade in Europe,* in which he wrote:

The tradition that all professional soldiers are really comrades in arms has, in tattered form, persisted to this day. For me, World War II was far too personal a thing to entertain such feelings. Daily, as it progressed, there grew within me the conviction that as never before in a war between many nations, the forces that stood for human good and men's rights were this time confronted by a completely evil conspiracy, with which no compromise could be tolerated.

In the final analysis the whole Allied program of demilitarization and dismantling seemed to be an exercise in fatuity, or as James A. O'Donnell, *Newsweek*'s correspondent, put it:

. . . like undertakers performing an amputation on a corpse. For five years we have been blowing up bunkers, cutting holes in air raid shelters, dismantling factories, silting harbors, banning the production of toy soldiers and pop-guns and 're-orienting' the German mind. Having stripped Germany of every possibility of defense, the irony of the sudden appeal to the Germans to get in there and defend what we believe in is obvious. It is like mentioning a rope in the home of somebody who has been hanged.

However, there was one man who had the breadth of vision to see the outlines of a great opportunity in the disturbing and perplexing question of rearming Germany. He was Dr. Konrad Adenauer, the first chancellor of the postwar West German government, who was installed in office on September 15, 1949, at the age of seventy-three. At that time the veteran Rhineland politician was considered a spent figure from the dim and distant pre-Hitlerian times, whose anti-Nazi record was his sole qualification for a return to the political arena. Dr. Adenauer had been lord mayor of Cologne from 1917 to 1933, when he was removed from office by the Nazis.

He had been resurrected for this post by the Americans, who had taken the military surrender of the city. However, he was again removed from his office by the British military government, which subsequently took administrative control of the city, in October 1945. The British were to later pay for this action in diminished influence in the postwar government headed by Adenauer. But in 1945 there was little to indicate that Adenauer, already on the pension rolls, was to have a second and more illustrious career ahead of him in which his achievements were to be favorably compared to those of Bismarck, the architect of modern Germany.

Adenauer was on friendly terms with the Americans, particularly with John J. McCloy, the U.S. high commissioner. In their almost daily contacts, McCloy kept Adenauer well informed about the Pentagon's objective to create a German army within the framework of the NATO alliance. He was also aware that the U.S. was taking the lead in the proposed rearmament of Germany while the British and French were not yet per-

suaded of the immediacy of a Russian threat. Adenauer knew that the U.S.,
with its superior military resources and its industrial power and wealth,
would eventually be the arbiter of West Germany's fate.

Adenauer not only accepted the inevitability of an early German rearmament, he welcomed it as the instrument with which to free his country
from the Allied occupation rule and to obtain almost complete political and
economic freedom for the fledgling Republic. He was confident that the
Americans were prepared to pay that price for West Germany's somewhat
grudging participation in the NATO defense system.

In a speech at Bielefeld on January 14, 1951—just a week before
General Eisenhower's personal invitation to the Germans to become the
"comrades-in-arms" of their Allied masters—Adenauer set forth the conditions for Germany's future military cooperation with the Western powers.
He demanded for Germany "absolute equal rights" with the other NATO
powers, a treaty guaranteeing an Allied defense of West Germany in the
event of a Russian invasion, an end to the occupation statute and Allied
supervisory control, financial support for the period of the German buildup
of its defense forces, and finally no concerted action by the Allies that
would block West Germany's advances toward full sovereignty.

Adenauer offered his compatriots a glimpse of the future that he
thought would stir the Germans out of their postwar apathy: the early end
to Allied military rule; political and economic freedom for the German
people; and a restoration of German sovereignty. But these visions never
came into focus because they seemed so unreal and impossible of achievement compared to the ugly realities which the average civilian had to endure each new day. Every morning as he stepped out of his doorway, the
physical devastation and sense of loss that met the eyes blotted out any
rose-colored images of a distant future. Not enough time had elapsed to
dull the memories of World War II and what it had wreaked on the lives
of those who survived it.

There was a widespread revulsion to the war and all things associated
with it which had sunk deep into the German psyche. The militarists had
become disillusioned and converted to pacifism. It must be remembered
that the great Nazi victories of the war were won in the earlier years, and
the battles had been fought on somebody else's real estate. In the last year
of the war the tide turned savagely; bombs and shells began to fall on
German homes and factories, power plants, water mains, sewers, and so
on. The birds of prey of the *Totaler krieg* the total war, which Hitler and
his armies had inflicted on Rotterdam, Warsaw, Stalingrad, Belgrade, and
throughout the European world, now flew home to roost in the rubble
and ruins of German cities, towns, and villages. When it was all over there
was no hero's welcome as there had been after World War I for the 2.5
million soldier survivors of this war. The German soldier's combat record
was degraded for having served at the command of the Nazi war crim-

inals. So they joined with the civilians in the general rejection of rearmament, with the popular slogan, *"Ohne mich!"*—best translated into the vernacular as "Count me out of it!"

In the immediate postwar period, the Berlin blockade had profoundly disturbed the Germans, who were frightened at the prospect that the growing tension between the two great powers might lead to open warfare, with Germany the scene of the first battlefield. Then the East German Communist regime announced the creation of a "people's army," which the West Germans visualized as the prelude to a "European Korea," with Germans fighting Germans under orders from Moscow and Washington. Again, *"Ohne mich!"*

The Socialist party was strongly opposed to rearmament; so were the six million organized trade-union workers. Ludwig Rosenberg, Socialist and leading trade union executive, echoed the views of his colleagues when he advocated that West Germany follow the lead of Sweden, ". . . which is officially neutral in the cold war, but personally pro-western and nobody accuses the Swedes of being pro-Russian because they do not want to join the European Defense Community."*

On the right side of the political spectrum, German big business, including the great Ruhr firms that had supplied the weapons for the armed forces of Kaiser Wilhelm II and Hitler, had no wish to get back into that line of production. Even Adenauer admitted that the opposition to arms production developed because the Ruhr was only a short flight from the Iron Curtain and "nothing attracts enemy bombers like an arms industry."* Besides, the reviving German industry was producing, at the peak of its limited capacity, a wide range of consumer and capital goods for hungry markets at home and abroad. To switch over and retool for arms production was just not economic good sense, because it meant surrendering a share of the expanding world markets and losing momentum in the reconstruction and modernization of Germany's heavily bombed industrial establishment.

It was not until 1954 that Adenauer was given the mandate of the Bonn *Bundestag* authorizing him to negotiate the rearmament of West Germany. On October 3, 1954 he signed the Treaty of Paris, together with the representatives of the U.S., France, and Great Britain, ending the Allied occupation of West Germany. The treaty acknowledged that the Federal Republic of Germany was now a sovereign state. In return for this restoration of its independence and full political and economic freedoms—except for certain stipulations agreed to by the Bonn government —Adenauer now pledged Germany's full support and participation in the common defense of western Europe against the threat of Communist aggression. With this treaty in hand, West Germany rejoined the family of nations as a dues-paying member.

West Germany's reluctant decision to rearm and participate in the defense of Europe was largely dictated by economic self-interests rather than any political aggrandizement; sovereignty gave West Germany the freedom and the incentive to develop its economic strength and resources.

Hitler was right when he promised us a 1,000-year Reich. That's what we have today: 12 years of nazification under Hitler and 988 years of denazification under the Americans.

—*A popular comment circulating in the U.S. zone in 1948*

What then was National Socialism? It was a historically unique phenomenon, dependent on an individual and on a moment, a phenomenon which can never re-appear in the same form. It was a state of intoxication, produced by a gang of intoxicated experts, kept up for years. It was a machine for the manufacture of power, for the safeguarding of power and for the extension of power.

—GOLO MANN, *German historian**

2] The Denazification of Germany

The opening lines of General Eisenhower's first proclamation to the defeated Germans set forth the primary objectives of the American and British armed forces. He said: ". . . we shall obliterate nazism and German militarism. We shall overthrow the Nazi rule, dissolve the Nazi party and abolish the cruel, oppressive and discriminatory laws and institutions which the party has created. . . ."

The Allied denazification of postwar Germany was an ersatz revolution imposed on the defeated by their conquerors. Its motivation was the conviction that the Germans had been so contaminated by the doctrines and practices of nazism that they had neither the will nor the capabilities to cure themselves of this ideological sickness. Hence their conquerors would undertake the purging of the German body politic, to restore it to health and democracy.

This number one war aim was soon codified into Law 38 of the ACC, with the approval of the American, British, Russian, and French military governors. In theory this law embodied a uniform policy for the "eradication of nazism" from the minds and hearts of some sixty million surviving Germans. However, once Law 38 became statutory, each of the Allied signatories went their own separate ways in carrying out the denazification of its respective occupation zone.

The Russians, for example, approached denazification as another phase of the long struggle between communism and capitalism. The Russians and their East German Communist allies eliminated in large measure the top layer of society—the landowners, industrialists, bankers, and businessmen—by summary arrest and conviction, followed by execution or deportation to the Soviet Union for forced labor, all in the name of denazification.* These unfortunate men of substance and their families suffered the loss of their personal properties while their lands and business enterprises were confiscated or nationalized.

Denazification in the Russian zone of occupation was governed by the basic principle that virtually any adult who did not have a vested interest in the preservation of a capitalist society could be "persuaded" by one means or another to perform tasks of value to a Communist-oriented society. It also offered an escape hatch for those members of the working and middle classes who had been Nazi party officials or members. They could avoid the penalties for their past political affiliations by demonstrating their loyalty and obedience to their new Communist masters. If, for example, a Nazi joined an anti-Fascist political party—another way of describing the Soviet-sponsored Socialist Unity party (SED) before March 31, 1946—he was considered to be politically rehabilitated, thereby earning an exemption from the denazification process and its penalties. This decree was in violation of Law 38.

This measure gave an ex-Nazi an incentive to throw in his future with the Communists, while the political organism of the Soviet military government was also strengthened in its increased membership.

When the new East German Communist government was installed in office, the door to ex-Nazis was opened wider. It issued a blanket waiver of denazification for all ex-Nazi officials and former German army officers if they were not guilty of any war crimes. They were restored to full citizenship with the right to engage in any profession. The objective was to tie their individual postwar careers to the Communist state, thus assuring it the support of an important segment of the adult male population.

Another group which was excluded from denazification comprised scientists and engineers who were the pillars of German technology. By agreeing to continue their work and research for the Soviet Union, they obtained political clearance at the price of having to work in Russian plants and laboratories.

Soviet pragmatism was neatly justified by a high-ranking Russian officer who said: "As we Russians are unlikely to be affected politically, we use the brains of the Nazis as much as possible."*

In sharp contrast to the Russian handling of denazification, the French evolved their own pragmatic philosophy concerning ex-Nazis, particularly industrialists, businessmen, and technicians. There was not much heavy industry in the southwest corner of Germany which had been taken over by the French. However, the French zone also included the Saar, an industrial principality of coal mines, steel mills, and other manufacturing plants. To maintain continuous production of coal, steel, and other goods, all of which were shipped to France as part of reparations, was more important to the French than to take punitive action against former Nazis, especially if they were the industrialists and manufacturers managing the mines, mills, and factories in the Saar.

In fact, the French experienced little trouble with any of the Saar's *Herr Direktoren* and managers, who went back to their desks to continue their work under French supervision—except for Hermann Röchling. Seventy-four years old and owner of the Saar's largest complex, *Röchling-werke,* he had been a strong Nazi supporter with known anti-French views. At the war's end, fearing French retribution, Röchling took refuge in the U.S. zone.

For two years the French made proposals to Röchling, inviting him to come back to the Saar and resume direction of his industrial empire. Röchling's return to the Saar would have been interpreted as giving approval to France's economic annexation of this industrial principality; Röchling rebuffed all offers. The French, their patience exhausted, finally issued a warrant for his arrest as a war criminal. He was extradited from the U.S. zone, tried, convicted, and sentenced to seven years imprisonment, for what, in reality, was his unwillingness to collaborate with the French.

In a moment of candor, quite revealing of his government's basic principle concerning denazification, General Perrin-Pelletier, deputy French military governor, told a Ruhr press conference in 1946: "We French take the point of view that every German was or still is a Nazi, and if you don't want to kill off all the Germans, then you have to work with these Nazis. In the Saar we did not make the idiotic mistake of denazification."

In short, the French showed the greatest political realism of the Allied powers concerning this prickly issue of denazification. They reasoned that the total defeat and collapse of 1945 would purge the Germans of any lingering nostalgia for Adolf Hitler; Allied denazification would only pile coals on Newcastle.

The British approach to denazification was singular; they operated on the principle that it was essentially a judicial proceeding rather than a political purge or a moral reform. The primary objective of British denazification was to find and punish those Nazis who were guilty of legally recognized criminal acts and to apply the German criminal code as far as possible in the prosecution and conviction of these Nazi criminals. The British denazification tribunals followed accepted legal procedures and were presided over by regular judges rather than by political appointees, as was the case in the three other zones.

Hence, instead of trying to bring every Nazi official before a denazification tribunal, the British confined their indictments and trials to members of the criminal organizations of the Third Reich, as identified by the International Military Tribunal at Nuremberg. This category comprised members of the SS Corps, the SD (*Sicherheitsdienst,* or security arm of the SS), the Gestapo, and the core of leadership of the Nazi party. All in all, only about 10 percent of the civilian population was involved in the denazification proceedings in the British zone, compared to over 30 percent in the U.S. zone. While the British zone had the largest population (22.7 million) of the four occupation sectors, they carried out only 22,296 trials, as compared to 169,282 trials in the American zone (with a population of 18 million), and a reported 18,000 trials—a doubtful figure—for the Russian zone (population 17 million). There were 17,353 denazification proceedings in the French zone (population 3.8 million), mainly to provide a police record of ex-Nazis for military-government purposes.

In retrospect, there seems little doubt that the British denazification program was the most equitable and effective in its efforts to eradicate the hard-core of Nazi political-criminal elements who managed to survive the collapse of the Third Reich.

The U.S. military government was confident that it could successfully obliterate nazism from that part of the German body politic resident in the American zone. The Public Safety Branch of OMGUS (Office of Military Government U.S.) under Col. Orlando Wilson, professor of criminology at the University of California, was given the job of administering the denazification of the 13 million surviving German adults in his bailiwick.

Colonel Wilson and his aides believed they had the necessary tools with which to successfully achieve the objectives of denazification. The ACC Law 38 made it mandatory for all Germans to provide explicit and detailed information about their past political attitudes and activities. The Americans and British prepared a *Fragebogen,* a detailed questionnaire, designed to extract every scrap of information from each German, and to disclose all aspects of that person's conduct and affiliations during the Hitlerian years. No excuses were accepted for failure to answer all the questions. No one could "take the Fifth Amendment" and avoid self-incrimination. In fact, the *Fragebogen* was an instrument specifically designed to elicit self-incriminating information; its purpose was to expose all Nazis and to measure the extent of their individual services to the Nazi Third Reich. There were severe penalties of long prison terms threatened for anyone caught falsifying his *Fragebogen* or failing to answer all of its 131 searching questions.*

Under the abnormal circumstances of the chaotic postwar period, it would seem relatively easy for the Germans to falsify their questionnaires. How could the Allies know for sure who was a Nazi and who wasn't? How could one separate the sheep from the goats? Except concerning the top level of Nazi party, the government, and the armed forces, the Allies had only sketchy information about the makeup of German society. Besides, most of the public documentation of a society such as the vital statistics of births, deaths, police records, and so on had been destroyed in the shelling and bombing of the German cities and towns.

However, the American counterintelligence corps had been tipped off that a cache of Nazi party documents could be found in a deserted paper mill in a Munich suburb, ready to be pulped into cellulose. The water-soaked documents proved to be the master membership files of the Nazi party, which had been kept in the Brown House, its headquarters. The documents included the names and other personal details of 8 million members of the Nazi party, as well as 4 million members of the party's auxiliary organizations.

This information, also available to the British and French authorities, made it risky for an ex-Nazi to deny or to falsify his past political record. Hence there was a surprising response in the U.S. zone to the 13 million *Fragebogen* that were issued. On the basis of their incriminating replies, 3.6 million Germans were indicted for war or political crimes. That was over 20 percent of the population in the U.S. zone, which included almost 4 million refugee Germans from the east.*

As prescribed by the military government and later written into German law, those indicted were to be tried and judged according to the following categories:

CLASS I. *Hauptschuldige* (major offenders), which comprised all of the top-ranking Nazis, including Hitler's intimate circle, prominent government officials, *Gauleiters,* SS generals, etc.

CLASS II. *Belastete* (offenders), identified as Nazi "activists, militarists, and profiteers," who openly and strongly supported Hitler's war making, including the industrialists who profited immensely from the Nazi conquest of Europe.

CLASS III. *Minderbelastete* (lesser offenders), covering those Germans who came into the party as young men and, while being active Nazis, had not committed any serious political or war crimes.

CLASS IV. *Mitlaufer* (followers), the small fry who could not avoid some form of allegiance to the Nazis, to keep their jobs, etc.

CLASS V. *Entlastete* (exonerated), the few Germans who could prove anti-Nazi opposition to the regime.

It was soon painfully evident that the American military government had bitten off far more than it could chew as far as denazification was concerned.* The wide-ranging *Fragebogen* had netted a case load of 3,596,000 Nazis, indictable for trials by tribunals. The American military government had neither the staff nor the stomach to sort out this bundle of dirty political linen. Bear in mind that as a result of the accelerated army redeployment program, the trained and qualified military-government personnel were being shipped home along with the combat troops. There just wasn't enough experienced, knowledgeable American manpower left behind in Germany to carry on the massive denazification program. At the rate the earliest denazification tribunals were able to process their cases, it would take eight-and-a-half years to clear up the backlog of 3.6 million ex-Nazis.

A series of amnesties by the U.S. military governor in 1946 exempted the young, the disabled, and those in the *Mitläufer* category, reducing the case load to 930,000. These Nazis were put through the denazification mill in a total of 169,282 trials. But by then the Americans were beginning to have their doubts about the whole program. As Clay admitted in his memoirs: "Perhaps never before in world history has such an undertaking to purge society been attempted. . . . Looking back, it might have been more effective to have selected a rather small number of leading Nazis for trial without attempting mass trials."*

Clay's hindsight spotlights the fundamental error of the whole American denazification program. A massive political purge of the defeated nation was not only unnecessary, but it was also to prove counterproductive, with its own subtle backlash. What the Americans and other Allies, to a lesser degree, failed to realize was that the denazification of Germany was achieved with the defeat of Hitler's armies: in their unconditional surrender; in the devastation visited on the German cities and towns; in the millions of soldiers and civilians dead and disabled; and in the incalculable losses of property and assets, public and private. Defeat was the catharsis that denazified the surviving Germans, except for a handful of die-hard war criminals who were hiding from their pursuers.

When Adolf Hitler committed suicide in his Berlin bunker in the closing days of the war, his discredited and bankrupt ideology died with him. Surviving Germans were drained of all resistance to their conquerors. As for hard-core Nazi fanatics, most of them were behind barbed wire. Allied directives called for the automatic arrest and internment of all top-ranking Nazis, as well as all officers and noncoms of the SS, SD, Waffen SS, and other paramilitary organizations, down to the level of sergeant. In the U.S. zone over one hundred thousand of these hardened Nazis were held in concentration camps for almost three years, and then turned over to German denazification tribunals for trial. Since the surrender they had been insulated and isolated from postwar German life.

Nazism in those early postwar years was as dead as Dillinger, a fact that most American security officers found hard to believe. During the first two years of the occupation, the U.S. Army counterintelligence corps organized all its resources to apprehend any individual or group of Nazis trying to establish organized resistance to the military-government controls or to reorganize a Hitler movement. Working together, the British and American security agencies staged three roundups from 1945 to 1947. The first was "Operation Nursery," which netted a handful of young Nazis who sought to perpetuate the Hitler Youth Movement. Two other raids corralled a number of high-ranking and junior SS officers (*Schutzstaffeln*) and SA officers (*Sturmabteilung*) of the Nazi party. All sought to keep alive small corps of believers in the Nazi credo; they set their future objective as the revival of Germany "into a powerful nation." They financed their activities, which mainly consisted of keeping in touch with each other but not in any overt challenge or sabotage of the Allied military controls, through black-market operations.

It amazed the Allied authorities that no overt resistance surfaced. No American or British soldier was ever killed or murdered for political reasons by an underground resistance group. No Allied soldiers were fished out of West Germany's canals or rivers with their throats cut, as happened to German soldiers during the Nazi occupation of France and the Low Countries.

What surprised the U.S. counterintelligence corps during the first year of occupation was the flood of mostly unsigned letters, tens of thousands, from Germans denouncing other Germans as Nazis and calling for their exposure and punishment. It took a great deal of time and energy to sift through this hate mail, but it never lifted the lid on any Nazi underground movement.

The time had come to dump the problem of denazification into the laps of the Germans, a convoluted bit of OMGUS* reasoning that had a queer logic of its own: if denazification is going to turn to be the "snafu" it shows every promise of becoming, then let the Germans get stuck with it.

The denazification program, designed by the Americans, was turned over to the Germans with a collective sigh of relief, for it was a task too big and too complex to be carried out by an occupation power. But somebody was guilty of political naïveté on a grand scale in assuming that a nation, which wholeheartedly had endorsed Hilter and nazism in peace and war, could turn around and be its own prosecutor, judge, jury, and defendant for the crimes committed in the name of nazism. Brushing aside this paradoxical situation, the U.S. military government issued orders that the three *Länder* (states) of the American zone pass a "Law for the Liberation from National Socialism and Militarism" in March 1946. This legislation continued the denazification program along the guidelines originally established by the Americans, but it quickly descended to the levels of influence peddling and old-style Tammany Hall politics.*

On September 26, 1945, OMGUS issued Law 8, which barred any member of the Nazi party or any of its auxiliary organizations from resuming his former employment or working in a different profession or craft. The only work permitted these ex-Nazis was menial labor, such as street-sweeping and garbage-collecting.

This attempt to put former Nazis into economic quarantine, at a time when unemployment was rife and hunger was stalking the land, showed little knowledge of the realities of life in the Third Reich and scant comprehension of the reaction of postwar Germans to this punitive measure.* For example, thousands of schoolteachers, as well as hundreds of thousands of government employees in the Hitler years, were put under heavy pressure to join the party to safeguard their employment. At the same time important Ruhr industrialists such as Friedrich Flick, August Thyssen, and Emil Kirdorf contributed millions to the Nazi party but never accepted the many invitations to join it. Others performed important services for the Nazis but never became members of the party. Heinrich Müller, who was wartime chief of the Gestapo, did not enter the party's ranks until 1939.

This employment segregation, which originated with Colonel Wilson's regime, was continued when the Germans took over administration of the denazification program on June 1, 1946. However, prior to this date the Americans had ousted 241,193 ex-Nazis from their public-service jobs, while 101,000 Nazis faced mandatory changeover from their white-collar positions to pick-and-shovel jobs. In this mindless purging, over 80 percent of the schoolteachers in the American zone and 50 percent of the doctors were required to close their books, shut down their clinics, and accept outside work such as shoveling away the tons of rubble littering the cities and towns. Three hundred thousand civil servants who had been Nazi party members were also subject to new careers in street-cleaning and rubble removal. But without their services the whole structure of military government in the U.S. zone would have collapsed, so an administrative waiver permitted them to remain at their desks.

These developments led to a change in the political climate. The Germans began having second thoughts about denazification and its implications for them. For example, the flood of denunciations against Nazis whose cases were shortly to be tried, which had been reaching American and German denazification officials, suddenly dried up. Many Germans who had submitted damaging affidavits about the past Nazi activities of fellow Germans or who had offered to appear as witnesses for the prosecution withdrew their sworn depositions and failed to show up as witnesses in court sessions.

The Communist party (KPD) was quick to realize that it was a political mistake to continue to support the denazification program in the U.S. zone. In July 1947 party headquarters instructed all its members that henceforth they could no longer serve as members or prosecutors of any denazification tribunal. Prior to that decision, the participation of KPD members in the denazification program had been far more vociferous and organized than any other political group. For example, in Catholic Bavaria, where the KPD had received only 6 percent of the total vote in 1947, its members held 16 percent of all the appointed positions as judges or prosecutors of the denazification tribunals. The KPD had sought to use the denazification program as a weapon to attack and to damage the landowners, industrialists, and other leaders of the bourgeoisie. Yet during the second year of occupation, the Communists saw for themselves that denazification was being discredited and was serving no further purpose as far as the KPD was concerned. A backlash of antipathy and resentment was rising among German civilians. When the KPD realized that further association with and support of this political purging would boomerang against them, they cut loose from it.

It was also becoming apparent that having a record as an "anti-Nazi" was losing the value and respect it had won earlier from the mass of the population. Instead, such a political identification was becoming a social liability. Some Nazis who had claimed that they had actually been members of an anti-Nazi underground resistance movement within the Nazi party began to change their stories. They submitted revisions to their *Fragebögens* that either diluted or neglected to mention their previous claims of anti-Nazi activities. It became acceptable to admit to a small degree of Nazi partisanship as proof of having been a "good German."

I remember eavesdropping on a lively conversation between three German businessmen while traveling on a Frankfurt streetcar. They were discussing their impending appearances before a denazification tribunal. Two of them had claimed they had only been Class IV Nazis, or *Mitläufer* (followers). The third man, who somewhat proudly characterized himself as an anti-Nazi, said he expected to be certified as a Class V *Entlastete* (exonerated) because of his past record. However, his two friends were insistent that he change his plea. One of the friends plucked at his coat lapel, and pleaded, *"Lieber Gott!* Otto, can't you think of something positive you did for the Nazi party during the war, so you can be listed as a *Mitläufer?* That shows you made a mistake like millions of us other Germans, but you weren't a war criminal! Being a *Mitläufer* is the best. You pay a small fine, but after that, you can still live with your neighbors because you are still just like them."

On September 9, 1947, the denazification tribunal in the Regensburg internment camp sentenced Erich Teich, a thirty-four-year-old cow-herder and sergeant in the *Waffen* SS, to a three-year prison term as a Class II Nazi activist. The court further ordered a confiscation of 10 percent of Teich's personal assets and formally barred him from any employment, except as a common laborer, for a five-year period. As a final slap he was forbidden to own or drive a motor car.

Teich was never a member of the Nazi party. Until the war had conscripted him, he lived on a farm at Freising, Bavaria, where he milked a herd of cows. In 1941 he was drafted into the police force to substitute for men who had gone into combat. He was later transferred into a military police unit stationed in occupied Holland. This unit was then incorporated into the *Waffen* SS, which was the new combat force of Heinrich Himmler's SS *Korps*. Teich rose to the rank of sergeant, but his heart certainly did not belong to Hitler. In the spring of 1945 he was court-martialed and given a two-year prison sentence by the Gestapo for *Zersetzung der Wehrkaft,* that is, displaying defeatist tendencies. But before he could be sent to prison, Teich was taken prisoner by the advancing American troops, still holding his sergeant's rank. After being detained for two years in an American internment camp for SS prisoners, Teich was handed over to a German denazification tribunal (*Spruchkammer*). Because of his rank as a *Waffen* SS sergeant, he was found guilty of being a Class II Nazi activist.

The *Spruchkammer* ignored the fact that Teich, in theory at least, was eligible to be certified as a "victim of fascism" for the two-year prison sentence handed to him by the Gestapo. This should have given him a political exoneration, with a Class V certificate.

A review of contemporary denazification findings and relevant developments serve to highlight the absurdities of denazification. A United Press report from Nuremberg, October 13, 1948, stated:

Twelve former Nazi Gauleiters are still awaiting trial in the Western zones. . . . Denazification trials have resulted in some surprising verdicts. General Franz Halder, Hitler's army chief-of-staff, acquitted recently in Munich, Eduard Jadamczik, former Gestapo Chief in East Prussia has been cleared, and Gunther Reinecke, chief SS judge was also acquitted.

From the October 28, 1949, *Stars and Stripes:*

Munich, October 27, Karol Baron von Eberstein, former Munich Chief of Police and a SS general, was classified as a "Minor Offender," Class III, yesterday by a denazification court. The court gave him a suspended sentence of one year and ordered confiscation of 30% of his property.

From a Reuters dispatch, October 10, 1948, dateline Düsseldorf:

Hugo Stinnes, Ruhr coal and steel magnate, was acquitted here today by a special denazification tribunal, representing political parties and the trade unions. The committee declared that the fact Herr Stinnes had held the honorary title of leader of the defense industry and was a member of the Brownshirts (*Sturmabteilung* of the Nazi party) could not be regarded as incriminating.

Other denazification tribunals handling the cases of well-known and important Nazis reached the following decisions:

Heinrich Morgen, Deputy SS judge, Class V, exoneration; SS General Steiner, Class III, minor offender; SS General and Reich Economics Minister Kurt Schmitt, Class III, minor offender; SS *Obergruppenführer/* Brückner (full general), who was Hitler's personal adjutant, three-year prison sentence; SS Brigadier von Dornberg, protocol chief and ambassador to Switzerland, exonerated; Arno Breker, close friend and official sculptor for Hitler, minor offender, et cetera, et cetera.

Once the Americans had loosened their control and supervision of the denazification program, the natural play of political and economic forces to be found in any community began to influence events and developments. The power of the city's leading businessmen and industrialists, as well as other members of the local establishment, were mobilized to affect the verdicts of the denazification courts, because most of these individuals had been staunch supporters of Hitler's regime. The owner of a factory could exert substantial pressure on a *Spruchkammer* by his power to hire and fire local workers. Few if any of the local inhabitants would care to testify against a man who provided their weekly pay packets, even though everybody knew the factory owner might have been a Class II Nazi activist offender. The city's or town's leading Nazis usually fended off retribution for their past by being judged as harmless Class IV Nazi followers. This verdict involved a small fine; the case was closed and everybody returned to their gainful employment.

A typical example of a pressure tactic employed in a community was disclosed in the denazification trial of Hans Hensoldt, owner of a large optical plant in Wetzlar. He had been indicted as a Class II Nazi. In his closing remarks to the Wetzler *Spruchkammer* handling this case—some of whose members worked in the Hensoldt plant—the defense counsel for Herr Hensoldt stated in open court what was often threatened behind closed doors in other cases involving industrialists. He said: ". . . you people will have to be very careful of what you do in this trial, because the descendants [of Hensoldt] will get back at you some day."

A primary tactic employed by the more powerful and affluent ex-Nazis was to utilize every legal maneuver to postpone or to delay their appearance before a *Spruchkammer*. Those whose political services to Hitler could not be lightly dismissed by any tribunal wanted to evade the day of reckoning for years, if possible. With every passing day, the power and influence of the U.S. military government was decreasing, the German sympathy for those facing denazification was growing, and the verdicts were becoming more lenient. Big-name Nazis usually had adequate financial resources with which to hire the best available legal talent to fight for postponements and appeals. They could also mobilize powerful and influential friends to testify on their behalf. Time was on their side.

That explains why Teich, cow-herding peasant and *Waffen* SS sergeant, got a three-year prison sentence and why, at the same time, twelve *Gauleiters,* regional political bosses of the Nazi party, escaped any judgments by the denazification tribunals.

Prof. A. J. Ryder, who was a senior education officer of the British military government, serving many postwar years in Germany, has observed that "Denazification was a substitute for a revolution which Germany never had."*

Denazification did make a lasting imprint on the German postwar mentality. It made Germans aware that politics can be a dangerous game to play: "One pays a high price for coming to power; power stupefies."*

It discredited the years of indoctrination that the state was man's supreme achievement: it showed the *pâpier-maché* façade that despotism erects to disguise itself as legitimate government.

Defeat, after the five years of World War II, destroyed German militarism and nazism and freed the minds and the energies of the surviving Germans to concentrate on the more immediate and basic problems of rebuilding their lives and fortunes. This was done by excluding, in large measure, the elements of politics from their daily existence, and by fully utilizing their economic resources, industrial productivity, and technological talents.

This was the true revolution of postwar Germany.

There is no doubt that JCS 1067 contemplated a Carthaginian peace, which dominated our operations during the early months of the occupation.
—GEN. LUCIUS D. CLAY, Decision in Germany

The Potsdam directives themselves had incorporated one sort of left-wing planning objective, probably the most absurd in history.
—From "The German Lesson" in the
Economist, *October 15, 1966*

3] The Deindustrialization of Germany

In settling their respective accounts with defeated Nazi Germany, the victorious Allied powers were in general agreement on the following broad objectives:

1. Germany's power to wage war must be completely and totally destroyed. That meant, as set forth in the Potsdam Agreement, "to eliminate or to control all German industry that could be used for military production." Few if any manufacturing plants could escape the strictures of this blanket decree, which had only to be invoked by a military-government official to put any industrial establishment out of business without recourse or appeal. For example, a factory making safety pins has a military potential; it could easily be retooled to produce firing pins for rifles.

2. Germany must pay heavy reparations to compensate in part for the tremendous losses of property and physical assets, not to mention the millions of human casualties, sustained by those nations that were victims of Hitler's aggressive warfare and military occupation. As Germany was totally bankrupt when the war ended, reparations would have to come out of what remained of Germany's industrial properties and the labor of its manpower.

3. Germany, which for generations had been "Europe's machine shop," must now be stripped of its "dangerous concentrations of economic power." This

called for a massive dismantling of an interlocking economic structure, whereby seventy industrial combines or cartels and six banks controlled two-thirds of Germany's industrial production.

4. Germany must henceforth live under a level of industry plan, which would permit the nation to exist on approximately half of the industrial output and standard of living that Germany enjoyed in 1938, a median point between the great depressions of the thirties and the economic recovery occasioned by Hitler's crash rearmament program prior to World War II.

As envisaged by the planners, the accomplishment of these related objectives was possible under a wide-ranging deindustrialization of defeated Germany. In more precise terms, it meant the emasculation of Germany's productive powers and capabilities, thereby reducing its economic potential to that of a third- or fourth-rate industrial nation. As in the other "Ds" of the Four-D program, the gap between the plan and the achievement of this most important "D" was never to be bridged. Ironically, the program to make an industrial eunuch of Germany was to have unexpected and contrary results. The deindustrialization cleared away the old and obsolete of Germany's industrial plants, equipment, and management, and thus prepared the foundation for what was soon to be Europe's most modern, efficient, and economically powerful nation.

The British had the Ruhr, the greatest concentration of German industry in their occupation zone while the U.S. zone was predominantly agricultural. However, the Americans produced the master plan for deindustrialization of defeated Germany. This was largely incorporated in JCS 1067 (Joint Chiefs of Staff policy directive 1067). The original architect of JCS 1067—working through President Roosevelt—was Henry Morgenthau, Jr., secretary of the treasury. An amateur farmer and an amateur statesman, Morgenthau was one of the most bitter enemies of Hitler's Reich. He drafted the Morgenthau Plan, which in a subsequent modified form became the basic American policy toward defeated Germany. Deindustrialization was the heart and soul of the Morgenthau Plan, the ultimate objective of which was to eliminate Germany as a modern industrial state, economically crippling her for generations to come. Germany would be permitted to manufacture only light consumer goods and be forced to live on her agricultural resources. This was called the "pastoralization" of Germany.

The original Morgenthau Plan was the most drastic and punitive of all proposals. It called for the destruction and removal from Germany of all industrial plants and equipment which could be used for war-making purposes—all heavy industries, such as steel mills, automotive plants, machine tool factories, and the like. Only the manufacturing of consumer goods, such as furniture, Meissen chinaware, German beer, and such would be licensed by the occupation authorities. The first Morgenthau Plan even recommended the closing down of the great Ruhr coal mines, which for decades had formed the foundation for the industrialization of the Reich. Germany would then be dependent on foreign coal for fuel and power, and so would other European nations whose economies required coal from the Ruhr.

Designed to wreak political and economic vengeance on Germany, the original Morgenthau Plan was considered unworkable and untenable. A special committee of the U.S. War and State departments, set up in 1942 to study the problem of treatment of a defeated Germany, rejected the Morgenthau Plan on the grounds that the whole economy of Germany could not be drastically altered and restricted without adversely affecting the economies of many other European nations.

The postwar situation of Holland and other small neighbors of Germany illustrates this interdependence of European economies. Holland was invaded by the Nazis in May 1940 without warning. The Dutch were subjected to the darkness and oppression of the Nazi occupation for four long years. They emerged as anti-Nazi as any other nation in Europe. The Dutch, however, cannot afford the luxury of vengeance; theirs is a small country. The great part of their industry and trade has been and must be tied in with that of Germany. Their barges service the Rhine River, carrying their own and German cargoes; their vegetables, cheese, milk, and butter have a ready market in Germany. The economic health of Holland is dependent on that of Germany, regardless of politics. If Germany was to be transformed into an industrial dust bowl, then immediately Holland, Belgium, France, Switzerland, and other countries would suffer in direct proportion. It is interesting to note that the Morgenthau Plan was never endorsed by the governments in The Hague and in Brussels.

U.S. State and the War department specialists agreed that Germany's industrial machinery and her coal were absolutely vital to the economic health of not only Germany but western Europe as well. However, they fully approved the destruction of those munitions and airplane factories that were left intact after the heavy Allied air raids and ground fighting. They also recommended the international control of certain strategic materials vital for war making such as aluminum, synthetic rubber, nitrogen, etc. The special advisers, however, recognized that in a modern state such as Germany, industrial machinery must not be arbitrarily destroyed for political reasons but most be reorganized and controlled so as not to cause economic dislocation throughout western Europe. This principle was accepted by the American Joint Chiefs of Staff in 1942.

Morgenthau, however, managed to persuade Roosevelt of the merits of his plan as a substitute for the program put before the Quebec meeting of the American-British War Council in September 1944. At this meeting Morgenthau made his recommendations. Prime Minister Churchill was forced to accept, or at least give lip service to, the Morgenthau Plan because the British were in desperate need of a large dollar loan; as the price for British endorsement of his plan, Morgenthau promised to give the British government a lend-lease advance of several billion dollars. However, at Quebec the U.S. State Department and the army continued their strong protests against the Morgenthau blueprint. As an alternative, they recommended strict postwar controls of German industry and the destruction of all arms and munitions plants, but not the destruction or dismantling of nonmilitary industrial plants for reparations, as Morgenthau demanded.

Besides, other experts asked, "What are we going to do if Germany cannot feed herself?" To this question there was the natural reaction of many who said, "In view of how many millions have died as a result of Nazi Germany's war-making and political and racial persecution, why should we worry about them? They showed no such consideration for those who were their victims." But that essentially is a short-range view. Something more constructive and intelligent than economic dismemberment was called for—to prevent the return of conditions and situations in Germany that had existed after the last world war and which led to Hitler's dictatorship.

John J. McCloy, the first U.S. high commissioner, succeeded Clay as the senior American representative in Germany and was a key figure in this bitter, behind-closed-doors struggle. As the assistant secretary of war, he was a member of this small group of planners and policy-makers. He made his views clear: "The question is not whether we want the Germans to suffer for their sins. Many of us would like to see them suffer the tortures they have inflicted on others. The only question is whether over the years, a group of 70,000,000 people . . . can be kept within the bounds on such a low level as the Treasury proposes." He pointed out that poverty in Germany would induce poverty elsewhere in Europe.

The JCS 1067 was the final compromise between what Morgenthau demanded and what the State and War departments proposed. But the fight didn't end there.* Even after General Eisenhower had presented JCS 1067 to the European Advisory Council in London as the final American policy for defeated Germany, both the State Department and the Foreign Economic Administration opposed it. Thus American policy toward defeated Germany was divided and discordant to the end of the military occupation. The full details of JCS 1067 were kept "top secret." Hence the American policy appeared to the public to have no fixed course, possessing a sort of Jekyll-Hyde character as time went on. Occasionally its oppressive nature would show itself, often unnecessarily so because there was little overt German opposition to the U.S. military government. Then it would reveal a generous and common-sensical treatment of the Germans as military-government officials filed off the rough edges of JCS 1067. But it was difficult for the Germans to ascertain the true character and purpose of the U.S. policy toward them.

The elements of this conflict between official U.S. occupation policy, as exemplified by JCS 1067, and the true opinions of many of the top American war leaders were set forth by General Clay in his occupation memoirs, *Decision in Germany*. He writes about the "philosophy of occupation" as outlined by one of America's elder statesmen, Secretary of War Henry L. Stimson, during a private luncheon at General Eisenhower's residence in Bad Homburg in July 1945. Clay reports on Stimson's views as follows:

He recognized the needs for controls, favored adequate security measures and believed that the arrest and trial of Nazi leaders and war criminals were of the utmost importance to future peace. *He would have no part of a policy based on vindictiveness and was certain that in the long run the American people would give their approval to an occupation that was decent and humane and which was conducted under the rule of law. He could see no purpose in the deliberate destruction of the German economy because he was convinced that its reconstruction was essential to create an atmosphere in which it might be possible to develop the true spirit of democracy.* He knew that the innate kindness and decency of the American people would lead them to disapprove the exercise of our supreme authority in Germany in other than the traditional American way. Both General Eisenhower and I were impressed by his talk and it had a *lasting effect on my conduct of my responsibilities.* [Italics added.]

The revised Morgenthau Plan, as embodied in JCS 1067, provided for:

1. The summary removal from their business affairs and the arrest and trial of all top-level industrialists—the owners of the great Ruhr family concerns, as well as their appointed managers—for having encouraged and profited from Hitler's aggressive war-making.
2. The breakup of Nazi Germany's "excessive concentrations of economic power," as exemplified in the great Ruhr coal and steel combines, the giant I. G. Farben chemical monopoly, the domination of the "Big Six" banks, which represented over 55 percent of the total assets of Germany's 655 commercial banks.
3. The dismantling of all armament plants, as well as heavy industrial plants selected for reparations. The original dismantling list involved almost 1,600 enterprises, together with their equipment.
4. Establishing a ceiling on industrial production in all important industrial sectors to hamstring Germany's future economic development. For example, prewar steel production was 22 million tons a year; the new ceiling on steel limited the output to 5.8 million tons yearly.
5. Outlawing certain sectors of industrial production, such as synthetic gasoline and rubber, atomic research and development, certain types of machine tools, certain chemicals and plastics, electronics, and so on, which were deemed vital for the growth and maintenance of any military establishment.

It was an ambitious program, designed to be applied to defeated Germany as a whole. However, with Germany divided into four zones of occupation, each with a military governor who was supreme and who could decide, in concert with his government, how to deal with the Germans, it was applied only spottily. Individual nations chose whether to make postwar existence harsh or bearable for the Germans; and whether to snuff out all hopes for a betterment of their miserable daily existence or to encourage some confidence that their travail would end in the foreseeable future.

JCS 1067 was a blueprint for the control and limitation of German industry, but the three major industrial areas of Germany were not within the control and jurisdiction of the Americans and their JCS 1067. The *Ruhrgebiet* was in the British zone, the Saar in the French zone, and the Silesian industrial basin in East Germany under Russian rule. The British, French, and Russian military governors did not regard JCS 1067 as the operational guideline for their respective zonal administrations. They had other ideas, quite at variance with Washington's blueprint for postwar Germany.

While there was theoretical agreement among the wartime Allies for the economic dismemberment of what remained of Germany, it was soon apparent that each of the occupying powers went its separate way in carrying out the deindustrialization of Germany, as dictated by its own self-interests.

The French were eminently pragmatic and logical. They argued: "If the objective of the Allied occupation is to reduce and to immobilize Germany's economic powers, then let us make the industrial Ruhr area an independent state, which we can control ourselves and which will produce goods and services, according to our own needs and specifications."* The French were very clear on the basic principle of divide and rule. They would have preferred a revival of the pre-Bismarckian Germany, a land of quarreling and competitive fiefs and ducal principalities united only by cultural and religious bonds and *Muttersprache* bequeathed to them by Martin Luther. As that was obviously not on the agenda, the French military governor emphasized his opposition to the turn of events by consistently voting against every American and British proposal to deal with defeated Germany as a political and an economic whole.

The French zone of occupation was primarily agricultural, with some light and medium industry, largely concentrated in the Saar. Inasmuch as the French planned to annex the Saar, there was no incentive to dismantle its industrial plants and equipment as reparations. Instead, factories were put back into production and their output was shipped to France as reparations. A French military-government report in 1947 neatly explained things: "The German population has been put to work in the principal centers of production, *especially those which are necessary for the recovery of the French economy.*" [Italics added.]

The French also extracted other reparations in the form of timber cut from the Black Forest, German ships, coal and steel from the Saar and Ruhr, and German POWs. At the end of the war, almost 500,000 German soldiers were working in French factories, construction projects, and on French farms until they were released in 1947 and 1948. Some 116,000 ex-POWs stayed on in France as contract laborers.

One aspect of the Allied occupation of Germany distinguished the French: they enjoyed their brief few years as the military master of their ancient foe more than did the British, Russians, or Americans. The French zone was the smallest of the three western zones, but it had the largest force of occupation personnel. The French military occupation was also the most *costly* to the German taxpayer. For the period 1946–49 inclusive, the occupation expenses of the three western zones took an average of 34.5 percent of the total taxes collected by the German authorities. For the same period, the cost of maintaining the French military personnel involved 53 percent of the local German tax revenues. Prof. Alfred Grosser, German by birth but French by education and citizenship, commented on this state of affairs in his book on postwar Germany:

In order to represent the French Republic worthily in a country believed to respect only force and to admire munificence, a large part of the [French zone] occupation budget was spent on luxury. Fleets of cars, armies of servants, lavish entertaining, game preserves, special trains and steamers, such was the example set by the higher grades, and imitated as far as possible by the lower satraps.*

The victors, particularly the Americans, were determined not to repeat a costly mistake of World War I: settlement of accounts with Germany. After 1918, the attempts to extract monetary reparations from the postwar German republic was largely a gigantic financial hoax, sustained by the international bankers, who profited hugely from the intricate and complex transactions that ensued. In actual reparations, the Weimar government paid out the equivalent of $7 billion to France, Belgium, and other Allied nations; none of this went to the U.S. After disastrous postwar inflation, the Germans did not have the money to meet the reparation installments they had agreed to pay. So the German government floated one big bond issue after another in the U.S., to which the Americans subscribed approximately $7 billion of their own wealth. Later, the Germans defaulted on these bond issues, an action which led to the Hoover moratorium. In short, American investors paid Germany's reparations bills for World War I. Washington was determined there would be no repetition of that expensive error after World War II.

It was also realized that World War II was a total war—that is, war to the bitter end: until that final day of reckoning when the guns no longer had ammunition to fire; the tanks had no fuel for their sorties; and the *Goulaschkannonen* could not fill the mess tins of the hungry soldiers. When the firing stopped Germany was bankrupt, having exhausted its reserves of men, munitions, and morale, and unable to carry on any longer.

The old saw, "You can't get blood out of a turnip," comes to mind, but the wartime Allies had evolved a plan to harvest the turnips of defeated Germany in the form of reparations. First, the signatories to the Potsdam Agreement announced there would be a reduction in Germany's postwar living standards, so as not to exceed the average of the living standards of all the European countries involved in World War II, including Britain and Russia. How to find a norm between the daily existence of a Ukrainian peasant, a Serbian goat herder, a French factory worker, and a London stevedore was not spelled out. In *Realpolitik* this agreement was actually the authorization for the victorious powers to pull down the ex-enemy state to whatever level of living standards the reparations traffic would bear.

Second, the Potsdam Agreement authorized reparations to be paid out of Germany's physical equipment and what few remaining German-owned liquid assets, such as gold, foreign securities, and exchange, remained. Raw or processed materials such as coal and chemicals, capital equipment such as modern industrial plants, machinery, ships, rolling stock, and so on would be allocated to the claimant countries on a proportionate basis.

However, at the Yalta and Potsdam conferences, Stalin had demanded the equivalent of $10 billion in reparations from Germany. Inasmuch as none of the other Allied powers publicly disputed or rejected this claim, it acquired legitimacy with the passage of time. Russia was to get 75 percent of her reparations from the Soviet zone of occupation and the remaining 25 percent from the three western zones. In return for this agreement, the Russians agreed to ship food from East Germany to West Germany and to permit free movement of commerce across the Iron Curtain frontier. When the Russians failed to supply the food, reparations from the western zones were cut off.

The Russians, too, were "Morgenthau-minded," but one must remember the Soviet Union had suffered millions of casualties and sustained damages and losses of catastrophic proportions. They wanted compensation out of defeated Germany in whatever form was immediate and possible. Their guiding principle was, "If it is transportable, take it!" Teams of Russians descended on the Soviet zone and, aided by German prisoners, proceeded to strip it of its infrastructures. Virtually anything that could be was detached—plumbing fixtures, railroad tracks, telephones and switchboards, buses, municipal power plants, streetcars, machine tools, whole factories—nothing escaped their attention.

But the Russians soon made some painful discoveries about their economic scavenging. They did not possess sufficient knowledge of the physical functioning of a modern industrial nation, and they were to pay a high price for their lack of technical know-how. Dismantling was easy, but it was quite something else to transport this industrial loot a thousand miles or more across a war-ravaged eastern Europe to the Soviet Union to reassemble the industrial machinery and put the factory back into business. German workers had carried out the actual dismantling, and they knew their short-term jobs were taking away the opportunity for long-term employment in the area of the dismantled factory. So the Germans were in no mood to be helpful or cooperative. Equipment was damaged or mislaid in dismantling; vital parts of the machinery got lost. Packaging was done sloppily, exposing the industrial machinery to rain and snow.

The Soviet railway system was overworked, short on rolling stock and locomotives, and in war-damaged condition. Massive bottlenecks in the movements of reparations shipments soon developed, due to an inadequate communications system and a shortage of experienced transportation personnel. Much of the reparations traffic simply got lost or was sidetracked on some spur line. If and when a shipment actually arrived at its destination in Russia, it was unlikely that cadres of skilled industrial workers and mechanics could be gathered together in short order to sort out the shipments and find and reassemble the factory and its machinery. The greater part of the massive reparations traffic ended up as so much junk, rusting and abandoned in the vast expanses of Eastern Europe and Russia.

This breakdown in the reparations pipeline was confirmed in large measure by a number of westerners who traveled by railroad from Germany to Russia in those early postwar years. They reported seeing railway sidings and freight yards piled high with boxes and uncrated goods which were clearly the components of German manufacturing plants that just never reached their destinations. It was believed by Allied intelligence sources that the Russians were only able to salvage about one-third of their reparations shipments out of Germany. Yet if these damaged goods were useless to the Russians, they also represented capital assets that were lost forever to the German economy.

The Soviet practice of indiscriminate dismantling of industrial plants and equipment and the looting of other capital goods for shipment to Russia proved to be shortsighted and counterproductive. They realized their mistake fairly early and cut down on their dismantling program. On May 21, 1946, Marshal Vassily Sokolovsky, military governor of East Germany, announced an end to dismantling in the Russian zone. However, this practice continued sporadically until April 1948. According to Allied intelligence sources, after the war the Russians dismantled over 1,300 German factories, including 380 taken out of West Berlin before the Americans, British and French settled in to their enclaves. In addition, over 4,500 miles of railway trackage was removed by them for the postwar reconstruction of the Soviet railway system.

Belatedly the Russians realized it was far more practical and profitable to take their reparations out of Germany's current production. Let the factories remain in Germany; repair them if necessary; feed their assembly lines with essential raw materials; reemploy their skilled workers; and then confiscate a large percentage of the finished products as installments on the reparations account. The Soviet Military Administration began to comprehend some of the elements of economic geography. The Russians discovered that industry is attracted to one area and not to another because of location and the availability of raw materials, labor, and adequate transportation. Applying these lessons, they decided, for example, that it made more sense to leave the giant new I. G. Farben synthetic fuel plant at Leuna—in close proximity to its basic raw materials, the brown coal deposits of Saxony—than to dismantle the whole installation and attempt to reassemble its complex mechanism somewhere in the depths of Russia.

The Russians then introduced a new phase in the economic enslavement of East Germany. They created a number of Soviet corporations, *Sowjetische Aktiengesellschaften* (known as SAGs), which took legal title to a number of industrial firms that previously had been on the list to be dismantled. The Russian propagandists described this development as the "socialization of industry for the benefit of the working classes."

By this expropriation maneuver, the Soviet Military Administration secured a hammerlock on private industry in East Germany, including such well-known firms as Farben's Leunawerke, the Leica Camera Company of Jena, and Meissen Porzellanwerk of Dresden. In this fashion, the Soviet Military Administration commandeered the continuous output of a large number of manufacturing firms. By 1948 these Soviet corporations employed one-fifth of East Germany's labor force and accounted for one-third of its total industrial production.* The amount of total output the Soviet Military Administration confiscated for reparations from each industrial sector varied. For example, from the new SAG textile plants in Chemnitz, 80 percent of the output was shipped to Russia. In short, the Russians took all that traffic would bear. It is reliably estimated that the Russians extracted between 50 and 100 billion marks ($12.5 to $25 billion) worth of reparations out of East Germany. They left only enough for the Germans to prevent a collapse of the local economy. This expropriation by the Russians of German industry nourished the slowly rising curve of hostility to Red rule that years later culminated in open revolt and the mass exodus of East German workers to the West.

In West Germany, 1,546 industrial plants were to be dismantled, of which 336 were war plants (205 aircraft and 131 munitions and weapons factories). More than a year later, in October 1947, a final dismantling list was made public; it contained only 683 industrial installations, including the 336 war plants noted above. However, there never was a final or a conclusive accounting of the entire dismantling program, which was subject to continuous erosion by political and economic forces and developments. It soon became apparent that the destruction of West Germany's industrial capacity was running counter to the enlightened self-interest of the Americans and, to a lesser degree, of the British and the French.

First and foremost came the matter of the growing expenses of playing the role of both ruler and reformer of a large segment of the defeated enemy. The Americans soon realized they would have to lay out about $700 million a year of their own tax dollars to prevent mass starvation and political disorder in West Germany, due to the collapse of the economy and the failure of the Russians to deliver the promised food supplies from East Germany. Then there was the inability of the Americans and the British to stop the Russians and the French from dragging their feet on the economic and political unification of Germany. The plans made in Washington and London were predicated on dealing with Germany as a whole, not with a country divided into four separate and independent zones of occupation. However, as General Clay explained to his superiors in the Pentagon:

[The Russians] did not intend to permit . . . a breakdown of the zonal barriers, or to place the resources of East Germany into a common pool, unless they were assured of a large share of the productive output of all Germany without payment. They expected we [the Americans] would finance the deficit and continued reparations from production.*

There it was in a nutshell! The Russians wanted their cake and the eating of it too. What this meant in monetary terms can be seen from the following figures. The original dismantling list of 1,546 industrial installations from West Germany had a book value of RM 1.98 billion ($600 million pegged at a 30-cent mark). The Russians had demanded total reparations of $10 billion from Germany, of which 25 percent or $2.5 billion was to come out of West Germany. Even if all of the 1,546 industrial plants were to be dismantled and handed over to the Russians, there would remain a reparations deficit of $1.9 billion. This amount would somehow have to be extracted out of the moribund West German economy over a period of years. In short, under such an arrangement the West Germans would have little if anything left over to supply their own vital needs, including food imports. That was the deficit the American taxpayer would have to meet in the foreseeable future, as viewed by Clay.

The Americans had, in effect, paid Germany's $7 billion reparations account for World War I. Now it appeared they were once again being placed in the position of paying Germany's reparations—this time for World War II. Clay and his immediate advisers were determined not to repeat that mistake.

Also exerting a decisive influence on the evolving U.S. policy in Germany was the cold war, now in full sway. U.S. officials were convinced that the Russians would seek to turn the West German civilians against the Americans and attempt to disrupt the political and economic affairs in the western zones through their agents in the German Communist party. U.S. authorities were apprehensive, as reflected in a comment by Clay:

The Soviet policy of Communist world domination which had been checked by the war, was brought out of moth balls and clearly formed the basis of their day to day planning, which is still, however, on an expediency basis.*

American policy on the all-important issue of deindustrialization was in the throes of a drastic change. On May 25, 1946, Clay sent a long *tour d'horizon* cable to the Pentagon in which he reviewed the current impasse vis-à-vis the Russians. In this message he called for a halt in the dismantling program with these words: "If economic unity proves impossible, only those plants in the U.S. zone which were designed solely for the production of war munitions should be removed."

This was probably the first official recognition on the part of the U.S. High Command that to continue to reduce or destroy Germany's industrial capacity was to directly and adversely affect long-range American foreign policy interests, while at the same time assisting, unwittingly, the achievement of Soviet objectives in Europe.

In fact, the notorious JCS 1067 was replaced by a milder policy directive, JCS 1779, quietly introduced without any fanfare in July 1947. Its preamble set forth a new premise that " . . . an orderly and prosperous Europe requires the economic *contribution of a stable and productive Germany."* [Italics added.]

However, while there was a growing consensus that the physical dismantling of Germany's nonmilitary factories and their assembly lines violated the canons of common sense, there was no relaxation of other aspects of the deindustrialization program as set forth in JCS 1067. The program to break up Germany's well-entrenched cartel system, as well as the "excessive concentrations of economic power," was to continue. In short, the structure and administration of Germany's intertwined industry and finance could be dismantled, so to speak, even though the factories received a reprieve from their earlier death sentences.

The intransigence of the Russians and the French on the question of unification led inexorably to closer American and British bizonal coordination of their occupation objectives. While the British controlled the Ruhr, the greatest concentration of industry in all of Germany, they agreed to mesh their economic and political policies with the Americans. In return the Americans supplied most of the funds, as well as the emergency food supplies, necessary to prevent starvation and riots in their two occupation zones. As a result, in February 1947 the American and British military governments issued virtually identical laws, with the announced objective of eliminating cartels, trusts, and other restrictive or monopolistic arrangements, as well as "excessive concentrations of economic power."

Law 56, which was applicable to the U.S. zone, laid down the arbitrary principle that all business enterprises employing 10,000 people must be considered as a *prima facie* case of "excessive concentration of economic power." It then became the responsibility of the managers of the corporation to prove or to convince the American authorities that the firm did not fall into that category. Law 56 further stated that any firm having its headquarters and 10,000 employees within the U.S. zone was subject to automatic deconcentration unless granted an exemption by the American military government. The comparable decree for the British zone was somewhat different. It did not require mandatory deconcentration of any firm having the bulk of its operations within the British zone. Also, the great Ruhr coal and steel trusts were to be subject to a special deconcentration process, as outlined under a different statute, Law 75.

The first hurdle, which was never cleared away, was how to define exactly what "an excessive concentration of economic power" was. What were to be the criteria to measure excessiveness: Was it the number of subsidiaries, gross income, owners or shareholders, or its percentage of the total production of its industrial sector? It was like asking, "How high is up?" No reasonable or acceptable answer could be found.

In 1946 the decartelizers of the U.S. military government submitted to the ACC their own bizarre formula defining an "excessive concentration of economic power." Falling into this category would be any corporation employing more than 3,000 workers whose output was 25 percent or more of the total production of its industrial sector, or which had a gross income of RM 25 million ($7.5 million at a 30-cent mark rate). However, this proposal was rejected at the outset by the British and Russians as unacceptable.

There was constant controversy within the confines of the economic division of U.S. military government about the application of JCS directives 1607 and 1779. James Martin, a left-wing protégé of Vice-President Henry A. Wallace, headed the decartelization branch. It was known that Wallace flirted with communism in those early years. Clay tells us that:

The decartelization group was composed of extremists, sincere but determined to break up German industry into small units regardless of their economic sufficiency . . . Unfortunately the reorganization of Ruhr industry suffered from the controversy.*

At this point an explanation about the "merchants-of-death" syndrome is needed.* This syndrome afflicted many of those who formulated the deindustrialization program in Washington and who sought to execute it in its entirety in occupied Germany. In 1935, under the chairmanship of Sen. Gerald P. Nye, the U.S. Congress conducted a highly publicized investigation into the munitions industry and how it allegedly fanned the flames of war to fill its coffers with profits from the sale of armaments. The American press was filled with reports of the international arms traffic and intrigues of the "merchants of death" such as Krupp of Essen, the fabulous Sir Basil Zaharoff, Vickers-Armstrong, Skoda, and others, as well as their American counterparts E. I. DuPont de Nemours of Delaware and other U.S. firms. The Nye munitions committee had a strong impact on the so-called liberals and New Dealers of that time. The fact that Hitler received the financial support of the Ruhr barons of the great coal and steel trusts and that they, in turn, won fat contracts to produce his tanks and guns when Germany's prewar rearmaments program went into production, caused the German industrial and financial community to be included in the "merchants-of-death" category. This thinking in Washington carried over into the formation of policies to reduce and to eliminate the powers formerly enjoyed by the Ruhr barons by limiting the postwar German economy.

Examples of the problems of deconcentration which sparked off "disagreements and disloyalties within the military government"* were the recommendations of the decartelization group to dissolve Henschel & Sohn (a manufacturer of locomotives) and Vereingte Kugellager Fabriken [VKF] (a Swedish-owned ball bearing plant). Henschel & Sohn did produce most of Germany's locomotives, but its only customer was the state-owned railway system. Germany had lost over half of her locomotives in the war and the Henschel plant could at least be utilized to repair some of the damaged engines, which were desperately needed to transport supplies of food, coal, and other necessities. VKF, one of two ball bearing plants in Germany, accounted for most of Germany's production in this limited but vital field. The other ball bearing plant was scheduled to be dismantled for reparations.

Clay vetoed the dissolution orders for these two firms because their continued production was absolutely essential if German industry was to function, even in a limited fashion. The left-wing hard liners in military government, headed by Martin and his colleagues, carried their protests to the U.S. press and to Congress, charging that Clay was protecting the employment and the property of ex-Nazis. This malicious gossip faithfully reflected the East German Communists and Soviet propagandists who attacked Clay as being pro-Nazi in his administration of the U.S. zone.

The deconcentration program was carried out in three major sectors: the breaking up of the large coal and steel combines of the Ruhr; the survivors of the Big Six commercial banks, and the giant I. G. Farben trust—the world's largest chemical firm in prewar times. The unsuccessful attempts to corporately dismantle I. G. Farben will illustrate the futility of this program. Today the three major successor companies of I. G. Farben—Bayer-Leverkusen, Farbwerke Hoechst, and BASF (Badischeanilin und Sodafabrik) of Ludwigshafen—are each bigger than their parent I. G. Farben ever was. In 1974 in a listing of the ten largest chemical companies in the world, BASF of Ludwigshafen with total revenues of $6.02 billion ranked no. 1; Hoechst was the third largest (after DuPont) with annual sales of $5.77 billion, followed by Bayer-Leverkusen in fourth place with gross income of $5.51 billion. (Source: *Business Week,* September 7, 1974)

Before World War I the German chemical industry accounted for 80 percent of the world's production of dyes and related products. After the war, the German firms lost their foreign assets, patents and trademarks. In 1926, six leading chemical firms joined together to form I. G. Farben. By the mid-1930s, it had become the world's largest chemical company, with branches and subsidiaries on every continent and in every country, under the administration of Prof. Dr. Karl Duisberg. At the end of World War II, about 60 percent of the production capacity of I. G. Farben was located in the Russian zone, 20 percent in the French zone, 11 percent in the British zone, and the remaining 9 percent in the U.S. zone. I. G. Farben's properties in the U.S. zone included forty-three manufacturing plants and over a hundred additional establishments, as well as the headquarters of this chemical giant in Frankfurt. This sprawling office building—at the war's end it was the largest in Europe—became the European Pentagon, as headquarters for the U.S. military governor and the American armed forces in Europe.

The broad objective of the deconcentration of I. G. Farben was to create a number of smaller, independent companies out of the portfolio of subsidiaries that comprised the giant chemical complex. Each successor unit was to be self-supporting and competitive with the other chemical companies that would emerge from the deconcentration process. At the first go-around eighty successor units were selected for debut. However, what appeared to be feasible and logical on paper proved to be a virtually impossible achievement in practice. The physical task of disentangling the skein of interlocking and interdependent Farben divisions and subdivisions thwarted the talents of even the most facile and cunning lawyers.

For example, at each of the major groupings of Farben plants at Ludwigshafen, Hoechst, and Leverkusen, hundreds of subsidiaries were jammed together, somewhat resembling a clutch of small stores huddled together in a big shopping center. Along the banks of the Rhine River at Ludwigshafen, BASF had grouped together over three hundred factories on a site only two square miles in area. All of them shared common sources of fuel, energy, transportation, raw materials and equipment, and so on. At Hoechst and Leverkusen there were similar groupings of semi-independent production units. Under those circumstances the physical as well as the corporate deconcentration just could not be worked out.

As a result, the original deconcentration list was revised to forty-two successor companies, then to twelve units, and finally to five—leaving virtually intact the physical establishments of Bayer-Leverkusen, Farbwerk Hoechst, and BASF at Ludwigshafen, plus two smaller firms, Chemische

Werke Hüls and Cassella Fabwerke Mainkur of Frankfurt. Farben stock-holders received nine new shares in a successor firm for ten old shares.

When they were members of the same I. G. Farben corporate family, the major units such as Bayer, Hoechst, and BASF did not compete with each other; they supplemented each other's activities and output. This traditional approach was continued when the deconcentration process was legally completed. While there were some areas where production and sales overlapped, there was a general understanding that each of the "Big Three" successor units would follow its own line of chemical products. As one of the lawyers explained years later: "They operate something like this: If BASF produces red dyes; then Hoechst will produce the yellow colors and Leverkusen the blues."

In recent years there has been growing competition among the Big Three, particularly in the world markets outside of Germany. However, the old Farben tradition of management hangs heavily on all their shoul-ders. There is a particular Farben school of management which is why, as the *Economist* commented: "The German chemical industry is one of the traditional powerhouses of Europe."

Germany has dominated the chemical industry ever since the 1860s when it was founded in the *Kaiserreich*. The abundant supplies of raw materials from the great Ruhr coal mines made possible its steady growth. The industry was created by bold-thinking scientists whose imaginative experiments in their laboratories led to one commercially valuable prod-uct after another. As a result, from generation to generation, Farben com-panies and their predecessors have been directed and managed by scientists and technicians, rather than businessmen, throughout the century of their spectacular emergence as an industry which affects the life of every German. Since they went through the deconcentration wringer in the early 1950s, they have become more versatile, more progressive, and more profitable than the old I. G. Farben could have ever hoped to be.

Prof. Kurt Hansen, chairman of Bayer-Leverkusen, has some thought-provoking comments about the special character and vitality of the Ger-man chemical industry which enabled it to survive two world wars and, after each debacle, return to its vanguard position. He said: "From the beginning in Germany, we had only technical men at the top; *we think that only scientists can have the feelings for technical change*—particu-larly in the last few years when change has been so much faster. It is easier for a technical man to learn about finance than for a finance expert to learn about chemistry."

Professor Hansen is fully at home in the international business world. He was born in Yokohama and, after obtaining his doctorate in chemistry, managed Farben sales in the United States. He is quietly confident that the German chemical industry can hold its own against American competi-tion in this field. In an interview with a British newspaper he explained:

The Americans are good at making things bigger and cheaper; but they are not so good at inventing. Most of their inventors are first-generation immigrants from Europe. The Americans are much more commercially-minded than we are. But they still need to have *Denker und Dichter* (thinkers and poets). We should not try to always copy American management; they like to make charts with boxes and fit men into *them*. We like to find our men first and then fit *them* in. [Italics added.]*

In retrospect, it is now quite obvious that the U.S. military-government officials who set out with so much self-assurance to break up the German chemical industry either did not know about or did not take into consideration the unique management traditions of I. G. Farben. Managers with the mentality of *Denker und Dichter* are obviously not people who can be expected to rest content in little boxes.

We Americans have never been particularly good at explaining or selling the merits of our system, or defending it in an argument. . . . We are rank amateurs when it comes to explaining to the other fellow what democracy means . . .

—Excerpted from a U.S. Army indoctrination pamphlet, issued to all occupation troops in Germany, November 1948

4] The Democratization of Germany

Demokratur, a postwar addition to the German language, expressed the cynical reaction of the Germans to the political contradiction they perceived between what the Americans preached and what they practiced. Formed from *Demokratie* and *Diktatur,* it focused on America's dilemma of "dictatorship by democracy."

After the first flush of occupation, the American High Command added a fourth "D" to the master plan of correcting the mistakes of the past and organizing the future for some 18 million Germans residing in the U.S. zone. The message went out to all units that, in addition to the demilitarization, denazification, and deindustrialization of the surviving Germans, they were also to be democratized.

This seemed a logical step in the reform and rehabilitation of the conquered people. But U.S. policy-makers were woefully deluded in their wishful thinking that democracy, as practiced in America, could easily be exported and made to work in central Europe. No doubt this conviction stemmed from the healthy state of America's ego. After all, wasn't it obvious that the U.S., a functioning democracy since its debut on the international scene in 1776, was now the world's richest and most powerful nation? In that euphoric state of mind, the Americans were confident that the Germans were ready for conversion to the alien political philosophy of democracy. After their traumatic experience with the autocracy of the *Kaiserreich* and the Nazi dictatorship, as well as defeats in two world wars, the Germans would obviously be seriously reappraising their past beliefs and political values. Why not dry democracy? Look what it had accomplished for the Americans.

However, a German dictionary equated "democracy" with "government by the people," with basic civil rights, equality before the law, and protection against arbitrary police powers. That state of affairs did not coincide with what the German encountered in his daily existence under Allied military-government rule. He enjoyed no basic civil rights. His residence could be searched without a warrant. He could be arrested and held indefinitely without *habeas corpus* or a chance to confer with a lawyer. The Germans had been subjected to this shelving of civil rights since the advent of Hitler. Now with the Allied occupation, police power again reigned supreme,* although torture and the concentration camps of the Nazi regime went out of existence. Phones were tapped; mail was opened and subjected to arbitrary censorship. If a German was traveling, he was liable to be searched at one of the many control points. If he was carrying food, it was usually confiscated on the assumption that it was purchased on the black market. When the venereal disease rate climbed in the occupation army, the military government put pressure on the German police to take remedial measures. As a result, German girls, whether prostitutes or not, could be picked up by the police and forced to submit to physical examinations for VD. If infected, they were shipped off to a detention camp where they were hospitalized behind bars.

The Germans expected a harsh peace. Hitler had promised them that if they failed to win the last battle of the total war, their daily existence would be unbearable should they manage to survive. Hence, in the U.S. zone the initial phases of demilitarization, denazification, and deindustrialization did not come as any surprise. If the Americans had not introduced the fourth "D" of democratization, they could have avoided the ensuing dilemma. Trying to impose democracy on the defeated, depressed, hungry, and homeless Germans, who had to spend each waking hour trying to eke out a living and had little time or inclination for reflecting on political affairs, gave the Germans the first opportunity to criticize their conquerors by raising the simple question: "Do you practice what you preach?"

In June 1946 the U.S. Third Army sponsored a "Think and Win" contest for American personnel stationed in Germany. The contest was designed to focus their attention and interest on the problems and the objectives of the American occupation of defeated Nazi Germany. In short, how best could we accomplish our stated mission in making Germany into an acceptable member of the family of nations?

First prize was awarded to Staff Sgt. B. F. Husband of the 38th Finance Detachment. Apparently, Sergeant Husband was more interested, as were the judges of the contest, in the routine mechanics of U.S. occupation than in the long-range and difficult goals of the military government of the defeated enemy state. For his invention of a new type of manila folder for interoffice communications Sgt. Husband received a fifteen-day furlough. This was, indeed, a remarkable contribution to the statecraft of military occupation.

This little episode illustrates the peculiar colonial attitude that top-ranking Americans demonstrated in Germany. There was a self-imposed form of mental, as well as physical, isolation from German civilians—the very people we were supposed to be informing and influencing onto the high road to a democratic way of life.

The army indoctrination courses for the GIs constantly stressed that he was the "ambassador of democracy" and, consequently, he should conduct himself in Germany in such manner as to be a credit to his country's standards and beliefs. Oddly enough, the ordinary GI was more of an ambassador than the phrasemakers realized. Whether he behaved correctly or not, it was the ordinary American soldier who rubbed elbows with the Germans in the street, who sneaked into their cafés and homes in search of company or excitement; he was the American the defeated people came to know. The attitude and actions of the ordinary soldier provided a yardstick by which Germans measured and evaluated the U.S. However, when American troops first breached the German frontier on September 12, 1944, Eisenhower, as Supreme Allied Commander, issued his now-famous "nonfraternization" order to all troops. This forbade any social contact and relationships between members of the armed forces and the German people, military or civilian. While the war was on, this ban made sense as a measure for military security. Once peace came, its wartime validity ceased to exist. On surveying the results, there is ample evidence to indicate it was a major political and psychological error on the part of Eisenhower and the Allied High Command—formulated without regard to realities or the consequences of the war.

The moment hostilities ended, the pressure of the war disappeared. The GI figuratively dropped his gun into his duffel bag and forgot about being a combat soldier. American and Allied soldiers began to fraternize with German women in open and widespread disregard of Eisenhower's order. Fraternization, however, did not just pertain to sexual relations between the conquerors and the frauleins; it covered the whole range of social intercourse. In its total application, an American soldier was forbidden even to talk to a German child or give away a piece of candy.

Many Germans were eager to talk to the Americans, for the collapse of nazism left them spiritually bankrupt. Always impressed by power, the Germans, particularly educators and business and professional men, were sincerely curious about Americans. They had never seen them before, at least not in such numbers, and they wanted to make open and direct contact. But the nonfraternization order excluded the Germans as being socially unfit, as carriers of some form of political leprosy. So they turned away, back to their own cares and concerns. An opportunity was lost, and it was never to return again.

There are those men who will belabor the Churchillian platitude that "once a German, always a German; arrogant in victory, cringing in defeat." That may be so, but Eisenhower missed an opportunity to use his GI ambassadors to influence the Germans. The combat veterans were a true reflection of America and our way of life, of its good and bad qualities; they were young, virile, democratic, informal, and friendly civilians in uniform. If they lacked culture and education, as measured by European standards, they made up for this deficiency in their genius to produce and build. The U.S. had organized a way of life that captured the imagination of Europeans; but we pulled down the shades just as a few prospective German clients were timorously peeking through the shop windows.

The Germans noted the widespread violations of the nonfraternization order. They concluded that the American High Command, as well as Eisenhower, as the author of this SHAEF directive, were stupid in their attempts to enforce the unenforceable. This resulted in diminishing respect for the conquerors. But, more important, it salved the guilty consciences of the Germans. A German editor in Frankfurt summed up the views of his many compatriots on this phase of German–American relations: "Eisenhower thinks that the Allied soldier is either too good or too immature to associate with the ordinary German; that he will be contaminated by mixing with us. But the soldier doesn't think so. Most of them go with our girls. We can't be so bad after all, if the Allied soldiers don't accept what their leaders tell them." That was the comforting ratiocination of the defeated people.

Official U.S. history for the period commented that the Germans felt that the nonfraternization order was "proof of the justice of the Nazi cause, or otherwise it would not have been necessary for the Allied High Command to take so much trouble to insulate their troops from German propaganda." At the same time, the Germans enjoyed a private laugh behind doors when they contrasted this Eisenhower order with the official policy of the American military government to encourage the growth of democracy in this defeated country.

Having taken such a strong and inflexible stand on the social relationship between the Americans and the Germans, Eisenhower found it difficult to retreat gracefully from this untenable position. But retreat was forced upon him and his successors. Two months after V-E Day, American soldiers were allowed to talk to Germans openly on the streets, but not inside homes and in cafés. Months later, however, the occupation soldiers were permitted to enjoy normal social contacts with German civilians.*

Incidentally, the German approach, when they were occupying Europe in the early stages of the war, was the exact opposite of the Eisenhower policy. The Nazi propagandists encouraged their soldiers to fraternize with the defeated French, Belgians, and Dutch. The Nazis realized the political value of fraternization and were trying to propagandize Hitler's "New Order in Europe." The Germans sought to contact and enlist the interests and sympathies of every age group and every stratum of society in the occupied countries; they wanted to win friends and influence people, especially those under the heels of the Nazi occupation forces.

During World War II, in close collaboration with the Nazi Propaganda Ministry, the *Wehrmacht* published *Signal*—a bimonthly picture magazine strikingly similar to *Life* in its format—in every country occupied by the German armed forces. This propaganda magazine was translated in over twenty languages and reached a peak circulation of almost three million. *Signal*'s basic theme was that the German soldier was everybody's best friend because he was fighting to preserve Europe's civilization and way of life from those who would destroy them: namely, the Jews, the Russians, the British, and eventually, the Americans.

In sharp contrast, one of the first acts of the U.S. Army on settling down in Germany was to build a series of ghettos for itself in the principal centers of occupation in the American zone. Actually these were "ghettos-in-reverse." Their American residents could enter or leave at will but the Germans could not come inside unless they had a special pass. In Frankfurt a ten-foot-high, barbed-wire fence was erected around a mile-square area, fittingly called "the compound," another derivative of colonialism. Inside this area was the massive I. G. Farben building serving as U.S. Army headquarters, plus the residences of high-ranking officers, WACs, and other personnel. The compound was a little America, complete with a shopping center, movie theaters, athletic club, schools, churches, and the other amenities of civilization. Any American who wished to invite a German to his office or home inside the compound, either for business or pleasure, had to sign his guests in and out of the area. A prominent German, such as a state minister or president desiring to confer with military-government officials, and a fraulein entering to spend the night with some American, received exactly the same treatment.

Walter Kolb, lord mayor of Frankfurt, protested that the continued existence of a compound was antidemocratic and certainly not intended to encourage good relations between the Germans and Americans. The local wits often asked: "When are the Americans going to liberate themselves from their own postwar concentration camps?"

The excuse given for these compounds rested on the premise that military installations had to be cordoned off from the general public and residential areas, and must be surrounded by barbed wire to protect their inmates from thievery and annoyance at the hands of the indigenous population. Two months after the Frankfurt compound fence was pulled down, however, the rate of theft dropped sharply, the local provost marshal reported, to his surprise.

The wives of U.S. Army personnel who had recently arrived to live in Germany with their husbands strongly endorsed the barbed-wire protection policy. When the army compound in Hoechst, an industrial suburb of Frankfurt largely populated by the skilled workers of I. G. Farben plant, was stripped of its protective fences, the American women strongly protested. In a letter to army headquarters, they expressed fears about daily contact with the German working classes, "a much lower type of people surrounding us." The concurrent campaign of both the military-government unit and the U.S. Army to persuade the German people of the virtues of democracy apparently had small impact on the embattled wives of the Hoechst compound.

Some of America's better-known liberals were surprised and critical of the enforced separation of the American soldiers from the German civilian population. Roger Baldwin, head of the American Civil Liberties Union, aptly reported: "Instead of 'Jim Crowism' in the American zone of Germany, there is 'Hans Crowism'. . . ."*

Baldwin was referring to the outward aspects of nonfraternization, such as Americans using the main entrance of the building while the Germans had to enter by a side door, or separate and not equal toilet facilities inside. In major cities such as Frankfurt and Munich there were separate street cars for the Americans on which no German could ride.

These social barriers were slowly dismantled. By 1947 the Americans stationed in Germany could invite members of the population into their homes. In announcing this concession, the U.S. Army stated that "the change of policy was authorized as a means of exemplifying the principles of democracy . . . and as a morale builder."

With the arrival of the "dependents"—official terminology for army wives and their children—the American occupation took on a new character. The isolationist, or colonial, aspects of the occupation were strengthened by the influence of American wives. In the summer of 1947 there were more American women in Germany than soldiers in the U.S. zone constabulary, the mobile striking force responsible for quelling any disorder and guaranteeing the security of the American occupation. There were 31,000 women over eighteen years of age, comprising the wives and daughters and a small group of War Department female employees.

Prior to the arrival of the wives, the American military personnel were becoming acquainted with the Germans—or at least with the frauleins. Now a new note of discord became apparent on the social scene; competition between wife and fraulein became a bitter, if little chronicled, social conflict. No one can say who won this war. Fraternization with the frauleins had been a pleasant and educational pastime for the American soldier. As a male, he was accepted as superior to the female; the fraulein was neither coy nor prudish about entering into a liaison; and she was grateful for small favors—cigarettes, soap, candy, and other PX gifts made a big difference in her standard of living. So when the American women arrived in Germany, they were looked upon in a new and more critical light and many were placed on the defensive.

Collectively the wives rallied and began a counteroffensive. This took several forms. For example, dances and parties that were attended by fraulein guests were in many instances boycotted by the American wives. It became apparent that fraternization was here to stay; so a proposal to form the occupation equivalent of a "junior league of frauleins" was adopted by the USFET (U.S. Forces, European Theater). If they passed the strict requirements laid down, German girls would be given social passes which permitted them to attend army-sponsored entertainment such as movies, dances, and parties. To qualify for a social pass a fraulein had to submit to a medical examination for venereal disease; produce a certificate from her pastor that she was of good moral character and another from the local police station that she had no criminal record; and clearance from the U.S. military government that she had never been a Nazi.

The junior league of frauleins was a fiasco. For one thing it presumed that German girls were so avid for American company that they would submit to almost any official indignity to attend the social functions of the conqueror. But few decent German girls, with any pride, would make the rounds of the doctor, pastor, police, and military government, gathering certificates of their physical, moral, legal, and political probity, just so she could attend a Saturday night GI dance.

There was an abstract, out-of-this-world quality about the democracy that the Americans pushed onto the Germans. But for the German, it had little to do with the realities he faced. He could not bring it into focus in relation to his existence. Democracy put no bread on his plate; gave him no heavy coat for protection against the frost of winter; no bricks with which to rebuild his bombed house. It was no guarantee of steady employment. It promised freedom. Freedom from hunger? From unemployment? From his bare-bones existence? No, it did not relate to his daily struggle to survive in those early postwar years. Rather, there was a communications gap between the occupiers and the occupied that could not be bridged.

In the autumn of 1948 the U.S. military-government detachment for the state of Württemberg-Baden began an energetic campaign to popularize a town-hall forum to show the Germans how democracy functions in small-town communities in New England. Under the protective sponsorship of the Americans, German audiences were encouraged to speak out openly and frankly at these meetings, criticizing their local public officials. However, the whole program received a setback from which it never recovered by what happened in a small community in the Stuttgart region. A German rose to his feet in a forum session and delivered a long harangue critical of the local town administration. The next morning a policeman came to his house and dragged the protesting German before the local magistrate, who promptly fined him the equivalent of twenty-five dollars for public abuse of the town officials. That ended further German participation in the town-hall program in Württemberg-Baden.

In November 1947, thirteen young students at Frankfurt University began publishing a monthly magazine called *Die Pause*. Because they expressed criticism of their educational system and, by inference, of the U.S. control of it, and displayed other definite though not subversive opinions about life in Germany, they were called to military-government headquarters in Wiesbaden. The student journalists were reprimanded and told it would be better to confine their editorializing to more adolescent subjects, such as scouting, because their magazine was a school publication.

The twenty-year-old leader of the group and editor of *Die Pause* angrily replied: "About eighty percent of our readers were in the German army and saw active combat service. They are interested in problems that are more adult than scouting."

The American program for democratization would have fallen into greater disarray if it had not been for Clay, the executor of U.S. occupation policy in Germany. Clay was a rare bird, an urbane and politically sophisticated army officer with a firm grasp of realities. He had to carry out Washington's orders to democratize the defeated Germans as quickly as possible, thus to immunize them against the virus of communism. But Clay's order of priorities managed to temper and make more acceptable the execution of U.S. policy. He often stated his thesis that democracy will only be acceptable to the Germans when their economic and political affairs are in good order. He did not permit himself the self-delusion that the U.S. military government could reform or transform the Germans from nazism and militarism to the democratic way of life through military occupation. He argued that job security and decent living, buttressed by a stable economy must come first. Then the ground would be fertile for the seeds of a new political doctrine.

The British military government, whose officers were more knowledgable and experienced in dealing with the Germans than the Americans, also had arrived at Clay's conclusion. The *British Zone Review,* the official publication of the British military government, in its August 1948 issue pointed out that the Western Allies had not been able to offer a better substitute for the nazism which young Germans had followed blindly into defeat. In a detailed study, the *Review* criticized the Allied military governments for their "failure to reeducate" the Germans politically; for the maladministration of the various denazification programs, "which is creating the foundations of a future resistance movement in Germany"; for the "fundamental mistake" in attempting to reorganize the political life in a country with a "shattered economy"; and, finally, for their erroneous assumption that democracy can be imposed on a society by a foreign army or group. The *Review* reached this pessimistic conclusion:

In any event, political education is difficult in Germany today. Democracy is not taught in a sunny schoolroom but in a gray ruin. Napoleon sought to impose democracy on Germany and the German people; but instead merely intensified their nationalism. In the days of the Weimar Republic democracy came again, after a lost war, as an imposed blessing, and was rejected. Today for the third time, the victor nations bring the opportunity of democracy to the German people, but synchronized with its arrival come hunger and distress.

The Americans ignored an important component of democracy. Where democracy has been successful, it first has been victorious. It does not develop out of defeat; that is the spawning ground for totalitarian governments. The U.S. survived and thrived in its first two hundred years of democratic rule because it never was conquered or defeated in a fight to the finish. But modern Germany has had no such background. When Germany was powerful and wealthy, it was ruled by strong men whose power and mandate remained unchallenged in peacetime. To be sure, Kaiser Wilhelm II and Hitler lost their wars. The Kaiser's abdication and Hitler's suicide cut the mystic political bonds that had once united them with the German people. By their last acts, the Emperor and *der Führer* acknowledged they had failed the Germans.

Touring West Germany in the immediate postwar years one saw that the outward memorabilia of nazism—the busts of Hitler, the swastikas engraved in the pediments of public buildings—were missing from the scene. The only statues still to be found standing on their stone pedestals were dozens of frowning Bismarcks and a lesser number of the more historically remote Frederick the Great. They were two strong men. They had won *their* wars. They had made Germany respected. Frederick the Great forged the Kingdom of Prussia into the military foundation on which Bismarck built modern Germany.

This preservation of memorials to the Bismarckian and Frederickian eras recalls a statement of Willy H. Schlieker, one of the first of the *Wirtschaftswunderkinder,* economic miracle whiz kids. Herr Schlieker, who fashioned a fortune and an industrial empire out of the postwar debacle, was slightly contemptuous of the American program to make democrats out of his politically apathetic compatriots. He said: "You Americans made one big mistake in your efforts to democratize us Germans and that is why it never worked properly. You didn't do your homework. In the beginning you neglected to de-Kaiserize us."

A 1949 editorial in the *Wiesbadener Kurier* acutely reflects the postwar disinterest and distrust of the German civilians concerning political beliefs and values preached by the Americans:

The Hessian Minister for Education has informed the U.S. press that it would not just do merely to profess allegiance to democracy; one had to be prepared to die for it too . . . We have died twice; once for the Kaiser and once again for Der Führer, so why shouldn't we, for a change, be prepared to die for democracy? . . . But, no thanks, let's risk it once to end our lives in a bed, without any heroics at all!

BOOK II

THE FOURTH
AND RICHEST
REICH

4

We are not here as carpetbaggers.
—GEN. LUCIUS D. CLAY

THE FOUNDING
FATHER

AFTER World War II, in order to fill the political vacuum created by the military defeat of Nazi Germany, the U.S. had to engage itself directly in the creation of a new and pro-Western German nation or suffer the loss of Europe to the Russians by default. This state of affairs was seen clearly by others. The *Economist* pointed out that America had now become "a great European power." The New World had embarked on an unprecedented experiment—a gamble is, perhaps, a more accurate description—of state-making in the Old World. By comparison, America's previous interventions in the banana republics of Latin America were mere child's play.

The situation was all the more remarkable because it evolved in a rather haphazard and unplanned fashion. A handful of determined men, directed and inspired by a regular U.S. Army officer and engineer by profession, took the first positive steps to create a new postwar balance of power on the European continent.

Even Clay, the military governor of the U.S. zone, and his immediate colleagues did not grasp the full import of their early decisions or envision the far-reaching consequences of their actions. Certainly the Truman administration in Washington and the American public did not smell what was simmering on the back burner. Their attentions were concentrated on headline-making developments elsewhere: the Soviet political take-overs of the Balkan states; the Communist threats in France and Italy; the civil wars in Greece and China, and so on. All these developments were more dramatic and eye-catching than what was taking place in occupied Germany. It was generally assumed that "the problem of Germany" had been resolved with the defeat and occupation of the Third Reich. But that was a gross misconception.

Germany was being governed by the four occupation powers in uneasy and discordant concert; she had become the principal combat zone of the cold-war struggle for political control of this "heartland" of the European continent. Germany, a nation of 70 million people who are highly integrated by their social, cultural, and historical relationships, straddles the Continent from the Baltic to the Alps. It is *Mitteleuropa,* the meeting place and point of balance between the West and the East. He who tips the scales one way or the other can change the political and economic patterns of Europe. Germany, even though truncated by the Iron Curtain, holds the key to Europe's future.

In attempting to calculate the basic causes or motivation for the cold war, it is helpful to recall the doctrines of the late Sir Halford Mackinder, dean of British geographers and founder of the school of geo-politics. In his classic book, *Democratic Ideals and Reality,* first published in 1919. Sir Halford saw that Germany and Russia were so situated on the European landmass that should they join together, or should one control the other, a Russo-German combination could rule the world. He based his conclusions on the following thesis: modern transportation and communications have reduced the continents of the world to islands. Europe, Asia, and Africa constitute not three continents but, in his words, one "World Island" which is the true center of gravity of world power. The Western Hemisphere is only a "lesser island," smaller in size, without the manpower or the natural resources to enable it to successfully challenge the World Island. The Mackinder geo-political doctrine identified the "Heartland" of the World Island as central and eastern Europe taken together and so situated geographically and strategically to dominate the World Island as a whole. From this premise he formulated his caveat for western democratic nations: "Who rules Eastern Europe commands the Heartland. Who rules the Heartland commands the World Island. Who rules the World Island commands the world."

Prof. Karl Haushofer, the first German geo-politician, was greatly impressed with the Mackinder heartland thesis. He in turn strongly influenced the strategic direction of Hitler's warfare. The *Führer's* long-planned Operation Barbarossa to conquer Russia confirms his geo-political conviction that there can be only one dominant power in eastern and central Europe: Germany or Russia. Nor was Hitler alone in his convictions. The Kremlin also seemed to be guided by Mackinder's geo-political concepts, but could not act until Germany's military power had been decisively broken in defeat. After World War II, with his Red Army, Stalin attempted the political conquest of the heartland but was stopped short of his objective to extend the Communist writ to the banks of the Rhine River. Mackinder's thesis did not take into consideration the emergence of the U.S. as the strongest military power in the world. However, as the war in

Vietnam clearly demonstrated, there are certain geographical and tactical limits on the overseas deployment of America's manpower and intercontinental nuclear missiles. The U.S. cannot on its own invalidate the heartland thesis; it can at best block Russian dominance of central and eastern Europe only by supporting strong and politically independent Germany.

It is strange that a professional army officer, not a diplomat or politician, first recognized the postwar problem of Germany in its true perspective and how it affected the U.S. and the Western allies. It was General Clay who almost single-handedly reversed the punitive and unrealistic American policy toward defeated Germany and then forced the U.S. government to follow in his turbulent wake. And as the record now clearly shows, Clay was the founding father of the *Bundesrepublik Deutschland*.

Clay has been described as "the General Patton of the cold war," a grudging tribute by one of his many critics to his imaginative and successful strategy and tactics in defeating Soviet attempts to force the Western powers out of Berlin through a ground blockade of the city. Clay organized the *Lüftbrücke,* the airlift, which supplied a city of two million people with the necessities of life. U.S. Air Force cargo planes flew twenty-four hours a day, seven days a week, through fog and sunshine, rain and snow, for ten months, eight weeks and three days without a break in operations. Besides being a magnificent demonstration of the tactical capabilities of the military air transport, the airlift exposed to the whole world the Russian policy toward West Berlin: submit or starve. It was a propaganda victory of Waterloo proportions for America.

However, Clay's unique contribution to the postwar evolution of West Germany went far beyond the successful airlift. The fifty-two-year-old military engineer saw through the complexities of the problem of Germany to a solution: Germany, a nation with the greatest industrial potential on the Continent could not remain a pariah in the family of nations. The Germans must have the freedom and incentive to rebuild their lives so that they could achieve the political and economic security that the *Kaiserreich* and the Third Reich had denied them. But this insight, or change of heart, did not come as a sudden full-blown vision. The cumulative effects of the harsh realities of existence in occupied Germany brought about a new understanding of the nature of the problem.

The Russians sensed the geo-political dangers for them in the changing American attitude and approach to the defeated Germans. The blockade of Berlin, which was imposed on March 31, 1948, was also aimed to frighten the Americans, to throw them off balance. But Clay's steadfastness in the face of Russian threats and brinksmanship was worth a division of troops. The Soviet High Command never expected that the Americans could or would manage to stay on in Berlin and support themselves and the two million civilians who were growing more hungry and restless with every passing day.

Stubborn and unflappable, Clay enjoyed greater freedom to maneuver than did his Russian counterpart, Marshal Sokolovsky, who had to refer all his ideas and suggestions to the Kremlin in Moscow for approval before taking action. On the other hand the American military governor could and did adjust his strategy and tactics to the problems as they confronted him each day, without having to wait for the Pentagon's green light. As a result, Clay dominated the German scene. He was a twentieth-century proconsul, similar to the Roman proconsuls who governed the borderlands of their far-reaching empire to hold back the barbarians who were ever poised to ravage and pillage at the slightest opportunity.

As U.S. military governor, Clay enjoyed far wider plenipotentiary power than any one of his Russian, British, or French counterparts. He exercised a range of powers with relatively little interference from the Pentagon in Washington. He was the only one of the Allied military governors who could virtually formulate his own on-the-spot occupation policy, largely because of the lack of more precise directions from his superiors in Washington. Once asked to explain how and where U.S. policy for Germany was developed, Clay replied: "At those various Foreign Ministers Conferences, *we* would have conversations out of which our Germany policy would develop."* He explained further that by "we" he meant himself and former Secretary of State James F. Byrnes, a fellow Southerner and close personal friend, and Byrnes' successor, Gen. George C. Marshall. Clay admitted that the decisions arising out of these conversations probably had not been set down on paper as a matter of record to be studied or even fully explained to the officials in Washington. The result was that Clay was not only tailoring his own concepts of policy out of these informal meetings with Byrnes and Marshall, but that his recommendations were generally acceptable to these two high-ranking officials. James Byrnes, when serving as secretary of state under President Truman, trusted Clay's judgment and his recommendations on German policy. So did General Marshall, who knew of Clay's capabilities from his previous wartime assignment in the Pentagon. Clay's mandate was sufficiently flexible that he was able to turn the course of U.S. occupation in Germany, committing America to the creation of a West German state as a new line of defense in the political confrontation with the Russians. Clay was responsible only to his military superiors in the army chain of command. That meant he reported to the Pentagon and not to the State Department, whose professional diplomats were highly censorious of the political wheeling and dealing of a four-star U.S. military governor over whom they had no control. The irritation of the State Department policy-makers concerning General Clay's decisive role in policy-making was best expressed by one of its officers who commented: "Every time we go into a Foreign Ministers Conference, we first have to make a treaty with our General Clay."*

Lucius DuBignon Clay was born in Marietta, Georgia, on April 23, 1897, the youngest son of U.S. Senator Alexander Stephen Clay, whose family was part of Georgia's social and political elite. Young Clay was raised in a Deep South that was still nursing its lasting and bitter memories of the American Civil War and its aftermath. The scorched-earth tactics of General Sherman's destructive march through Georgia to break the backbone of the Confederacy's resistance was still a reality of daily existence. Following the assassination of President Lincoln, the vindictive military occupation by Northern troops, which propped up their puppet state governments with their bayonets, remained fresh and vivid in the collective mind of the South. The wholesale looting by the hordes of northern carpetbaggers, who descended on the South like a swarm of wasps on a picnic table, was not easily forgotten. These were the drops of vinegar that the sons and grandsons of the Confederacy imbibed with their mother's milk. The experience of what can happen to people who have lost a war, of the price that can be exacted by the victor and must be paid, were in the subconscious mind of Clay when he took up his appointment in Germany. It colored his views about America's policies toward defeated Germany. After taking over as head of the U.S. military government, he surprised a Berlin press conference with his comment: "We are not here as carpetbaggers."

The guiding principle that he applied to the administration of the military government and the occupation of Germany was expressed one day in this remark: "I tried to think of the kind of occupation the South would have had if Abraham Lincoln had lived. I have kept in mind the kind of reconstruction that Lincoln had promised, as compared to what actually did happen."*

Another major influence on Clay's administration of the U.S. military government was his professional career as an engineer. He was a graduate of West Point in 1918 and selected the Army Corps of Engineers as his branch of military service. In times of peace an army engineer is likely to devote many of his work days to nonmilitary projects. That is because the Corps of Engineers has responsibility for the maintenance of all navigable waterways in the continental U.S. and its overseas territories. As a result, Clay spent most of his years between the wars directing and supervising the construction of dams and other hydroelectric projects in the U.S., the Panama Canal Zone, and the Philippines, where he also served as chief of engineers under Gen. Douglas MacArthur. Clay's first physical involvement with military operations in World War II was to repair the heavily damaged harbor of Cherbourg so that it could serve as a major supply base for the Allied troops fighting in France. After taking command of Cherbourg in November 1944 he quintupled the volume of military supplies moving through Cherbourg in the first thirty days. In the following April 1945, he came to Germany to take charge of military government in the U.S. zone.*

For a noncombat army engineer like Clay, progress and accomplishment were to be measured in terms of the construction and repair of facilities such as the hydroelectric projects which serve a community and better the people's way of life. In Germany, however, he was called on to carry out a punitive and destructive deindustrialization program, to dismantle factories, to deliberately depress the standards of living of a defeated nation, as a matter of a high policy of his government, and to curtail its industrial productivity when there was a war-ravaged Europe to be repaired and replenished with the necessities of life. This was more than an anachronism to an engineer; it was contrary to the values and standards in which he had been educated.

So it was in character for Clay to organize the first large-scale reconstruction project in Germany in the immediate postwar era—make the Rhine River navigable once again. This giant artery of commerce was a shambles at the close of the war. Thirty-five bridges from Switzerland to the Dutch frontier had been dynamited by the retreating Germans and their wreckage completely blocked all the water traffic which was vital to the economic functioning of western Europe. More than a thousand barges had been scuttled and sunk, adding more obstacles to navigation. Clay set the U.S. Army engineers with heavy-duty equipment to work together with German technicians. Within the first year of occupation a navigable channel had been cleared from Basel to Rotterdam. Six shipyards were put back to work with American equipment, with the result that 750 barges and 108 tugs were soon operating again. The Rhine River moves the bulk of the coal mined in the Ruhr; one river barge can transport the equivalent tonnage of a 35-car freight train. Without this Ruhr coal, industrial production as well as electrical power for civilian and military activities would be paralyzed.

Early in the occupation, Clay began to privately question the wisdom or relevance of the master policy directive, JCS 1067, which set the guidelines for American military rule in Germany. His reaction to the official policy, conceived during the heat and stress of a major war, was in line with the conclusion reached by former President Herbert Hoover. In 1946, when the acute food shortage in Germany became the number one priority project, President Truman asked Hoover to make a survey of the problem of feeding Germany's postwar population. After studying the postwar scene, the former president capsulized the dilemma facing the decision-makers in Washington and the military government in Germany in how to treat with the defeated ex-enemy. Hoover reported to Truman: "You can have vengeance, or peace, but you can't have both."

The master policy directive JCS 1067, which Clay was later to describe as the imposition of a Carthaginian peace on a defeated enemy nation, was not only unworkable, it was also likely to be counterproductive and to encourage the Germans—or at least a large number of them—to seek out a *modus vivendi* under Communist rule. Clay's education in the *Realpolitik* of postwar Europe was also stimulated by the folklore of the Deep South of his youth, which kept ever green in his consciousness the "peace with vengeance" imposed on the defenseless southern states by the victorious North after Lee's surrender at Appomattox.

In the spring of 1946, when the cold war was intensifying its psychological pressures on the Allied High Command and the German civilian population alike, Clay reached the conclusion that there was no possibility of any four-power agreement on the future of Germany as a whole. The Russians wanted no political or economic unification except on their terms, which were obviously unacceptable to Washington. Failing this, the Russians wanted a separate and politically insulated East German satellite which would serve as a buffer state between the Soviet Union and the Western powers. The French did not want a united Germany, even in defeat. They fought every inch up and down the conference table against all proposals to end the present four-power zonal quartering of Germany. Divide and rule was the guiding principle of the French vis-à-vis their traditional enemy.

Thus, if there could be no whole Germany to which a master policy could be applied, the next best thing in Clay's opinion was to create a segment of Germany that could be made to function as a nation, at least economically. Clay's objective was relatively simple: turn the country back to the Germans and then turn them loose to rebuild their war-shattered economy with a minimum of further financial aid from American taxpayers. It would be easier to organize a West German state out of two zones of occupation as a starter than to continue the fruitless and exacerbating negotiations with the Russians and the French.

In a long cable to the Pentagon on May 26, 1946, Clay reviewed the situation in Germany as it appeared to him. He pointed out that as a result of Russian and French intransigence:

. . . after one year of occupation, the [four] zones represent air-tight territories with almost no free exchange of commodities, persons and ideas. Germany now consists of four small economic units, which can deal with each other only through treaties, in spite of the fact that no one unit can be regarded as self-supporting . . . economic unity can be obtained only through free trade in Germany and a common policy for foreign trade designed to serve Germany as a whole. A common financial policy is equally essential. Runaway inflation, accompanied by economic paralysis may develop at any moment. Drastic fiscal reforms . . . are essential at the earliest possible date . . . Common policies and nationwide implementation are equally essential for transportation, communications, food and agriculture, industry and foreign trade, if economic recovery is to be made possible . . . as it stands now economic integration is becoming less each day with the Soviet and French zones requiring approval for practically each item leaving their zones, and with the British and our zones in self-defense moving in the same direction. The postwar level of industry to be left to Germany, which serves as a basis for reparations, is based on the treatment of Germany as an economic unit. Its execution under other conditions would be absolutely impossible, as it would leave economic chaos in Germany. *It would particularly affect the U.S. Zone which has no raw materials and would create a financial liability for the United States for many years.* [Italics added.]

The American military governor then went on to sketch out his proposal for a solution to the problem of Germany through the creation of a federation of 9 to 15 states (*Länder*), organized either by economic areas or by traditional political divisions. Clay further advised the Pentagon to expect stiff resistance from both the Russian and French governments to his proposal for a new postwar German state, but added as an alternative solution the fusion of the American and British zones as the embryo of a dimly envisioned independent West Germany. Clay rationalized his way to this zonal merger as follows:

However, if agreement cannot be obtained along these broad lines in the immediate future, we face a deteriorating German economy which will create a political unrest favorable to the development of communism in Germany and a deterrent to its democratization. The suffering of the German people will be a serious charge against democracy and will develop a sympathy which may well defeat our other objectives in Germany.

The British and U.S. Zones together could within a few years become self-supporting, although food would have to be provided during this period until industry could be rehabilitated sufficiently to provide requisite exports to support food imports . . . it is our proposal to effect this merger before winter, even though we would much prefer to obtain Allied unity in the treatment of Germany as a whole.*

The following July, Clay attended the Foreign Ministers Conference in Paris, and while there gave Secretary of State Byrnes the details of his state-making project. It would be a fusion of the British and American zones—the industrial Ruhr joined to the food-producing farmlands of Bavaria, Hesse, and Württemberg-Baden—to be governed in the initial stages by an economic administration of chosen German officials. Clay also won the support of two important U.S. senators in the field of foreign policy: Tom Connally of Texas, chairman of the Senate's Foreign Relations Committee; and Arthur H. Vandenberg, senior Republican member of that committee. It was agreed that Byrnes would announce this major change in policy toward Germany in a speech to be delivered in Stuttgart on September 6, 1946.

It was a dramatic occasion. The international press had been alerted that Byrne's speech would be a front-page news event. The setting was the opera house in the midst of the heavily damaged city center. In addition to U.S. government and military personnel, the audience included a guest list of leading German officials and personalities, who were seated in the front rows of the orchestra. On the stage facing them were Byrnes, Senators Connally and Vandenberg, and Gen. Joseph T. McNarney. Clay sat behind the German guests to savor their reaction to Byrnes' speech.

Secretary Byrnes made three major points. To reassure the Germans of security against any Communist takeover, he promised that "as long as the occupation force is required in Germany the army of the United States will be part of that occupation force."

He said the time had come for the Germans to have freedom from occupation controls so they could become self-supporting by their own efforts. This could best be done by merging the British and American zones and, through bizonal agencies, evolving common financial, industrial, and social policies.

Finally, Byrnes declared that the Germans must be given a greater measure of self-government. In his flat and southern drawl, Byrnes evoked an emotional climax with these words: "The American people want to help the German people win their way back to an honorable place among the free and peace-loving nations of the world."

The speech, with a running translation, was carried live by German radio. A British observer commented on the effects of this political blockbuster: "At the time they were spoken these were bold words and they came to the millions of Germans who heard or read them as the first glimmer of dawn after a long, dark night. Their moral impact was incalculable."*

Having been convinced of the need for a change in the basic occupation policies, Clay began one of the most astute courses of personal diplomacy displayed by any of the so-called soldier-statesmen of World War II. He was constantly aware that even within his own military-government ranks hatred and distrust still set the tone in relations between the conqueror and the conquered.* If he was to successfully revise the punitive and negative character of the occupation, he would have to win the support of the American people, particularly their representatives in the U.S. Congress. As Clay began to emerge on the international scene, a new facet of his personality became apparent; he was an adroit and successful practitioner of the art of public relations. Clay utilized this talent to win over the sympathies of the U.S. and Allied correspondents in Germany, as well as their editors and commentators back home. In the summer of 1946 the first of a series of group tours of West Germany was organized for prominent and influential Americans who were described as the "thought-leaders and provokers" of the U.S.

In the succeeding two years, hundreds of members of the U.S. Congress, leading business executives, and the elite of the press, radio, and media came to see and to be briefed on Clay's plans for the ultimate creation of a new, pro-Western German state. With few exceptions, these visitors returned home with the light of understanding shining in their eyes. The military governor was strengthening his hand by building up an important political constituency in America, supporting what he was trying to achieve in Germany.

While Byrnes' speech was gratifying to those Germans in top-level political and economic circles—who could read its implications correctly—it did not evoke a similar response from the masses. The man on the street did not seem in any hurry to grasp at the opportunity for greater freedom and to assume the greater responsibilities required to go it alone. Many took their cue from Kurt Schumacher, the crippled survivor of Hitler's concentration camps, who had emerged to become leader of the Socialist party in West Germany. Schumacher kept reminding the Allies, "Total victory means total responsibility."

It was his way of saying that if the Americans, British, and French were to be the masters and the defeated Germans were to be their slaves, then it was the master's moral responsibility to provide the necessities of life for the slaves.

Behind this German apathy and distrust over the evolving U.S. occupation policy was the widely held conviction that the Americans were actually attempting to create their own West German satellite state, which was to be directly under the control of Washington. Public mood equated it with the East German Communist regime controlled by the Kremlin. The Germans had an understandable lack of enthusiasm for being puppets of the great powers in their cold-war skirmishing.

But Clay was prepared to combat this negative attitude and bring about a conversion of those on the sidelines. He wanted to mobilize the support of the German officials of the four *Länder* (Bavaria, Hesse, Württemberg-Baden and the city-state of Bremen) of the U.S. zone behind the American-British conviction that the time had come to form an independent federal government for West Germany.

Clay summoned the four minister presidents to meet him in his Frankfurt office. The military governor went into the room accompanied only by his interpreter, Robert Lochner. His political adviser, Ambassador Robert D. Murphy, was excluded. Clay sat opposite the four stolid, elderly German politicians. The atmosphere was described later as "very frosty." Clay opened the conference by bluntly declaring: "Gentlemen, you have deserted me in the struggle against the Russians for Berlin. . . . Either you are sympathizing with the Russians or you are frightened of them. I can find no other explanation to account for your negative attitudes."

The military governor in crisp but emphatic language, as if he were a drill sergeant and they were fresh recruits, called on them to snap out of their political lethargy and to openly express their opposition concerning the Russian political aggression clearly to the public. If they failed to do so, Clay hinted, he would make it known publicly that they were abandoning their fellow Germans under siege in Berlin. The effect of this brief encounter was to bump the German minister presidents off the fence they had been straddling and to help hasten the formation of a West German government.

Clay previously had very little personal contact with German civilians. Except for occasional meetings with their officials, he purposely remained isolated from the people he governed, so as to strengthen the influence and prestige of his position in their eyes. To the man on the street he was a remote and somewhat awesome personality, surrounded by the military trappings of his office. Many credulous civilians actually believed that he was Morgenthau's brother-in-law, because Clay was responsible for the Four Ds to punish and to reform the Germans. Those knowledgeable in the English language relished the aphorism going the rounds that "American democracy has feet of Clay."

Yet, when intelligent Germans came into close personal contact with him, they were very surprised to discover the wide gap between the image they had of the U.S. military governor and the relaxed and informal four-star general who was the antithesis of a military master of a defeated enemy nation. An example of this reaction was provided by a German editor when he had his first close-up meeting with Clay during a press briefing in the latter's office in the Farben building.

Clay was seated behind his large desk; grouped around it in a semi-circle were Allied correspondents and the German guest. Clay was a chain smoker, but in this meeting he had exhausted his supply. Leaning across his desk to the journalists, he asked: "Will somebody pass me a cigarette?" Several extended their packs, Clay took one, lit up, and the press conference continued. It was discovered that this bit of byplay later became the talk of local journalistic circles through the description given by the German editor: "No German General, or even one of our so-called 'democratic' Ministers today, would ever invite the press into his office to talk on such a friendly give-and-take basis. But what was more amazing to me; General Clay thought nothing of borrowing a cigarette from one of the journalists.

"You know in prewar Germany and even today, that would never happen. If Clay had been a German General, there would have been an aide offering cigarettes on a silver tray. A German General would have thought it beneath his dignity to accept a cigarette from a visitor to his office, especially from a member of the press. Besides he would not have given the journalists a chance to talk with him, unless he was ordered to do so by his superiors. . . . I just don't understand Clay and some of your American traits."

After the military governor opened up his frequent press conferences to German journalists—as part of his public-relations program to elicit some degree of German understanding and support for his master plan—the climate of public opinion became less critical of the *Amis,* a slightly derogatory German expression for Americans similar to the American usage of *krauts,* for the Germans. The civilians began to view the U.S. military governor in a new light, especially when they became aware, through the press, that he was a man who had definite and positive ideas about Germany's future and that he was working on a program to repair and reconstruct their war-gutted nation. Ordinarily these abstractions would have had little effect on the German civilians, whose own precarious daily existence commanded their time, energies, and thoughts. But Clay and the *Amis* began to have an impact when the German civilians learned that the American government was doling out hundreds of millions of dollars in army relief funds. In addition to the $740 million of GARIOA money (Government Aid and Relief in Occupied Areas), Clay was controlling the spigot out of which $3.5 billion of Marshall Plan funds and supplies would pour to prime the pump of the moribund German economy. For the first time since the occupation, the *Amis* were taken seriously, having demonstrated some talent for *Realpolitik* in the eyes of the Germans. The Germans could grasp the elements of the emerging new balance of power; American green dollars would now confront the Red Army battalions in the political *Nervenkrieg.*

The cold war that was being waged, which developed so quickly in the early postwar days, frightened the Germans because a few hundred miles to the east were millions of Red Army soldiers, guns in hand. They had not been redeployed to their homeland as the Americans had gone back across the Atlantic. But the menace of a Russian takeover of western Germany began to recede in the minds of thinking Germans when they contemplated the enormity of America's economic power and resources, now being mobilized to compensate in part for the Soviet military domination of eastern Europe. From that point on the act of building the postwar eco-political state of West Germany was launched in the German psyche.

5

Disintegrating forces are at work, the patient is sinking while the doctors deliberate.

—SECRETARY OF STATE GEORGE C. MARSHALL,
*commenting on the Foreign Ministers
Conference in Moscow, March 1947*

The genesis of the Federal German Republic can be traced to the American offer of economic fusion between the zones of occupation in July 1946.

—*From the* Times *of London, April 30, 1967*

BIZONIA TO BONN

THE COUNCIL OF FOREIGN MINISTERS met in London in December 1947 in a last-ditch attempt to work out an arrangement about Germany's future status in the family of nations that was mutually acceptable to the governments in Moscow, Washington, London, and Paris. A futile exercise in diplomacy, it started and ended in a hopeless deadlock. However, this cleared the decks for the official merger of the British and American zones, as originally proposed by Clay and then pushed through by the U.S. government. On February 6, 1948 the ersatz state of Bizonia—as it was christened by the German press—first appeared on the postwar maps of Europe. It was a hybrid creation, sired by political expediency out of Soviet intransigence, but it was to have a future because it was the unwitting embryo of the future Federal Republic of Germany.

At the outset, Bizonia was an *ad hoc** improvisation, an economic marriage of the British and American zones, designed to arrest the rapid decline of the economy and the slipping standards of living. The British and American military governments, even with the best intentions in the world, could not solve this crisis out of their own supreme powers and resources. They did not have at their command the adequate cadres of experts, who had the requisite background and experience necessary to administer at the ground level the economy of their two merged zones. They had no alternative but to turn to the Germans. So a German-staffed economic administration was formed to bring some order out of chaos and to get the industry, commerce, and finance of the bizonal area moving again.

Bizonia had some of the physical attributes of a government: its economic council of fifty members served as a quasi-legislative assembly; an economic director's office and five quasi-ministerial agencies for food and agriculture, finance, transportation, civil service, communications and economic planning served as the executive branch; while a judiciary system was included to enforce the decrees and regulations of the new administration. Each of the quasi-ministries was located in a different city, while the economic director and the economic council were set up in Frankfurt. The director's office was housed in an abandoned German army barracks, while the council shared what remained of the bombed-out stock exchange with a local theatrical company, which put on occasional performances of comic opera.

The first objective of the bizonal administration was to pool the limited resources of the two zones, principally food and coal, so as to stimulate the stagnant industry to produce more for export trade and thereby enable West Germany to contribute to its own self-support. The number one priority was to boost the lagging Ruhr coal production. Coal was Germany's prime source of fuel and energy, as well as its most available and ready export item. However, the thousands of unemployed miners, who were eager to return to the pits to earn some money, could not sustain their back-breaking labor on the existing daily food ration of 1,550 calories. Just maintaining average productivity, a coal miner requires a food intake of about 4,500 calories per day. To meet this deficiency Clay allocated dollars to be spent for added food rations for the coal miners, plus other work incentives such as tobacco, beer, and *schnapps*. The extra rations produced result: Ruhr coal production climbed from 110,000 tons per day to 280,000 tons, compared to normal prewar production of 370,000 tons per day.

It soon became apparent that Bizonia was only the halfway house in Germany's road back to some semblance of normalcy. The economic administration by the Germans only shadowboxed with reality. For example, the various agencies responsible for the segments of economic improvements such as food and agriculture, transportation, communications, and others had little independent authority to carry out their duties. The substantive controls over the West German economy, as well as the instruments of economic power, remained in Allied hands. Clay and British General Sir Brian Robertson controlled the allocations of vital supplies and goods, the exports and imports, and the collection and spending of all revenues as they deemed necessary to keep the waterlogged West German economy afloat in the high seas.

Though designed to have the appearance and functions of a government, the German-staffed bizonal administration was not a government; nor was it permitted to operate like a government. In fact, it had so little authority and prestige that the various *Länder* governments ignored or violated its ordinances with impunity. The concept of Bizonia as a quasi-government was the natural outgrowth of the policy decisions of Clay and his Washington mentor and friend, Secretary of State Byrnes, that West Germany's economic revival must come before full political independence and freedom of action were granted to the occupied and truncated country. However, Clay had no mandate, nor was it likely that any authority would be given by the U.S. Congress, to permit German officials to spend the GARIOA funds of the U.S. Treasury; nor was Clay prepared to recommend the surrendering to any large degree the allocation of U.S. funds and supplies to the economic council and economic director of Bizonia. This impasse signaled that the time had come to create a new and independent West German state, economically and politically tied to the Western powers, especially the U.S.

Then an unexpected act of political aggression in neighboring Czechoslovakia sounded a note of alarm in Washington and other Western capitals that the cold war might be coming closer to overt military action. On February 28, 1948, the democratic and pro-Western government in Czechoslovakia was overthrown in a ruthless *coup d'état* engineered by the Communists, which involved throwing Foreign Minister Jan Masaryk to his death from a fourth-floor window in Prague's Czernin Palace. The specter of further westward expansion of Soviet power became a definite possibility in the not-too-distant future. The Western national hastily began to reconsider their options about Germany and its role in the defense of Europe. The note of urgency ringing in the Allied councils was echoed in a long leader in the *Economist,* which read:

In short, the competition for the soul of Germany is now no longer avoidable—and it is the soul that must be won. . . . It is well to re-state the essence of the problem. It is to recreate a Germany with the full powers of a centralized government with unimpaired industrial capacity—anything less will make a Democratic Germany less attractive to the Germans than a Soviet Germany.

There were several immediate effects of the Communist coup in Prague. A Western European Union, primarily defensive in character, was formed by Britain, France, and the Benelux countries. The growing threat of Soviet aggression caused the French government to change its policy toward Germany. Henceforth Paris would no longer treat the French zone in Germany as a separate political entity, but would join it to the British and American zones. Bizonia would become Trizonia.

More important, however, as it concerned Germany's economic future, the French agreed to the creation of an International Ruhr Authority which did not involve the political separation of the Ruhr area for Germany. The Western Allies were closing up their ranks in the face of a common danger.

The Communist take-over in Czechoslovakia had one definitive result; it strengthened the growing conviction of the Americans that Germany would remain divided by the Iron Curtain into an East German satellite of Russia and a West Germany, which must be made economically and politically strong and independent so as to be immunized against the virus of communism. That could only be accomplished by the creation of a West German government, allied to the Western European Union and to the U.S.

The crossing of that Rubicon was revealed in a speech delivered by Gen. Sir Brian Robertson, the British military governor, to the *Landtag* (state parliament) of North Rhine-Westphalia on April 17, 1948. Sir Brian announced that a provisional West German state would be created. Speaking on behalf of his American and French colleagues, he told the Germans: "For the time being we must accept the fact that an Iron Curtain splits Germany. Come forward, determined to make the best of the larger part of your country which is on the right side of the Iron Curtain. The rest will come in time."

While he did not mention the Soviet Union by name, he called on the West Germans to support the ideals of western civilization in the face of the common enemy, adding: "Make up your minds to stand against these gentlemen, who, with democracy on their lips and truncheons behind their backs, would filch your German freedom from you. . . . The prospects are good; go forth and seize them. . . . We all form part of Europe."

Sir Brian closed his speech in German, an oblique admission that the hitherto subservient role of the West Germans to the Allied military authorities was soon to be drastically revised and improved. He said: "Is it strange that I talk to you like this? Yes, it is strange! But we are living in strange times, they have no parallel in history."

This Düsseldorf address was another milestone in the evolutionary development of West Germany. However, it was not recognized for its long-range implications by the Germans. The Robertson speech did not excite much friendly comment in the press; most editorial reaction was cautious or passively negative. But the foundation had been laid for the *Bundesrepublik* and work could now begin to create the institutions and instruments of government for a West German state.

While Bizonia was short-lived, it was the period of gestation for the *Bundesrepublik,* when its character and form were achieved. It was also the time when the most important decisions affecting the future of the new West German state were made. The embryonic West German state seemed put together on a two-tier assembly line as it progressed from the blueprint stage to the completed model. On the upper tier were the Allied authorities, mainly concerned with the outward appearance of their creation—an economically viable vehicle, patterned after western-style democracies. At a lower level were the German officials of Bizonia, arguing furiously about the mechanical aspects of their new government: how it would function; how it would provide security with good mileage and few breakdowns. However, this was the most important level of political and economic engineering because the decisions reached by the Germans themselves were to be incorporated in the institutions and basic code of law of the new Republic when it emerged from the womb on September 17, 1949, with the official convening of the new federal parliament (*Bundestag*) in Bonn.

It was at this lower level that both the vitality and the viability of the Federal Republic of Germany were assured, with the result, as Prof. Alfred Grosser, the noted Franco-German historian, pointed out in his study of the formation of the *Bundesrepublik:*

When the institutions of the Federal German Republic were set up, they were able to function more or less harmoniously *because the brunt of the work had already been accomplished; the important decisions were made before the decision-making machinery* existed. When the new state was born, the period of dramatic changes was already over—indeed its birth was a sign of that very fact.* [Italics added.]

The comparatively brief existence of Bizonia was marked by a short but decisive struggle that determined the very character and substance of the new postwar Federal Republic of Germany. It was a conflict between two strong men who dominated their respective political factions: Adenauer, who at the age of seventy came out of virtual retirement to take over the leadership of the conservative CDU; and Kurt Schumacher, the tough-minded, intolerant, and crippled survivor of Hitler's concentration camps, whose anti-Nazi record clearly established him as the leader of the SPD.

Both the CDU and the SPD seemed roughly equal in party followers. At the outset the political contest appeared only to involve a struggle for the control of the administrative machinery of Bizonia. In reality there were vital and fundamental issues at stake: whether the as yet unborn West German state would have a free-enterprise system or a Socialist planned economy; whether it would be a decentralized federation of states or a strong federal and centralized government; whether if would be international in outlook and align itself with the Western democracies or whether it would adopt a position of nationalistic and total independence from West and East alike—a figurative "pox on both your houses," which Schumacher's fiercely neutral attitude exemplified.

At the time, the conflict between the Conservatives and the Socialists was largely obscured from the outside world because the press was paying more attention to the actions and decisions of the Allied authorities—who seemed to have Germany's destiny firmly in their hands—than to the quarreling German politicians. In general, the members of the international press failed to see the real issues at stake or to grasp the long-range implications of the political scrimmaging. It was not what it appeared to be, a competition for the scraps of power that might fall from the table of the military governors; it was a real struggle for the authority and the instruments of power to direct Germany's clouded future.

Those two outstanding political figures of the early days of Bizonia,

Adenauer and Schumacher, seemed to have been resurrected from their political graves to enter upon the most decisive and influential periods of their careers. Their contest as to whom would dominate the emerging bizonal administration was to have far-reaching repercussions. Because of their inherently strong and positive personalities, the basic political and economic issues involved became polarized around them. Adenauer, the Catholic and sophisticated conservative Rhinelander, was more internationally minded in his thinking, calling for the formation of a weak central government and a stronger federation of states, welded together with the free-market economy. Schumacher, Prussian-born, of Protestant upbringing, demanded a strong central government and a strong presidency, with overriding financial and fiscal powers, functioning in a Socialist planned economy. Schumacher was to develop a strident nationalist outlook; he did not want Germany's postwar future and fortunes tied to the Western powers or the Communist bloc.

Both men were critical of the Allied occupation policies and practices, and in particular the moralizing tone of the American preachments about the need for reform and rehabilitation of the German people. Adenauer kept his criticisms private, restricted to his own circle of intimates. The Rhinelander was convinced that West Germany could not make a political or economic recovery on its own; it must have the support and help of the Western powers in traversing *Der Weg zurück,* the road back.

On the other hand, Schumacher was openly scornful of the occupation policies and practices, castigating the Allied authorities as "fools and villains." Schumacher was an intolerant ideologue, fanatic in his conviction that the Socialists alone came onto the postwar scene with clean hands, having earned the moral and political right to govern West Germany because of their long and proven anti-Nazi record. Few colleagues within his own party dared to question the arguments and beliefs of this World War I veteran who lost an arm in combat on the eastern front; this political martyr who spent ten tortured years in the Dachau concentration camp for his biting criticisms and unwavering opposition to Hitler and the Nazi party while serving as a deputy in the prewar *Reichstag.** Few of his followers challenged his convictions that the SPD alone represented the best hope for Germany's future—that the Socialists, if they were in control of a strong federal government with a planned economy, could navigate an independent course between the twin menaces of authoritarian foreign capitalism, as exemplified by the United States and its Marshall Plan, and the Communist totalitarianism of the Soviet Union.

The contest between Adenauer and his CDU cohorts on one hand and Schumacher and his SPD legions on the other started in the British zone, the most populous of the occupied enclaves. Both Adenauer and Schumacher grasped the obvious reality that the British zone, with its great

North Sea ports and its congested *Ruhrgebiet,* the machine shop of Europe, would dominate political and economic developments in West Germany.

The first serious scrimmage for power between the two men came with the formation of the bizonal economic council and affiliated governing agencies. Because the CDU and SPD appeared to be fairly equal in their voter strength, based on the recent local elections in the British zone, it was proposed that a coalition administration for Bizonia be formed of CDU and SPD nominees, plus a few representatives of the smaller parties. In return for Socialist participation in this arrangement, Schumacher demanded that the key economic and financial directorships be given to the SPD. Ever conscious of the Socialist objective to establish a planned economy, Adenauer and his coalition partners vetoed this proposal. Following this rejection, Schumacher turned his back on the bizonal administration; the Socialists became the party of opposition in the economic council. However, with the majority control of this pseudolegislative assembly firmly in his hands, Adenauer proceeded to do the reverse of what Schumacher had planned for the nascent West German state; he began to lay the foundation for a free-market economy. He staffed the bizonal administration with businessmen, bankers, economists, and capitalist-minded politicians whose broad, if vague, objective was to minimize wherever possible government power and influence on the private sector of the economy.

The next phase in the struggle for the ideological soul of West Germany came with the drafting of a federal-type constitution, as proposed by the Allies to the minister presidents of the eleven West German *Länder.* The shadow of the ill-fated Weimar Republic after World War I hung heavily on the deliberations of the minister presidents. They sought a *modus operandi* which seemingly gave them a republican constitution within a framework of change and flexibility, instead of rigidity and permanence. Instead of summoning a constituent assembly which would then draft a formal constitution, as was the case with the Weimar Republic, the minister presidents created a parliamentary council which in turn would draft a code of basic law (*Grundgesetz*) as the legal framework for the new Federal Republic of Germany.

The parliamentary council sat for nine months under the presidency of Adenauer. The chairman of the steering committee, which actually drafted the basic law, was a leading SPD member, Prof. Carlo Schmid, a witty and skillful negotiator. For a great part of this period Schumacher was sick in bed, though calling the signals for his deputies in the council. Professor Schmid, a plumpish, genial, and friendly man with a good sense of humor, was a sharp contrast to the thin, dour, acerbic, and aloof Schumacher. Schmid's persuasive and pleasant personality may explain why the final draft of the basic law was more in line with SPD doctrine than with what the CDU was demanding.

However, in March 1949 the three military governors rejected the draft of the basic law, on the grounds that it provided too much power and authority to the federal government at the expense of the various state governments, particularly in matters affecting taxation and revenue spending. The Germans had to amend this draft before it could be approved and further progress made toward ending military occupation. Adenauer was in favor of amending the basic law, but Schumacher was not. He held his fire until he addressed a full conference of the SPD in Hannover on April 19, 1949.

Rising from his sick bed, Schumacher, in a burst of impassioned rhetoric for which he was famous, voiced the historic "No" of the Socialist party, rejecting Allied demands to amend the basic law. He told the SPD congress: "You can only be a German patriot, and not a patriot of the eleven German *Länder*. That is the whole difference between the Socialist-Democratic party and the C.D.U."

To the surprise and consternation of Adenauer, the Allied authorities withdrew their objections to the basic law as drafted by Professor Schmid. By the end of May it had been ratified by the various state assemblies and was officially promulgated as the basic law for the Federal Republic of Germany. The first national election for a federal parliament (*Bundestag*) was scheduled for August 14. Once in office, the *Bundestag* would then vote for the first chancellor as head of the government, and for a president, as the chief of state.

Schumacher reaped the plaudits of the press and public because his flat rejection of the demands of the Allied military rulers was the first successful show of resistance offered by the Germans. As the *Frankfurter Rundschau* editorialized: "Schumacher's *'Nein'* should determine the destiny of Western Germany."

Though the election for the first national government was several months away, it appeared that the SPD leader had become an odds-on favorite to be West Germany's first chancellor, a view confirmed by public-opinion polls. However, Adenauer remained strangely unperturbed by these developments. He had reason to be. He was about to explode a political bomb that would decisively affect the results of the first postwar national election.

While Schumacher was confident of his victory, he was even more convinced that he was striking the proper political and economic chords that evoked an affirmative response from a majority of the German voters. He promised them the rewards of a planned economy and the nationalization of heavy industry. No longer would the arbitrary decisions of the *Schlotbarone* ("chimney barons," Ruhr slang for the owners of the great coal and steel trusts and combines) control their daily lives and incomes. He gave voice to a strident nationalism that the Germans should be free of the political pressures and influences of Moscow and Washington, to navigate their own way on the world scene. Schumacher was disdainful of his wily opponent Adenauer, a veteran of decades of political combat; this was a costly mistake. During a mass meeting in Heidelberg on July

22, 1949, to which all the international press had been invited, Adenauer exploded his political bomb. He charged that Schumacher's "historic *Nein*" at Hannover was a sham; his highly emotional rejection of the Allied demands to amend the basic law was political trickery, because the Socialist leader had been tipped off in advance by a British officer that the Allies would withdraw their objections if there was any serious German resistance. Adenauer accused Schumacher of shabby tactics in creating the illusion that he was the one person who dared make a strong stand against the Allied authorities, Schumacher knew there would be no risk whatsoever in this wrestling match with a paper tiger. The angry SPD leader tried to deny the story, but Adenauer added insult to injury by disclosing the name of a British officer who had revealed to Adenauer the details of the advance information given to Schumacher. The British authorities belatedly tried to cover up this embarrassment, but it was difficult to do so, because for years it was widely known that the postwar British Labor government in London had shown favoritism to the SPD in the earlier days of the occupation.

Sir Christopher Steel, the chief political officer of the British military governor in Germany, admitted to the press that the SPD had received special help and encouragement from the British government. In speaking to selected British correspondents, Sir Christopher did not go into specific details about the nature of assistance given to Schumacher and his SPD colleagues. He said that the objective of this sub rosa help was to "make the SPD a bulwark against communism."* While true in part, the Labor government in London was actually more interested in establishing a Socialist government in the new West German state which would cooperate with its British sponsor and offset the ever-increasing American influence and power in Bonn. British officials were well aware that Adenauer, leader of the conservative faction, would be pro-American and anti-British if he became chancellor.

Adenauer appeared to be trailing Schumacher in the public opinion polls right up to the election day of August 14, but he was to prove himself the smarter and more successful politician. He was better attuned to the real hopes and aspirations of the forty-five million West Germans. He was confident that Schumacher was not seriously influencing the Germans when he projected such abstract and remote issues as nationalization of the heavy industries, a Socialist planned economy, an independent foreign policy line in the cold war, rejection of the Marshall Plan, and a choice between socialism or democracy. Instead, Adenauer based his campaign on what he perceived to be the real concerns of the German people: more food, adequate housing, secure employment, and other necessities of life. The political party that persuaded the Germans that it could meet these pressing daily needs would get their votes; Adenauer's campaign motif was *Magenpolitik*. He was right; for in this and in subsequent national elections the Germans voted as their stomachs dictated.

In the closing weeks of the first postwar national election, Adenauer introduced Erhard, head of the bizonal economic council, into the fray. Erhard was responsible for the economic recovery that was getting underway with some force and momentum. Erhard, on his own initiative, had jettisoned all rationing and price controls and launched his free-market economy just after the currency reform of June 1948. The worthless reichsmark had been replaced by the deutschemark, which was gaining greater acceptance with every passing day. This new money enticed goods back onto the store shelves and into the marketplaces. The Germans could work and spend as they pleased, and have something to show for their labor. For the first time the future displayed a rosy tinge, a promise of easier and better times ahead.

Erhard was a definite political asset to Adenauer. In the last stage of the 1949 election he could point to the specific improvements in the standards of living of the Germans and take credit for them on behalf of Adenauer and the CDU. Above all, with his open countenance, his simple but confident reiteration about the state of the economy—*"Es geht wieder,"* "It's working again"—he gained credibility with the public.

Finally it is difficult to understand the rationale of Schumacher's embittered and continuing attacks on the Marshall Plan, which was to provide almost $4 billion in money and supplies to the stagnant West German economy. No German could be unaware of the American relief program because it was highly publicized in the press and other media. Every box or crate, every railway freight car or truck containing or transporting goods financed by the Marshall Plan, was marked with stencils or signs to that effect. There was little reason for the Germans to look this gift horse in the mouth, as Schumacher was doing. Perhaps he recognized, instinctively, that the Americans represented the greatest obstacle to his obsession to create a truly Socialist state in West Germany. Hence, he reacted with great hostility to this "American imperialism," as he described it.

The popular mood prevailing in West Germany after the Marshall Plan was in full swing was best revealed in a brief letter from Frankfurt, printed in the Paris edition of the *New York Herald Tribune* in March 1949:

Dear Sir:

If a man has to have a master, it is better to have a rich rather than a poor one.

Sincerely,
A German Reader

This bit of street-corner wisdom apparently escaped the attention of the lonely and crippled ideologue, Kurt Schumacher, in his long and fruitless political planning and maneuvering.

The results of the August 14 election, for which there was a turnout of 78.5 percent of all eligible voters, came as a surprise: the CDU captured 31 percent of the voters; the SPD 29.2 percent; and the Free Democrats

(FDP) 11.9 percent; with the balance scattered among a host of splinter and one-issue parties. It was a severe blow to Schumacher. He had fully expected to win and begin the transformation of this embryonic West German nation into a Socialist state. But the West Germans had not seen fit to give him the mandate he so passionately desired; their order of priorities was quite different.

Instead the West Germans had opted for a middle-of-the-road formula, the *Soziale Marktwirtschaft* of Prof. Ludwig Erhard. Seldom have the accidents of history proved to be so beneficial to its victims as the economic doctrine that came to Bonn with this virtually unknown and untested market researcher from Furth, Bavaria.

6

Currency reform was a bold leap taken into semi-darkness.
—*The* Economist *of London, October 18, 1952*

OPERATION BIRD DOG

A FEW DAYS before June 20, 1948 convoys of U.S. Army trucks converged on the modernistic Reichsbank building in Frankfurt's Taunusanlage, where they loaded up with large wooden boxes. Each convey was escorted by troop carriers, armed with heavy-duty machine guns, and manned by American soldiers. As the trucks completed their loading, they fanned out from Frankfurt with their military escorts to all points of the compass. The wooden crates contained some 500 tons of new deutschemarks, which had been printed in the United States. The army convoys would transport the new currency to banks and post offices throughout West Germany. Then, on June 20, the new deutschemark would be substituted for the now virtually worthless reichsmark in a swift and unprecedented monetary reform which bore the code name, "Operation Bird Dog."

Because it involved a nationwide operation and the assistance of thousands of officials and employees of the German banks and postal service, the impending currency reform could not be completely covered up from the public. Rumors were rife that the reichsmark would be outlawed and some new form of legal tender would replace it. There was a flight from the discredited reichsmark; Germans bought goods—whatever was obtainable and price was no object. The stores and market places in West German cities and towns appeared to be drained of all their merchandise. Germans, particularly those black marketeers who congregated at the railroad stations, walked around with fistfuls of reichsmarks, trying to find something to buy, regardless of the sky-rocketing prices. Ration cards, which authorized the limited purchases of necessities such as food, clothing, shoes, and household furnishings were no longer honored in the shops. The shop windows and shelves were barren. Many stores just pulled down their steel shutters and locked their doors, putting up signs that they had nothing more to offer.

Eric P., a slick and slippery character, posed as a friendly German textile trader with international interests during the *blitzkrieg*. His wartime job had been to ingratiate himself with the American press corps in Berlin and to report on their attitudes to the Gestapo. In the spring of 1948, Eric was again in Frankfurt. He was still well tailored and well fed, and his obvious affluence in this time of hunger was intriguing. He lived in a handsome brick residence with extensive gardens in an outlying suburb that had been untouched by the war. It was surprising that this house had not been requisitioned by the U.S. Army for the use of a high-ranking officer. But there was a ready explanation; a framed notice on the front door, in German and English, duly signed and stamped, gave notice that this house was under the protection of a Central American banana republic. Hence it was off limits to Allied occupation forces and Germans.

Inside, in a pleasantly furnished room, two coquettish *Hausmädchen* who obviously doubled as Eric's bed warmers served French champagne. The former textile trader disclosed that he had developed a new profitable occupation as a *Grosshändler,* or a sort of wholesaler in the black market. He bought and sold through agents or dealers who dealt directly in the black markets throughout West Germany. A tour of the spacious house revealed rooms filled with a variety of black-market items, including hundreds of cartons of American cigarettes, food—piles of smoked sausages, cans of coffee, and tins of butter—as well as furnishings, antiques, sets of silver, porcelain, figurines, chinaware, paintings, Persian rugs, and assorted *objets d'art.* Eric explained how his establishment had come under the protection of a Central American country. A member of that nation's military mission, attached to the U.S. military government headquarters in Berlin, was actively engaged in the lucrative traffic of selling his country's passports to those ex-Nazis, who had sufficient resources and the urgent need to escape the clutches of the denazification tribunals and find a safe haven in South or Central America. These passports cost about $5,000 each, or the equivalent in gold or hard currency. Eric was an active partner in this passport traffic and his trading volume was sufficiently high to merit being given a pseudodiplomatic cover address for his extensive operations in Frankfurt. Later Eric was forced to liquidate his entire *Grosshandlung,* after the U.S. counterintelligence corps got wind of his activities. However, he managed to escape from Germany, using one of his illegal Central American passports.

The occupation forces were about the only sources of popular negotiable and black-market items. As the GIs walked out of their barrack areas or strolled the midtown streets, they were constantly propositioned to sell anything they could obtain from the army PX. The panic-buying fever hit an all-time high when on June 19, 1948 a carton of Lucky Strike cigarettes was quoted at 23,000 reichsmarks; at the official but unacceptable rate of exchange of RMs 10 to $1, this meant a tidy $2,300.

For almost two years the Americans had been working on a plan for currency reform, devising an acceptable substitute to replace the inflated and worthless reichsmark. The everyday standard of value in the marketplace was the ubiquitous American cigarette; goods were priced in terms of single cigarettes, packs of twenty, or cartons of ten packs. The Lucky Strike was more than a black-market item; it had become a commercial instrument. The Germans had evolved a pragmatic sense of values which met the needs of the marketplace. Germans had become so conditioned to the cigarette economy that the Lucky Strike and other Allied brands were accepted as a crude but negotiable form of money. This German attitude was best illustrated by an incident that took place in early June 1948 during a press conference given by the U.S. military governor in his Frankfurt office. At this point in time there was much speculation in the German press about currency reform and what might be expected. During the press conference, a serious-minded German reporter asked Clay if the current rumors were true that the U.S. Treasury was to make a loan of fifty million cartons of American cigarettes to give a support base for any new German currency. The Germans were well aware they had no reserves of gold or silver for this purpose; nor was it reasonable to expect the American government to loan West Germany sufficient dollars or gold to prop up the deutschemark.

However, America was the land of cheap and plentiful tobacco and a commodity loan in terms of cigarettes was something quite conceivable to any German who had to buy and sell in the black market, which included virtually everybody. Cigarettes had acquired their own special commercial value, so that a new West German currency that was backed by fifty million cartons of Lucky Strikes piled up in the cavernous underground vaults of the old Reichsbank building would have an immediate credibility and an acceptance by the public.

The initial reaction of Clay and the attending Allied journalists at the press conference was amusement at the seeming naïveté of the German reporter. Yet second thoughts quickly tempered their reaction. For it was obvious that the American cigarette had become a functioning substitute for the reichsmark. Tobacco had acquired a monetary character, like gold and silver. Clay's answer recognized the psychological gap that had to be bridged when he replied: "If a new currency is introduced, this will be done to stimulate the German economy; and if it accomplishes this, the new currency will be acceptable as a valid money."

The Allied-imposed *Währungsreform* (currency reform) did not by itself come as a great surprise to the German public. The grapevine had spread the word and the rush was on to get rid of reichsmarks for whatever the market would offer. However, what really shocked the Germans was what it meant to their individual monetary holdings. A British MP described the Allied currency reform "as one of the harshest acts of confiscation imposed on a people by their conquerors. Yet it saved Germany."*

The changeover in currencies involved drastic fiscal surgery, amputating about 93 percent of the paper wealth of the Germans in terms of savings, securities, and pocket money. At the time of currency reform there were about 70 billion reichsmarks in circulation, compared to 18 billion at the start of the war. Bank deposits in reichsmarks had increased from RM 30 billion to about RM 150 billion during the same period, while the national debt had jumped from RM 12 billion to over RM 400 billion when the war ended. In addition, there was an overhang of about RM 300 billion for war damages and other related claims to be settled.

All currency and bank deposits held by individuals and firms had to be registered. These were converted into the new currency at a ratio of one deutschemark for 10 reichsmarks. At the outset every German could exchange only 400 reichsmarks for 40 deutschemarks; two months later he could make another exchange of 200 RMs for 20 DMs. And that just about ended it for the great mass of the population, as few persons kept savings accounts of more than a few hundred worthless reichsmarks. Debts were also scaled down for individuals and firms alike, on the same ratio of 1 DM for 10 RMs. The 400 billion RM national debt carried over from Hitler's Third Reich, as it pertained to the German bondholders, was just erased from the public ledgers, so to speak. However, foreign claims against Germany were not waived, but were made subject to settlement by direct negotiations between defeated Germany and its creditors at a later date.

On the eve of currency reform, the U.S. Army delivered 10 billion deutschemarks to the German banks and post offices. Of this total, approximately 6.1 billion deutschemarks were exchanged in the first few weeks, wiping out in the drastic process hundreds of billions of marks in securities, reserves, bank accounts, mortgages, and bonds and stocks in RM denominations. It appeared to complete the impoverishment of West Germany in one coordinated mass maneuver. Yet this was not the case; in fact, it was the first step to economic recovery.

In the summer of 1948 the paradox about the currency reform was not clearly evident. There were very few Germans who would accept the truth of the matter: that the monetary changeover did not result in a mass confiscation of their reichsmark holdings. In reality, this arbitrary action was directed at the elimination of an already discredited and worthless money from the national economy; the public's flight from marks into goods before currency reform was a clear indication that the Germans themselves had repudiated the reichsmark. In the final analysis individual Germans suffered little or no loss through currency reform. Their reichsmarks, whether in savings accounts or in securities, had already so depreciated in purchasing power as to be beyond hope of recovery; there was literally nothing more to lose.

Instead, currency reform provided the Germans with money that quickly proved to have acceptable purchasing power. This fiat currency attained a valid exchange value vis-à-vis the U.S. dollar. This development seemed to be in violation of economic theory and practice, especially Gresham's Law that "bad money drives out good money."

One can only surmise that by the odd juxtaposition of favorable circumstances, a huge dollop of good luck, plus wishful thinking, on the part of the recipients, and other psychological stimuli, the billions of deutschemarks handed over to the public were somehow transformed practically overnight in the eyes of the Germans into "good money." The financial alchemy practiced by Dodge, Colm, and Goldsmith,* who drafted the original *Währungsreform,* transmuted some 6.1 billion deutschemarks, which the Germans received for their reichsmarks, from just handsomely engraved bits of paper into a functioning currency having a value of approximately $600 million at the current rate of exchange. In effect, that amounted to giving each of the 24 million adult Germans the equivalent of $25 for his 60 invalidated reichsmarks. For the national economy, this was like a transfusion of good rich blood into the veins of a semicomatose patient suffering from an acute case of anemia.

An integral aspect of the economic miracle was the acceptance of this new deutschemark as valid legal tender, as money that had a purchasing power. One of the factors contributing to its credibility with the general public was its appearance; in size, texture, printing, and color it bore a physical resemblance to the U.S. greenback dollar. This was not so surprising, as both the dollar and the deutschemark were printed by the U.S. Mint in Washington, D.C. But the deutschemark had not an ounce of gold or silver in reserves to support it, nor was there any likelihood that it would be convertible into dollars or other hard currencies in the foreseeable future.

Yet the black market, the most sensitive of economic indicators, quickly reflected the basic German reaction to the new money. On the morning of June 20, the first day of currency reform, the deutschemark was being quoted at 45 to the U.S. $1 in Frankfurt's flourishing black market at the Hauptbahnhof. However, by the end of the day, the deutschemark had noticeably strengthened and was being traded at ten to $1. In the following weeks the deutschemark fluctuated between ten and fifteen to the dollar, except for a brief period when it slumped below twenty to $1. This was caused by French military-government officers flooding the Swiss currency exchanges with deutschemarks, resulting in an immediate drop in the going trading rates. When this financial hanky-panky was exposed and diplomatic protests filed with the French government in Paris, the deutschemark recovered. By February 1949 it had risen to six to $1.

The credibility of the deutschemark was also purposely aided and abetted by its scarcity. The fact that every German, rich and poor alike, received only DMs 40 on the first exchange and then had to wait two months to get another 20 added to the illusion that the deutschemark was a currency with inherent value. That was a psychological gambit on the part of the Allied planners that paid off handsomely by winning public acceptance for the 500 tons of high-quality fiat currency that replaced the 70 billions of tattered and discredited reichsmarks.

There was no official rate of exchange for the deutschemark; but for purposes of export bookkeeping it was pegged at 1 DM to $0.30. Later, when economic recovery was well underway, the deutschemark was made convertible to hard currencies at DMs 4.20 to $1. In subsequent revaluations, as the new mark became one of the hardest currencies in the world, the dollar itself began to fluctuate in relation to the stable deutschemark, in the range DM 2.50 to $1 by the mid-1970s.

Within hours after the first deutschemarks had been distributed, on June 20, the standards of living for the West Germans began to improve. The stores, whose shelves had been empty for weeks previously, suddenly blossomed in a profusion of goods for sale. Other merchants set up their wares on the sidewalks. A surprisingly wide variety of merchandise was suddenly back on the market again. The food shops, which the farmers previously had refused to supply, were now bright with displays of fresh vegetables, slabs of golden butter, homemade sausages, buckets of fresh eggs, and other mouth-watering luxuries.

The reaction of the public was mixed: pleasure at being able to once again find something to buy, and anger at those who had withheld their food from the marketplaces. One hapless farmer's wife sampled the accumulated wrath of the hungry city dwellers when she arrived in the Frankfurt main station with two baskets of fresh eggs on the second day of currency reform. She was immediately surrounded by a crowd of hostile women.

"Where were those eggs last week? And the week before?" demanded one red-faced angry *Hausfrau*. With that, she picked up a handful of eggs and pelted the farmer's wife. Others gleefully joined in, until the victim was a sodden yellow mass from head to foot.

The whole atmosphere and character of German cities and towns changed almost overnight, as economic life began to quicken. The new deutschemark attracted surprising reserves of merchandise of all types and kinds—shoes, clothing, office equipment, cameras, furniture, pots and pans, even surplus U.S. Army equipment appeared in the marketplaces. Almost miraculously, drugs and medicines, which for months past the local pharmacies had said were unavailable, could now be purchased by those with a prescription and money. Where had all these goods been hiding? It was useless to ask questions; it was sufficient that there were some goods for sale in the shops. Prices in all categories had risen substantially; but they could be exchanged for the new deutschemarks. It was proving to be an acceptable and valid currency.

The black market began to wither away and the cigarette economy also began to collapse. For the first time, the Germans began to smoke the cigarettes which they had long hoarded as money.

The Germans began the first of a series of buying sprees that would be spaced out in the months and years to come as their incomes rose and steadied, and as the variety and quantity of goods began to reappear in the stores. However, at the outset the Germans went on a food binge. Starved for fats and proteins for years and forced to exist on a drab diet of 1,550 calories a day, now they could eat and drink as much as their wallets permitted. Food was no longer rationed: fresh meat and vegetables, bacon, lard, butter, eggs, and *Schlagsahne*—wonderful, thick whipped cream to smother cakes and pastries. All these were now available in the markets and also in the few remaining restaurants and cafés which were reopening their doors. The Americans in Germany, who jealously guarded their commissary privileges as insuring adequate food in a land of semistarvation of pre-*Währungsreform* days, now found it pleasant and interesting to eat "on the German economy," as they described their culinary safaris outside their guarded compounds. Meanwhile, encouraged by the expanding markets, the farmers began moving their food output to the markets every day instead of holding it for sale to black marketeers. Within a year, by the summer of 1949, food production had shown such improvement that the average West German worker was consuming more and better food than the English worker in austerity-ridden Great Britain. Reports of these developments provoked angry editorials in the popular newspapers in London, asking the rhetorical question: "After all, who won the war anyway?"

It would be a mistake to give the impression that a veritable cornucopia of goods inundated the West Germans with the advent of the new deutschemark and the free-market system promulgated by Erhard. Yet the contrast between their impoverished daily existence in the predeutschemark days and what happened after the historic June 20 currency reform was so sharp as to convince everybody that they had climbed the fence into greener pastures. And they had—in the eyes of Allied observers at that time. Henry Wallich, the noted economist, who was born in Germany and is now a member of the U.S. Federal Reserve Board, was with the U.S. military government in Germany at that time. He described how currency reform:

. . . [it] transformed the German scene from one day to the next. On June 21, 1948 goods reappeared in the stores, money resumed its normal function, the black and grey markets reverted to a minor role. . . . The spirit of the country changed overnight. The grey, hungry and dead-looking figures wandering about the streets in their ever-lasting search for food came to life as, pocketing their 40 D-marks, they went on their first spending spree.*

What contributed to making June 20, 1948 such an important economic watershed was the fact that actually there had been far more extensive hoarding of food and consumer goods by both manufacturers and the storekeepers than the Allied authorities had believed. But this was to prove to be a fortunate circumstance, because the new currency brought these goods back on the store shelves and display windows where they were quickly snapped up by purchasers with their new deutschemarks. If this supply of hoarded merchandise had not been available, the new currency would obviously not have been accepted so universally as a credible medium of exchange, for the range of its purchasing power would have been sharply reduced in markets without goods for sale.

The American and British financial experts collectively held their breath, wondering how long this favorable state of affairs would continue. Erhard was taking a big risk.

Währungsreform was the first phase of the complex and delicate process of political and economic reconstruction.* Despite outcries from the Communist party, which was still legal in the western occupation zones, that currency reform "was a crime against the German people," the 45 million West Germans did not view it in that light. Since the new money replaced the old, their daily existence was definitely and rapidly improving. For the first time in years they could enjoy the pleasures of eating and drinking, or buying a pair of shoes or some pots and pans, without having to stand for hours in a queue or submitting a ration card in order to spend their money.

The reports on currency reform and how the daily lives of the West Germans were improving because of it began to spread by word of mouth throughout Communist-controlled East Germany, despite stringent measures by Russians to insulate their 17 million people from this development. Illegal border crossings from east to west doubled and then tripled, marking the beginning of a population hemorrhage that was to bleed the Russian zone of several million of its young and skilled workers. The flood of eastern refugees was to continue until the Communists had to imprison their population behind high barbed-wire fences, mine fields, and an army of border guards who shot to kill anyone trying to leave their *Volksparadies* without permission.

The Soviet Military Administration had to carry out its own currency reform shortly after the reichsmark had been repudiated in West Germany, but theirs was a clumsy and ineffective operation. For the new East German mark had no more value or purchasing power than the old reichsmark; nor did it attract to the marketplaces a flood of consumer goods and food, as happened in West Germany. Proof that life in the west was far more attractive than in the Soviet zone was unwittingly supplied by the Russians. To commemorate the tenth anniversary of the outbreak of World War II, the Russians organized a "Peace Day" celebration for September 1, 1949. The border controls were relaxed for the occasion, in the expectation that this would entice several hundred thousand West Germans to visit their friends and relatives in East Germany. Quite the reverse happened.

According to an official accounting, 43,000 East Germans "invaded" the American and British occupation zones; they came over for something to eat and drink. The West German shops and cafés in the border crossing points did a rushing business. To pay for their food and drink and other purchases, the East Germans were happy to exchange 5.4 of their Russian zone marks for each new deutschemark. This development was front-page news in the West German papers on the following day, and further strengthened the credibility of the deutschemark in the eyes of the West Germans.

7

Nothing is more difficult to take in hand, more perilous to conduct, or more uncertain of its success, than to take the lead in the introduction of a new order of things.

—NICOLO MACHIAVELLI, The Prince, A.D. *1513*

In the order of importance, Germany has replaced the bureaucrat with the businessman.

—PROF. LUDWIG ERHARD, *1957*

THE PROFESSOR'S
GREAT GAMBLE

SELDOM is a man given the opportunity of originating a new social order from the point of dead zero, so to speak, without any accompanying violence or revolution. The peaceful creation of a new and better society—politically and economically—is the ever-recurring dream of the ivory-tower scholars and the more imaginative politicians and economists who wish to play an active role in its development. However this utopian concept seldom achieves a closer brush with reality than study and debate in the groves of academe.

Yet there was one man of this era who enjoyed the unique distinction of having designed a new social order, of taking the initiative to put it into practice and then making it work successfully. That individual was Prof. Ludwig Erhard, whose creation of *Soziale Marktwirtschaft*—his vision of capitalism with a social conscience—was the prime mover in lifting a broken and defeated nation right out of its turbulent history and feudal traditions and transforming it into one of the most productive, prosperous, and stable societies in the Free World.

Bavarian economist Erhard is, without challenge, the architect of the new postwar Germany. He supplied the formula and the direction of its postwar growth, which enabled it to become the third strongest economic power in the world in the relatively short span of a single generation.

Erhard had looked down the long corridors of German history and grasped an essential truth that had escaped the consciousness of the German people and their leaders for the past century and a half. Germany's struggle to be a major world power could best be accomplished and preserved by economic development rather than by military or political measures. Germany's strength lay in its superior industrial capacity. Its future could be secured not by making weapons with which to conquer more *Lebensraum,* but by the manufacturing of capital and consumer goods and services to capture the export markets around the world.

Erhard's contribution consisted in making the postwar survivors of West Germany accept this essential truth and react positively to it. He focused the attention of the Germans on the economic recovery of their defeated and bankrupt nation. He channeled their energies into the nuts-and-bolts, the hammer-and-saw, the brick-and-mortar restoration of their homes, factories, power plants, transportation, stores, and cafés. He gave them tax exemptions as incentives to achieve their individual repair and rebuilding projects. They had little time or interest for anything not connected with the *Wiederaufbau,* reconstruction.

The introduction of Erhard's *Soziale Marktwirtschaft,* a doctrine of ever-increasing productivity, meant exposing the West Germans to the uncontrollable laws of supply and demand, the free-enterprise system, after twelve years of totalitarian controls and the direction of all phases of their economic life. In short, Erhard denazified the German economy to make it work again. It was a shock to the Germans' nervous systems, now having to face grim prospects of no job security, no assured supply of food through a ration system, no more controls on the prices of essentials. One had to work or starve, produce or fall by the wayside. There was no social security cushion to support the weak and incompetent. *Der weg zurück*—the road back—was a long, hard passage, the survival of the fittest.

But Erhard promised his fellow Germans a bright new day would dawn for them if they all worked hard and accepted today's spartan existence as a down payment for tomorrow's rewards. He held up before their eyes the example of the United States of America; how one nation became the greatest power of the postwar world because it had concentrated its energies and talents primarily on its own economic development. In his constant exhortations, Erhard told his listeners: "Free enterprise has given the American citizen a living standard and a chance for self-expression unparalleled in the rest of the world."

Ludwig Erhard began life in humble circumstances. He was born in Fürth, in Franconia, on February 4, 1897, the son of a peasant who left his farm to open up a small dry goods shop in the town. Erhard was an early victim of infantile paralysis, but recovered sufficiently to be a soldier in World War I. He was severely wounded in the fighting at Ypres. Returning home, Erhard was not strong enough for full-time work in his father's store, so he attended the Nuremburg Commercial College where he majored in economics. He took his degree at the University of Frankfurt, where he studied under Prof. Fritz Oppenheimer. Oppenheimer who sought to reconcile the conflicting doctrines of Socialism with capitalism, gave Erhard his first inspiration for *Soziale Marktwirtschaft,* which the Franconian later described as "free enterprise that is alive to its social responsibilities."

Because he refused to enroll in the Nazi Association of University Teachers, Erhard was denied a position at the university from which he had graduated. He spent the next sixteen years on the staff of the Institute for Market Research in Nuremburg, but his refusal to join the Nazi Labor Front organization cost him his post as deputy director. He then founded his own market-research company. In the late 1930s, Erhard came into contact with the University of Freiburg's school of economists, headed by Prof. Walter Eucken, who were still advocating free-market economics in the face of the totalitarian system imposed by the Nazi government. By 1943, Erhard became convinced that Germany had lost the war and he began to plan for the postwar period.

He developed and refined his own economic philosophy and devised a policy of application for a Nazi-free postwar Germany. His privately circulated views caught the attention of Karl Goerdler, mayor of Leipzig, who was destined to head the new postwar German government if the July 20 conspiracy had succeeded in killing Hitler. Goerdler is reported to have favored Erhard to be a minister in the new government if ever it came to power.

Shortly after the end of hostilities, Erhard was appointed economics minister for the state of Bavaria by the U.S. military government, because he was one of the few anti-Nazis to be found who had some knowledge and experience in modern economics. And in 1947, when he became director of economic affairs of Bizonia, Erhard came face to face with the harsh realities of the postwar economy.

He headed a small group of German officials who worked out the details of the currency reform. Erhard agreed, in principle, to the substitution of the deutschemark for the worthless and inflated reichsmark. But he argued that much more was needed if the prime objective of the program, the beginning of economic revival, was to be achieved. From his office in an old *Wehrmacht* barracks building in the suburbs of Frankfurt, he had been bombarding the I. G. Farben headquarters of Clay with a stream of memos. With missionary zeal, Erhard claimed that currency reform must be accompanied by an abolition of all rationing, as well as price and wage controls. Only if the German people were given the unlimited opportunity to buy what each individual needed and wanted and to sell their individual goods and services for what the open market would pay, could economic recovery get underway.

However, his suggestions evoked no positive response or signs of interest when he submitted them to the American and British occupation authorities. Erhard's program was considered another harebrained economic formula and one of many remedies proposed to revive the bankrupt country. When viewed in the light of the acute shortages of food and other necessities of life, it was considered unthinkable to impose a free-market system by abolishing all rationing and lifting price and wage controls. Rationing at least had the negative virtue of spreading food and consumer good shortages evenly among the people; "fair shares" for all, so the Allied planners rationalized.

In effect, Erhard wanted to denazify the West German economy, to strip away its Nazi heritage. The whole bureaucratic structure of rationing, as well as wage and price controls, and originally been created by the number two Nazi Hermann Goering as part of the master plan to achieve *Autarkie,* so as to make the Third Reich economically self-sufficient. After the war ended, the Allied occupation authorities had left intact the German administration of economic controls, despite their Nazi origin. They did not dare risk the chaos and disruption, including food riots, which they predicted would follow, if all rationing and price ceilings were invalidated.

However, Erhard saw things in a different light. He believed the economic baggage of the past was an impediment for the future. Unless it could be jettisoned, there was little chance for economic revival. He was also realist enough to know that if ever his package of economic measures— which he rated as imperative and equal in importance to currency reform— was to become a reality, he must take the initiative on his own responsibility. It was also extremely doubtful whether as Bizonia's economic director he had the authority to adopt a policy that would run counter to the Allied guidelines. In any event, he would surely be risking his career by embarking on what was to prove to be a history-making gamble with far-reaching consequences, domestic as well as international, for West Germany and the North Atlantic community of nations. So, in the face of storm warnings, Erhard pushed an emergency law through the economic council on July 7, 1948 and then made a nationwide radio broadcast to explain that he "had just thrown into the waste basket in one fell swoop hundreds of decrees, promulgating economic controls and price limitations."

In an unprecedented executive act, he had overturned the Allied-controlled West German economy. In its place he offered the alternative, as he pointed out in his radio address: "Only when every German can freely choose what work he will do, and can freely decide what goods he will consume, will our people be able to play any active role in the political life of their country."

This is the core of Erhard's economic philosophy. He was convinced that if the Germans were to effect a comeback in a hostile postwar world, they must undergo some drastic reappraisals of traditional attitudes. They must be weaned from their age-old dependence on government as a guide and director of their individual lives. They must think for themselves; depend on their own efforts to survive. By freeing themselves of their past, they could achieve full political and economic maturity.

The importance, as well as the impact of Erhard's new free-market system, and the discarding of the rationing and price and wage controls, were largely obscured by the first major crisis of the cold war. On June 24, 1948, four days after the introduction of currency reform, Marshal Sokolovsky announced the complete Russian ground blockade of West Berlin with its three sectors occupied by American, British, and French troops and a civilian population of 2.3 million. All shipments of fuel, food, and goods for Berlin by railroad or waterway were halted at the western frontiers of Communist East Germany by the barricades manned by Russian soldiers. Only the three air corridors to West Berlin were open to the military and civilian aircraft of the Western powers. These could not be blockaded by the Russians, except by shooting down Allied planes in flight, an act that would have meant open war between the Americans and Russians.

This international crisis, which was to endure for almost a year, was further heightened by the growing concern among Germans and Allies as to whether or not the American-organized airlift could supply the necessities of life for a civilian population of 2.3 million West Berliners and for the American, British, and French military forces stationed in the beleaguered city. This required the daily airlift of 4,000 tons of fuel and food for the German population and an additional 500 tons for the Allied military garrisons. After a slow start, due mainly to a shortage of cargo planes, the airlift had reached an average of 5,000 tons daily by the following December. By early spring this cargo total had risen to 8,000 tons per day, which equaled the preblockade volume of fuel and food into West Berlin carried by rail and waterways.

The success of the airlift forced the Soviets to end the blockade on May 10, 1949, ushering in a definite though short-term lull in the cold war as it concerned Germany. However the constant tension engendered by the blockade of Berlin, that small island of democracy behind the Iron Curtain, coupled with the heroic dimensions of the *Lüftbrücke*—the air bridge—tended to overshadow the concurrent political and economic developments in West Germany which followed on the heels of the currency reform of June 20. Hence Erhard and his new economic system were somewhat neglected by the international and domestic press in their coverage of West Germany during this crucial and formative stage of the new *Soziale Marktwirtschaft*.

The basic mechanics of Erhard's economic program were never really spelled out in any specific detail, but they were mainly concerned with two broad objectives:

1. To encourage the revival of production of goods: capital goods for export; and consumer goods for which the Germans could spend their money, thereby further stimulating the economic revival.
2. To keep prices down, so as to avoid inflation at all costs. The monkey on Erhard's back was the fear of inflation that would sabotage his free-market economy at the outset.

The German people too could not erase the painful memories of rampant inflation, which destroyed the value of the reichsmark and robbed them of their small savings, their pensions, and property after world wars I and II. So anti-inflation measures were a must in their eyes.

In this connection, West Germany embarked on a new course in its search for economic stability which differed from the other postwar nations of Europe. It is noteworthy that no special efforts were made by the government to create jobs for the growing army of unemployed—approximately 2.2 million by February 1950. Dr. Andrew Shonfield, the British economist, pointed out in his study on Germany's economic policies of the early postwar years: "Most notably, the new objective of full employment on a permanent basis, which occupied a leading place in the thinking of postwar governments of the Anglo-Saxon world, hardly figured at all in Germany."*

At the time of the currency reform there were about 450,000 workers without jobs. Twelve months later the number of unemployed had risen to 1.5 million, and then hit its peak early in 1950. This pool of excess skilled workers was to be a very effective anti-inflationary tool to keep labor costs down and to act as a brake on the cost-of-living index, as well as to encourage the productivity of the individual workers. When industrialists were paying their employees in inflated reichsmarks, they could afford to keep many of them on the payroll to handle minor repairs, maintenance work, and so on. After all, to pay 250 reichsmarks to hire a semiskilled worker for a month was not considered a serious outlay for labor; it was just the equivalent of 2½ packs of Lucky Strikes. But, when the factory owner had to pay the worker 250 deutschemarks for the same time and output, he began to seriously revise his labor expenditures. DM 250 was the equivalent of $20–25 in hard currency, depending on the latest exchange rate.

So the manufacturers trimmed their labor forces of all but the most productive workers. From this point on the laborer began to feel intense competition from his fellow workers for the declining number of jobs. To hold his place at the workbench or on the assembly line, the average worker had to increase his individual output. Absenteeism immediately decreased from 20 percent to less than 5 percent in the Ruhr coal and steel companies. A regular job acquired a new dimension; it provided a wage in a currency that demonstrated real purchasing power.* This was one of the incentives to spur the worker on to produce more goods per hour of his labor. As a result, the economic revival took a massive surge upward. In the twenty-two months following currency reform, while unemployment rose from 3.2 percent to 12.2 percent, industrial production rose by 83 percent. Overtime pay was virtually tax free, so workers put in as many extra hours as possible.

At this early stage the trade unions were powerless to prevent workers from being dismissed for redundancy. Unions could not call a strike because they had no funds to support a walkout; currency reform had wiped out their reserves.

* * *

With the end of rationing and price controls, the costs of food and consumer goods understandably began to climb, though they never reached the levels of the black-market economy. The price of eggs tripled in a month's time. Other shortages became manifest. The newspapers, reflecting the growing apprehension of the public as the winter of 1948–49 drew closer, began to editorialize for some form of price controls. On November 12, 1948 there was a one-day general strike in the Ruhr to protest the rising cost of living coupled with growing unemployment. Erhard was the target of angry street demonstrations. Signs were carried by the strikers calling for "Erhard to the gallows!" Many of Erhard's colleagues urged him to make some concessions in the face of public outcry. Adenauer made plans to absorb Erhard's ministry into his own office if the professor's gamble showed signs of losing. It was Erhard's supreme test, but, as a man who had defied the Nazis, he was not about to cave in to public pressure. He was more tough-minded than expected. He knew that any hint of a return to price controls and rationing would trigger off a wave of panic buying which would quickly empty the markets and the shops of their slim stocks of food and consumer goods. He was also confident that the millions of dollars of Marshall Plan aid and grants that had been pouring into the West German economy would shortly turn the tide. The best and quickest way to bring down prices and dampen inflation was to provide more goods.

At this point Erhard practiced what seemed like economic heresy. He rejected all suggestions that the economy of West Germany must be coddled and protected; that it must grow in an incubator chamber, as sickly babies must be cared for after birth. Despite strong objections from American and British authorities, Erhard reduced the tariffs* on imported goods. This had a twofold purpose: to prevent German manufacturers from increasing their prices; and to make them face international competition so as to sharpen their commercial and industrial capabilities. Next, he organized the crash *Jedermann* (every man) program; he supplied necessary cloth and leather for the manufacture of cheap clothing such as shoes, suits, shirts, and women's dresses. On Christmas Eve 1949 Professor Erhard broadcast a promise that "prices will drop by springtime." He was right, and from that point on the West German economy was truly on *der Weg zurück,* the road back, gaining momentum every day.

By mid-1950 the first dividends of the *Soziale Marktwirtschaft* began to show themselves; prices of food and other necessities began to drop from their winter peak. In the next decade the cost of living index rose only 16 percent compared to 45 percent in Great Britain and over 50 percent in France. During the first year after currency reform the West German GNP doubled and in the second year passed its 1938 peak, when prewar industrial output had reached its highest peacetime level.

The German workers began to receive their rewards for hard work and long hours at minimum wages. For example, for the years 1950–57, while the national income rose by 112 percent, wages and salaries after taxes increased by 119 percent. As the whole economy showed marked improvement, a revitalized social-security program was introduced in stages throughout the next few years, which meant cheap health insurance, sick pay, free medical care, unemployment insurance, and old-age pensions. Keeping prices down and meeting the public's deep-seated craving for economic security in times of want kept the Adenauer-Erhard government in top power for sixteen years and the Socialist opposition, with its demands for a planned economy, on the outside looking in, with a growing sense of political frustration.

Once Erhard had gotten a firm grip on the first economic crisis, the shortages of food and consumer goods, and the attendant rising prices, he turned his attention to getting his free-market economic system underway. Coupled with currency reform, Erhard's program of *Soziale Marktwirtschaft* proved to be favored by time and circumstances.

In the planning and in the execution of the physical repair and reconstruction of their war-shattered country the Germans enjoyed freedom of initiative and action. Currency reform provided them with a money that had purchasing power, so after years of deprivation, the Germans could buy the necessities of life, albeit at higher prices.

Currency reform, followed closely by the elimination of rationing and price controls, brought forth a surprisingly large stock of hoarded goods into the stores and marketplaces. These developments unchained the energies and abilities of the Germans to exploit to the hilt their new-found economic liberation. Now they were able to utilize their intelligence, their energies, and their one remaining social asset: the hundreds of thousands of skilled workers to crank up the industrial machinery once again. This pool of trained labor, the largest in Europe, was the one important industrial resource left to the Germans that could not be marked down for reparations, dismantling, or deconcentration.

The key operative word for the new free-market system was incentive. It was the fuel that would get the wheels of industry and commerce turning again. Incentives encouraged the Ruhr steelmaker to repair and fire up his great blast furnaces; the laborer to work hard again at wages below what his trade union wanted but could not collect; the banker and the investor to provide funds to finance the repair and reconstruction of the Ruhr when there was virtually no collateral to support these credits; the small shopkeeper to restock his shelves with consumer goods in a tight money market. There were incentives for almost everybody who had a stake in the German economy to make their small contributions to its early revival.

Erhard's economic formula was simple and based on the fundamentals of human nature. The bottom line, so to speak, was the recognition that for the great majority of Germans, the desire to escape the grinding poverty of their daily existence and to acquire some modicum of financial security for the foreseeable future was the dominant motivation of their waking hours. Tax incentives and "orderly financial housekeeping"* were the instruments by which Erhard would carry out his new program.

When the military government took over the administration of defeated Germany, the ACC in Berlin promulgated a stiff new income-tax schedule. It was specifically designed to siphon off some of the excess billions of the estimated seventy billion inflated reichsmarks in circulation, which gave the economy the resiliency of a waterlogged sponge. This postwar tax schedule was described by American economist Henry Wallich, a member of the U.S. Federal Reserve Board, as: ". . . in outward appearance probably the fiercest piece of income taxation ever inflicted on a Western country."*

Professor Wallich, who had been born in Berlin and came to America as a young man, was then serving with the U.S. military government in Germany.

The Allied-imposed income-tax tariffs were carried over after currency reform took effect and were for a number of years the highest income taxes in the western world. For example, an unmarried man earning DM 3,000 a year ($714) paid a tax of DM 285 ($67). As personal incomes rose, so did the tax rate. On an executive salary of DM 100,000 ($23,800), an income tax of DM 48,600 ($10,500) was levied. This stiff progressive rate, rising as high as 95 percent, kept an effective ceiling on executive salaries. The tax rate for a business firm was also high, with the lowest tax rate set at 55 percent of profits.

Erhard worked hard to get the approval of the Allied authorities for his new tax-reform program, so as to give German workers, as well as businessmen, more money to spend, as well as to save, and to invest in development projects and thus further lubricate the reviving economy. But at the outset the Americans balked, arguing that it was manifestly unfair to grant tax reductions to the Germans while U.S. taxpayers were giving Germany hundreds of millions of their tax dollars in Marshall Plan aid. However Erhard gradually wore down their resistance to his proposals. He managed to convince the Americans that it made good business sense to permit tax exemptions for money that would be invested into the repair and reconstruction of industrial or commercial enterprises. Such investments would stimulate the economic recovery by providing more consumer as well as capital goods to be purchased and more jobs for the German workers, thus adding substantially to the public's overall purchasing power. As a result, Erhard argued this would reduce Germany's dependence on the Marshall Plan much sooner than originally anticipated, with a consequent multimillion dollar savings to the U.S. taxpayers. Erhard's salesmanship, which had previously won Clay's approval of the controversial end to food rationing and wage and price controls, now convinced the Allied financial experts of the economic merits of revising the income-tax code in April 1950 to include a new schedule of tax incentives.

However, Erhard's tax-reform package did not eliminate the high income taxes for individuals and corporations. In fact, to make the incentive program effective, the taxes had to be kept high. Then tax exemptions could be made which were sufficiently large to encourage widespread participation in his economic pump-priming program. Savings and profits that were invested into government-designated industrial or commercial projects that would stimulate and strengthen the economy would be tax free. This was the quickest and safest way to acquire the wealth which had been wiped out by war losses or through the currency reform. It meant tying up this money for a certain period of time in these investments. If the German investor couldn't spend it in order to keep his funds free of income taxes, he could borrow money at a bank with these investments as his loan collateral. At the outset, the government designated certain industries as basic to the economic well-being of the country, such as the Ruhr's coal and steel industries, the electrical power companies, housing, shipbuilding, and so on. These industries were given large depreciation allowances, which could be used to offset against income taxes for the amounts invested in these sectors. Also for industrial and commercial firms in general, if their profits were not distributed but plowed back into further reconstruction or expansion of the individual enterprises, such profits were also tax free.

Erhard launched his free-market economy on the conviction that, in large measure, war-shattered German industries could finance their own repair and reconstruction from their own resources if there were sufficient incentives involved. German businessmen responded to these incentives with greater support and enthusiasm than the Bonn government ever expected. For example, in 1953 and 1954 the sum of DM 2 billion was raised for the repair and reconstruction of many of the great iron and steel plants in the Ruhr. Of this amount, DM 1.3 billion came from tax-exempt profits of the Ruhr steel firms which had managed to resume their operations in a limited fashion. This utilization of tax incentives revved up the motors of other sectors of West German industry.

However, the most successful graduates of Professor Erhard's economics course in "how-to-pull-yourself-up-by-your-own-tax-exempt-bootstraps" were the shipbuilding and housing industries. Because of extensive war damage, especially Allied bombing, the influx of millions of refugees, plus hundreds of thousands of displaced persons released from slave labor camps, as well as almost 3 million Allied soldiers, the housing shortage in postwar Germany was the most acute of any nation in Europe. The Bonn government showed ingenuity and imagination in encouraging private financing of housing. Any investments in new housing were exempt from income taxes. In addition, workers were encouraged to keep their savings in a *Bausparrkasse,* a special housing-construction bank. These savings from wages were not only exempt from income taxes, but also earned a small amount of interest. The *Bausparrkasse* in turn loaned out the savings of the general public to new housing projects at low interest rates, acting largely as a nonprofit middleman. In addition, the housing industry received from the government substantial grants and subsidies which increased in volume as the national economy improved. As a result of these developments, housing construction began to climb swiftly from 215,000 units in 1949 to over 440,000 by 1952, finally leveling off at over 500,000 new units yearly.* Of the total funding for housing construction, over 55 percent came from tax-exempt private savings and investments, with the balance from government grants and some Marshall Plan assistance of about 3 percent. It must be also borne in mind that as construction of housing increased throughout West Germany, this exerted a powerful stimulus for other associated industries—such as home furnishings, household appliances, plumbing, electrical supplies, glass, concrete and other materials used in the building of houses and apartments.

On a cold brisk morning in December 1953, Theodore Schecker, managing director of Howaldtswerke, the biggest shipbuilding yard in Germany, furnished a striking example of how the industrial recovery of the *Bundesrepublik* had moved into high gear. On a sideboard against a wall stood a model of a 400-ton fishing trawler. "That's what we started with," said Herr Schecker, gesturing toward it.

He then pointed out the window to the quayside, where the gleaming white 755-foot long *Tina Onassis* lay moored. "And that's what we are building now," he continued, "some of the world's biggest oil tankers." In those two brief sentences, Schecker had summed up the story of the dramatically swift postwar comeback of the German shipbuilding industry and the rebirth of the German merchant marine.

In the winter of 1945, Allied air raids had reduced about 90 percent of this North Sea port's harbor installations and its shipyards to a shambles. The city of Hamburg itself was about 50 percent destroyed; Bremen, Emden, Lubeck, Kiel, and other West German shipbuilding centers were also devastated. To top it off, the Allies had forbidden any further construction of merchant-marine vessels, except small coastal craft to be operated by Germans, and no naval ships whatsoever. West Germany was no longer a maritime power. From a prewar merchant marine of 4.4 million tons, Germany was left with only 35,000 tons of shipping afloat, of which the largest was the MS *Sodemann,* a 1,500-ton coastal steamer.

A shipping expert from the U.S. Consulate at Hamburg explained that a "tax gimmick and the Korean War" changed it all. In Hamburg's busy and pulsating harbor, the air resounded to the clanging of steel on steel and the staccato chattering of riveting guns at work on ships being built in the brisk closing days of 1953. On the main slipway of Howaldtswerke, the then-world's-largest oil tanker—the 47,000-ton *Al-Malik Saud Al-Awai* (*King Saud I*)—was taking shape, shortly to be added to the growing fleet of the then unknown Aristotle Onassis.

The Allies had neglected to forbid the Germans to construct ocean-going vessels for foreigners such as the host of Greek shipping tycoons, including Onassis, Niarchos, Livanos, and Kulukundis. These Greek shipping magnates discovered the postwar potentials of the German shipyards for the quick construction of oil tankers and cargo vessels, because of the availability of Europe's most skilled labor force at bargain-basement rates. The Greeks virtually put the German yards back into business.

The tax gimmick that helped to unchain German money and financing for the swift repair and reconstruction of the shipbuilding industry was the famous paragraph "7-D" of the federal tax code. Almost every resident of Hamburg—from a bartender in a grubby St. Pauli pub to the business executive in the exclusive Übersee Club uptown on the Alster—was aware that a few lines on the statute books contributed to the comeback of this great seaport and its industries. Under "7-D" any German who invested in shipping and shipbuilding was granted tax exemption for the amount involved; legally speaking, even spending money to buy a row boat qualified for the tax exemption. By 1953, "7-D" had already attracted DM 1.5 billion out of the DM 2 billion invested in ship construction. Money came from all over Germany. Among those who acquired interests in shipping were Dr. Rudolf Oetker, the "pudding powder king" of the West German food industry; the Reetsma Tobacco firm; as well as a host of businessmen who had never even put foot on an ocean-going vessel.

In 1951, after the outbreak of the Korean War, the Allied authorities scrapped the last of their controls on German merchant-ship construction, except for naval craft. The Korean War brought a spurt in world shipbuilding and the German shipyards were flooded with orders for over 2 million tons of new tankers and freighters. This encouraged a speed-up in the repair of war-damaged yards and harbors. In Hamburg's huge harbor were 2,800 ships of all sizes that had been sunk during the war and abandoned by their owners. With the advent of the Korean War, these wrecks became assets. Twenty-four freighters, totaling 74,000 tons, were raised, repaired, and put back into service. Other wrecks were sold for scrap-steel value. By 1953 the harbor had been 70 percent repaired and put back into full operation. By the 1960s, Germany's restored merchant marine numbered 2,700 ships, with a total tonnage of 6.5 million GRT (Gross Registered Tons) on the high seas.

However, the early quick pace of the reconstruction of the West German shipyards was so unexpected that the Bonn government decided to eliminate the famous "7-D" tax shelter at the end of 1954, as being no longer necessary. In fact, fears were expressed in the *Bundestag* debates that continuation of this tax incentive would lead to surplus shipbuilding capacity within a few years.

There is another important factor to be considered when studying the amazing comeback of postwar German shipbuilding and other sectors of their heavy industry. War damage and dismantling cleared out the old and obsolescent machinery. The shipyards and factories alike could install the newest and most modern equipment and utilize the latest methods to save time, money, and manpower. These technological advances made the Germans fully competitive, and more so, on the world market with other shipbuilding countries. By 1958 the Germans were the number two shipbuilders in the world, just behind the also-defeated Japanese. The resilient Orientals had erected an entirely new and modernized shipbuilding industry on the wreckage of their old slipways at Yokohama, Kobe, Nagasaki, and other seaports. Germany had done the same, though they could never compete with the low cost labor in Japan.

For example, in both these defeated and devastated countries the modern techniques of electronic controls and computerization were applied to shipbuilding. Inasmuch as building ships is a labor-intensive industry, any innovations that cut production time and labor costs improve one's competitive position. These technological advances were introduced later in the British, American, and Scandinavian shipyards. The *Times* of London pointed out in a detailed report in June 1955 on the resurgent German shipbuilding industry: "Hard thinking by engineers accompanied Germany's swift return to the front ranks of the world shipbuilding countries. Methods are changing in all the big German shipyards in the same general direction."

There was another tax incentive for encouraging fresh money into the shipbuilding industry which also applied to other industries. It was a remission of taxes on profits earned on export sales. These exports earned hard currency for West Germany, which in turn further strengthened the deutschemark on the home front. Thanks to the cabal of the Greek shipping tycoons, almost 70 percent of the ships built in German yards were sold to foreigners.* The profits on these orders for new ships qualified for special export tax exemptions. This permitted German shipbuilders to quote lower prices and increase their competitive advantages on the world market.

The international economic situation was favorable to the Germans. As one of the immediate fallouts of disastrous and wealth-consuming World War II, there existed everywhere, except in the U.S., serious shortages of goods, both of capital equipment and consumer products. The German manufacturer found a ready market at home and abroad for virtually anything he could produce in his war-damaged plants, and production could be increased as quickly as manufacturing plants and equipment could be repaired or expanded. The busy industrialist could market his products without having to employ a sales force, so great was the hunger for goods, not only in Germany, but throughout Europe, Asia, and Africa.

Hence it was not surprising that in the postwar hierarchy of West German industry the sales director, unlike his counterparts in America and England, was a low man on the executive totem pole for at least the first decade of economic recovery. On the *Vorstand* (the board of managers, comparable to an executive management committee of a U.S. firm), the director in charge of production ranked first, followed by the director of finances and the director for labor relations or personnel. The chief sales executive was not included in top-level management. In those early noncompetitive days, a manufacturer's main problems were centered in the procurement of raw materials, the actual production of finished goods, and the transportation and distribution of these goods to the marketplaces. The selling of his output was the least of his worries. Even the *Arbeitsdirektor,* labor director, who had the responsibility for keeping up the productivity rates of the workers, was more important to daily management than the sales director.

Profits of a manufacturer were consistently high—a 30 to 40 percent return was considered normal. If the manufacturer—who was earning a 35 percent profit on his yearly turnover—had the forbearance to defer an improvement in his daily life-style and invested his surplus earnings in the reconstruction of his plant, in new machine tools, and so on, he could quickly build up his personal wealth by the steady compounding of his tax-free investments. He could in a few years of plowing back his profits be a deutschemark millionaire, as many astute businessmen learned to their satisfaction.

The pay scale for German executives was low by comparison with executives of the same caliber and responsibilities in the U.S. and Britain, mainly because of stiff personal income taxes. An annual salary of DM 100,000 ($23,800 when the deutschemark became fully convertible in 1955) was considered to be a top-rank executive income for many years, until the taxes were reduced to more reasonable levels. This anomaly caused German business executives to accept comparatively low salaries, but to concentrate on the tax-free perks that were commensurate with an individual's rank and position in a company. The Bonn government was very broad-minded and generous in permitting companies to give their executives large expense-account allowances to compensate for deficiencies in their cash compensation.

Hence, a top executive would receive a tax-free residence, servants, and full maintenance of house and gardens; a lavish entertainment allowance, which covered food, drink, and other basic living expenses for himself and his family; the full-time use of a car, chauffeur, and full maintenance.* In addition, he would be recompensed for all travel expenses, which included summer and winter vacations in and out of Germany. Thus, if postwar Germany had the highest income taxes in the western world, it also enjoyed the biggest individual tax deductions, at least for the executive class. Bonn recognized that there must be incentives to stimulate the constant flow of managerial talent upward from the ranks of white-collar employees into the executive suites.

An American banker, resident in Frankfurt, summarized it neatly and cynically. He said: "I am happy to have lived long enough to see and to enjoy the expense account's 'finest hour.' "

Erhard was a nonconformist in a world that had long lived with the conformity demanded in a totalitarian state. In the years when he had been a politcial outcast for his anti-Nazi views he had studied German history and pondered his country's mistakes. So when the time came for him to take the wheel, he knew what course to navigate. He had a clear line of policy concerning what defeated Germany must do in order to effect its economic comeback. Against the advice of all but a few of his intellectual intimates, he launched his big gamble on the future of his war-ravaged country.

He gambled that the instruments to achieve his objective would be financial and economic orthodoxy; he ignored the heavy political pressures and panaceas involving socialism, planned economy in all its manifold aspects, and so on. He gambled on human behavior: that men were primarily motivated by their never-sleeping appetite for material gain, coupled with their deep-seated instinct for self-survival; in short, by their quest for security and protection against want and helplessness in a troubled and feckless world.

But if Erhard believed man seldom acted out of love or charity for his fellow man, at least he was convinced that the individual—a man who is free to act on his own initiative—has the power and intelligence to acquire a large measure of economic security for himself and his family. If thousands of Germans felt and acted in this fashion, their collective efforts would be a powerful stimulus in Germany's drive to achieve full economic recovery. Erhard did not think that a government *per se* was capable of providing security on a continuing basis for its individual citizens through any social, political, or economic formula or ideology; man, not his government, is ultimately responsible for his own fate; that was the essence of Erhard's credo.

Erhard gambled on his evaluation of the world's economic situation after World War II. The tremendous scale of physical damage, together with the squandering of the wealth of nations as they continued to fight to the war's bitter end, resulted in a global shortage of capital goods and equipment: trucks, motors, machinery, railway engines and cars, construction equipment, tractors, cement works, chemical plants, steel mills, farming machinery, electrical generators, communications equipment, and on, and on. Despite the damages it had sustained, West Germany still had the industrial capacity to produce much of this needed capital goods and engineering equipment. West Germany had the largest pool of cheap skilled labor available on the Continent: its only remaining asset. At this point in time, Germany needed an upsurge in world trade in heavy industrial goods and equipment; for which it would be able to employ its latent industrial capacity to provide a flood of exports. Then, as the *Economist* pointed out: "Just at the right time, the miracle happened. In June, 1950, the Korean War boom burst across the trading world."

With the onset of the Korean War, a flood of orders poured in for German machinery, tools, heavy industrial equipment, and so on, and this unexpected development laid the solid foundation for West Germany's economic comeback. It was, of course, something that Erhard had not figured into his plans; but his new free-market economy could adequately cope with the sudden spurt of industrial production because it was completely flexible. So Ludwig Erhard's gamble on the future of his divided country paid off handsomely.

When Erhard first appeared on the public scene in 1949 as a member of Adenauer's cabinet, he was generally unknown to the public at large. But a few years later, when Germany's economic recovery was in full bloom, he began to receive both domestic and international accolades. One tribute that came from the *Times* of London, in a report of Erhard's invigorating defense and promotion of modern-day capitalism, described Prof. Ludwig Erhard as "the irrepressible reincarnation of Adam Smith."

8

The German people have already decided against a planned economy by an overwhelming majority. . . . We shall continue along the road of the economic policies on which we have already successfully travelled.
>—KONRAD ADENAUER, *on taking office as*
>*chancellor of the first postwar German*
>*government, September 20, 1949*

I cannot avoid smiling a little when, as chief of an occupied nation, I sit down with the leaders of the occupying countries, such as Mr. Eden and M. Bidault. In spite of the fact that Germany hasn't yet full sovereignty, its economic and political impact is fully felt in world affairs.
>—KONRAD ADENAUER *in an interview with*
>Time *magazine, January 4, 1954*

ADENAUER, THE ABSENTEE LANDLORD

WEST GERMANY'S early postwar return to the world stage was largely due to a unique development; for all practical purposes, it had a two-tier government. The upper level was predominantly concerned with international and domestic political affairs under the control of Adenauer, the seventy-three-year-old chancellor, and head of the conservative Christian Democratic coalition. The lower level was responsible for the administration of the West German economy, under the baton of Economics Minister Erhard, ably abetted by his collaborators Finance Minister Fritz Schaeffer and the president of the central Bank Deutscher Länder, Dr. Wilhelm Vocke.

The first postwar government, situated in the sleepy university town of Bonn, was surprisingly successful because the politicians did not intervene in economic affairs and the economists and fiscal experts did not get involved in political matters or problems. However, despite this apparent dichotomy, the two tiers were in full agreement as to the major policy objectives. All their respective plans and efforts were devoted to restoring the defeated and bankrupt nation to political respectability, acceptance in the western community of nations, and economic good health and solvency.

Postwar West Germany enjoyed much good fortune and luck in its first

quarter century of existence on the map of Europe. The reentry of Adenauer into postwar public life was certainly one of the most providential
events of the brief postwar history of this embryonic Fourth Reich. The
time and the circumstances called for the emergence of a good and moral
man, who was also a recognized anti-Nazi, to lead the German people out
of the depths of defeat and despair. Only a man recognized for his essentially reputable character could acquire the status necessary to negotiate
with the Allied authorities on behalf of his millions of voiceless German
constituents, and to win concessions for them, so as to ease their way back
to some semblance of normalcy and security.

Adenauer fulfilled these qualifications. A man of Catholic background
and convictions, he was a devoted father of a large family. No taint of
scandal touched either his public or private life.

Adenauer was deeply versed in the arts of municipal government. As a
young lawyer, he became a member of the city council of Cologne in 1906
when he was thirty years old. His career in government was abruptly ter-
minated twenty-seven years later by the Nazis, when, as lord mayor of
Cologne, he refused them the permit to fly their swastika banners from the
city's bridges on the occasion of a visit by Hitler. At the close of the war
he was called out of retirement by the U.S. military government and re-
installed as Cologne's mayor.

In the eyes of his compatriots, Adenauer was a man whose first loyalty
in the postwar years was to his defeated country. Despite his long and
close-working relationship with the Allied authorities,* he never acquired
the degrading image of a collaborator in the eyes of the German populace.
He maintained an air of detachment in all his official relations with the
Allies, not currying their favor but rather constantly chivvying them for
concessions or changes in the occupation controls that would make life
easier for the Germans.

U.S. High Commissioner John J. McCloy, a highly regarded Wall Street
corporation lawyer and veteran negotiator in his own right, bore the brunt
of Adenauer's quiet, behind-the-scenes, arm-twisting tactics. In one session Adenauer raised a minor point about a paragraph of the impending
occupation statute. McCloy was heard to mutter as he perused the long
document, pencil in hand, "Oh, all right, that's concession Number 122
so far."

When Adenauer felt he was on sure ground, he would even refuse to
obey the orders of the military overlords, or at least ignore them. For example, after the British army took over the military government of
Cologne and its environs from the Americans in the summer of 1945, the
relations between Adenauer and the British area commander, Brig. John
Barraclough, grew steadily worse. Barraclough claimed that Adenauer was
not showing sufficient initiative to repair and reconstruct Cologne, which

had been about 85 percent destroyed by British bombing raids. Adenauer's reply was that he had neither the tools nor the manpower and supplies with which to make repairs. Barraclough summarily dismissed Adenauer from his post and ordered him to live outside the city of which he had been lord mayor for sixteen years. Adenauer never let the British forget this grievous political mistake.

Air Marshal Sir Sholto Douglas, who was British military governor and known for his anti-German views, felt the bite of Adenauer's temper at a cocktail reception in Düsseldorf in 1949. According to a report published in the *London Daily Telegraph* the British military governor walked over to Adenauer and, in a breezy, condescending fashion, asked: "And what is your political background, Mr. Mayor?"

"Oh, I just became mayor of Cologne in 1917; then I was dismissed by the Nazis for political unreliability in 1933; reinstated by the Americans in March 1945; and was dismissed by the British for incompetence in October," Adenauer replied with a straight face.

Sir Sholto Douglas stared speechless at the unsmiling Adenauer and walked on.

Adenauer was also a superb politician. A man of strong convictions, he had an amazing clarity of vision. He could readily distinguish between the realities and the illusions of the political scene. He always spoke clearly, precisely, and simply; his message reached all his listeners. He avoided the rhetoric and bombast that echoes the politician's unending search for public acclaim.

To these assets he added another talent; he always knew what he wanted, and this single-mindedness impressed his followers as a conviction that he was doing the right and proper thing. Only in his last few years as chancellor, when he was in his mid-eighties, did the natural deterioration of old age adversely affect his insight and political judgment.

Adenauer learned from Germany's past mistakes; this guided him in the planning of the new postwar West Germany. The Second Reich of Bismarck and Kaiser Wilhelm II and the "thousand-year Reich" of Adolf Hitler had been intensely nationalistic and militarily aggressive. The time had come to make a 180-degree turn away from Germany's history and traditions; to discard the last shreds of nationalistic thinking and identification, which would be replaced by a new international outlook in policy and practice. Adenauer would be the leading advocate of the new internationalism; he would be the "good European, as friend and neighbor." As he often remarked to his intimates: "Europe is my guiding star."

Adenauer rationalized that only by adopting this course of action could a penitent Germany redeem itself in the eyes of the Western democracies and be accepted back inside their ranks. Only by becoming European rather than German could the pariah nation win back a place in the European confraternity. It was a mixture of political morality and international public relations, for which Adenauer revealed surprising talents. His number one priority was to end the centuries-old conflict and antagonism between Germany and France. Adenauer saw that by effecting a permanent reconciliation between these two pillars of Western Europe, one of the historic flash points of continental warfare could be eliminated. Such a reconciliation would be a great step forward for postwar Germany in regaining social and political acceptance for the defeated ex-enemy state. Finally, West Germany would firmly commit itself to be staunchly anti-Communist, and be willing to fight for the defense of Europe as the friend and ally of the Western democracies and particularly the United States of America.

Adenauer was acutely aware that a stiff price must be paid to achieve these objectives. The Germans must work their passage back. They must accept rebuffs, distrust, hostility, as well as sacrifices of their material wealth to be invited back into the councils of Europe. But there was nothing to be gained in other directions. It would be a hard and bitter struggle to get the German people to follow him, for these goals seemed distant and unachievable.

Adenauer sensed that the great masses of the West German people were with him in shutting the door on the past, which was too painful to think about at great length. They too had paid a great price for following Adolf-the-Pied-Piper with his swastika-bannered flute: in their millions of war dead and disabled; in the losses of their homes and property, their savings, pensions, and jobs; in being reduced to poverty and being subjected to the will of their military conquerors. Adenauer grasped the realities that his principal opponent, Socialist leader Schumacher, failed to be aware of: the great majority of West Germans were in no mood for any political adventuring in new fields, or for any new ideologies, such as communism or democracy. Both of these had little appeal to the Germans. The question of the reunification of West Germany with its eastern Communist half, split off by the Iron Curtain, evoked little if any nationalistic or jingoistic reactions. Nor were most Germans concerned with the socialization of industry, the benefits of a planned economy, or other current political and economic issues.

The masses wanted new housing, a job with some promise of permanence, and an income in a stable currency with real purchasing power. The Germans wanted no more military service, and no more government control and interference in their lives. They wanted to be left in peace, so that they could devote their time and energies to rebuilding their lives and to acquiring some degree of economic security. They did not want their efforts to disappear in another catastrophe such as they had in World War II.

Adenauer knew that the German people were prepared to work and work hard to achieve these simple and vital objectives. As a result, he was guided in the domestic policy-making of his government to concentrate on the *Magenpolitik,* stomach politics, that would serve the needs and the demands of the West German people. If Adenauer could improve their daily lives and make progress in satisfying their craving for security, the people would repay him with their votes at election time. Adenauer was right on target in his political evaluation.

However, even before the first national election in West Germany on August 14, 1949 to choose the membership of the new federal parliament, there was confirmation available that most Germans would vote as their stomachs dictated. The case in point was the 1947 plebiscite in the Saar. This 783-square-mile industrial principality on the western frontier had long been contested by the Germans and the French because of its rich coal mines and conglomeration of steel plants. Its nationality changed with the fortunes of war, though its population of one million is ethnically German. By possessing the Saar, France would have a total steel production approximately equal to Germany's; however, with the Saar and the Ruhr together, the West Germans would clearly dominate the European steel industry.

After World War I, the Saar was detached from Germany and placed under French control until a 1935 League of Nations plebiscite was held, in which 90 percent of the Saarlanders voted to be Germans again. After World War II, the Americans, who overran the state, turned the administration of the Saar over to the French. Then, in order to legitimatize this political booty, the French scheduled another plebiscite in September 1947 to ratify a new constitution for an independent Saar and to approve its economic union with France.

One striking aspect of the electioneering was the absence of any ideological or political appeal by the French to the Saarlanders to vote for democracy. Instead the Saarlanders were informed by the French and their German collaborators that they could look forward to the day when they could travel with a French passport and become liberated from defeated and poverty-stricken Germany. On the eve of the plebiscite, Gilbert Grandval, the French high commissioner, painted a roseate picture for his German listeners of how, if they voted to join France in an economic union, their principal shopping streets "would soon resemble the Champs Elysées" in Paris in the abundance of the good things of life on display that would soon be available to them. With a shrewd appreciation of the basic and prevailing interests of the population of the Saar, the French propagandists promised more food for the Saarlanders; a stable and a convertible currency—the French franc—that had real purchasing power compared to the inflated reichsmark; and the prospect of greater economic security for all.

The French had accurately gauged the mood of the Saarlanders. More than 80 percent of them approved economic union with France and a political divorce from Germany. This victory for the French was solid proof that *Magenpolitik* and not nationalism governed the voting returns in the Saar, which has been for generations a cockpit of Franco–German conflict. In the 1935 plebiscite, over 90 percent of the Saarlanders had voted to return to the arms of *der Vaterland*. Now in 1947, in the chaotic aftermath of World War II, the economic union with France—its material benefits so enticingly spelled out by the clever French propagandists—outweighed any latent nationalistic or patriotic feelings the Saarlanders had formerly displayed for the Third Reich.

Tables were to turn once again. By the end of 1955, the West Germans were living well, as well as the French if not better. The future looked bright for forty-eight million West Germans; again the political attitude of the Saarlanders changed. Another plebiscite was held and on December 18, 1955, 63 percent of the Saarlanders voted to rejoin the burgeoning new *Bundesrepublik*. By December 1956 the Saar was again tucked inside the frontier of West Germany under the wings of the German eagle.

Adenauer, who had taken over the leadership of the CDU, the dominant conservative political amalgam in West Germany, had early recognized the necessity of stressing the basic economic issues and problems and what he and the CDU were doing and would continue to do to solve them. With this election strategy he stood the best chance of winning against the Socialists, the principal competition for the administration of the new government of West Germany. In line with this approach, he invited Erhard, who had until then stayed aloof from party politics, to join the CDU and head up its economic team. Erhard had already achieved a certain aura of success and popularity because of the currency reform and the ending of rationing and price and wage controls. The entry of Erhard into the election was seen as a promise that the daily lives of the West Germans would continue to improve if the CDU took over the government. Schumacher, leader of the SPD, recognized the danger to the Socialist cause implicit in Erhard's political debut. Schumacher tried to denigrate the plump Bavarian economist with insults such as his scathing description of Erhard as ". . . the fat propaganda balloon of private enterprise, filled with the putrid gases of decaying liberation."

Schumacher also stressed the economic aspects of the political struggle for power in West Germany; but he did not, or could not, handle the bread-and-butter issues in the same convincing manner as Adenauer, Erhard, & Co. The SPD leader spoke in broad terms of the concepts and reforms that he would undertake if his party won the election, such as the need for planned economy, nationalism of heavy industry, and so on. These evoked little noticeable response, except from his own party followers. There were also times when his rhetoric was either too exaggerated or just plain misleading. For example, he repeatedly emphasized that this first national election presented the German people with ". . . the unique opportunity to deprive the remnants of the big business cliques in Germany of their power."

In election summer of 1949 it was very difficult to find evidence of the "power" of the "big business cliques," or that the thinned-out ranks of the so-called Ruhr barons were engaged in any operations or maneuvers inimical to the best interests of the German people. The handful of leading Ruhr industrialists who were still free to move about, those such as Hans Günther Sohl of August-Thyssenhütte and Wilhelm Zangen of Mannesmann, were trying to preserve their equipment against the day Germany could again fire up the blast furnaces and provide jobs for thousands of Ruhr workers.

Adenauer, together with Erhard, was an avowed enemy of socialism; but he made it clear that he was not against social reforms. As such, he approved of Erhard's vision of a socially responsive free-market economy. In this context, social reforms meant providing the German people with a comprehensive, all-purpose social-security system which was to become the most far-reaching and expensive program, proportionately, of any of those in the Western democracies.* In 1950 the social-security outlay for federal and state governments was about $2.3 billion and by 1977–78 the annual West German social-security bill was a staggering $125 billion (based on the then current dollar-deutschemark exchange rates).

The whole social-security program with its generous pensions, lavish medical care, health insurance, and substantial unemployment payments was the Adenauer–Erhard answer to the public demand for economic security. Before each of the national elections in 1953, 1957, and 1961, the Adenauer administration pushed through the parliament healthy increases in the various social-security payouts. Even the Socialists could not muster sufficient opposition in the *Bundestag* to hold down the escalating social-security handouts. Nobody ever votes against Santa Claus.*

The results of the August 14, 1949 election came as a great surprise: for the press and the political observers, including the opinion polls, had predicted that Schumacher and his Socialists would win. However the CDU and its Bavarian sister party, the CSU, took the lead, polling 31 percent of the votes. The Socialists came second with 29.2 percent, followed by the Free Democrats (FDP), essentially liberal and centrist, with 11.9 percent. The Communist party (KPD) fell far behind expectations, polling only 5.7 percent of the vote. This dismal showing was largely due to the damage to the Communist image as the people's party caused by the ruthless Russian blockade of Berlin recently broken by the Allied airlift. The balance of the votes were spread among ten splinter parties, representative of sectional and special interests. They were soon to fade, as the two major parties tended to increase their popular appeal and polarize the political scene. As leader of the CDU, Adenauer was elected chancellor by a slim one-vote margin. He took office on September 15 at the age of seventy-three, as head of a coalition government formed with the aid of FPD and the German party (*Deutsche Partei*).

Schumacher never fully recovered from the bitterness of this defeat.

He had been so confident that he, not that "old man" Adenauer, knew what the public wanted and needed and would reap the rewards of his political prescience. His rejection by the public in favor of the conservatives Adenauer and Erhard and their "ridiculous" free-market system was unacceptable. He described the new government as a tool forged by the Allied high commissioners, "a western counter-action to the Russian action in setting up a totalitarian regime in the eastern zone."

Within a few months the Adenauer–Schumacher wrangling reached a new high in vituperation. Adenauer had just concluded an agreement with the Allied high commissioners for the internationalization of the Ruhr, in return for concessions to the German government from the occupation authorities. However, the agreement drew a storm of angry protests from Schumacher and the SDP when it was brought into the *Bundestag* for ratification. To answer this outcry, Adenauer explained to the deputies: "The Allies told me that the dismantling of industry would be stopped only if I satisfied their demands for security. Does the Socialist Party want the dismantling of our factories to continue to the bitter end?"

In reply, Schumacher rose to point his finger at Adenauer and shout out: "You're a liar! . . . You are nothing but the Chancellor of the Allies!"

This insulting taunt caused the speaker to expel Schumacher for three days. Meanwhile other Socialists joined in to attack Adenauer's pact with the Allies. Finally, his patience exhausted, Adenauer snapped at the opposition benches: "Who do you think lost the war anyway?"

The chancellor's stinging reminder of the not-too-distant past silenced the opposition for this session.

Acting as chancellor and his own foreign minister, the seventy-three-year-old Adenauer took on a heavy load of work and responsibility. However, the elder statesman's energies enabled him to stay on top of his new government and its conflicting ideas and personalities.

Adenauer was a throwback to the old traditions of the Prussian civil service. Before Hitler had politicized and nazified the national civil service, it had been an honorable and proud profession in the prewar Germanies and by virtue of its inherent capabilities and *esprit de corps,* it had survived the collapse of the *Kaiserreich* after World War I. The old-line civil service considered itself a unique class, devoted to the arts of governmental administration. There were few men in Bonn who could match Adenauer's experience and background or who could teach him any new tricks about how to run a government. Before Hitler came to power, Adenauer had been offered the chancellorship, but he preferred to remain in Cologne.

Adenauer took over the direction and control of the political side of the Bonn government, domestically and internationally, and quietly asserted to his close intimates: "I am seventy percent of this government."

It was soon recognized in the upper echelons of Bonn that he was in truth the *Herr im Haus,* the unquestioned head of the governmental family.

In fact, what evolved became known as *Kanzlerdemokratie* (chancellor democracy), an allusion to the democratic form of government that was clearly under the thumb of one man, the chancellor. However Adenauer could and did delegate authority and responsibility, but only to those few capable and trusted men concerned with economic administration: Erhard as minister for economics, Schaeffer as minister of finance, and Vocke, president of the central Bank Deutscher Länder. The central bank of issue was made independent of any government controls by a specific paragraph of the constitution, but its president was given the right to participate in the weekly sessions of the cabinet.

Adenauer knew little about basic economics, except to be generally conservative in his outlook, and he displayed little interest in the mechanics of this somewhat esoteric discipline.

Terence Prittie of the *Manchester Guardian,* a veteran Adenauer watcher, wrote in his detailed biography of the chancellor concerning his relations with his cabinet:

A feature of these was Adenauer's absolute readiness to decentralize to a limited extent. He gave Ludwig Erhard virtual *carte blanche* in the economic field where he had already proved so resoundingly successful, and about which Adenauer professed and preferred to remain ignorant. Schaeffer had almost equally total authority in the realm of finance, and the Ministers of Posts, Transport, Housing, Food and Bundesrat Affairs, Refugees and Marshall Plan aid were encouraged to get on with their jobs with a minimum of direction. . . . The picture of Adenauer as an interfering autocrat is an entirely false one. He was frankly uninterested in various functions of government and had no time for them. He placed great reliance on his key Ministers, Erhard, Schaeffer, and Heinemann (Minister of Interior) and was justified in doing so.*

Adenauer maintained his own independent contacts with the West German business world. His closest personal friend and adviser was Robert Pferdmenges of Cologne, a powerful and wealthy financier and a partner in the Sal Oppenheim Bank, which had close ties to Ruhr heavy industry. Pferdmenges became a deputy in the *Bundestag,* where he was in constant contact with the chancellor. A Protestant and a successful businessman and banker, Pferdmenges was able to give Adenauer a political, social, and economic point of view which was complementary to his own. The Cologne banker and amateur politician was also pro-American and pro-European in his outlook.

However, as a result of the freedom of action and policy-making given to Erhard, Schaeffer, and Vocke, a two-tier system of government began to develop: Adenauer and his immediate teams of advisers on top were mainly concerned with the political side of federal administration, as well as the relations with the Allied high commissioners; while Erhard, Schaeffer, and Vocke enjoyed almost complete autonomy in the management of the national economy.

Erhard constantly fought for an end to *dirigissmus*—the government's attempts to direct and control the economy which had been the practice under Hitler. It was the one promise that was completely fulfilled. In fact, Adenauer went several steps further by not interfering with his own cabinet ministers' administration of the economy. However in time Adenauer began to disclose that he somewhat resented losing control of the economic administration of the country. For example, he created quite a flurry in a public speech at a Cologne banquet in May 1956 when, for the first time, he voiced public criticism of Erhard, Schaeffer, and Vocke. The fact that he publicly aired his complaints about Vocke's discount policy, Erhard's tariff reductions, and Schaeffer's complex income-tax regulations—matters that should normally have been raised in a cabinet meeting behind closed doors—provided a one-day sensation. But Erhard let it be known that Adenauer's interference in economic affairs "was beyond all reason" and Adenauer retreated from a confrontation with the experts.

Adenauer worked overtime on political and foreign affairs, and, for all practical purposes, he played the role of an absentee landlord concerning the national economy. He did not concern himself with the management of economic affairs and he did not disturb his "tenants," Erhard, Schaeffer, and Vocke in their specific tasks. However, he collected his rent in the form of the political dividends that increased as the economic revival of West Germany began to rapidly accelerate. The growing attention that the world press paid to the amazing economic comeback reflected prestige and admiration for Adenauer. In April 1953 he made his first visit to Washington, where he was welcomed by President Eisenhower as a friend and potential ally. In December 1954 he was named "The Man of the Year" by *Time* magazine. Step by step, Adenauer succeeded in loosening the chains that once tightly bound defeated Germany to the chariots of its conquerors. By the late 1950s, Adenauer was often described in the German press as "the greatest chancellor since Bismarck."

In the eyes of many Germans, no higher praise was possible. But what was partially obscured by the adulation and smoke of incense burners was the simple fact that the burgeoning economy, plus Germany's potential as Europe's greatest industrial power, made all this possible.

If Adenauer was the captain on the bridge of the ship of state, proudly navigating it back into the harbors of the transatlantic community of nations, then Erhard was the fireman in the engine room below decks. He kept pouring on the coal that fueled the fires that made the steam, which turned the turbines, which powered the ship to "Full speed ahead!"

9

Of course, the Germans have many advantages. They regard work and not football pools as their national sport. They have virtually wiped out their internal debt. They have no rearmament so far to bother them. On the other hand, they were, literally, eating out of the dustbins in 1945 and 1946. They have had occupation costs to bear. Their country was smashed in ruins. They have had this colossal influx of refugees. But—and this is the crux of the matter—you can time their amazing recovery almost to the hour, from the currency reform of 1948—and if that wasn't monetary discipline then I'm the Dean of Canterbury.

—HAROLD WINCOTT, *London* Financial Times,
July 22, 1952

. . . All the politicians and all the voters, when on the verge of making a decision, should tap their purses and tell themselves: 'My money must remain stable. No more controlled economy!' Everyone should always keep that thought in mind; the one who makes savings deposits, the housewife, the worker, in short, everyone of us without distinction.

—DR. WILHELM VOCKE, *chairman, the central
Bank Deutscher Länder, in a June 21, 1952
speech to insurance company executives*

DISCIPLINE PAYS
DIVIDENDS

IN THE EARLY HOURS of June 25, 1950, the Communist armies of North Korea under the command of Marshal Choe Yong Gun, crossed the 38th parallel and invaded South Korea in an oriental version of the *blitzkrieg*. Their objective was to sweep the pro-American government of President Syngman Rhee out of power and take full control of the five-hundred-mile-long Korean peninsula that juts out from the mainland of China toward the islands of Japan. The Communist invasion of South Korea, a country under the protection of U.S. forces, sent a wave of shock throughout West Germany, as well as through the whole non-Communist world. The immediate questions in every German mind were: Was the invasion of South Korea part of a global assault of the Communist bloc on the Western powers? Would the massed legions of the Soviet Union invade West Germany to push the American and Allied forces back across the Rhine River and beyond? Was West Germany the next big Communist target? But, when the U.S. Marines landed at Inchon behind the North

Korean armies, bringing swift defeat and disintegration to the Communist invaders, the waves of panic subsided. In a few months it became apparent that the Korean War was to prove to be immensely beneficial, politically and economically, for West Germany.

First of all, it convinced the Allies, especially the Americans, that West Germany must actively participate in the joint defense of Western Europe against the threat of future Soviet aggression.* The Germans alone had the great collective fund of experience and knowledge about what it means to engage in combat against the massed legions of Russia.

Achieving this objective meant creating a completely new political relationship between the erstwhile conquerors and their ex-enemy. This development served to confirm the sagacity of Adenauer, who had correctly foreseen that the day would come when West Germany would be needed as the military ally and friend of the Western powers. The Korean War gave him a quantum boost in his bargaining powers vis-à-vis the Allied high commissioners sitting high above the Rhine in their Hotel Petersberg headquarters, across the river from Bonn.

The industrial capacity of the Ruhr must be mobilized and put to work to strengthen the economies of the free world. In sure and predictable moves, the Allied controls on German industry were removed one by one. The 11.1-million-ton ceiling on the production of steel was lifted, followed by the drastic reduction and then elimination of restrictions and controls on other strategic products such as aluminum, synthetic fuels, synthetic rubber, ball bearings, electronic equipment, and certain chemicals. By the end of 1952 the Ruhr had been freed of all its chains. As Theodore H. White, an acute observer of the international political scene, commented: "For the Germans alone, the Korean War brought quick, complete and unconditional profit."*

One immediate result of the outbreak of the Korean War was the swift development of a worldwide shortage of steel. This was triggered when the U.S. government embarked on a multibillion-dollar program to procure military supplies and equipment for the U.S. and United Nations' forces fighting in Korea. Steel was in short supply around the world. American buyers appeared in the Ruhr where they competed with agents from Communist East Germany to purchase hundreds of thousands of tons of scrap steel salvaged out of the broken bridges, buildings, and other damaged industrial plants and equipment making up the infrastructure of this congested industrial area.

The chiaroscuro of industrial shortages and deficiencies in postwar Germany took on some quixotic turns. For example, after the Allied controls on production had been lifted, the renascent Ruhr steel industry was faced with a new crisis: a shortage of coking coal. While the Ruhr sits on billions of tons of coal—the foundation of its industrial concentration—mining was hampered by the inability to get pit props, normally supplied from the eastern European forests. Out of this industrial pileup emerged a bright young German blessed with imagination and vision that ranged far beyond the confines of his introverted nation. His name was Willy Schlieker, the first of the new postwar breed of business entrepreneurs, who found a simple solution by "bringing coals to Newcastle." The self-educated son of a Hamburg longshoreman, Willy looked across the Atlantic and grasped his big opportunity. He contracted to buy high-quality West Virginia and Pennsylvania anthracite at $10 a ton, plus $15 a ton extra to transport it to the coke-hungry Ruhr. He found ready buyers for all the coking coal he could import from America, which reached a total volume of 72,000 tons monthly. For each ton of U.S. coal, he demanded and got a ton of Ruhr steel, which he then sold to U.S. buyers at a high profit. Out of this coking coal crisis, Willy amassed a quick fortune of $8 million; with this he began to build an industrial empire consisting of steel mills, shipyards, and so on, ultimately worth $150 million.

In addition, there were acute shortages in a wide variety of heavy industrial products necessary for making armaments and for waging war, such as machine tools, trucks, engineering and electrical equipment, motors and machinery of all descriptions, earth-moving equipment, and so on. In Germany and throughout Western Europe, there was a seller's market for the materials, tools, and equipment needed to complete the repair and reconstruction of World War II damages which were still to be taken care of when resources permitted. The Western nations had been deprived of easy access to the normal production of their industrial societies for years because of the military priorities of the war and its aftermath. The public's appetite for consumer goods—clothing, furniture, household appliances, radios, bicycles, as well as food—was increasing with every passing day. There was even a brief period when the cheap Reynolds ballpoint pen, sold in the PX, was a prized status symbol throughout Europe.

West Germany was uniquely positioned to take full advantage of the global demand for capital and consumer goods. Despite the widespread physical destruction of manufacturing plants and equipment and the dismantling that followed the war, Germany had the latent production capacity to produce a wide range of products. Germany also had the largest pool of skilled industrial labor in postwar Europe. The energies and ingenuity of these workers could be put to work comparatively cheaply because of rampant unemployment outside the factories gates. Finally, the nation's economy was fortunately saddled with an undervalued currency in relation to the U.S. dollar, the pound sterling, the Swiss and French francs, and other monies. In May 1949, Allied authorities had set the value of the deutschemark at 3.33 to $1. In the following September it was arbitrarily devalued to 4.20 to $1. This rate was to prove highly advantageous to the German exporters, but that was not immediately apparent. Later, when Germany's competitors on the world markets, particularly the British, examined what contributed so much stimulus to Germany's successful export drive at their expense, the money men in London and Paris called for the elimination of the export leverage enjoyed by the undervalued deutschemark.*

The Korean War set the stage for the economic recovery of West Germany. After the initial reaction of fear and panic that Communist aggression in Korea might be followed by a Soviet invasion into Western Europe had subsided, the two-tier government in Bonn swiftly went to work to exploit the political and economic opportunities that had opened up as a result of the conflict being waged in the distant Pacific theater of war.

Adenauer envisioned his responsibility as chancellor in this crucial period as being something of a good shepherd leading his flock out of the wilderness to greener pastures. Sensitive to the burdensome legacy of international hatred and suspicion that Germany had inherited from Hitler, he saw the Korean War as opening the door to Germany's return to the family of nations. He rejected any nationalistic feelings or sentiments he may have felt in favor of transforming himself and his image as a father figure to his people into becoming "a better European than a German." In that self-appointed role, Adenauer was to lead his truncated country in successive stages into the Schumann Plan, the European Coal and Steel Community, the Council for Europe, NATO, and the European Economic Community, which is better known as the Common Market.

The chancellor had prepared the groundwork for this postwar process of the internationalization of his nation. When Adenauer had been president of the parliamentary council of Bizonia, it had drafted a constitution for the new *Bundesrepublik;* under Adenauer's pressure, the new constitution contained a clause (Article 24) that specifically authorized the federal parliament to "transfer sovereign powers to intergovernmental institutions" such as a projected "United States of Europe." This was another of the basic decisions that set the course of the Bonn government before it took office in September 1949. No other nation had legally prepared itself in advance to surrender, when necessary, a substantial measure of its sovereign powers to supranational agencies or institutions. Adenauer had taken the first step to lead the "hated land of the Hun and the Nazis back to moral respectability" and to earn for himself "a seat in the highest councils of the Western powers."*

The Korean War boom, which quickly developed in Germany, was to accomplish what was completely unexpected: by June 1951 West Germany was self-supporting. Its export trade was in high gear, and by mid-1951, Germany's balance of payments had moved firmly and strongly into the plus column and was to remain solidly entrenched there for the next quarter of a century. By the middle 1970s, Germany had piled up greater gold and dollar reserves than any other nation in the world.* If not the most powerful, this new *Bundesrepublik* was certainly the richest Germany in the long history of Europe.

*   *   *

Erhard, Schaeffer, and Vocke shared several common objectives, which explains why their fiscal and financial housekeeping made such an outstanding contribution to the economic revival of West Germany. They regarded inflation as the number one threat to economic growth and stability and their convictions were buttressed by painful and vivid personal memories. Each in his own lifetime had seen his family's savings and investments wiped out in the raging inflation following World War I.* Then after World War II, they and their fellow Germans went through the inflation wringer again, when the reichsmark as a monetary yardstick gave way to the ubiquitous Lucky Strike cigarette. As finance minister, Schaeffer had promised that inflation would come to Germany "only over my dead body." In his official capacity he had an arsenal of fiscal weaponry with which to combat inflation. So did Dr. Wilhelm Vocke, president of the central bank (Bank Deutscher Länder, or BDL), who could control the money supply of the country.

So these three economic leaders of the Bonn government had no compunction about stepping on toes to keep prices down in their crusading fervor against inflation. Erhard, Schaeffer, and Vocke were all high-collar, old-fashioned, and orthodox in their views on the necessity of operating with a balanced budget. In this fiscal area they were supported by Article 110 of the new West German constitution, which states that the "budget must be balanced as regards revenue and expenditures." In later years, the legal experts at the finance ministry found a few loopholes which they claimed authorized deficit spending, but such practices never entered the minds of the original trio of economic managers. Schaeffer, as finance minister, not only stayed well within his budget, but he also began to accumulate budget surpluses each year as federal spending, particularly for defense, lagged far behind the incoming tax revenues. By 1956, Schaeffer had built a tidy little nest egg of over DM 6 billion (approximately $1.5 billion), which he said would eventually be paid out for defense contracts. He called his treasure trove the *"Juliusturm,"* a description derived from the hoard of gold and silver that Kaiser Wilhelm II had cached in the Julius Tower in Spandau for wartime contingencies.

The economics and finance ministers and the head of the BDL shared the conviction that Germany's only road to economic recovery must involve a tight-money policy. In the final analysis that meant West Germans must finance their own revival in large measure—by their own savings, by accepting a minimum of social-security spending, by continuing to pay high taxes, and, in general, by not rocking the boat. This economic discipline was painful and was not accepted without protests. However, this pull-yourself-up-by-your-bootstraps course in economic recovery was to make spectacular progress in the decade of the 1950s.

Finally, as a corollary to this policy, as soon as circumstances permitted, Erhard, Schaeffer, and Vocke employed all their resources and talents to transform the deutschemark, which had begun life as a fiat currency without an ounce of gold or silver to support it, into a currency as stable and as hard as the Swiss franc. There were disagreements among the three as to when the deutschemark could be made freely convertible with other currencies and, thus, attain the status of a hard currency if it could hold to its parity value. Schaeffer was fearful that there might be a run on the deutschemark by the Germans, exchanging their money for dollars or Swiss francs, unless there were sufficient reserves behind it. However by 1958, when the central bank had piled up gold and dollar reserves plus a large credit balance in the European Payments Union totaling $7.3 billion, the deutschemark was unleashed to become freely convertible and took its stance as one of the hardest currencies of the world, in company with the U.S. dollar and the Swiss franc. In a review of the amazingly successful fiscal and financial operations of Erhard, Schaeffer, and Vocke, the *Economist* remarked: ". . . it is their stern monetary policies that made the Mark into the dollar of Europe."

According to the Bonn constitution, ministers are appointed and dismissed by the federal president at the suggestion of the chancellor, as head of the government (Article 64). In office, a minister follows "the general policy guidelines" laid down by the chancellor but he "shall conduct the affairs of his department autonomously and on his own responsibility" (Article 65). It is understandable that the economic affairs of the new West German state should be largely fashioned and directed almost independently, as the economics and finance ministers decided upon in their own offices. Of course their policy-making was affected by the views and operations of the central bank, but Dr. Vocke was usually in general agreement with the broad objectives and practices of the ministers.

For example, Vocke took pride in being dubbed in the press as the guardian of the deutschemark. Equally conservative and financially orthodox was the pfennig-pinching Schaeffer, who was described in a Bonn newspaper as a man who " . . . handles the government's money as if he earned all of it himself and had to account for every pfennig to his wife every night."

Schaeffer focused his eagle eye on two areas: governmental income and spending. No matter how important it might be, any measure that involved a reduction in revenues or an increase in federal outlays was certain to draw a critical blast from the Ministry of Finance.

Schaeffer, a thin, birdlike man with a balding head, was considered by most political observers as the most competent and efficient minister in the Adenauer cabinet. He came out of Bavaria with close ties to the peasants of southern Germany and the Catholic church, two of the most conservative political forces in the country. Schaeffer was one of the few men who dared openly to talk back to Adenauer. His feisty attitude had caused him to be twice ousted from public office. He had been appointed minister of finance in the Bavarian government in 1931 and removed from office by the Nazis. In 1944 he further aroused their anger and was put in the Dachau concentration camp. At the end of the war, he was resurrected by the Americans and installed as minister president of Bavaria. He was later removed from this post because he refused to give up the services of several Nazi officials who were on the blacklist of the U.S. military government.

Schaeffer was constantly embroiled in controversy because he demanded all the tax revenues that the traffic would bear; for his ruthless pruning of the spending plans of his fellow ministers in order to keep his budget balanced; and for using every opportunity to squirrel away government funds in his Julius Tower against the proverbial rainy day, an unlikely event that went further into the future as the economy revival changed from a trot to a gallop. Other politicians, as well as bankers and businessmen, opposed Schaeffer's money hoarding, arguing that the awakening economy could make better use of surplus funds in financing foreign and domestic trade and investments.

Vocke was a banker's banker, who spoke softly but carried a big stick and did not hesitate to use it to keep the forces of inflation at bay and to hold down prices. He did not shrink from making decisions that ran counter to the government's policy line if he felt the general economic situation required him to do so. Vocke's independence of mind and policy was shown clearly in his highly criticized decisions shortly after the start of the Korean War. The worldwide demand for steel caused orders to the Ruhr steelmakers to jump from one million to eight million tons. There was a sudden demand for capital funds with which to repair and to expand the Ruhr's steel mills to cope with this rush of orders. Vocke, as president of the BDL, took two drastic and highly unpopular actions to stop any inflationary boom before it could pick up momentum: he raised the minimum cash reserves to be held by the commercial banks by 50 percent; he, then boosted the discount rate from 4 to 6 percent. He was heavily criticized by political and business circles, which viewed his credit-restricting action as seriously handicapping the industrial recovery now stimulated by the global demand for steel. However, several years later the BDL was quietly able to report:

Germany acquired a favorable competitive position in 1952 and 1953. Whereas the upward price spiral inspired by the Korean crisis continued in some of the most important countries, the level of prices in the Federal Republic fell considerably.

During this two-year period, the West German index of retail prices rose by only 7 percent, while in Great Britain the same index rose by 35 percent. By taking the intelligent, long-range view that keeping prices down inside Germany, including labor and production costs, was the number one priority, Vocke's unpopular decisions in this instance helped to vastly improve Germany's competitive trading position on the world market.

This set the stage for the West German export boom that was to continue unabated for years to come and to contribute immeasurably to the recovery of the *Bundesrepublik*.

The BDL was originally created by the Allied authorities in March 1948 to serve as the fiscal instrument for the economic administration of Bizonia. Its organization and functions were largely patterned after the U.S. Federal Reserve Board. The BDL was given almost complete independence in its relations with the federal government in Bonn. The BDL's charter stated that the central bank was obligated to "give consideration to the general economic policy of the federal government and to support it within the scope of its task." This escape clause permitted Dr. Vocke, who in those early days was the dominant personality at the BDL, to take a policy line independent of the government's if he felt it was in the best interest of the national economy. By controlling the money supply and the costs of borrowing money, he could effectively exert an anti-inflationary discipline which was often resented by the business and political communities.

At first encounter Vocke gave the initial impression of being a serious schoolmaster type. His quiet and reserved manners gave no clue that he was "regarded by many economists as one of the great central bankers of his time."* He was born in Bavaria in 1886, the son of a poor country parson. However, young Vocke managed to attend four leading universities, emerging as a lawyer. He became a government official attached to various financial offices until, in 1919, at the tender age of thirty-three, he was appointed a director of the central Reichsbank, the youngest in its history. He served through the wildcat inflation of the early 1920s and then, in conjunction with Dr. Hjalmar Schacht, worked out the details of a currency reform and the stabilization of the new *rentenmark,** which replaced the quintillions of worthless reichsmarks. This traumatic period, which saw the flood of bogus paper money issued by the government in carload lots sweep away the life savings and wealth of millions of Germans, deeply affected the economic beliefs and decisions of Vocke. In 1939, Vocke's strong opinions caused him to write a memorandum to the bank's staff in which he was critical of Nazi rearmament and its inflationary effects on the German economy. The result was his dismissal from the board of the Reichsbank, by special order of Hitler. To his dying day Vocke was convinced that inflation was a cancer that could destroy the economy of a nation unless it was brought quickly under control. After the end of World War II, when he was called from retirement by the British to become the first chairman of the BDL, he carried these convictions with him in the performance of his new postwar career.

As the man who could independently control the supply of money, who could make the money market tight or loose through raising or lowering the discount rates, Dr. Vocke was in a position to apply his conservative economic beliefs to the renascent new German state. His influence on economic planning and decision-making was all the more pervasive because he had the talent of simple and clear exposition of his ideas and opinions. He laid down a basic principle: the BDL would be a much more effective financial and fiscal agency if its policies and operations, as well as its general economic intelligence, were shared with the public. He organized the publication of a monthly report in both German and English, which gave its readers an accurate and understandable picture of the evolving West German economy, complete with detailed statistical tables; on numerous occasions he wrote the monthly report himself. It was a quality information service that no other central bank furnished. Vocke died, while still in office, in 1958.

By 1958, Germany's expanding economy and booming world trade required the transformation of the BDL into a truly functional central bank renamed the Bundesbank. In this changeover, the Bundesbank actually acquired a stronger grip on the daily management of the nation's monetary affairs. Dr. Karl Blessing, a leading foreign currency expert, was Vocke's successor. Another "high priest of financial orthodoxy," as he was described in the monthly newsletter of the Merck, Finck banking group, Dr. Blessing's career paralleled Vocke's in some respects. Blessing served in the Reichsbank before World War II, and he too was ousted by order of Hitler for his criticisms of the inflationary tendencies of the Nazi rearmament program. He then became director of the German operations for Unilever, the British-Dutch food and soap combine. During the war he helped organize the *Wehrmacht*'s oil supplies, returning to the Unilever organization when the war ended. He served as president of the Bundesbank from 1958 to 1969, and practiced what he preached: a pay-as-you-go system, with balanced budgets and a stable currency for West Germany. He was given a large measure of credit for averting a major recession in 1967 by his use of the discount rate in controlling the money supply.

In its formative years, West Germany's central bank had been directed by strong and independent personalities who opposed loose, uncontrolled government spending, especially in the Keynesian sense of stimulating the economy, and worked for tight credit restrictions to combat the ever-present inflationary forces.*

After the last shot had been fired in World War II and an uneasy peace had settled on a traumatized globe, the victors and the vanquished alike, with the possible exception of the United States, faced not only the physical repair and reconstruction of their daily existences, but also the restructuring of their political and economic standards. Prewar ideologies and philosophies were in large part discredited; prewar economic patterns were found wanting. Britain had lost an empire which had once made it the world's richest nation. France had crumbled before the Nazi war machine and emerged from the war as a second-rank power. Nazi Germany had conquered a continent, seeking *Lebensraum* and economic self-sufficiency in the name of *Autarkie,* only to lose all and reap total disaster. Old-fashioned capitalism and other rightist economic formulae such as Mussolini's corporate state had been weighed and found wanting. Meanwhile communism, backed by the military might of the Soviet Union, as well as Marxist socialism, increased its appeal in postwar Europe, as war-weary millions sought more order and security in their lives. There was a mass groping for new ways in which to develop the maximum potentials of the nation's industrial and commercial assets, without creating political disturbances at home and abroad.

Communism only came to power in areas controlled by the Red Army. But elsewhere in Europe after 1945 there was an advance of socialism, mainly because of "the myth of historical necessity," wrote Prof. Wilhelm Röpke, the economic mentor of Professor Erhard. Viewing this postwar revival of socialism in Europe, Röpke found:

. . . the appeal of this myth to the intellectual laziness of the average man was, of course, bound to multiply as the zero hour of history seemed to have struck. . . . That is what happened at the end of World War II. Everywhere in Europe and overseas, socialism—as a curious mixture of planning, socialization, repressed inflation, war economy, welfare statism and post-Keynesianism —was triumphant. . . . Now we can realize what it meant when, soon after the war, a group of countries emerged whose leaders were bold enough to question the timetable of history and set the helm on the opposite tack. . . . The really shattering blow came from West Germany when, five years ago, Erhard and his associates answered the collective bankruptcy of inflationary collectivism by a resolute return to the market economy and monetary discipline, and when, in addition, they were successful beyond the hopes of the most optimistic.*

One may or may not agree with Professor Röpke's analysis of postwar developments, but the quotation cited above expresses something of the evangelistic faith in orthodoxy that motivated the Freiburg school of economy, which itself was the seedbed of the postwar revival of West Germany. For in those crucial postwar days, West Germany faced the choice of either a planned or a free economy. The former called for increasing production of goods through easy credit, large governmental spending, and strong central planning of investment and foreign trade, while the expected inflation would be managed by price controls, rationing, and a tight rein on foreign trade. These measures, plus sharply progressive taxation, hitting at the affluent, would serve social needs such as redistribution of wealth, social-security benefits for the masses, and weekly support handouts for the unemployed. That was the choice made by the British when, at the end of the war, they booted out Winston Churchill and installed a Socialist Labor government in his place. As the Western powers sadly witnessed, from that point on all was downhill, as Great Britain wasted away the economic muscle that contributed to its world-power status.

The alternative, which was Erhard's socially responsive free-market economy, was based on the premise that production would be increased and unemployment reduced by improving the economic machinery itself, and not just by fueling it with increased public spending, or as they say in Washington, "not by just throwing money at it." The Erhard school preached a minimum of government interference, a balanced budget, a stable currency, and complete freedom of trade. This meant, in short, living within one's income, husbanding the national wealth and resources, and plowing back savings and profits into the rebuilding and modernization of the nation's industrial and commercial machinery. Professor Erhard, as well as his colleagues Schaeffer and Vocke, were distinctly not welfare-minded, especially at this early stage of economic revival. There was to be no German equivalent of Lord Beveridge's womb-to-tomb social-welfare system, introduced by the first postwar Labor government in Whitehall. There was to be no emphasis on leveling out the inequalities between the rich and the poor in matters of income and consumption. As Professor Wallich cogently pointed out:

The outstanding aspect of the German system was the wide range of incentives it offered. Some were built-in—the urge to overcome the consequences of a lost war, to reestablish one's personal status, to recover one's material possessions. From an *incentive point of view, a lost war seemed to be much more effective than a war barely won.* [Italics added.] The system gave freedom of action to the strong. It was hard on those who could not make their own way . . . It was a harsh system but in keeping with the situation. The war ended in crushing defeat and there was no illusion that peace would be enjoyable. "Fair shares" [as advocated by British Socialists] might have overburdened the strong and all might have sunk together. By being able to save their own skins first, the strong were put in a position where they could pull the rest after them. The rapid advance of the economy helped everybody. . . . The rapid rise in income took the place of the redistribution [of wealth]. In this sense, the *Soziale Marktwirtschaft* . . . produced socially positive results.*

Yet, the conservative-minded, budget-balancing government of Adenauer, Erhard, & Co. recognized that to maintain social harmony, to avoid political discord on the home front, and to promote economic recovery, there would have to be some arbitrary adjustments in the distribution of individual wealth of the West Germans. By mid-1948, German officialdom, as well as the Allied occupation authorities, could get a fairly reasonable approximation of what the lost war had cost the Germans in terms of human casualties and material losses. It was found that some sixteen million adults in West Germany—of whom eight million were refugees from Communist-held Eastern Europe—had lost all, or most of their material possessions, such as their homes and household goods, as well as any personal savings. Millions of these, including all the refugees, now faced an uncertain future with nothing but the shirts on their backs and little else. The new Bonn government had no financial or other resources with which to provide some form of assistance to this large body of destitute citizenry.

However, to meet this situation the Bonn government evolved a unique, mandatory program to partially bridge the gap between those who managed to save something out of the wreckage caused by World War II and those who ended the war penniless and empty-handed. It was based on this simple, nonideological principle: Germany lost the war but every German must have lost it *equally,* as far as possible.

The Bonn parliament, in 1952, passed legislation creating the *Lastenausgleich,* or "equalization of burdens" program. To an American or Englishman, *Lastenausgleich* seemed to be a Socialist-inspired share-the-wealth program, but to the Germans it had no such political or economic connotation. The official government *Bulletin* in its August 30, 1953 issue, explained the background:

Not only these sixteen million people had lost the war, however, but also those other inhabitants of Germany who had suffered no direct material loss. It was therefore only a question of justice to distribute the burden as equally as possible among all and to compensate the former at least in part.

When Finance Minister Schaeffer introduced the equalization program to the Bonn parliament, he said the government considered this the only way to prevent millions of Germans who had lost everything and saw little hope for their future from venting their anger and frustration by joining antidemocratic political movements. *Lastenausgleich* was, in reality, a Socialist-type project by its very character, if not by definition or origin. But it was created by a conservative administration and the Socialist opposition in the parliament had to support it into law. It gave almost one-third, the lower impoverished one-third of the West German population, a reason to hope, as well as a small stake in the future. That in itself helped to defuse a socio-economic problem that had great explosive possibilities if left unattended. Though incredibly complex—the equalization law was over 200 pages long and covered over 400 categories of tax levies and compensations—the program worked something like this:

Ludwig Schmidt, a butcher in prewar Essen, lost his *Metzgerei* and his family home and furnishings above the butcher shop in one of the Allied air raids. He was left without a pfennig of assets at the war's end. He put in a claim for his butcher shop, his family apartment, and all the material possessions that were destroyed by the bombing raid. The equalization office granted him a war-damage compensation of DM 4,200 or about $1,000. This is only 20 percent of the value of what he had actually lost in the war, but 20 percent is better than nothing and it provided him with a small stake to begin life anew in a rebuilt Essen.

Schmidt's aged uncle, Franz Gebhardt, who had formerly lived in

Danzig (now the Polish seaport of Gdansk), was no longer employable because of his years; he was granted a monthly pension of DM 40–60 for the rest of his life as a partial compensation for what he left behind in Communist Eastern Europe.

Meanwhile, Helmut Dockweiler, who lived in neighboring Wuppertal, was one of the Germans who had to shoulder their share of financial assistance to the Schmidts and Gebhardts of the immediate postwar scene. As required by the equalization law, Dockweiler, a small business entrepreneur, had to report in detail the full extent of all his material possessions. He had a small machine shop, a six-room detached house, plus the normal amount of household goods consistent with his lower middle-class status. Fortunately for him, his business and home escaped war damage and his future showed promise as orders piled up.

Dockweiler's material wealth was assessed at DM 35,000 (about $8,300), as of June 22, 1948, the date of the currency reform. He was required to pay a 50-percent capital levy on this assessment, amounting to DM 17,500, which could be settled in regular installments over a 30-year period. Considering that the value of his home and machine shop increased as the economic revival got underway, the equalization burden was not to prove too burdensome for Dockweiler.

In the first twenty years of the operations of the *Lastenausgleich* program, about 84 billion deutschmarks (approximately $28 billion) was extracted from the pockets of the upper two-thirds of West Germany's population and handed over to the impoverished, disaster-stricken lower one-third. Yet, in view of the volume of this monetary turnover, among its many effects on the lives of its recipients, the equalization program served to lubricate the reviving national economy at a time when it needed all the help it could obtain. *Lastenausgleich,* as expected, was an imperfect and criticized solution to bridge the gap between the "haves" and the "have-nots" of an industrial society but it was better than nothing at all.

Yet in a long and detailed survey of how the recovery of West Germany got started, Dr. Blessing wrote in 1954: "To the economist the financing of the recovery of West Germany is an exciting chapter. . . . What makes the financing of the reconstruction so exciting is the fact that it was *not* carried out according to *traditional rules.*"*

This equalization-of-burden project illustrates the pragmatic approach that the West German leaders engaged in to solve a serious problem, which involved bypassing traditional rules. The conservative government had no apologies to make for employing a Socialist-type measure to correct an inequity that otherwise might pose a serious threat to the maintenance of a capitalist system. It must be remembered that Erhard described his system as the *Soziale Marktwirtschaft,* the "socially responsive free-market economy." *Lastenausgleich* was a good example of the freedom of action permitted the conservatives operating under the umbrella of social responsibility.

IO

You German workers are a funny lot. French and English workers want to know how they can be helped in their miserable predicament. You Germans must first be convinced that you *are* in a miserable *predicament*. As long as you have a piece of foul sausage and a glass of beer, you don't notice that you lack anything. That is part of your damned attitude, that you don't need much.

—FERDINAND LASSALLE, *founder of the German labor movement, addressing the first Workers' Association meeting in 1863*

The German trade union structure was built up from scratch after Hitler's war; it is therefore incomparably better suited to the modern age than is Britain's nineteenth-century leftover mess.

—NORMAN MACRAE, *The German Lesson, the* Economist (*London: October 15, 1966*); *an economic survey of postwar Germany.*

LABOR LEARNS FROM
THE PAST

IN THE CLOSING MONTHS of World War II, Hans Boeckler, the leader of the underground movement of the German trade union, was a fugitive from the dreaded Gestapo. After the abortive July 20, 1944 plot to kill Hitler, Boeckler had been listed for immediate arrest as a possible member of the assassination conspiracy. Boeckler escaped capture by hiding out in remote mountain villages in the Bavarian Alps. When he emerged into the postwar world, Boeckler had arrived at some very definite and positive conclusions as to the role that organized labor must play in the rebuilding of his country and its return to normalcy. The plans that he formulated were to have a decisive and far-reaching effect on the economic revival of West Germany.

Under Boeckler's strong leadership, the trade-union movement concentrated on acquiring economic power, rather than overt political power, as the prerequisite to achieving its major objectives. Henceforth the postwar trade-union movement, officially at least, would be politically neutral in national and local elections. It would avoid getting entangled in the conflicts of the political arena. This was a sharp break with tradition. The German trade unions had always been politically motivated since the first

Workers' Association had been founded in 1863 by Ferdinand Lassalle, shortly after Bismarck came to power. The fortunes of organized labor from its earliest days had been bound up with the struggling Socialist party. In 1877 the Socialists achieved their first impressive electoral victory, winning twelve seats in the *Reichstag*. The following year Bismarck forced through a law banning all political activity for the Socialist party. Only those party members who were deputies of the *Reichstag,* enjoyed parliamentary immunity from police harassment, while continuing to have the right of free speech. The trade unions' journals were also closed down by Bismarck's laws and their assets confiscated. Thus political power, in terms of membership in the national parliament, began to assume top priority in the eyes of the Socialists and the trade unionists. Political power was seen as necessary to survival, as well as for the growth and influence of the trade unions.

Meanwhile, after Lassalle died prematurely in 1864, his role as the leader of the embryonic trade-union movement was later assumed by August Bebel, who also became head of the struggling SDP. A carpenter by trade, he was a self-educated man. The great historian Theodor Mommsen said that if Bebel's brain could have been divided among a dozen Junker aristocrats east of the Elbe, each one of them would have enough cerebral power to outshine any of his peers. Bebel spent five of the next twenty years in prison for his political activity, charged with spreading doctrines dangerous to the state. He and his lieutenants were intensely politically minded men. The SDP, more than the trade-union movement, was constantly under attack from Bismarck's government. Hence political power in the form of a bloc of Socialist deputies in the *Reichstag* was the only effective weapon with which to defend the SDP against the government's efforts to eliminate it from the political scene.

In 1890 the Socialists won 35 seats in the *Reichstag* and polled 1,400,000 votes nationwide. Bismarck had resigned and the new Kaiser Wilhelm II, seeking to win popularity with the workers, had the anti-Socialist laws repealed. However, five years later the Kaiser labeled the Socialist deputies in the *Reichstag* a "gang of traitors" and added that socialism must be wiped out. However, this was no longer possible, for the trade-union movement was growing in power and influence. As the industrialization of Germany accelerated in the last years of the nineteenth century, trade-union membership increased tenfold, from 250,000 to over 2,500,000.

At one point there was almost a complete marriage between the trade unions and the SDP. In the 1906 party conference at Mannheim, a resolution was offered to make the trade unions subordinate to the policy decision of the Socialist party. This was defeated and marks a milestone in the history of organized labor. From that point on, the German trade-union movement adjusted its immediate goals to the world in which it had to exist, rather than to work for the establishment of a Socialist state.

Trade unions flourished in the years before World War I. The government did not interfere with the right to organize workers into cadres of unions. Wages and working conditions improved as a result; skilled workers began to earn as much as six marks a day, or about $8–9 a week. By contrast with the worker's lot in other European nations, conditions in Germany were far superior. Samuel Gompers, president of the American Federation of Labor, visited the Ruhr in 1909 and reported that the German worker appeared to live in a period of "the greatest production, the highest general intelligence and the best reasons for hope for his class that the history of the world has ever recorded."*

After World War II, Hans Boeckler was determined that the trade-union movement would learn from the mistakes of the past. In Boeckler's opinion, the principal mistake was the erroneous premise that political power was necessary to provide a firm foundation for the movement. Another long-held trade-union dogma was the belief that if there were sufficient numbers of Socialists in the prewar *Reichstag,* the economic objectives of organized labor could be achieved.

However, a quick review of recent history disclosed that these assumptions were false. The trade-union leaders and the Socialists, who represented the biggest single party bloc in the *Reichstag* in the immediate post-World War I period, had not been able to prevent the massive inflation of the reichsmark of 1922–23, which had wiped out the savings and property of the working classes. Nor in the following years had the trade unions and Socialists been able to prevent Hitler, their deadly enemy, from seizing power in 1933 and replacing a failing democracy with a dictatorship. Once installed in office, Hitler had swiftly liquidated the trade-union movement, arresting its leaders and confiscating the assets of the unions. The Nazi Labor Front, a captive labor movement, took over as the leadership of the working classes. Prior to Hitler, there had been three trade union organizations: the Socialist group, the Catholic labor organization, and a so-called liberal trade union. These three often quarreled with each other, to the ultimate harm of the whole labor movement.

Boeckler set out to achieve three major objectives in the postwar re-creation of a national trade-union movement: there would be one big master union; the trade-union organization would be politically neutral and not allied to any party, which meant separation from the Social Democrats; and organized labor would share with the owners and their executives in the day-to-day management of German industry.

This third objective was revolutionary in its concept; perhaps evolutionary is a more precise description. Taken to its logical conclusion, it meant abandoning the traditional and major socialist tenet that "nationalization of industry" was the best and most expeditious method to ensure that the wages and working conditions demanded by workers could be guaranteed permanently. In its place, Boeckler proposed *Mitbestimmung,* that it, joint management of industry by representatives of the trade unions and owners on an equal basis. In short, instead of trying to take over a factory and run it themselves by nationalizing the industrial plant, the workers, through their representatives, would sit down with the owners at the directors' table to coordinate company policies and practices.

If the conservative elements of the new West German state enjoyed a special relationship with the U.S. military government, the postwar trade-union movement and the Socialist party developed their own special kinship with the Labor government in London and its representatives in British occupation forces in Germany. The British occupation zone included the Ruhr, the industrial heart of West Germany, where the Socialists and the trade unions marshaled their greatest strength. The British regarded the surviving trade-union leaders as the only group of anti-Nazis who could be trusted. Hence the British authorities gave full encouragement and support to Boeckler and his deputy, August Schmidt, head of the coal miners union, as they began to organize the postwar trade-union movement.*

The British also strongly cautioned Boeckler against creating a single trade union to represent all the workers of a wide variety of industries and service trades. It would be too unwieldy and subject to splintering, as various dissident factions rejected the master policy decisions. The British brought over two leading trade-union officials from London to confer with Boeckler. As a result, he accepted their recommendation to form a single union for each of the major industries and service trades and then to group them all together in a federation of trade unions. Thus, the Deutscher Gewerkshaftsbund (DGB) was officially formed and launched in a trade-union conference in Munich in October 1949. Hans Boeckler was elected chairman of the federation, which then comprised over 5 million workers. By 1953 national membership had climbed to six million out of a national work force of 17 million.

The new postwar labor organization was designed for the present and the foreseeable future. It was a clean break with the pre-Hitler past and with the traditions and outlook of the jerry-built structure of a one hundred politically divided craft unions which existed before the Nazis came to power. The old and underlying motif of class warfare and other Marxist ideology became muted in the early postwar months and years, as the trade-union leaders focused their attention on the material needs and demands of the workers. In short, organized labor began to emerge from its postwar cocoon as an economic commodity rather than a political force.

This change resulted from the new organization structure of the DGB, which now comprised sixteen industrial and service trade unions ranging from the largest, I. G. Metall with 1.6 million members, to the Artists Union with 33,000 members. The unique feature of this postwar arrangement was that each union represented and bargained for all grades and types of workers within each industry. A prime example of this umbrella-type labor union was I. G. Metall, which covers anyone who works in any way with metal. Thus, I. G. Metall represents the iron and steelworkers in the Ruhr, the auto workers at the Volkswagen plant in Wolfsburg, the machinery builders in Essen, the electrical equipment employees at Siemens in West Berlin, and so on; i.e., anyone who processes, fabricates, distributes, or repairs industrial products made of metal.

For example, when the management of Daimler-Benz at Stuttgart and the trade-union representative meet to negotiate a new wage contract, I. G. Metall speaks for all the workers on the assembly line, in the offices, and in the adjoining production facilities. By contrast, in a British automotive plant, separate contracts must be negotiated with each of fifteen different craft unions which cover all types of labor involved with British car production. The advantages of this German innovation to both business and labor alike are obvious. It meets the needs of the time and the circumstances. Another important simplification of labor-management relations is that all wages are negotiated in percentage points rather than in deutschemarks and pfennigs. For example, if I. G. Metall asks the Ruhr steel producers for a 12-percent pay increase and settles for an 8-percent boost, then everybody (except management) connected with steel production—from the men operating the giant blast furnaces to the night watchmen and typists—will get an 8-percent jump in their weekly pay envelope at all the Ruhr steel mills.

There is none of the trade-union practice, as employed in the U.S., of picking out the weakest or most vulnerable firm in an industry, and extracting a favorable wage contract from it, which then sets the pattern for the other stronger firms in the same industrial group. Negotiations and contracts within an industry differ, due to geographical circumstances or regional subdivisions of the unions. I. G. Metall, for example, may agree to a wage contract with Daimler-Benz at Sindelfingen in the southwest corner of Germany, and then negotiate a slightly different wage contract with the workers in the giant Volkswagen plant at Wolfsburg in the northeast corner of the country, because of variations in the cost-of-living indices throughout West Germany.

Though each of the sixteen master unions that make up the federation is autonomous and theoretically independent, the DGB sets the broad policy lines and strategy for labor-management disputes. The control which the DGB exercises over the sixteen unions is largely the power of the purse; the DGB can withhold or grant financial support to strikers. Without the financial backing of the DGB, no union can risk calling a strike that may collapse for lack of funds to pay the living expenses of the strikers.

The German trade unions have never been as convinced of the effectiveness, or as willing to support strikes as a means to settling labor-management disputes, as their fellow Europeans, such as the French, Italians, and the British trade unionists. Even August Bebel, the political firebrand who went to prison for his strong political convictions about the rights of labor in Bismarckian times, often cautioned his workers against a strike. He feared that utilizing the weapon of a major or general strike would earn the labor unions the enmity of the general public.

This same feeling still permeates organized labor in Germany today. Hence the DGB established an elaborate formula for calling an official strike. The DGB must be consulted first. If it does not object to the strike proposal, the matter is put to the full membership of the industrial union concerned. If 75 percent of its members vote yes, a strike can be called and the union becomes eligible for strike funds. At this point the DGB steps in to direct the strike action and to negotiate directly to settle the dispute. Failure to follow these procedures makes any strike unofficial under German labor laws. The workers and unions can be forced to pay damages commensurate with the losses of those firms that were involved in the strike.

Both Hans Boeckler and Christian Fette, his successor as head of the DGB, recognized that the trade unions must accept a greater degree of responsibility for the actions of their members if they wished to acquire a greater participation in the management of the national economy. Hence the DGB supported the Wage Agreements Act, in which the mutual obligations of the employers and the unions were spelled out. This makes all collective agreements legally binding on both parties and provides for financial penalties in cases where unofficial strikes or lockouts are called.

In those early formative years, West Germany was almost 100 percent strike-free, but this was largely due to an overhang of about 1.3 million unemployed men on the labor market during the 1949–51 period. The Korean War boom began to create new jobs as the repair and reconstruction of the manufacturing plants and equipment spurted forward.* Labor peace continued—except for a spate of wildcat strikes of short duration in 1955—without much interruption during the following years. For example, for the years 1957, 1958, and 1959, the number of working days lost through strike action in West Germany was as follows: 2,386,000, 712,000, and 62,000. For the same three years, the number of strike days lost in Great Britain was 8,412,000, 3,466,000, and 5,251,000. West Germany and Britain were comparable: the *Bundesrepublik* had 20 million workers and a total population of 52 million in 1959; Britain had 21.8 million workers out of a total population of 51.6 million.*

But there were other compelling reasons for the fact that West Germany had fewer and less costly strikes than any of the major industrial nations. Until the middle of the 1950s the DGB had no cash reserves with which to finance a major strike. However the incentive to strike was lacking because, from 1951 onward, the gross weekly earnings of the industrial worker began to steadily forge ahead of the cost-of-living index. For example, the following statistics show this development:

	COST OF LIVING*	INDUSTRIAL WAGES (IN PERCENTAGES)
June 1948	152	100.7
June 1949	169	130
June 1950	156	150.5
June 1951	169	181
June 1952	171	187
June 1953	169	201

* 1938 = 100.
SOURCE: Economics Ministry

This was one of the first dividends of the conservative and anti-inflationary economic policies of Ministers Erhard and Schaeffer and Dr. Vocke of the Bundesbank. It was to result in a long and sustained period of tranquil labor-management relations. However the greatest stimulus to labor peace came from the instinctive need of the workers for their own economic security. In general, the trade unions recognized that everybody was in the same boat; the bosses and the workers alike were making the same voyage, sharing the same perils of the high seas. They would not reach the safety of the home port unless everybody, the bosses and workers, acted with a sense of responsibility and discipline in this time of uncertainty and peril.

There was an understanding, a gentlemen's agreement, between labor and management during the first years of the 1950s. For example, when it could be shown that a manufacturer was plowing back a goodly share of his profits into the reconstruction and modernization of his factory—thereby increasing its productivity and its sales—the workers in general refrained from demanding wage increases. This was not exactly altruism. It was, rather, an act of enlightened self-interest on the part of organized labor. The owner bettered his competitive position on the domestic and export markets through his capital investments in new plant and equipment; at the same time he was providing greater job security for his workers. As long as the owners kept reinvesting their earnings in their respective industrial enterprises, the trade unions did not apply pressure for wage increases.* When multiplied by thousands of instances, as was the rule in West Germany, it was one of the major factors for the economic miracle that was to surprise the Western world by its swift blossoming in the 1950s and 1960s. It was another confirmation of the old maxim: don't hassle the goose that lays the golden eggs.

*   *   *

Just before he died in 1951, Hans Boeckler said during an interview:

Mitbestimmungsrecht [the codetermination law] is my last trade union fight and I mean to see it through. You do not know the German industrialist as I do, and whatever else happens after I am gone, I want to be sure at least our trade union movement sits behind closed doors and knows what is going on. We will at least have a chance of preventing the kind of sell-out by industry to Hitler that we experienced in 1933.*

The idea of worker participation in the management of an industrial company is not new in Germany. It first surfaced in the 1848 revolution; it was again revived and made a part of the constitution of the abortive Weimar Republic after World War I. Article 165 of this constitution laid down that:

Manual and non-manual workers are authorized, as equal partners with employers, to participate in the determination of their terms and conditions of employment and in the overall development of the productive forces of the nation.

But not until the end of World War II did *Mitbestimmung* codetermination, become a reality. The British military government arbitrarily imposed codetermination on what remained of the great Ruhr coal and steel industries. The British were going to make sure that never again would the Ruhr barons be in a position to utilize their great industrial power to promote their own political or economic objectives without outside supervision and controls. This could be done by giving representatives of the workers equal status on the boards of directors of the Ruhr firms. This action was fully supported by Hans Boeckler, who wished to perpetuate it by the passage of a *Mitbestimmungsrecht* by the Bonn parliament. There were several strong motivating factors behind Boeckler's compulsion to make codetermination the law of the land.

Trade-union leaders who survived World War II were somewhat on the defensive for not having put up a stronger and more determined effort to block Hitler and his cohorts from coming to power; Nazis were helped by the money and the influence of the Ruhr barons. A *Mitbestimmungsrecht* on the statute books would help atone for that historical mistake.

However the concept of actual participation in the management of heavy industry on an equal basis with the owners quickly captured the imagination and enthusiasm of the DGB leadership. It fulfilled the desire of the workers for a "living ideology," as Professor Wallich pointed out in his survey:

The strength of German labor had in the past derived largely from the intensity with which it adhered to its Marxist creed. Now the old belief in socialization was waning, but German labor could not conceive of itself without some ideological banner. Co-determination—the German word *Mitbestimmungsrecht* has much more punch—seemed to have the makings of a new faith.*

It has been argued by some observers of the postwar German scene that Boeckler and the DGB devoted more time and energy to promoting codetermination than they gave to boosting the weekly incomes of the working classes. However, this does not seem to make them derelict in their responsibilities to the West German laborer. The trade-union leaders set their sights on the executive suites of the big corporations; if they could share with the owners in the actual management of industry, such matters as wages and working conditions of their members could be satisfactorily handled, all in good time.

What was involved in the eyes of businessmen and conservative politicians was a thinly disguised grab for economic power. In the ensuing controversy, Boeckler and his colleagues would have to muster all their political and economic resources to gain victory and seats at the directors' tables in the corporate board rooms throughout the *Bundesrepublik*.

After the August 1949 national election installed a conservative government in power, Boeckler realized that the DGB would have to settle for the continuance of the codetermination imposed by the British on the Ruhr's coal and steel industries. He could not hope to get a *Mitbestimmungsrecht* covering all industrial firms. So Boeckler prepared his groundwork carefully. He polled the coal and steelworkers union and found 95 percent in favor of making codetermination permanent under German law. He then announced there would be a strike of these two unions in February, 1951 to underscore the DGB's demand for a *Mitbestimmungsrecht* for the coal and steel industries. This done, he called on Chancellor Adenauer.

The two men were contemporaries; both were born in 1876. Both were old friends, and in pre-Hitler times, had worked together in the administration of the city of Cologne. Boeckler, a metal worker with a passion for social justice, had entered politics, becoming a member of the Cologne City Council while Adenauer was lord mayor. Adenauer was not opposed to codetermination in principle; he had stated that the new *Bundesrepublik* must have "an economic system suited to our times." But he told Boeckler that using the threat of a major strike to force parliamentary approval was not the way to achieve his objectives. Boeckler agreed to let the cabinet, together with representatives of Ruhr industry, work out the draft of a law that would be approved by the *Bundestag*. However before they parted, Adenauer asked Boeckler to henceforth have the DGB drop all further demands and plans for the socialization or nationalization of industry. Boeckler did not make any specific promises, but after codetermination became law, organized labor ended its open advocacy for public ownership of industry. This was acceptable, for codetermination seemed to offer to the working classes all the advantages of public ownership and it wouldn't cost a pfennig.

A few weeks before the *Mitbestimmungsrecht* was approved by the two major parties, the conservative Christian Democrats and the Socialists,

Hans Boeckler died of a heart attack. He was given the equivalent of a state funeral, attended by the president of the *Bundesrepublik,* Theodore Heuss, Chancellor Adenauer, political leaders, bankers, prominent industrialists, as well as thousands of mourning workers. Flags were at half-mast throughout the republic. These honors paid to the dead man seemed to signal the new era in labor-management relations that was dawning. Indeed, whatever else *Mitbestimmung* accomplished, it ushered in a long period of labor peace and productivity that was to further strengthen the economic recovery of West Germany.

But *Mitbestimmung's* bark was worse than its bite. The Ruhr's industrial hierarchy, as well as its bankers, had feared that the smooth running of the coal and steel industries would be thrown out of gear when the representatives of the workers took their places on the various *Aufsichträte,* the supervisory boards of directors of the big corporations. They had expected that organized labor would start raiding their treasuries for higher wages and fringe benefits at the expense of profits and capital investments. They feared that the new labor-nominated *Arbeitsdirektor,* the director of personnel, who was equal to the other chief executives, would further interfere with functioning by coddling the workers with fringe benefits and other costly concessions.

The law provided for equal membership on the board of directors for representatives of trade unions and the owners, plus a neutral chairman. The odd man on each *Aufsichträt* was the chairman who cast a deciding vote in any deadlock. He was usually an outsider, but a respected member of the community, such as a university professor, acceptable to both sides.

But the specter of an invasion of the executive suites by uncouth, rough-speaking workers, nominated as *Herr Direktoren,* making impossible demands and thoroughly disrupting the normal operations of coal and steel companies just did not materialize. On the contrary, organized labor suddenly found itself caught in a dilemma. Within the ranks of labor, the trade-union leaders could not organize a cadre of men with adequate educational and intellectual backgrounds who could cope with their new duties and responsibilities as *Herr Direktoren.* This situation would obviously place them at a disadvantage as they sat across the table from the professional and experienced directors of the corporate elite of the Ruhr. As a result, the trade unions hastily recruited economists, lawyers, and other educated men to serve as the representatives of the workers. For example, I. G. Bergbau, the coal miners union, had to nominate seventy-five men to fill the labor directorships on the supervisory boards. Only two of these appointees had actual coal-mining experience.

This employment of outside talent by the labor unions no doubt made their teams of labor directors more intellectually presentable; but there is question of how much these pseudolabor directors knew about the problems and demands of the steel workers and coal miners at the meetings of the *Aufsichträte*.

This deficiency in trade-union officials forced the DGB to establish three schools in Hamburg, Frankfurt, and Dortmund to train young men for future appointments to the supervisory boards of directors of German industry, as well as in all aspects of labor's future relations with industry and the business community in general.

In addition, the labor federation canvased German universities with attractive job offers for graduates to make a career in the field of economic administration from the labor side. Specialized training programs in this area of labor-management relations is a progressive step forward—and also a step further away from Socialist doctrine, which had dominated labor's thinking since the middle of the nineteenth century.

Another related development arising out of this shortage of executive talent has been the enlisting of the same top executives of the DGB and the coal miners and steelworkers unions as new codetermination directors for the giant Ruhr corporations. In 1961, for example, eight top executives of DGB served on twenty-three supervisory boards in the coal and steel industries. Ten top officials of I. G. Metall held twenty directorships, while the head of this union, "Iron Otto" Brenner, sat on five separate boards. The eleven top executives of I. G. Bergbau held twenty-three seats on various boards.

What was the extent of the power and influence that the labor representatives brought to bear on the great Ruhr coal and steel industries? Perhaps the answer can be found in the fact that at this writing in 1977, the labor-management relationship in the Ruhr is pretty much what it was. There have been no great structural changes in these industries as a result of *Mitbestimmungsrecht*. The predicted economic revolution has not taken place; the free enterprise capitalistic system is still operating at a profit. If anything, the great experiment in industrial partnership between labor and the owners has tended to make the trade unions more management-minded.

In 1952 I had to make a detailed survey of *Mitbestimmung* for the *Wall Street Journal*. I find in my notes some candid comments by prominent industrialists and bankers which I could not print at the time. Hermann Winkhaus of Mannesmann told me bluntly that, on the basis of his experience sitting on the board of his firm from the earliest days of *Mitbestimmung*: "As long as things go along good, there won't be any trouble. If we could have four years of unbroken prosperity, I can educate these labor directors to see the light on how business should be conducted, but if we have bad times, they will take their orders from the DGB."

Herr Winkhaus had many times four years to educate his labor colleagues in the arts of management. Dr. Johannes Zahn, head of Trinkaus Bank and a member of five boards of directors in the Ruhr coal and steel industries, said during the same year: "It has become a general practice for the representatives of management and the shareholders to hold informal meetings in advance of regular board meetings. Then we discuss and decide among ourselves questions of business policy and operations. . . . Then the regular board meetings, which are attended by the labor directors, are devoted to discussions and decisions about social welfare, pensions, and other routine matters. In times of stress and recession, we have our doubts whether the trade unions can control the workers. We shall wait and see. Our primary task is to get the labor directors onto our side. I think it can be done."

Codetermination has changed perceptibly the economic and political opinions of the representatives of the workers serving on the boards of directors and as personnel managers of the coal and steel firms. It shook many of them loose from their deeply ingrained Marxist beliefs. After all, Marx's *Das Kapital* gave no guidance regarding the need for capital investments, sometimes at the expense of increased wages for the workers; or on how to meet a payroll of several thousand workers each month. Nor did Socialist dogma reconcile the conflicting demands of the workers for higher wages and better working conditions with management's different priorities on profits and survival in a very competitive world at home and abroad. The first lesson was simple: a modern industrial plant cannot be operated at a profit by adherence to a set political principle. The second lesson was equally fundamental: the job security of workers depends on the firm being operated in a businesslike manner. The new labor *Herr Direktoren* were now part of management; if their firm's sales began to drop and workers had to be laid off as a result, they too would share in the blame and criticism directed at management. Hence the new labor representatives had to educate themselves to the realities of industrial administration. If anything, this situation introduced a note of caution in their policy and decision-making.

Perhaps the most subtle and pervasive influences that gradually induced the new *Herr Direktoren* of the labor unions to become more management minded were personal financial considerations. Once installed in the corporate board rooms and executive suites, their incomes and living standards increased handsomely. A worker appointed to serve on a board of directors of a coal or steel firm would receive an annual fee ranging from DM 5,000 to DM 50,000, for attending the regular board meetings, usually one every three months. In addition, he received all the "perks" and other emoluments that were given to the directors representing the shareholders. If the coal or steel firm had a profitable year, the directors usually received substantial Christmas bonuses, as well as a share in the profits. For example, in 1960, Willy Richter, chairman of the DGB, received DM 47,498 and Ernst Striefler, a top official of I. G. Metall, was paid DM 31,972 for services as labor directors on the board of August-Thyssenhütte, the Ruhr's biggest steel company.

A trade-union member who received an appointment as *Arbeitsdirektor,* or personnel director, became a member of the *Vorstand*,* which is the top executive committee of a large corporation. The *Arbeitsdirektor,* as a full-time administrative officer, received the same salary and perks as the two other members of the *Vorstand,* the production and finance directors. This meant, for example, in the case of Bernard Jung, the new personnel director of Hibernia, A. G., the big coal mining company at Herne, a salary of DM 50,000 per year, compared with the DM 10,000 he formerly earned as a local trade-union official. He was given a furnished suburban villa complete with a maid, and full maintenance and taxes paid by Hibernia. Jung was also authorized a lavish expense account to cover a substantial portion of his normal living expenses. He was given a Mercedes with a chauffeur plus gasoline expenses. Socially speaking, he was no longer *Genosse*—Comrade Jung—but *Herr Direktor* to those whom he encountered inside or outside the executive offices of Hibernia A. G. As *Arbeitsdirektor* of Hibernia, Jung was appointed to a four-year term in office by his labor directors on the *Aufsichträt.* He can be dismissed only by them. The law makes him independent of and equal with the two other members of the *Vorstand,* but he must follow the general policy lines set forth by the supervisory board.

None of the old-line Ruhr industrialists would admit publicly that *Mitbestimmung* was not the threat to normal operations that its opponents had predicted. However, many expressed confidence, privately, that the new labor nominees could be converted to a managerial attitude. As an example of a conversion, they cited the trade unionist who became *Arbeitsdirektor* of Edelstahlwerk at Krefeld. In his new position he was responsible for maintaining the productivity level of the workers. He became convinced that many of them were not giving a full day's labor for their day's pay, so he installed time clocks; the subsequent protests by the employees cost him his executive post.

In 1952 the Works Council Act (*Betriebsverfassungsgesetz*) was passed, which gave the workers one-third representation on the boards of directors of all companies with twenty or more employees. In addition, in each of these companies a works council (*Betriebsrat*) was created to act as spokesman and guardian for workers' rights on all matters concerning wages and working conditions. The *Betriebsrat*'s members are elected by the workers in each company. It is protected by law from any interference or restriction whatsoever by management. While the Works Council is an effective representative of the worker in the executive suites, the one-third worker participation on the *Aufsichträt* in companies covered by the Works Constitution Act "has been largely illusory" and inconsequential.*

After months of long, loud, heated debate and negotiations, the Socialist-Free Democratic coalition government managed to agree on a compromise law in March 1976 extending *Mitbestimmung* to all industrial corporations employing two thousand or more workers. However this law does not give organized labor a 50–50 split of the directorships on the

Aufsichträte. Instead, one of the members of labor's panel of directors must be a senior salaried executive (*Leitende Angestellte*) of the firm involved. In any deadlock, he will obviously cast his vote with the representatives of the shareholders, thereby assuring that their views will prevail in crucial decisions.

The tone of moderation that permeated the German trade unions explains in part why there was so little opposition from organized labor to the automation and computerization of German industry beginning in the 1960s. German workers did not react with fear and anger to the introduction of electronic controls that took the place of workers on the assembly line, as, for example, did the Luddites who rioted and destroyed the textile-weaving machines in England in 1811 because they caused the unemployment of hand workers.

Through the works councils, each phase of automation was explained in advance and the companies found other jobs for men who were displaced by the computer-controlled machinery. Equally important, there was the understanding that automation was an integral part of the modernization of German industry which would make German products more competitive on world markets. In the final analysis, this meant greater job security for the German workers and made automation understandable and therefore acceptable. This frame of mind also explains why public opinion polls for years consistently showed that job security ranked first in the demands and objectives of the workers themselves, even ahead of the prospect of higher wages.

Organized labor and management have coexisted in a fairly amicable fashion in postwar Germany to their mutual profit—much more so than in Britain, France, and Italy. One of the important factors contributing to this state of affairs has been a unique instrument of continuous negotiations—*Konzertierte Aktion,* concerted action. In reality this instrument has been designed to perpetuate and to foster the large measure of consensus that has flowered between labor and management since *Mitbestimmung* became the law of the land.

Concerted action was introduced by Prof. Karl Schiller, the right-wing Socialist who became economics minister in the grand coalition government of the CDU–SPD for the 1966–69 period. It was a part of a comprehensive measure to promote economic stability in the face of rising prices. In practice, concerted action calls for regular conferences—three to four times yearly—between leaders of German business and industry, the trade unions, experts of the ministry of economics, as well as representatives of the Bundesbank and the government's council of economic advisers ("the five wise men"). The conferences are purposely kept small and informal, to encourage the frank and ready expressions of ideas and opinions, as well as a free and uninhibited exchange of economic information. These exchanges of information and opinions lead to better understanding and knowledge of the economic problems involved—such as how to handle the cyclical ups and downs of economic activity. They also serve to encourage compromise solutions in labor-management disputes.

For example, if in a concerted-action meeting the economics minister discloses the government's plans or objectives for the coming months, or if the *Bundesbank* president forecasts that the discount rate may have to be raised or lowered, then both business and labor leaders can make their plans with some degree of assurance. They are also encouraged to come to reasonable terms about wages and prices based on the information furnished them. How well concerted action operates was shown during the growing recession in 1975. Labor, business, and government experts concluded that new capital investments were crucial to economic recovery. As a result, labor agreed to keep its wage demands below 6 percent if business carried out the promised capital spending. After this agreement was reached, the two principals had some noteworthy comments. Heinz-Oskar Vetter, chairman of the DGB, said: "We have been engaged in a revolutionary social experiment. We have agreed to hold down our wage demands to give industry a chance to make the investments that will create new jobs. This fall and next summer will show if the other side has kept its part of the bargain."

On behalf of the Federation of Employers Association, Dr. Hans Martin Schleyer had this comment about his consensus partners: "The labor unions, despite all the conflicts we have had with them, have contributed to the stability and health of the economy in recent years by showing a great deal of responsibility."*

Hence it would appear that the *raison d'être* of concerted action is being achieved and that it is likely to remain operative. Shortly after that crucial concerted action session, Chancellor Helmut Schmidt paid his official Bicentennial visit to America in July 1976. Accompanying him and constantly at his side were two witnesses to labor-management consensus: Heinz-Oskar Vetter and Hans Martin Schleyer. Concerted action is a political and economic fact of life in today's Germany.

Hans Boeckler, founder of the West German trade-union federation, laid down the basic principle that organized labor must seek economic power and influence in order to accomplish its objectives in the chaotic postwar world. He rejected political action as the road to power. However, he had been thinking only in terms of *Mitbestimmung*—the concept of the owners and the workers as equal partners, sharing in the daily management of industrial corporations. While he did not live to see it, the surging economic recovery of West Germany has given organized labor far more economic power and influence, measured in tangible assets worth billions of deutschemarks, than Boeckler could ever have envisaged in his most optimistic frame of mind. To his credit, however, he pointed organized labor in the right direction.

The trade-union federation, together with its largest industrial unions, has become big business itself. It owns and operates West Germany's largest business conglomerate, the Beteiligungschaft für Gemeinwirtschaft A.G. (BGAG), with total assets of $25 billion and which, in 1977, produced a net income of DM 5.4 billion ($2.2 billion). BGAG, which employs over 40,000 persons, comprises a mixed bag including the newest addition to the coterie of *Grossbanken,* the Bank für Gemeinwirtschaft (BfG), with assets of $23 billion.* Also included in the BGAG portfolio is Co-op Zentrale, Germany's second biggest retailing chain, with an annual turnover of $5 billion from its 5,000 food and furniture stores; its 52 supermarkets; 9 department stores; 30 factories; Volksfürsorge Lebens-Versicherung, a major life-insurance company; as well as a large printing company; a computer service company; and an advertising agency. In addition, the DGB holds 51 percent and the BGAG 49 percent of the shares of Neue Heimat, Europe's largest housing-development agency. Through its 30 affiliates, Neue Heimat in turn is the owner of 230,000 housing units, making it the largest single real-estate proprietor in West Germany. And as a nonprofit company, it has tax-exempt status, which contributes enormously to its competitive position in the German real-estate market.

Today the West German trade-union organization is big, wealthy, and, based on its impressive total of assets, an economic powerhouse fully able to fend for itself in any confrontation with West Germany's corporate giants. The DGB now comes to the bargaining table for annual negotiations concerning wages and working conditions, as an equal to management —at least in terms of the economic muscle it can muster. For almost three decades the federation has been collecting its 15 percent share of all trade-union dues paid in by its millions of members. Because West Germany has been virtually free of any serious, sustained labor-management conflict since the end of World War II, the DGB has not had to dip into its reserve to support the workers who have gone on strike. In turn, its dues income has been invested in a variety of business enterprises which serve the needs of the workers. In effect, the DGB, together with the BGAG, has been transformed into a vast and mushrooming paternalistic commercial empire, flying the house flag of organized labor. The millions of its members buy their food, clothing, furniture, household appliances, and many other consumer items in the Co-op Zentrale stores; they rent an apartment from Neue Heimat or borrow its money to build their own house; they keep their savings in the Bank für Gemeinwirtschaft; and insure their lives with Volksfürsorge Lebens-Versicherung. Millions of German workers not only support the trade unions and DGB with their monthly dues, they also provide the greater part of the tremendous income that is the life-

blood of the multibillion-deutschemark commercial and financial conglomerate which has been created by organized labor in the last quarter-
century.

It is indeed ironic that the German trade unions, originally formed to
fight against repressive working conditions and a lack of economic freedom, imposed on the masses of laborers by the Ruhr barons in the nineteenth century, have become, in the last half of the twentieth century, the
embodiment of big business themselves. Organized labor now has a big
financial stake in the West German economy. Leaders of the trade-union
federation must now think in terms of profits and losses for its multibillion-
DM conglomerate enterprises, as well as higher wages and shorter work-
weeks for its millions of members. The DGB must shift from its traditional
worker policy outlook to become more management-minded, in the light
of its $25-billion stake in the nation's economy. The profitable growth of
commercial side of the trade-union movement, which seems to be another
case of the tail wagging the dog, is a confirmation of the special eco-political
character of the new postwar Germany. Despite ideological bloodlines going
back to Karl Marx, the trade unions, through BGAG, have invested their
savings and reserves, as well as their future, in the healthy functioning of
a capitalistic free-market economic system.

II

When the Germans began to reconstruct their economy, they built upon the familiar structural foundations and plan, much of it invisible to the naked eye, as if guided by an archaeologist who could pick his way blindfold about some favorite ruin.

—ANDREW SHONFIELD, Modern Capitalism,
Oxford University Press

DER WEG ZURÜCK
(THE ROAD BACK)

O N August 11, 1949, the *New York Herald Tribune* published an interview with Dr. Hjalmar Schacht, Germany's leading international financier of the period between the two world wars, which was surprisingly relevant concerning the role that industry would play in the postwar economic recovery of West Germany. At that time Schacht's ideas and opinions attracted scant attention: he was a prophet without honor in his own land, discredited and ignored by the public and business community because he had served Hitler as president of the Reichsbank for the years 1933–39. Though he was at times politically amoral and conceited, he had not lost his formidable financial acumen. Few in Europe could match Doctor Schacht's market sensitivity in the realm of international economic affairs.

The former central banker was making his comments at a time when the cold war was at its height and when the West German economy was taking its first hesitant steps along the road to recovery. He announced in his rather aggressive and condescending fashion that he had a plan for the recovery of West Germany that would not cost the Western world a single dollar. This would involve the creation of a European economic union in which Germany would produce most of the heavy industrial goods. In return for its goods and services in this field, West Germany could be paid off in food and consumer goods. Schacht—and everybody else for that matter—was aware that East Germany, which had produced the grain and potatoes and other basic foodstuffs for the German nation, was now cut off by the Iron Curtain. This necessitated finding new sources of food for the sixty million West Germans now deprived of their traditional breadbasket. The *Bundesrepublik* was also shut out of Germany's traditional export markets in Eastern Europe and the Balkans, which were now under Communist economic regimes. New outlets had to be found for the products of the Ruhr to keep West Germany's workers employed and fed.

Schacht expanded his plan to suggest that West Germany's big industrial firms be harnessed into massive development projects in Africa and Asia. These should be organized within the framework of America's Point IV Program of technical assistance, as laid down by President Truman. Schacht fleshed out his ideas as follows:

Creation of these projects would provide Western Germany with desperately needed outlets for its industrial products, and most important, it would furnish markets that are non-competitive to present Western European production . . . Germany's main problem for the future is to find some means of exchanging its industrial output and technical skill for the vast food imports that are necessary . . . unless Germany finds markets abroad sufficient to permit a decent standard of living, economic pressures will inevitably drive the country into making a deal with the Russians.*

Though Schacht's plan made little impact at the time, he had accurately pinpointed the essentials of Germany's problem of postwar survival. Ever since the turn of the twentieth century, Germany had been a heavily industrialized nation, straddling the center of the European continent. It processed raw materials into manufactured goods and sold them to the Russians and eastern Europeans, to the Balkans and middle eastern states, to the Mediterranean states in the south and to the Scandinavian bloc in the North, to pay for its large imports of food and raw materials. At the close of World War II, Germany had no export markets left. On paper, at least, it was a country without a present or a future; Germany could not change its geography or its infrastructure. Its traditional markets to the east were closed off by the Iron Curtain; the Western industrial nations were hostile to the ex-enemy state. But Germany, burdened down with Europe's greatest concentration of industrial capacity in the Ruhr, had to find new markets for her exports or perish like the prehistoric dinosaur. However, due to the curious juxtaposition of time and circumstances, this modern industrial dinosaur was given a new lease on life. What at first seemed to be a heavy liability proved in a relatively short period to be a hidden asset which would enable West Germany to begin *Der Weg Zurück,* the road back to a normal and stable existence. As Professor Wallich described the unexpected developments that marked the sharp turn upward in Germany's postwar fortunes: "It was her concentration on capital goods industries, her ability to supply machinery and equipment that floated her exports off, at ever-improving terms of trade, upon the rising tide of world demand."*

In short, West Germany was able to produce what other European nations needed: the tools and machinery with which to reconstruct their own industrial plants and to replenish their depleted inventories of capital goods. The war had stripped Europe of much of its industrial wealth and productivity. A fresh start had to be made. Germany could provide what was required. So, for example, in the two years, 1952–53, 50 percent of Germany's exports were capital goods: machinery, machine tools, motors, power and electrical equipment, railway rolling stock, ships, vehicles, engineering products, instruments and optical goods, and light steel and metal products. Another 30 percent of West Germany's export was made up of basic industrial materials such as iron, steel, coal, and chemicals. Exports of consumer goods for those two years covered only 10 percent of the total trade volume.

However, the vigor and drive of the reviving West German economy continued long beyond the initial export boom in capital goods. The strength of its recuperation is amply demonstrated in the following basic statistics for the years 1950–62 inclusive, as furnished by the Ministry of Economics:

	1950	1962	INCREASE/ DECREASE IN PERCENT
Gross National Product (millions of DM)	97,200	336,000	+247
Industrial Production (index 1950 = 100)	100	274	+174
Foreign trade:			
Exports (millions of DMs)	8,363	52,975	+534
Imports (millions of DMs)	11,874	49,498	+335
Surplus (−) minus	−3,511	+3,477	
Gold and currency reserves (millions of DMs)	1,100	27,700	+2,418
Employment:			
Wage and salary earners	13,903,000	21,239,000	+53
Industrial workers	4,797,000	8,037,000	+68
Unemployed	1,300,000	83,000	−94
Percent of total employed	8.8	0.4	
Real wages (index: 1950 = 100)	100	201	+101
Housing construction (number of unit dwellings)	561,300	571,000	
Social security benefits (millions of DMs)	13,000	47,400	+265
Tax revenues (millions of DMs)	18,801	84,800	+349

In order to understand the motivation behind Germany's postwar export boom, we must reach back into history, to the years after Waterloo, when the economic unification of pre-Bismarckian Germany was beginning. The first step in this process was the *Zollverein,* the customs union that unraveled a tapestry of tariff barriers which had been throttling the commerce of thirty-nine principalities and dukedoms of the German Confederation and the Kingdom of Prussia. The Germans who proclaimed the 1848 revolution in Frankfurt's Paulskirche were economic liberals who had been inspired by the free-trade doctrines of Adam Smith. But by 1878, Bismarck was persuaded by industrialists and the landed Junker aristocrats east of the Elbe to usher in the era of economic nationalism. This was to survive in varying forms until the entry of the Munich economist Prof. Ludwig Erhard on the scene in 1948.

Erhard was aware that the virus of nationalism of the Second *Kaiserreich* and the Hitlerian Third Reich had been among the prime causes for World Wars I and II. He remembered how after World War I the victorious Allies had botched the peace of Versailles. He had read and been influenced by the *Economic Consequences of the Peace,* by John Maynard Keynes. A brilliant young economist, Keynes had resigned from the British delegation at the peace conference to write a powerful critique on the contradictory and shortsighted Allied demands forced upon the defeated Germans. After World War I the Germans were presented with a huge reparations bill. They could not conceivably pay it because the Allied nations had erected high tariff barriers to shut out exports of Germany's capital and consumer goods. These gross errors of statesmanship were to have dire consequences in Germany: the political and economic chaos that followed; the mass unemployment of six million people; the swift rise of nazism; and Hitler's coming to power as dictator, all climaxing in World War II and the catastrophic end of the Third Reich.

Erhard looked back to the beginnings of modern Germany and saw how the industrialization of the Reich produced a new element in society: the industrial worker. The place of the worker in society and what was to be his share in the industrial pie was to become the controversial and insoluble "social question." The various formulae—socialism, communism, and national socialism, which Hitler and his cohorts developed —did not provide the answers to this question. The past attempts to find a catalyst to bridge the conflicting demands of the nationalistic and socialistic concepts of a society had proved to be counterproductive for contemporary Germany. But what about looking further back, beyond Bismarck's time to the first days of Germany's economic unification, to a time when the doctrines of free trade stirred the minds of men? In this somewhat convoluted fashion, Erhard arrived at his *Soziale Marktwirtschaft,* the socially-responsive free market economy, which 150 years ago was studied and described as *Smithianissmus,* after its originator, Adam Smith of Kirkcaldy, Scotland. Erhard and a handful of like-minded colleagues prepared the foundations for the export boom that was to produce the money and momentum for the amazingly swift economic recovery that followed in the next decade.

West Germany's inheritance from the past included much more than a reprise of the free-market liberalism of the Paulskirche vintage years.* The immediate and startling success of post-World War II trade was also due to some other prime factors. First and foremost, Germany had inherited an industrial structure which, despite its extensive war damage and postwar dismantling, could still produce a wide range of heavy industrial and consumer goods. Coupled with this was an abundance of incentives to speed up the repair and reconstruction of damaged plants and equipment.

Industry attracted the best available brains, executives who otherwise would have opted for a career in the army or in politics—both professions being in a rather depressed state at that time, and offering none of the rewards or challenges that the business world could provide. In addition, there were reserves of cheap and skilled labor available, including millions of refugees. Labor costs for industry were held down, which in turn sparked the exports of German-made goods. The entrepreneurs could earn large profits and build up equity by investing in tax-free industrial development projects. The Bonn government was extremely liberal in its tax-incentive programs. The high rate of West German capital investments continued, even after the excess labor had been absorbed. As the cost of living rose, so did wages. This development encouraged the imports of new technology, especially in the field of industrial automation equipment from the United States.*

However, Professor Erhard and the industrialists were on a collision course, though this development was not apparent in the early days of the *Bundesrepublik*. What was at stake was the extent to which the national economy could be controlled and directed. Erhard's professed liberalism was a commitment for a totally *free* economic system; that is, freedom from dominance and controls by both big government and big business. The federal government's power had been whittled down considerably with the creation of a federation of eleven states, each with its own taxing powers. The decentralization of economic power had also involved the world of industry and finance. Here the Allied authorities, particularly the Americans, had brought about major structural changes. To eliminate "excessive concentrations of economic power," the Allies had imposed Law 27, which enforced the dissolution of the large coal and steel combines and trusts of the Ruhr, as well as the Big Three nationwide commercial bank systems, the giant I. G. Farben chemical monopoly, and other industrial conglomerates. Also banned were cartels and unfair and monopolistic trading practices.* The future economic order was so planned and legislated that even if Erhard did not remain in office, German industrial firms would be limited as to their size and kept divided and competitive by anticartel laws.

The economic blueprint produced by Erhard and the Americans was to be strongly contested. As Dr. Shonfield pointed out:

German industry thought otherwise. It was highly organized in a hierarchical system of industrial associations dating back to imperial Germany and enormously reinforced under the Nazi regime—which had survived largely intact in the Federal Republic. The last thing that German industrialists contemplated was to establish a free market economy of small producers, in the Anglo-Saxon spirit. Their problem was, in any case, how to mobilize the economic resources and power on a scale required to do the job of reconstruction as rapidly as possible.*

In short, the German industrialists and bankers also welcomed a free-market economy, provided it gave them the freedom to operate their enterprises as they saw fit, without interference or controls from the government. Their attitude was fundamentally self-serving, with its own compelling logic. It seemed crystal clear to them that economic recovery could only be accomplished if they marshaled all their resources and collaborated with each other, fixing prices and sharing markets as far as circumstances permitted. The situation was desperate and required some coordinated bulldozing for new markets for their goods and services by big enterprises, which could undertake large-scale capital investments. The situation further required mobilizing large sources of risk capital by financial institutions for projects that bordered on outright gambling for big stakes. To the industrialist and his banker, it seemed obvious that they must have the freedom to return to operating within the cartel system. It was a way of doing business that had made Germany the leading industrial power in Europe before World War I.

In the United States, and to a lesser extent in Great Britain, "cartel" is a dirty word, identifying a business practice outside the code of ethics, one that is politically and economically reprehensible. In Germany, past and present, the *Kartell* is viewed in an entirely different perspective. It was invented in Germany, not as an instrument of economic exploitation or oppression, but rather as a form of economic self-protection which enabled groups or associations of business firms to survive in periods of economic crisis.

In 1873, Germany suffered its first industrial recession brought on by too much speculation.* At that time numerous firms within their respective industries formed associations for self-survival. Describing themselves as "children of the financial storm,"* they fixed prices and shared their diminishing markets with each other, because "nobody must starve and nobody must fail." Inasmuch as many of them weathered the rough period and later prospered, the cartel idea caught the imagination of the industrialists as a form of insurance against business failures and disruptive competition which can lead to such costly practices as price-cutting, dumping, and so on. So cartels proliferated in a wide range of industry and commerce. By 1900 there were 275 cartels in operation, covering the domestic and export markets. Kaiser Wilhelm's government encouraged the growth of cartels because they substantially strengthened the overall national economy. In fact, the government created a compulsory cartel in 1910 for the potash producers to prevent cutthroat competition in an industry that was deemed vital to Germany's continuing industrial and agricultural growth.

The biggest cartel of all was the Rhine-Westphalian Coal Syndicate, which controlled the production, sale, and distribution of coal, Germany's major source of fuel and energy. In fact there were even cartels formed by the wholesalers and transporters of Ruhr coal to strengthen their bargaining positions against the master coal syndicate. The process went a step further as the domestic consumers of coal formed the first consumer cooperatives, which brought large quantities of coal from the syndicate for resale to their members.

In general, there were four main types of cartels. First, there were agreements to share the market in which certain regions or groups of customers were allocated individually to the members of a cartel. Second, there were compacts to fix prices for domestic and export sales. Third, there were agreements fixing the total volume of production for an industrial group, in which each member was allocated a production quota. Finally, there were agreements to share in the profits of a cartel, according to a schedule worked out by the members. Of course, there were cartels that incorporated several of these features or objectives, listed above, for the cartel was essentially a flexible instrument, subject to changing markets and conditions for manufacturing.

The development of the *Kartell* was further stimulated in 1879 when Bismarck ended free trade with the outside world and erected tariff barriers. The new tariffs gave the industrialists a protective wall, particularly against the cheaper British imports, behind which they could fix prices and markets for their products inside Germany. The creation of new cartels tended to limit the competition that faced the members of the new *Verbaende*—the industrial associations that organized and operated the cartels. But this enabled them to arrange financing for their enterprises from the banks on much more favorable terms. This, in turn, increased their ability to dominate their respective markets. As G. P. Gooch, the noted British historian, reported:

The expedient has been of great value in fostering the production of wealth by economising effort, preventing waste, and giving each member of the group a fair chance; the manufacturing output of Germany increased more than threefold during the reign of Wilhelm II. Yet the system has its critics and its disadvantages are obvious. The tendency towards unification, however, legitimate and indeed inevitable, has resulted in a concentration of power in the hands of a few bankers and business supermen, who settle the questions of production, sales, prices, credits, new capital, interest and wages. The domestic consumer watches in angry impotence when the omnipotent *Kartell* sells its goods more cheaply abroad than at home and piles up fantastic profits.*

Surprisingly, there were no protests from the trade unionists and Socialists as the giant cartels and trusts concentrated economic power into fewer hands. As Prof. W. O. Henderson explained in his detailed study of the industrialization of Germany:

The attitude of the leaders of the Social Democratic party is more difficult to fathom. One might have expected men like Bebel and Liebknecht would have denounced cartels as organizations of capitalists filling their pockets at the expense of the workers. The failure of the German Socialists to mount an effective campaign against cartels may perhaps have been due to the fact that they realized that if ever they came to power *it would be much easier for them to nationalize an industry dominated by a few cartels than to take into state ownership an industry in which there were a large number of relatively small firms.** [Italics added.]

Hence, it is not so surprising that the press disclosed that the German Federation of Trade unions, in March 1954, had quietly notified the Bonn government that it "supported the recartelization of industry." Thus the DGB fired a warning shot across Erhard's bow, voicing their opposition to his proposed anticartel law, which was being studied by the Bonn parliament. The leaders of organized labor stated: "Cartels are a fact in Germany's economic life and should be recognized as such . . . there should be legal penalties for abuses of cartels rather than banning them."*

The attitude of the postwar German trade-union leaders was understandable and logical. They were strongly influenced by their conviction that the cartel system provided greater job security than a free-market economy that outlawed cartels. In effect, organized labor took the line that what was good for I. G. Farben or August-Thyssenhütte was good for them and the *Bundesrepublik*.

Between the two world wars the Weimar Republic played host to about 1,500 cartels. But after the Nazis took power in 1933 the *Kartell* reached its apotheosis. The monopoly capitalism of Weimar was transformed into what might be described as state, or nationalized, capitalism. The Nazis passed a series of laws that gave greater power and recognition to the *Kartell*. All producers in an industry had to join the cartel for that industry. The protection of the consumers against exorbitant prices by the cartels was discontinued. Cartels were virtually free to organize and operate as they pleased, and to be self-regulatory, as long as their practices did not impede or conflict with the decisions and policies of the Nazi government. As acting minister of economics, Dr. Hjalmar Schacht was appointed general controller of cartels by Hitler.

The Hitler dictatorship spawned the "excessive concentrations of economic power."* After the war, the American and British military governments were determined to exterminate all cartels, industrial trusts, syndicates, and other restraints of trade and commerce. In their occupation zone, the British issued Law 78, which abolished all cartels and forbade all restrictive practices in both domestic and international trade; the Americans passed a similar ordinance, Law 56. When Dr. Adenauer was negotiating with the high commissioners about ending military occupation, he promised in a letter to them that legislation would be enacted to perpetuate the Allied anticartel decrees. In 1952, Professor Erhard presented the *Bundestag* with the draft of a law against restrictions on competitive trade, but it was opposed by a bloc of conservative deputies who represented the anticartel sentiments of heavy industry. In succeeding months and years, this anticartel draft became one of the longest delayed and most hotly contested pieces of federal legislation ever introduced.

As the man who had imposed the *Soziale Marktwirtschaft* on the young republic, Erhard was firmly convinced that a free-market economy must be just that: free from domination and interference by both government and big industry. Elimination of the cartels—many of which had been revived and had, for all practical purposes gone underground in the face of legal prohibitions against them by the Allied authorities—would give the free-market economy the viability and flexibility that were necessary to a revival of business and industry.

Cartels could be, and were, quite informal in those early days. They were operative as long as the essential element remained intact, which was a working agreement among a number of firms to adhere to certain fixed business practices and prices. For example, there were the so-called luncheon cartels, which were kept functioning through regular luncheon meetings of the participants at which no notes were taken or records kept. The *Wall Street Journal* reported in December 1953:

Whatever actions the German government or the Allied High Authorities take, there is no doubt about the prevalence of cartel thinking these days—and it's noted that you don't necessarily have to have formal cartels to accomplish the cartel purposes; informal and unpublished agreements can easily do the trick. Indeed, a current wisecrack in this Ruhr city [Düsseldorf] goes as follows: "Why do we need a cartel if we have a telephone?"

German industrialists, raised in the traditions of the cartel system, resented the missionary and moralistic attitudes of the U.S. government in condemning a way of doing business that, in their eyes, had proved its worth and was fully acceptable to the community. An observer summed up their attitude by saying: "Competition is an accepted fact, but so are collective business decisions—if they are imposed by the right people."

During a 1953 discussion in Düsseldorf's Industrie Club, a prominent member of the Ruhr's *Machtelite* (power elite) called for an end to

"Yankee tutoring of the Germans on how to conduct their business affairs." As a clincher he added: "Sure, we are building cartels in Germany. We Germans can't afford the luxury of a free and uncontrollable market as [the] rich Americans do."

Meanwhile, big business was equally determined that the anticartel law promised by Adenauer must be blocked in the federal parliament. They thought passage of such a law would cripple all chances of economic recovery. Fritz Berg, a manufacturer of mattresses who was president of the powerful Federation of German Industries (BDI), was constantly on the offensive, attacking Erhard and his anticartel legislation. Berg contended that "free competition" actually means "less freedom" and "the destruction of all economic values." It was a contest that was not resolved until 1957, when an anticartel bill was finally passed by the *Bundestag*. It was a flabby compromise, filled with loopholes, to which both sides gave their reluctant approval. Erhard, even with all his popular support as the man who masterminded the economic recovery, could not overrun or outflank Herr Berg and his strong defenders of the cartel system in the *Bundestag*. The Ruhr industrialists had spent liberally to cultivate a large bloc of deputies in the federal parliament. According to a *New York Times* report on February 16, 1953 the Ruhr industrialists were collecting a fund of DM 35 million ($8.3 million) to finance political campaigns in the impending 1953 election of conservative members of the *Bundestag*.

So the anticartel bill, which finally emerged, actually permitted eight categories of cartels to be created. Each of these must have some economic justification such as: for survival in a period of recession; to achieve cheaper prices and lower production costs; for automation of an industry; and for exports and imports. Finally the minister of economics was empowered to grant exceptions and to approve new cartels if they served the broad interests of the national economy. The *Economist* commented on the face-saving tactics required to reach this compromise: "During the past two years, the parliamentary committees have kneaded and twisted its 80 paragraphs into their present elasticity."

But the contrast between the pro- and anticartel forces did not end there; each side still sought to extract greater concessions from the *Bundestag*. The *Financial Times* of April 4, 1962, headlined a report about this struggle as:

A BATTLE WITH THE AURA OF A RELIGIOUS WAR.

Nobody today claims any victory; but the Ruhr industrialists are aware that they did not suffer a defeat on this vital issue.

When the Allies decreed the breakup of the great coal and steel trusts of the Ruhr and other industrial conglomerates as being "excessive concentrations of economic power," the American and British authorities were unwittingly performing a great service for these business dynasties. By being subjected to a deconcentration process—as punishment for their participation in Hitler's wars of conquest—they were in reality undergoing a corporate health cure which was to trim much excess poundage off their bones. Instead of going into a business decline, because of the loss of various subsidiaries, these tradition-encrusted dinosaurs were about to be streamlined and rejuvenated. In a few years time they would be transformed into modern, aggressive companies, operating efficiently and profitably in the marketplaces at home and abroad. They would be staffed with a new generation of bright and ambitious managers, eager to prove their capabilities by moving as swiftly and energetically as the best of their competitors.

If any proof was needed that the Allied deconcentration of the big industrial trusts and conglomerates was not a setback, but actually a blessing in disguise, one need only to look at their latest annual reports. For example, before World War II, I. G. Farben was the biggest chemical company in the world. It was broken up into three big successor companies and two smaller units. They have made so much progress in the intervening years that today each of the three successor companies has a greater gross income than either DuPont or Dow, the two American chemical giants. In 1976 the gross incomes were: Farbwerke Höechst, $9.9 billion; Bayer-Leverkusen, $8.8 billion; and BASF-Ludwigshafen, $8.8 billion. By comparison, DuPont grossed $8.3 billion in 1976, while Dow Chemical had an income of $5.5 billion. Within three decades of the end of World War II, one of the five successor units of the original I. G. Farben trust, Farbwerke Höechst, had regained the title of biggest chemical company in the world, while two of its sibling survivors were within challenging distance of the leader. When one also considers that the annual gross incomes of these industrial triplets totaled $27 billion (in 1976), the original attempt to eliminate I. G. Farben as an "excessive concentration of economic power" was truly an exercise in futility.*

Another example presents itself in the breakup of Vereingte Stahlwerke, which before the war produced over 50 percent of Ruhr steel and was a conglomerate comprising 177 steel and coal companies. In the deconcentration process, it was broken up into thirteen successor companies, of which August-Thyssenhütte was a major unit. By March 1973, August-Thyssenhütte had completed a series of takeovers and mergers of many of the former unit companies of the defunct Vereingte Stahlwerke and had emerged as the number three steel company in the world, behind Nippon Steel of Japan and the U.S. Steel Corporation. August-Thyssenhütte's gross income for 1976 was $8.365 billion, right on the heels of U.S. Steel's income of $8.604 billion for the same year.

Before World War II, the Ruhr was dominated by the Big Six coal- and steel-producing trusts: Vereingte Stahlwerke, Krupp, Klöckner, Gutehoffnungshütte, Mannesmann, and Hösch. In addition, the Nazi government had built a massive new steel works at Salzgitter on top of iron ore deposits in central Germany. It was named the Herman Goeringwerk. In the past, the Ruhr expanded with vertical trusts and horizontal cartels. The Big Six steel companies acquired coal mines to provide coke, fuel, and energy for their steel mills. They also expanded horizontally, operating a wide variety of industrial plants, including shipyards and the manufacturing of heavy-duty equipment, as direct consumers of the steel pouring out of their mills. The Allied deconcentration program forced them to divest themselves of their coal mines and fabrication plants, to reduce their over-all economic power.

The successor units could have no interlocking directorates, as was the common practice in the past. In theory, each would have to survive by its own efforts or lapse into bankruptcy. The original owners received shares in the new companies, proportionate to their holdings in the parent firms.

Incidentally, the Hermann Goeringwerk as a government property couldn't be deconcentrated. It was partially dismantled and then, after the Korean War caused all limits on steel production to be lifted, the Salzgitterwerk, as it was renamed, was rebuilt with the help of a $4 million Marshall Plan grant. Its annual output today of 5.5 million tons is five times its productive capacity when it was working for the Third Reich.

The ink was hardly dry on the final separation decrees of the dismembered Ruhr trusts when the process of their reconsolidation was underway. Klöckner A. G. of Duisburg, which was the first of the Big Six to be put through the deconcentration wringer, was advertising in the press in December 1954 under the headline, "Back Together Again!" Klöckner announced that its *Töchtergesellschaften,* "daughter companies" as the successor units were known, had rejoined their parent firm in one form or another. The Allied decree barring any interlocking directorates was an early casualty, as the stockholders of the various firms voted to ignore the ban and to restore connections with the parent firms as far as possible. The Allied high commissioners chose to sit on their hands and take no disciplinary action when their complex and artificially contrived program began to disintegrate. The German public, almost to a man, was in favor of reconcentration: conservatives with Socialists, industrialists with trade-union leaders—all were united because of a widespread conviction that to carry out the corporate dismemberment of the Ruhr was to open the door to economic chaos and disorder.

Of the twenty-six successor companies to the prewar Big Six steel trusts, nine large steel companies had emerged to dominate the Ruhr steelmaking by the mid-1950s. By 1970 this number had been reduced to six firms in the Ruhr, Salzgitter, and two steel groups in the Saar. By 1975 reconcentration had progressed further so that there were only five steel combines in the Ruhr: the Thyssen group, Hösch-Hoogovens (a German-Dutch combine), Mannesmann, Krupp and Klöckner. In addition, there were the Salzgitter-Peine and Saar combines.

The new word for reconcentration was "rationalization," which was used to refer to any projects, methods of doing business, or developments that would make an industrial firm more productive, more efficient, and more profitable.

Rationalisierung was the explanation given for many mergers, take-overs, and projects of mutual collaboration between the eight steel companies that now dominated the industry. A good example of this was the Quadriga project set up by four of the big steel firms. This involved pooling their orders for certain types of steel. If a firm received an order for a type of steel that it could not produce at a competitive price, the order would be handled by the firm that could produce it the cheapest.

Another example of *Rationalisierung* was the deal between August-Thyssenhütte and Mannesmann, which substantially increased the industrial power and capacity of these two survivors of deconcentration. Thyssen had previously taken over Phoenix-Rheinrohr, a major producer of tubing and pipes of all types, and also one of the original units of Vereingte Stahlwerke. Mannesmann was also a large producer of tubing and pipes and the principal competitor of Phoenix on the world market for pipeline contracts. After detailed negotiations, Thyssen sold the tubing- and pipe-producing units of Phoenix-Rheinrohr to Mannesmann, which in turn sold its rolled steel mills to Thyssen. As a result of this deal, Mannesmann emerged as the dominant firm in the pipe and tube field in Europe; Thyssen added to its rolled steel capacity, giving it a clear lead as the number one steel firm in Europe.

One episode in the record of Allied assaults on the citadels of economic power in the Ruhr illustrates well the quixotic aspects of deconcentration. In this case a rich and powerful industrialist was able to make the loss of his properties work to his advantage; deconcentration put him on the road to becoming the richest man in postwar Germany, vested with more economic power than any other single individual.

Friedrich Flick was born the son of a peasant in the Rhineland in 1883 and died in 1972 at the age of eighty-nine; for half a century he was the stormy petrel of the German industrial world. He was a loner who had little in common with the great industrial clans of the Ruhr—the Krupps, Kirdorfs, Haniels, and Thyssens. He was an outsider to them, never accepted by them socially or trusted as a business collaborator. It was no small wonder that the Allies made a mistake when they thought he could be deconcentrated and removed from the Ruhr stage as one of the leading players. For the granite-faced Flick was a genius at wheeling and dealing behind the corporate façades of heavy industry. He operated through a small holding company and only a few intimates shared in his business manipulations and in his profits. His special talent lay in analyzing a corporate balance sheet, being able to spot its hidden weaknesses, ever alert to exploit its hidden assets.

Employed as a bookkeeper for a small steel company, he married the daughter of a textile manufacturer, a union which brought him a dowry of 30,000 gold marks. Shortly thereafter he became the director of the steel mill and was on his way to becoming a millionaire. When World War I broke out, Flick realized a fortune could be made in steel production, and did before the November 1918 Armistice. He was one of the few farsighted men who gambled that the reichsmark was going to be inflated at the end of World War I. So he borrowed heavily from the banks and invested in industrial properties, mainly steel mills and coal mines. As the mark collapsed in value, Flick was able to pay off his loans from his petty cash accounts.

By 1926 he merged his coal and steel group into the new trust, the Vereingte Stahlwerke, and served as its chairman; but he was always at odds with his partners. The Great Depression of the 1930s caused the value his holdings to drop drastically. He had to raise money, but knew he would suffer substantial losses if he sold any of his shares on the open market, with its depressed prices. A press campaign spread the rumor that the French were trying to buy Flick's shares of Gelsenkirchener Bergwerk A. G., one of the biggest coal mining companies in the Ruhr, which was also a key unit of the steel trust. Within a matter of days the government of Chancellor Heinrich Brüning bought Flick's shares for three times their stock-exchange price.

Flick was a rich man before World War II began; he held a variety of industrial properties, including steel mills and coal mines. After the war he was tried and convicted at Nuremberg for war crimes and sentenced to seven years in prison. Three-quarters of his industrial holdings, which were in Communist East Germany, were confiscated and he was acutely aware that his remaining industrial properties in West Germany might also be lost or deconcentrated by the Americans. During the years he spent behind bars, Flick gave much thought to his crisis, and when he was released from Landsberg prison in 1950 at the age of sixty-eight he was determined to make a comeback. He employed the legal services of H. Struve Hensel, a senior partner of the Wall Street law firm of Carter, Ledyard, & Milburn,* to negotiate with the Allied high commissioners for the most advantageous settlement of the Allied order for the forced sale of either his coal mines or steel mills.

The advice of the American lawyer was short and to the point: Hensel persuaded Flick of the wisdom of not fighting the deconcentration process but selling either his coal or steel properties, then taking his tax-free income and investing it in other industries where he would have complete freedom of operation. Also, the business situation in Germany at that time favored this course of action.

In the mid-1950s the economic revival was assuming boom proportions. Money was in short supply and it was expensive to borrow; short-term loans were commanding interest rates of up to 16 percent. Flick realized that if he could acquire sufficient funds, he could pick and choose among a wide variety of industrial enterprises that had great profit potentials but which needed some immediate working capital. On Hensel's advice he sold his large coal-mining properties, Harpener Bergbau and Essener Steinkohle, to a French syndicate headed by the de Wendel steel group. He received $26 million in dollars, plus another $19 million in blocked funds, which could be invested only in French-owned enterprises. The $45 million was exempt from any taxes whatsoever because of the forced sale of his properties.

With $26 million cash in hand, Flick began secretly to buy up shares in Daimler-Benz, the makers of the Mercedes cars, buses, and trucks. For $20 million he picked up 37.5 percent of the shares in the firm. When it became known that Flick was buying Daimler stock, the 50-DM shares began to take off like skyrockets, eventually reaching a price representing a 3,000 percent increase in their par value. Years after his death, when the Flick fortune had to be divided among the heirs, a 29-percent block of the shares in Daimler were sold by the Flick holding company to the Deutsche Bank for over DM 2 billion (approximately $800 million at the 1975 exchange rates), which represented a 4,000 percent return on the original investment.

With the balance of his hoard of cash, Flick purchased Feldmuhle (paper-making), Dynamit Nobel (explosives, plastics, and chemicals), Krauss-Maffei (locomotives, tanks, and military vehicles), plus shares in a steel plant in France and one in Belgium. He also retained ownership of four steel plants in Germany and substantial shares in 227 other industrial enterprises. Prior to his death, Flick was widely heralded as the richest man in Germany and probably the richest in all Europe, with the possible exception of J. Paul Getty, the oil billionaire. As for the Allied plan designed to eliminate him as an excessive concentration of economic power, the London *Financial Times* had a particularly apt comment:

Where Herr Flick differed from some of the other big German industrialists (notably Krupp) was in his appreciation that some of the Allied postwar demands to German industry were in reality a God-send. It was with the compulsory sale of his mining interests in the early 1950s that Herr Flick raised the capital to break into Daimler-Benz. In much the same way he entered other new industries such as chemicals and plastics.

12

It seems as if the German capacity for excellence, shifting from field to field, has now, after a succession of music, scholarship, and soldiering, settled on industry.

—SEBASTIAN HAFFNER, *London* Observer,
August 24, 1960

THE WIRTSCHAFT-WUNDERKINDER

I N TIMES of chaos and social upheaval, men of vision, daring, and talent find sudden buoyancy and rise through the turbulence to the surface of events. Two such men—each an archetype of the special postwar breed, the *Wunderkinder*—were Willy Schlieker and Hans Günther Sohl. One was a true entrepreneur; the other was an executive and re-builder of a great corporation. Their respective postwar careers accurately reflected the dynamic and imaginative contributions made by German businessmen to the economic comeback of the *Bundesrepublik*.

The national newspaper *Die Welt* christened Willy Schlieker the "favor-ite child of West Germany's economic miracle." Without challenge, he ranked first among Germany's *Wunderkinder*. In the range and scope of his achievements, during and after World War II, he was the leading one-man success story of the contemporary German business world—until the day he ran out of money. Possessing tens of millions of dollars in assets which could not be turned into ready cash, Schlieker had overextended himself. When this happened, the "establishment" of the Ruhr and Hamburg turned thumbs down on the man who had defied them, their cartels, and their clubby ways of doing business. In their eyes, Willy Schlieker was always a loner, a maverick, and a threat to their well-ordered existence.

Schlieker was a stranger to them, a man lacking proper social or family background. His father had been a Socialist dockyard worker, and Willy had a lean and hungry childhood in the grimy workers' flats in the Ham-burg docklands. He had no formal education; yet he became fluent in three foreign languages and a connoisseur of medieval art and furniture. After the war he started out to make his fortune with no assets except his lively imagination, his fertile brain, and an encyclopedic knowledge of the Ruhr steel industry. In a few short years, he was a multimillionaire, successfully doing business at home and across the Atlantic with the top brass of the big U.S. oil companies, President Romnes of A.T.&T., Walter Touhy of the Chesapeake & Ohio Railroad, leading Wall Street financiers, and rugged individualist John L. Lewis of the United Mine Workers. Willy possessed a quality that was rare among the managers and descendants of the Ruhr industrial dynasties; he had a flair for operating in a manner that attracted attention and made him stand out against the massed ranks of dark-suited, conservative-minded business executives of West Germany.

Willy's introduction to Ruhr heavy industry came just before World War II, when he was a sales representative for a steel export firm. He persuaded the Rumanian government to sign a contract for the construction of a steel bridge across the Danube. This coup caught the eye of the management of Vereingte Stahlwerke. Schlieker was invited to join the steel trust to become chief of its raw materials department. In 1941, after the *Wehrmacht* failed to capture Moscow, it became apparent that the war would be long and costly in men and munitions.* The whole system of procurement and production of military supplies had to be reorganized under a new ministry for rearmaments headed by Albert Speer, Hitler's favorite architect. Speer, who had no technical qualifications in this field, recruited Schlieker to become the special commissar in charge of all steel production in Germany and in Nazi-occupied countries. He was also made the final arbiter as to the allocation of steel among the fiercely competitive demands of the army, air force, navy, and consuming public.

In a quick upward move, Schlieker, only twenty-eight years old, was handed supreme authority over the operations of the great industrial combines and trusts of the Ruhr. He was given full power concerning the production of the great iron and steel companies—what they could produce and in what quantities. Iron-fisted control would have been tolerable; the mounting pressures of the war demanded it. But Schlieker went a logical step further and assumed full control of the allocation of their steel output. Until he took charge, the Ruhr steel producers sold their products to those who paid top prices on a first-come, first-served basis. This resulted in crippling shortages in some areas of weapons production, while surpluses piled up in other sectors. Schlieker added insult to injury by eliminating the very profitable cost-plus contracts the industry had with the government, which had meant extra millions of reichsmarks in their coffers. The Ruhr barons never forgave him for the losses he inflicted on them in their hitherto sacrosanct and cozy relationship with the government of the Third Reich.

His next contribution to the Nazi war effort was the creation of a central-allocations desk. When the *Wehrmacht* wanted tanks, heavy artillery, or any military item made of steel, the order was funneled through the

Schlieker Bureau. Each requisition listed the amount and type of steel used in the manufacturing of the specific item and this data was recorded on punch cards. Another set of punch cards covered the monthly output and type of steel produced by every mill and blast furnace in Germany and throughout Nazi-occupied Europe. With this system in operation, Willy could sit down with the military men each month and draw up a balance sheet covering all the various categories of weapons and munitions required and the amounts and types of steel available for their production. Henceforth, there would be no more crippling shortages in one area of armaments and overproduction in another area.

In the ensuing months, despite the savage and destructive mauling that was administered to the Nazi armies on the Russian front and despite heavy Allied air raids on the Ruhr and other industrial centers, German armaments production began to climb steadily. As the 1942 summer offensive opened, Hitler predicted that with 600 new tanks a month victory was assured. But victory eluded the *Führer* and the Russian front chewed up more than the monthly output of 600 tanks, like a hungry tiger devouring its kill. The waxing tide of Russian victories in the east and the Allied return to the Continent in the west increased the destruction of German armaments. Production targets had to be set higher and higher. The rollout of tanks jumped to 1,000 a month and by the end of 1944 to over 1,800 tanks per month, as did the production of other weapons and munitions. The Speer ministry was winning the battle of production, but the *Wehrmacht* could not wrest a similar victory on the combat front.

However, German arms production soon took a decisive downward turn. According to Willy, the Allies modified their bombing tactics in the closing months of the war. Instead of continuing to bomb the factories manufacturing armaments, the American and British forces began to concentrate on the rail lines in heavily populated sectors. This resulted in a paralysis of the internal German railroad network and the withering away of all industrial production, as raw materials could not be brought into the factories, nor could the finished goods be moved out to where they were urgently needed. In the middle of April, Hitler issued an order to set up the production of arms in the Austrian Tyrol; Schlieker was ordered south to handle this special assignment. However, after leaving Berlin one dark night, his car was rammed by a German army truck and he was found unconscious in a ditch with six ribs broken. His career was ended, or so he thought at the time.

At the end of the war Schlieker had to run the gauntlet of Allied intelligence officers. Everybody wanted to talk to the man who was able to muster the last available coordination and strength of German industry to produce weapons and munitions going into the last weeks of the war. The Russians got to him first and then installed him as the custodian of what remained of Friedrich Flick's industrial properties in East Germany. The experts of the U.S. Air Force next worked on him; they inquired about the effects of their wartime bombing on industrial production. Then he was turned over to the British, who brought him out to Düsseldorf to advise them on how to resuscitate the bomb-battered industrial Ruhr. Once again Willy was installed in charge of the allocation of raw materials and the production of steel for the purposes of general repair and reconstruction of the bombed-out cities.

However, Willy's enemies among the surviving Ruhr managers and owners were numerous, and they were out to get him. He was brought before a local denazification court in 1946 and charged with war crimes. They could not make the accusation stick because several prominent Socialists appeared as character witnesses for him. But he was convicted as a Class III (minor offender) Nazi, which meant the loss of his job with the British military government.

For almost two years pickings were slim for him; but in 1948 he bought the corporate shell of an export-import firm and began to operate as an independent trader in steel. At the end of the war the Ruhr was littered with piles of ingots, plates, bars, and other steel scraps that were left as waste because of the breakdown in arms production; Willy bought as much of this steel as his finances permitted. Hence, after the currency reform on June 20, 1948, he had some tangible assets in hand, instead of worthless reichsmarks. The tide turned for him in 1949 when the Russians and the East Germans began to buy steel. Within a short time, he had a virtual monopoly on the east-west trade in steel. As he later disclosed, during this brief commercial chapter on his life he sold about $18 million worth of Ruhr steel to the Russians and netted over $1 million in profits. He was one of the first, if not the first, postwar millionaires in West Germany. However, with the intensification of the cold war in Germany, Schlieker decided to retire from lucrative trading across the Iron Curtain; from a political standpoint, he would be jeopardizing his future—even though he kept the Americans informed of all his trading deals with the Russians.

But the Ruhr steel men were largely successful in elbowing Willy out of the domestic steel market. As he often explained, the Ruhr was like a Naturschutzpark—a game preserve—only open to the members and friends of the industrial establishment. No outsider was admitted. Willy was not only an outsider, but he had also been found guilty of lèse majesté against the Ruhr barons in the past. He was definitely on their blacklist, and they would not sell him any steel. But they failed to take two important factors into consideration. He was unquestionably the best-informed man concerning the physical state of the postwar Ruhr and its major components. In his capacity as the wartime boss of the Ruhr steel industry, he had made it his business to know everything about the individual firms, the extent of their war damages, their productive capabilities, the character and qualities of their respective managers and workers, and so on. Second, as Peter Schott of the Industriekurier described him, Schlieker was a "specialist in bottlenecks," which were widespread and serious obstacles to the postwar operations of German industry.

Schlieker was aware that the Korean War boom was causing a serious bottleneck in the growing shortage of coking coal, without which no Ruhr steel could be produced. He looked across the Atlantic and discovered that there was a surplus of high-quality Pennsylvania and West Virginia anthracite available at a price per ton, transport included, that could be shipped to West Germany and sold cheaper than Ruhr coal. Willy was the first to "carry coals to Newcastle" and many others followed him to exploit this bottleneck. But he was the pioneer in this new avenue of trade. He traded his Appalachian anthracite for Ruhr steel, which in turn he resold in the steel-short American market, earning about $6 million in profits from this particular bottleneck.

With his profits from U.S. coal, Willy proceeded to exploit another bottleneck. Because of the dismantling of August-Thyssenwerke, the production of electrical sheet steel—a vital component for the manufacturing of electrical generators, transformers, motors, and such—was virtually at a standstill. No widespread economic recovery was possible without electrical equipment to power the wheels of industry, and no electrical equipment could be produced without electrical sheet steel. So Willy bought the two small plants that had been the principal source of this specialized steel, as well as corralling the experts of August Thyssen, who had handled its production. Within a comparatively short time he had a virtual monopoly on electrical sheet steel and sat astride a vital sector of German heavy industry. He had broken his way into the exclusive *Naturschutzpark* and was now recognized as a member of the *Machtelite,* even if he was clearly unwelcome to the Ruhr establishment.

This was largely due to the fact that in Germany, as elsewhere, the owner of an industrial enterprise wields a bigger stick than the manager of the enterprise. At this stage of the game Willy was expanding swiftly; he built another steel mill to produce pipes and tubing cheaper than the *Kartell* in this sector of industry. His iron-and-steel-trading company was now grossing about $70 million a year. Next he ventured into shipping, buying a fleet of three freighters to fly the black-and-white flag of the Reederei Willy Schlieker. The next step was to invest in a small shipbuilding firm, which he swiftly expanded by buying part of the dismantled area of the great Blohm & Voss shipyard in the heart of the bustling Hamburg port area, fronting on the crowded Elbe. Willy had now returned, literally and figuratively, to the home of his birth and childhood.

The shipbuilding industry was booming and all the German yards in Hamburg, Bremen, Kiel, and Emden had their order books filled for several years ahead. A labor shortage developed, and this became an obstacle to Schlieker's plans to expand Schliekerwerft into a major shipbuilding enterprise. Advertising for workers in the local press did little good, as every other shipyard also had "Help Wanted" notices in the newspapers.

But Willy solved his labor problem with a promotional coup that was the talk of Hamburg's shipping and trade-union circles for months. He gave his workers a Christmas bonus, the first such gratuity offered by any of the shipyards to its employees in the postwar period. On the day before Christmas, *Weihnachtsabend,* as Schlieker's workers passed out the gates of the shipyard, each was handed a big, fat, live Christmas goose, festively decorated with red and green ribbons and "Seasons Greetings from Schliekerwerft." As the workers rode to their homes on the buses and street cars, or stopped in the local *Bierstube* for a Christmas grog, each, including the squawking goose, was a walking advertisement for Willy's enlightened labor-relations policies. The New Year rolled around and there were many new applicants for jobs at Schliekerwerft. Willy soon had corralled sufficient workers to carry out his expansion plans for the shipyard.*

Hamburg is an ancient and proud city-state, one of the legendary Hanseatic League, with a rich tradition of international trade and commerce going back to the Middle Ages. Hamburg has a cosmopolitan society, dominated by its old mercantile, shipping, and shipbuilding families who look unkindly on intruders into their own rich *Naturschutzpark.* So there was no welcome mat for Willy Schlieker when he purchased an elegant French-style mansion in the suburb of Blankenese.

However, Schlieker spared little time or interest in his relationship with Hamburg's oligarchic society. Instead, he was fully occupied with the problem of being able to compete against the long-established and experienced shipbuilding firms which were enjoying a flood of orders for new tankers from the Greek shipping tycoons. Before completing his planning for expansion, Schlieker made a quick visit to Japan to acquaint himself with the latest shipbuilding techniques of the Japanese, who were offering stiff competition to the German, British, and Scandinavian shipyards. He returned with a shipbuilding revolution in his briefcase.

Shipbuilding has always been a labor-intensive industry, employing a high proportion of expensive skilled workers in relation to the volume of production. Only by reducing his labor costs sharply could Schlieker have a chance to compete against the long-established and better-known shipbuilders, such as Howaldtswerke, Deutscherwerft, and so on. This Willy proceeded to do by introducing the computer and electronic controls and assembly-line production methods to the complex arts of ship engineering and construction. Schlieker's computer helped his technicians design ships for the most economical methods of construction and operation; his new automated and electronically controlled cutting and welding operations worked quicker and faster than human beings; his assembly-line building of a ship was similar to the construction of modern prefab housing units. Finally, the new technique developed by the Japanese of building a ship in separate sections—bow, stern, and midsection—and then joining them together in a dry dock, enabled Schliekerwerft to take on the contracts for much larger vessels than the size of his premises would normally permit. During the war the largest dry dock in the world had been excavated on the land that Schlieker had acquired for his shipyard, but the installation had been put out of action by the destruction of its lock gates. With financial help from the city of Hamburg, Schlieker had the dry dock repaired, which gave his shipyard the capability of handling the largest vessels afloat on the high seas at the end of the 1950s.

Schlieker was an easy man to work for; he knew his own mind, made decisions quickly and incisively, and had an extraordinary talent for handling journalists. They always had easy access to him, and he received them as welcome guests and not as intruders. Little wonder that he enjoyed such a favorable press locally and internationally. Willy seemed to be a man with everything going his way: he had money, power, growing fame, and popularity; a charming, gracious, and cultured wife; an expanding industrial and commercial conglomeration of twenty-three companies with gross revenues of about $200 million; luxurious homes in Hamburg and Düsseldorf and a chalet, complete with its own mountain, in the Bavarian Alps. It made one wonder what made Willy run so hard. He had reached a plateau of achievement where he could relax and enjoy the fruits of his labor; there were few other mountain peaks within sight for him to climb. Once asked what he wanted out of life, what his highest priority was, his answer was revealing: "I have had a lot of unpleasant encounters with some of my fellow Germans. I want to build up my position, as strong as a fortress, so that never again can anyone or any group do me any harm."

In many respects, Willy's answer disclosed his kinship with the average German. Past insecurity laid heavily on his consciousness; he wanted insurance against any repetition of the long and hungry days of poverty, destitution, and hopelessness. But it was this drive for complete economic security that brought Willy Schlieker to the brink of privation again.

In the last week of July 1962, Schlieker found himself unable to raise $3.5 million to meet debts due at the end of the month; his business empire went into receivership. The subsequent bankruptcy proceedings revealed that Schlieker had operated on a very slim capital basis of only $5 million. He had not laid away any cash reserves, but had plowed all his profits into the expansion of his enterprises and the modernization of their equipment. Undercapitalization and overexpansion were the causes of his business downfall.

With $50 million in new orders for ships on his books, Willy sought everywhere, unsuccessfully, to find the funds to stave off bankruptcy. None of the big banks would lend him a pfennig in his hour of need. The Ruhr establishment was especially gratified to see him forced to make his exit from their *Naturschutzpark*. The members of Hamburg's exclusive Übersee Club were pleased that the control of the city's most modern and competitive shipyard had been taken out of the hands of "that upstart"

Schlieker. After all, the son of a dockyard worker was never *salon fahig,* acceptable to Hamburg's socially elite.

Nursing his wounds, Willy commented: "My creditors stiff-armed me and never gave me a chance to save my properties."

The anti-Schlieker attitude of the leaders of the West German business establishment was confirmed in a long article in the weekly news magazine, *Der Spiegel* in November 1965. In a cover story about Hermann J. Abs, chief of the Deutsche Bank and the acknowledged leader of the German financial world, the magazine reported that the defense ministry had recommended that the Bonn government give Schlieker financial assistance in his liquidity crisis because his modern shipyard was needed for future naval construction. Chancellor Adenauer asked Abs for his opinion about government help to the maverick industrialist. Abs turned thumbs down, and this rejection pushed Willy over the hump into bankruptcy.

However, several years later, in 1966, it was quite a different scenario, when the legendary Krupp of Essen got into serious financial difficulties because it extended massive cheap credits to Communist-bloc countries. The financial establishment, headed by Abs, rallied behind Krupp to persuade the Bonn government to underwrite the $600 million which the firm owed to the Deutsche and 261 other West German banks. To prevent Krupp from sliding into bankruptcy, Bonn came to the rescue. As a condition, Krupp had to be transformed into a corporation, subject to the normal legal controls which it had previously escaped as a privately owned firm. Abs emerged as the new chairman of the board of Krupp. All of which can be explained by the fact that Krupp has been a charter member of *Naturschutzpark,* which had a fixed policy of closing its doors to the independent mavericks of the business world, such as Willy Schlieker.

Out of the wreckage, Willy managed to save his chalet and mountain in the Bavarian Alps near Berchtesgaden. But he could not savor the magnificent scenery from his chalet balcony while at the same time seeing his remaining assets lying idle and unexploited; so he built a ski resort on his mountain. To further absorb his restless executive energies, he has organized his own business consulting firm. Willy will be back on deck in the foreseeable future, because he is that kind of man.

In July 1963, the weekly news magazine *Der Spiegel* published a front-cover photo of West Germany's number one industrialist. The picture caption was brief: *Stahl Manager Sohl.* In so describing Hans Günther Sohl, who was then and still is widely acknowledged as the leading steel producer in Western Europe, this news magazine confirmed a known fact: the most important ingredient in the economic recovery of West Germany has been the "manager." This plain English word has been adopted into the postwar

German vocabulary, as well as its companion word, "management." Their usage marks a definite watershed between the comparatively small clique of somewhat provincial Ruhr industrialists who dominated the prewar German business world, and the new and more numerous postwar generation of successful executives—many of whom are individually described in the German press as *Der selfmademan*. In German, manager carries an added connotation; it refers to the modern, computer-experienced, internationally minded businessmen who have proved their competitive worth on the global marketplaces against the Americans, Japanese, British, French, and others. In short, *der Manager* is a master of modern business techniques, one who has contributed, by his efforts, to the economic rebirth of West Germany.

Sohl, often described in the press as "Mr. Steel," was born in Danzig in 1906. As a young man he was a gifted pianist and seriously considered a career in music. However, he completed his studies in Berlin, obtaining a doctorate as a mining engineer—*Bergassessor,* a title that he still uses. His special talents were noticed fairly early, for in 1932, at the age of twenty-six, he was appointed head of the raw materials division of Krupp. Sohl was considered something of a boy wonder and on the strength of his performance for Krupp, he caught the attention of Alfred Vögler, the head of Vereingte Stahlwerke. Sohl joined this company and became assistant chairman of the *Vorstand,* the board of management of the steel trust. During the war he took a leave of absence to serve with the new Speer ministry for arms production. At the end of the war he was interned along with hundreds of other government officials, Ruhr executives, bankers, and other prominent personalities who were subject to automatic arrest as suspected war criminals.

After two years behind barbed wire, Sohl was given his freedom. He had been noticed by the British military government for his obvious capabilities. He found early employment when he was appointed by the Allied control board to be the "liquidator," that is, to tidy up what remained of the once-powerful Vereingte Stahlwerke. This one-time giant of the German steel industry was in the process of being corporately and legally dismantled as an "excessive concentration of economic power."

However, Sohl viewed his appointment as something quite different than a liquidator of the Ruhr's industrial assets. He took the lead in halting the further dismantling of the steel mills and their equipment. He directed his special appeals to the American authorities, realizing that the U.S. was the dominant power concerning the fate of western Germany.

Sohl made a strong and persuasive case against further dismantling; he pointed out that if the steel mills and their equipment were all removed, thousands of workers could no longer find employment; this would result in political disturbance and economic chaos. Sohl offered, on behalf of the absentee owners, to assign majority control of the Ruhr mills about to be dismantled to either the French or some international agency, provided that the steel mills were left intact and could continue to operate. He was playing for big stakes. Of the total of four million tons of steel capacity the Allies had originally planned to dismantle in the Ruhr, 60 percent consisted of August Thyssen's plant and equipment. Sohl's proposal created quite a stir in Paris and, undoubtedly, it had a deterrent effect on the American and British occupation authorities; for shortly thereafter, the dismantling orders were canceled. The Americans did not want the French to gain a foothold in the Ruhr and play a further disruptive role in the development of the postwar West German economy.

Sohl was next appointed by the Allied authorities to be trustee of August-Thyssenhütte, one of the largest units of the Vereingte Stahlwerke before the war. When Sohl took over A-T-H, it was a shadow of its prewar size, with only 2,200 workers still employed, compared with a wartime payroll of 11,000. A total of 116,000 tons of plant and equipment had already been dismantled, half of which had to be scrapped. Production was down to several hundred thousand tons of steel a year. However, Sohl's vigorous and successful campaign against dismantling had impressed Frau Amelie de Thyssen, widow of Fritz Thyssen, who had inherited the steel trust from the original August Thyssen and the Countess de Zichy, her daughter. Frau Thyssen was a majority shareholder in Phoenix-Rheinrohr, a large tube and steel plant which had previously been a subsidiary of the steel trust; her daughter was a majority shareholder in Thyssenwerke. In 1953, Sohl was installed as chief executive (*Vorsitzender des Vorstands*) of Thyssenhütte, with the full support of mother and daughter.

Sohl is a short man, stocky in build, with a round, open countenance. He has a friendly personality, which attracts foreigners, particularly the Americans, an asset which has paid off in solid dividends. He is fluent in English, and it did not take him long to get on a first-name basis with such men as Roger Blough, chairman of U.S. Steel Corporation, and other American industrialists whom he met on his frequent visits to New York. Sohl's strength and success can be seen in his planning for the future and in his courage to back his decisions in the face of much skepticism and doubt on the part of his fellow Germans.

When he took executive command of August-Thyssenhütte, Sohl had three major objectives: to restore the firm to its prewar eminence as the largest single steel producer of the Ruhr by reuniting it with its former deconcentrated subsidiaries; to make it the most technologically advanced steel producer in Europe; and to realign the German steel industry into groups that could compete in the international markets of the future.

In April 1973, when Sohl retired after twenty strenuous years directing the renascence of A-T-H, he had just about accomplished his three objectives. In the previous month he had completed his last major acquisition, the takeover of Rheinstahl of Essen, one of the original major units of Vereingte Stahlwerke. This last addition made A-T-H the third largest steel producer in the world, after Nippon Steel of Japan and U.S. Steel. The expanded August-Thyssenhütte of 1973 was an industrial giant resulting

from the acquisition of eight other steel companies and their own subsidiaries, including two major shipbuilding firms. Taken altogether, the A-T-H
conglomeration had a total production capacity of 15 million tons of steel
annually and gross sales of over $5 billion.

Quite fittingly, the A-T-H headquarters is housed in the Ruhr's first skyscraper, the 26-story Thyssenhaus. Architecturally, the starkly modernistic
structure provides its own special identification; it resembles three giant
slabs of steel pressed together in a vertical position. A ground-floor wing
contains a beehive of IBM computers behind glass walls. It is also a schoolroom, where many German and foreign executives stationed in the Düsseldorf area receive their first lessons in the new art of electronic administration of big business, as part of Thyssen's policy of fostering industrial
collaboration.

However, the growth of Thyssenhütte into Europe's top steel producer
involved much more than a series of takeovers and mergers. Sohl was
aware, though few of his colleagues could see his point, that the widespread
bomb damages and dismantling suffered by the Ruhr presented Germany
with a once-in-a-lifetime opportunity with startling possibilities.

Sohl was convinced that a sustained and worldwide demand for steel
was about to develop, as the postwar industrial boom got underway in
Europe, America, and the Far East. This was no time to concentrate on
repairing steel plants and equipment that was on the verge of obsolescence.
He reasoned that it would be more difficult to borrow $10 million to recon-
struct a duplicate of a prewar steel mill that had been bombed or dismantled, than to raise $100 million to build a brand-new steel mill with all the
latest technological advances. Sohl was fortunate to have Robert Pferdmenges, the noted Cologne banker and friend and adviser of Chancellor
Adenauer, as chairman of the board of August-Thyssenhütte. With his help
Sohl was able to raise financing from all the major banks, the federal government, and the Marshall Plan funds. He managed to scrape together
about $150 million between 1950 and 1957, of which only $50 million was
invested in the repair and rebuilding of damaged blast furnaces. In addition,
he built new blast furnaces and began the massive construction project that
was to be Europe's most modern steel mill at Beeckerwerth on the flat
meadowland along the banks of the Rhine above Duisburg. In the 1970s,
A-T-H completed its companion installation, a monster blast furnace tower-
ing 350 feet above ground and capable of pouring out 10,000 tons of
molten steel a day (4 million tons a year), to feed the hot strip and cold
rolling mills of the neighboring Beeckerwerth complex. Sohl has often remarked that "a 4 million-ton plant can sell steel as much as $50 a ton
cheaper on the world markets than a 200,000-ton plant."

From the earliest days of his command of Thyssenhütte, Sohl sought to
catch up with the latest in U.S. steel technology; he wished to combine it
with German know-how, so as to grab the leadership of the Ruhr steel
industry. With the aid of a $10-million loan from the U.S. Export-Import

Bank in 1956, Sohl financed the purchase of American steel-making equipment and technical assistance from Armco Steel of Middletown, Ohio. This U.S. firm furnished him with the technical plans and expertise for the first installation of a broad-band strip mill, the opening phase of the Beeckerwerth project. Sohl also cultivated friendly relations with U.S. Steel, whose officials offered their help to the enterprising new chief of August Thyssen. However, even before the Allied authorities had lifted the limits on German steel production, Sohl had placed orders with German firms for the equipment that would escalate the productivity of A-T-H. He always had his eye focused on the ultimate profitability of any steel-making installation. As a director of Vereingte Stahlwerke, he is remembered for a maxim "famous throughout the German steel industry," according to *German International* (August 1969), which quoted him as saying: ". . . anyone who can't ensure that his company regularly earns enough money to pay at least a 14 percent dividend and put at least that much again into reserves, should let himself be buried."

August-Thyssenhütte earned handsome profits in the years after Herr Sohl became its chief executive. The industrial boom, which he had planned on, continued for years, until West Germany's first postwar business recession in 1966–67. Hence a large percentage of Thyssen's profits could be plowed back into investments in new plant and equipment. Its growth and modernization went on unabated, as did the improvement of its competitive position on world markets. Sohl merited his title of "Mr. Steel"; nobody else could match his performance in taking a virtually dismembered industrial complex with comparatively small output and transforming it, in twenty-five years, into the third biggest steel company in the world.

Sohl was the manager incarnate. Long before he retired from A-T-H to become president of the Federation of German Industries, he carefully fulfilled his last responsibility to his firm. A believer in continuity of policy and the maintenance of momentum of a great corporation such as Thyssenhütte, Sohl years ago had picked his successor and had rigorously trained him for the day when he would take over as chairman of the *Vorstand*.

In 1955, Sohl had spotted Dieter Spethman, a young lawyer and ex-naval officer, working for Gelsenkirchener Bergwerk, a coal-mining company. He took on Spethman as his personal assistant. In the intervening years, Spethman was moved around to various executive and managerial posts within the A-T-H organization, finally returning to Sohl's side as his finance officer. Spethman was only forty-six when Sohl retired in 1973, but he had been brought in on every important decision that Sohl had made in recent years. When Spethman moved to the head of the *Vorstand,* he was 100 percent Sohl-educated and Sohl-trained for the job.

In general, the leading German industrialists, merchant princes, and bankers have never been transformed into popular personalities in the same fashion as movie stars or football players. But there was a period after World War II when the managers and the *Wunderkinder* captured the public's interest and adulation. Their accomplishments, in the face of great odds and obstacles, in rebuilding their war-shattered business enterprises—becoming millionaires in the process—enshrined them, temporarily at least, in the pantheon of folk heros, taking over the pedestals recently vacated by the *Lüftwaffe* aces, the Rommels and other heros of World War II. These outstanding executives and entrepreneurs were credited with having stimulated the economic revival. In this role they were admired and acclaimed, because they restored the hopes and revitalized the morale of millions of their fellow Germans. Their individual achievements, their newfound wealth, and their *dolce-vita* standards of living, were seized upon by the popular press and illustrated weeklies as the only German success stories of the postwar scene. These *Wirtschaftswunderkinder* (economic miracle workers) were a welcome antidote to the numbing defeat and impoverishment occasioned by World War II.

These men were the architects of reconstruction; their primary task was to restore or rebuild their individual business enterprises in the dark days after the war, and make them productive and profitable once again. The problems they faced were harsh, but basically fundamental: how to put together plant and equipment or shop and inventory out of the wreckage left by the war; how to manufacture and finance their operations in an economy that was teetering on the edge of national bankruptcy. In short, it was a bootstrap operation for which there weren't available any plans, market research, or sophisticated tools of modern business.

Perhaps the most important common characteristic shared by these managers and entrepreneurs was that they were not competition-minded. At the outset of the economic revival they did not have to be; their problem was to fill the economic vacuum caused by the war. For all practical purposes Germany's national inventory of capital and consumer goods had been wiped out. Production of goods was first priority and the public demand, not only in Germany but also throughout Western Europe, was without measure. It must be borne in mind that in those early and crucial years of economic revival, the acknowledged leaders of Germany were the production men who worked out their own small economic miracles in getting manufacturing underway in an environment littered with war-damaged or destroyed industrial plants. Every item they could produce could be sold to someone, even before it left the factory premises. Salesmanship was not a necessary talent in those early days.

A production manager without peer in this postwar era was Heinz Nordhoff, who, single-handedly and from point zero, made Volkswagen into the world's third largest automotive firm in the short span of a decade. Nordhoff was born in 1899 in Hildesheim, near today's Volkswagen headquarters. He was educated as an engineer and, in the thirties, joined the staff of Adam Opel A. G., the General Motors subsidiary in Germany. He also spent some time at GM plants in Detroit, learning the techniques of U.S. assembly-line production. In 1939 when the war started, he was director of the Opel truck plant at Brandenburg, which soon switched over to military vehicles.

In 1938, with great propaganda fanfare, Hitler announced that the "people's car," the Volkswagen, would soon be produced by the Nazi Labor Front organization, to provide cheap autos for the masses. Over $110 million in advance down payments to finance the construction of the Volkswagen plant at Wolfsburg were paid over by Germans anxious to get first delivery of the people's car. But the war intervened and instead of producing Volkswagens, the Wolfsburg plant began to make a German military vehicle similar to the American jeep. The Wolfsburg plant was 60 percent destroyed by bombing during the war, and when the British army began to occupy the area it became a repair depot for military vehicles. A handful of former Wolfsburg engineers and some workers regrouped some of the machinery in a corner of the plant and produced the first two postwar Volkswagens. Surprised British officials encouraged the Germans to continue their piecemeal production by purchasing all the vehicles that were made. During the first year, 713 cars were produced under chaotic working conditions; every time it rained, production had to stop because the improvised assembly area had no roof.

In 1948 the British installed Nordhoff as general director of Volkswagen and gave him virtual *carte blanche* to produce as many of the streamlined little four-seater "Beetles" as machinery and manpower permitted. Nordhoff was starting from scratch; he had no tradition to follow, nor any stockholders to placate or interfere in his operations. In a 1953 interview he said: "That was a blessing for us. We didn't have people looking over our shoulders and saying, 'You can't do this, because we never did it that way.' We solved our problems as we encountered them, in our own way, not by what the book told us, but usually by improvisation. It is a very educational experience."

Working seven days a week, Nordhoff gradually brought order and continuity to the operation. He introduced some of GM's production techniques, as well as developed some techniques of his own creation. As far as his resources were concerned, he operated on the proverbial shoestring. At one point coal for fuel and energy and steel were in such short supply that Nordhoff had to barter new Volkswagens for these two scarce commodities. At the time of the currency reform, when the deutschemark replaced the worthless reichsmark, Nordhoff found it impossible to meet his next payroll in deutschemarks. He sent out an SOS to his dealers for help. He explained: "They came to Wolfsburg by whatever transport they could find, carrying all the money they could lay their hands on in their briefcases. It got us over the hump."

This demonstration of the support of his dealers, plus the fact that during his tenure as general director there was never a strike at Wolfsburg, illustrates the high degree of faith and loyalty that Nordhoff was able to command from his employees.

Nordhoff's basic approach to the production of Volkswagens was clear and concise: "Keep it simple and easy to produce and then improve on it." This formula was an outstanding success. Volkswagen became as well known on the roads of the world as Henry Ford's original Model T. By 1967 the Wolfsburg plant was completely repaired and modernized and was the largest automotive plant under one roof in the world; the firm was producing 3.5 million cars a year.* It had truly become the people's car, originally promised by Hitler, but finally delivered by production genius Heinz Nordhoff.

Nordhoff lived in a small detached house in a housing settlement populated by his workers and employees. He had enlightened labor and social-security policies. Wages were kept 5 percent higher at Wolfsburg than at other automotive plants in Germany. His workers had a generous pension system long before the national social-security program provided old age benefits for all the Germans. At Wolfsburg, his workers became convinced that he had found the way to provide for their economic security; they repaid him with high-quality productivity.

Nordhoff died in 1968 when Volkswagen was at its peak as the number one industrial company in Germany in terms of gross income. Since that time, after a succession of managers and policy quarrels between the *Vorstand* and *Aufsichtkrat,* Volkswagen has slipped down the list to seventh position; it has passed out of the miracle class.

Much has been written and there is more to be studied about the importance of the "manager" and the *Wunderkinder* in the amazing rebirth of West Germany as the most powerful economic nation on the European side of the Atlantic. In their day, they contributed more than the individual politicians to the renascence of their country. In a 1973 survey of the German scene, the *Economist* pointed out:

Germany's desperately keen, highly self-educated entrepreneurs, and its desperately keen, highly self-educated shop floor labourers turned with a common will to fashion a miracle from the only postwar asset which Germany had got: the shattered structure of industry. They did it so well that the beauty of it has blinded them ever since. It is this devotion to heavy industry . . . which provides the character of Germany's problem in future years.

13

Gemeinsam Leben ist besser. (Being together is better)
—Deutsche Zeitung, *November 8, 1962*

THE SEATS OF
POWER

ONE of the pervasive myths of the twentieth century is that the Ruhr barons, the owners of the great industrial combines of prewar times, ruled the German business world and dominated the nation's economy. This misconception has been kept alive by historians and journalists afflicted with less than 20–20 vision, as they surveyed the German scene from Bismarck's time to the present. In fairness to these chroniclers, the Ruhr barons, including the legendary House of Krupp, seemed to possess all the appurtenances as well as the appearances of men who wielded great economic power. They formed a close-knit, economic oligarchy of their own creation—the *Naturschutzpark,* as Willy Schlieker described it. They sought to exclude the public from any close scrutiny of their private lives and activities. Outwardly they appeared to be the real power brokers of the German economy. However, virtually at the elbow of every Thyssen, Kirdorf, Poensgen, Vögler, Reusch, Haniel, and others of the Ruhr *Machtelite* were their company's bankers. For the big commercial banks (*Grossbanken*) occupied the seats of economic power in prewar Germany, as they still do in today's *Bundesrepublik.*

In 1964 the conservative Bonn government issued a detailed survey to disclose the degree of reconcentration among the large corporations in postwar West Germany.* The survey was based on a sampling of 425 of the major corporations, whose aggregate capitalization amounted to three-fourths of the par value of all the issues on the stock exchanges of West Germany. Of this sampling, it was found that 70 percent of their capital assets was controlled by the banks.

Since the beginning of the twentieth century, the big commercial banks have functioned as if they were the legal partners of German heavy industry. In addition to providing for their financial needs, the banks have served industrial firms as advisers and planners of commercial growth and technological development. In his penetrating study of modern capitalism the

British economist Andrew Shonfield points to the unique and close relationship that has existed in Germany between industry and the banks:

German businessmen right from the start of the country's industrial development, have been influenced in some measure by the considerations of collective economic policy, whether applying to groups of firms thrusting for some special advantages, or to the whole of an industry. The banks have usually been either the leaders, or the active partners in this process; typically they were the originators of the original cartels. The banks have always seen it as their business to take an overall view of the long-term trend in any industry in which they are concerned and then to press the individual firms to conform to certain broad lines of development. *They saw themselves as essentially the grand strategists of the nation's industry. . . .** [Italics added.]

With the exception of Japan—where giant families of industries, trading companies, and banks are grouped together under the house flags of the Mitsui, Mitsubishi, Sumitomo, and other conglomerates—in no other nation have the banks maintained such a close, almost incestuous, relationship with their clients as has existed in Germany for the past hundred years.

It is one of the paradoxes of the modern West Germany economy that the big banks control about 70 percent of the shares of the nation's largest and most powerful corporations, not by right of ownership, but by voting the proxies of thousands of shareholders. This financial *droit de seigneur* is a unique German contribution to modern banking that originated in the latter half of the nineteenth century, when the industrialization of the *Kaiserreich* began to gather a full head of steam. The German bankers formulated this instrument of holding the proxies of the shareholders as a means to further protect and to supervise their loans and investments in industrial companies.

After 1870 the industrialization of Germany began its swift and lively expansion. Money was needed and the banks also increased their financing of new industrial plants and equipment by direct loans, by underwriting new issues of shares, or by investing their own funds in these enterprises. But because industrial development was a relatively new thing—with many uncertainties and doubts about its profitability—the banks began to seek greater safeguards and continued surveillance over the daily operations of the enterprises that they were financing. To this end a bank would ask for one or more seats on the board of directors of the firm it was helping. A bank would also suggest to the purchasers of new shares that they deposit these securities with the bank and give it the right to their proxy votes. This arrangement of increased supervision and control of an industrial enterprise by the bank gained acceptance with the shareholders, contributing to the greater safety of their investments.

This same system of the banks exercising the proxy votes of the shareholders of big corporations is alive and flourishing today. This financial practice largely results from the fact that the big banks are the only agencies authorized to buy and sell shares on West Germany's stock exchanges, except for a few licensed independent brokers (*freie Makler.*) The banks also effectively control these exchanges; because of this situation, they exercise a virtual monopoly on the securities market. When buying shares for an investor, a bank usually requests and generally obtains the purchaser's proxy vote. This voting right (*Depotstimmrecht*) can be exercised for a period of fifteen months and then must be renewed. A bank is under no legal obligation to reveal the owner of the shares that it will vote at a meeting of a corporation; it merely certifies it has possession of the number of shares it is voting.

There is a further and commonly used extension of this proxy voting through a system of *Stimmenleihe,* or loaned votes. This practice involves one bank lending its proxies to another bank for certain votes in which the latter bank has a special interest. This lending of proxies does not have to be referred back to the owners of the shares for their approval. It is usually the Big Three banks that exercise most of the *Stimmenleihe.* Hence, it can be readily understood how the use of the proxy voting in its varied forms gives the Big Three banks a major leverage in impressing their points of view on the managements of the various corporations in which they are interested. The special government survey on concentration in industry (*Bundestags-Drucksache* IV/2320) reports that 70 percent of proxy votes of shareholders were cast by representatives of the Big Three banks, the Deutsche, Dresdner, and Commerz banks.

The degree of cooperation between the Big Three reaches its apex in any situation that concerns the proxy votes of their own shareholders. As Andrew Shonfield reports in his book *Modern Capitalism:*

But when it comes to the really serious business, like dealing with the shareholders' votes at the annual general meeting of the banks themselves, the rule of collaboration among the Big Three is apparently absolute. Each dutifully delivers up to the bank concerned the proxy votes collected from its shareholders—with the result that an estimated 65–80% of all shareholders votes at the annual general meeting of any of the Big Three banks are controlled by the management of the bank itself. Here at the peak of the German system we arrive at the apotheosis of managerial self-government.

However assiduous as the banks are in mustering the proxy votes of the shareholders of the major German corporations, they are equally diligent in accumulating seats on the boards of directors (*Aufsichträte*) of these same firms. A trade-union newspaper, *Die Welt der Arbeit,* caustically commented: "The banks collect *Aufsichträte* like other people collect postage stamps."

The Bonn's government report on reconcentration tendencies in industry (previously cited in this chapter) gives a revealing insight on the special position that the banks occupy in their relationship to industry through the *Aufsichträte,* the supervisory boards of directors. The survey disclosed that only one-fifth of the largest corporations had no bankers on their boards. The remaining 318 corporations in the survey had a total of 573 bankers on their respective *Aufsichträte.* Apart from the directorships reserved by law for representatives of the workers, this gave the banks one out of every three seats on the supervisory boards of 318 of West Germany's biggest business enterprises.

In fact, the appetite of the big banks for directorships in as many business enterprises as they can handle provoked the passage of a postwar law, *Lex Abs,* limiting any banking executive to a maximum of ten directorships on the *Aufsichträte* in West Germany. The law was named after Hermann J. Abs, chief executive of the Deutsche Bank, who compiled a record that can never be equaled. As of 1964 he was the chairman of sixteen supervisory boards, vice chairman of six more, and a member of two more boards, while also serving as chairman of the *Aufsichträte* of the Kreditanstalt für Wiederaufbau,—a public bank with assets of DM 15 billion—and also of the *Bundesbahn*—the federal railway system, a DM 10 billion giant with 475,000 employees—in addition to his normal service as the *Sprecher* (speaker), or chief executive of the Deutsche Bank. This title is used to designate the *primus inter pares* of the management board of any bank, the members of which are all theoretically equal by law. While in his prime as West Germany's leading banker, there is good reason to believe that Abs was probably the second most powerful man in terms of influence and economic muscle, in the *Bundesrepublik,* after the Chancellor.*

However, to get a clearer perspective of the close relationship that has existed between the big banks and German industry, we must turn back to the middle of the nineteenth century, when a banking revolution was imported from France that was to set the character and pattern of major financial institutions for the decades of industrial development that were to follow.

West Germany's highly integrated and industry-oriented banking system can trace its origins back to a pair of dynamic and imaginative French financiers, the brothers Émile and Isaac Pereire. They founded the Crédit Mobilier in Paris in 1852. Their primary objective was to create a new financial instrument that would enable them to wrest control of France's banking system from the hands of a few big financial houses such as the Rothschilds. The Pereires attracted small investors who put their savings into shares of Crédit Mobilier. In turn, these funds were loaned or invested in public utilities such as railways, and industrial enterprises. The Pereires were very successful; they paid dividends as high as 40 percent in 1855. However as pioneers and innovators in new fields of finance, the Pereires were bitterly contested by James Rothschild, head of the Paris branch of the famed multinational banking family, but they survived the opposition of the old-line conservative financial houses.

Crédit Mobilier was created primarily to stimulate the industrialization of France and neighboring European countries. Though it crashed in a spectacular fashion in 1867, Crédit Mobilier was responsible for exporting this banking revolution to Germany in the middle of the nineteenth century. Industrial financing in Germany was actually initiated in 1852, when the A. Schaafhausen Bank of Cologne was reorganized by Gustav Mevissen as a joint stock company. He announced that the bank would give limited financial aid to industrial firms in the Rhineland that showed promise of future growth and profits. While the Schaafhausen Bank was successful in its new field of financing, the scope of its activities was rather small and it did not attract much attention. But by the turn of the century it had become one of the Big Six banks.

Meanwhile in 1853 a small syndicate of German bankers appealed to the Crédit Mobilier to invest in a new credit bank which would concentrate on industrial financing in Germany. With the help of the Pereire brothers, the Darmstadter Bank was organized, despite strong opposition from the Frankfurt Rothschilds and other orthodox financial houses. Rondo Cameron, an economist and student of that era of finance, has reported:

Although the initiative for the bank came from Germany, the inspiration, the idea, most of the capital and a large part of the practical experience, both in promoting it and in organizing its operations came from the Crédit Mobilier.*

The founding of the Darmstadter Bank is important because it was the first modern institution in Germany to finance large-scale industrial enterprises. It invested in railways and then branched out into textiles, coal mining, engineering, and shipping. It set a trend that was to become the primary concern of the big commercial banks in the coming decades: to finance and to promote the industrial development of the *Kaiserreich* and to eventually give Germany the economic leadership of the European continent before World War I.

The idea of these credit banks caught on in Germany. The public invested its savings by purchasing shares of the credit banks, which channeled this capital into industrial undertakings. A boom resulted from this influx of savings, and the investments began to pay off good dividends, enhancing the public's acceptance of this banking innovation. The increasing economic stimulation was noted by the English consul in Leipzig, who reported in 1856:

New railways are everywhere projected, and numerous mining and other industrial companies are being formed. . . . In Saxony alone 30 new coal-mining associations have lately been established for working the newly discovered beds of coal. . . . But the favorite of the day are the credit institutions or banks, upon the plan of the French Crédit Mobilier.

The period 1851–57 was marked by an economic boom. For example, credit banks provided the funds for the expansion of the railway system from 5,856 kilometers (3,513 miles) to over 11,000 kilometers (6,600 miles) by 1860. The enlarged railway network resulted in increasing the traffic of raw materials and manufactured goods; this movement of goods contributed to the growing industrialization. The coal fields of the Ruhr began to yield their buried treasures of fuel and energy as nearly a hundred new mines were tunneled into the ground. The production of iron and steel began to climb sharply, as did that of textiles and other manufactured goods. "The tall chimneys of industrial plants began to sprout like mushrooms," observed Max Wirth at the time.

The proliferating credit banks supplied the funding for the industrial revolution that came to the Kaiser's Germany with a rush in the last half of the nineteenth and the first years of the twentieth centuries. In contrast to Germany, there were no similar industry-oriented banks in Great Britain. One must remember that the industrial revolution first came to Britain. It was new and there were no precedents as to its profitability available to British bankers. As Prof. Asa Briggs of Oxford, an eminent British social historian, recently pointed out in the *Financial Times:* "Britain had the most intensive of all experiences of industrialization. There were no limitless resources, such as in the USA or USSR. It was also the most expensive since we were the first and we had the one with the most waste—because it was based not on scientific knowledge but on the ransacking of resources and great strength of will."

There was small cause for wonder that the British banks considered industrial enterprises risky and unsound, at least by comparison with the profit potentials of empire-building and in the exploitation of the resources of the new colonies. Great British fortunes were made overseas. However, by contrast, the Germans had the advantage of hindsight. They were at least a generation behind the British in industrial development, but they could see much more clearly the money-making potentials of the industrial revolution. The great German fortunes were made at home on top of the great Ruhr coal mines. The new generation of German bankers plunged into industrialization with enthusiasm. As another British historian, G. P. Gooch, wrote in his study of imperial Germany: "In no other part of Europe has the provision of credit for industrial undertakings played such a leading role as in Germany, where a willingness to take a risk has been rewarded with success."*

There were a handful of farsighted and confident pioneers in the field of commercial banking such as: Abraham Oppenheim of the Darmstadter Bank; Gustav Mevissen of the Schaafhausen Bank; David Hansemann of the Diskonoto Bank of Berlin; Gerson Bleichröder, the private banker and *éminence grise* of the German financial world, who was also Bismarck's financial counselor and confidante; and a few others. They saw the handwriting on the wall; Germany could become a great and strong industrial power, even surpassing Great Britain in the foreseeable future. Therefore the logical and profitable role for their commercial banks was to establish a close association and active collaboration with Germany's industrial establishment.

The big banks were the instigators in this working relationship, and, in many cases, they were the designers of the first industrial cartels. The Diskonto Bank created the Rhine-Westphalian Coal Syndicate, the first great coal cartel. The Darmstadter Bank organized the iron-smelting cartel, to be followed by the Union of Steel Producers. The Deutsche Bank and other financial houses assisted in the formation of the two cartels that controlled the Siemens-Schuckert and the Allgemeine Elektrizitats A. G. (AEG), groups of electrical companies. The first dye cartel followed shortly. The Schaafhausen Bank organized the cartel of wire manufacturers, and so on. Between 1879 and 1890 over two hundred industrial cartels were formed. This pattern of business relationships between competing companies was firmly imposed on the main industrial sectors of the German economy largely through the initiative of the big banks.

By the end of the nineteenth century the industrialization of Germany, centered on the Ruhr, was in high gear, brought about by the efforts and money of the Big Six banks which held sway over the bustling world of business. They were the four "D" banks—the Darmstadter National Bank, better known as Danat; followed by the Diskonto-gesellschaft, founded in 1856; the Deutsche Bank in 1870; and the Dresdner Bank in 1872; together with the Schaafhausen Bank and the Commercial Bank of Berlin. These banks reached their growth and national influence through the takeovers or mergers of the smaller credit banks, many of which were formed without sufficient assets to survive. With industry and commerce, banking and shipping making giant strides, the Germany of Kaiser Wilhelm II was on its way to winning the economic hegemony of the Continent.

The chaotic years after World War I saw a further concentration of German industry, a development masterminded and supervised by the *Grossbanken*. This trend was stimulated as a result of the whirlwind destruction of economic values caused by the uncontrolled inflation of the reichsmark to astronomical heights. The savings, pensions and possessions of millions of Germans were wiped out. Hugo Stinnes, probably the most foresighted and acquisitive entrepreneur of modern times, led all others in reaping the harvest of properties thrown on the market by the owners and shareholders who had to sell their equities just to survive. He was already a multimillionaire through the wartime profits of his coal, steel, and transportation operations. When postwar inflation began to get out of hand, instead of exporting his capital to safe havens outside of Germany as hundreds of businessmen were doing, he invested in a wide range of industrial and commercial enterprises. He borrowed money from banks and from other financial institutions to buy more properties, and he was able to pay off his loans in depreciated reichsmarks, whose exchange values declined steeply with every passing day. Stinnes established a bank in Holland as a refuge for the flight capital of German businessmen; he then used this money, in the form of "hard" Dutch guilders, to buy more business properties in Germany. When he died suddenly in 1924, Stinnes had acquired 1,388 companies in his bulging portfolio. A Socialist journalist reported that, at his peak, Hugo Stinnes controlled one-fifth of the total industrial production of the infant Republic.

When inflation was halted by the introduction of the *rentenmark,* pegged at 4.20 to $1, funds from the new American and British loans began flowing into the debilitated economy, reviving it like a blood transfusion. This launched a new industrial boom, further contributing to the concentration of heavy industry. In 1925, six large chemical firms came together to become I. G. Farben, the world's largest and most powerful chemical company. In the following years the new steel trust, Vereingte Stahlwerke, was created through the amalgamation of August-Thyssen-hütte and three other large steel companies. By the end of 1925 it was estimated that over 2,000 industrial and commercial cartels were in operation. The *Kartell* had become the standard operating procedure for normal business.

At the beginning of the Allied military-government rule of defeated Germany, the predominant U.S. policy toward the Big Banks, or what remained of them, and their role in the economic life of the nation was outlined by Gen. Lucius D. Clay as follows:

Their functions and power far exceeded those of our own banks and included commercial and investment banking, closely integrated with industry and the stock exchange. . . . Through interlocking directorates, voting control of stocks, and management of new financing, they wielded unbelievable power throughout the industrial field. To a considerable degree they had profited under the Nazi regime and they had not hesitated before the war began to acquire Jewish banking and financial enterprises at sacrifice value, nor afterwards to extend their holdings into countries occupied by Germany. Their dissolution was essential to the decentralization of financial and economic power in Germany and perhaps a major step to this end.*

Of the original Big Six banks of the time of Kaiser Wilhelm II, the only surviving *Grossbanken* after World War II were the Deutsche, Dresdner, and Commerz banks. Their home offices in Berlin, which were massive granite structures of forbidding appearance in the Behrenstrasse, lay in ruins. What remained of their offices and assets in the Russian zone of occupation were summarily expropriated by the Soviet military government. In West Germany the Allied occupation authorities issued Law 57 in May 1947, which compelled the dismantling of these *Grossbanken* as "excessive concentration of economic power." Each of the Big Three was broken up into ten successor banks: one for each of the nine West German states (*Länder*) and one for West Berlin. In theory, each successor unit was independent and on its own, with no legal or financial connections whatsoever permitted with the other siblings of the dissolved parent bank. But within a comparatively short time, unexpected developments intervened to render inoperative for all practical purposes this so-called economic reform of the banking system.

The increasing tempo of the cold war brought with it a 180-degree change in Allied policies toward Germany. Its economy had to be revived to help the Germans better their daily existence, and immunize them against the spreading virus of communism. The currency reform of June 1948 gave the first big stimulus to economic revival, but it soon became apparent that the repair and reconstruction of devastated West Germany would be seriously handicapped unless the dismantled banking system could be made to operate more effectively. The financial structure had to be more centralized and cohesive, but to achieve this meant flouting the letter and spirit of Law 57. However, German bankers took the initiative because they were aware, as were the Allied decartelizers, that the deconcentration decree of 1947 was already a cold-war casualty. Behind closed doors, the initial steps got underway to reconcentrate the *Grossbanken,* with the tacit approval of the Allied high commissioners.

After long and complex negotiations, the Bonn government was given the green light for a partial restoration of the commercial banks to their former status. The Allied high commissioners approved a law of March 1952 which authorized three successor banks, covering north, central and south Germany, for each of the Big Three banks. This meant that the Deutsche Bank was now permitted to operate under three separate administrations: the Norddeutsche Bank of Hamburg, the Deutsche Bank West of Düsseldorf, and the Süddeutsche Bank of Frankfurt.

The Dresdner and Commerz banks were also reorganized along the same broad geographical divisions. As a result, everybody in government and financial circles knew the March 1952 statute was only a stopgap measure, a necessary prelude to a full and final reconstitution of these financial institutions to their prewar forms and functions. The Americans, once the strongest advocates of eliminating the Big Three banks, were now reconciled to the inevitable reappearance of the Deutsche, Dresdner, and Commerz banks in their former roles as movers and shakers of the German business world. In anticipation of this likely development, U.S. High Commissioner John J. McCloy had extracted a promise from Chancellor

Adenauer that there would be no further reconcentration of the Big Banks for at least the next three years, as a condition for American approval of the 1952 statute. Four years later the *Bundestag* approved the law for the reconcentration of the Big Three banks (*Gesetz über Wiederzuzammenschluss der Grossbanken*) and the road was finally swept clear of all deconcentration obstacles.

In May 1957, almost ten years to the day after the promulgation of Law 57, the Dresdner Bank sent out a form letter to thousands of its clients, friends, and German businessmen announcing: "We have the honor to inform you that the three postwar successor institutions of the Dresdner Bank have again been reunited to form one single institution, the Dresdner Bank."

Similar announcements were made within days by the Deutsche and Commerz banks. A crowded decade after Law 57 had sounded the death knell of the *Grossbanken,* they emerged from a limboesque existence, restored to their rights and powers; they returned to the business world, led by skilled defenders and administrators. They were also well-endowed financially to handle the increasing volume of financing for the years ahead. Together, the Big Three had a combined balance of DM 17.7 billion ($4.2 billion) as follows: Deutsche Bank, DM 7.8 billion; Dresdner Bank, DM 5.4 billion; and Commerz Bank, DM 4.5 billion.

The economic recovery of West Germany would have been impossible without the Big Three and without their long and close relationship to the big industrial and commercial corporations. While this relationship may justify serious criticism because of its self-serving and monopolistic nature, only these financial giants could have reorganized the national structure of credit and financing and kept it intact and functioning in the crucial years after currency reform. They operated on the principle that while the country hovered on the brink of economic collapse, the situation called for innovative financing with a high degree of risk; conservative lending policies and traditional methods of financing would not move the debilitated economy out of the danger zone.

The Big Three loaned out all the money they could get their hands on. They financed the repair and reconstruction of firms whose plants and equipment were in ruins. The banks made loans based not on the balance sheets of these firms, but on their past track records and on their importance to a viable economy. Herbert von der Porten, who for many years was the Bank of America's representative in Düsseldorf and Frankfurt, said: "From the start in 1948, the German banks granted credit at a truly daring rate, often lending ten and even twenty times their own capital funds to one borrower. BASF (Badische Anilin und Sodafabrik of Ludwigshaften, one of the major successor units of I. G. Farben, the deconcentrated chemical trust) had nothing left but some real estate, bombed-out factories, ruined machines, some engineers and workers and the will to work, but the Deutsche Bank gave them the money to get going on the basis of deposits by the German public."

A striking example of this risk financing was at work in the reorganizing of the new Carl Zeiss Optical Works at Oberkochen. At the end of the war, the famed Carl Zeiss Optical Works at Jena in East Germany was taken over by the Soviet military government. One hundred of the Zeiss technicians and executives had been evacuated to West Germany by the U.S. Army, which was anxious to keep this pool of special talent out of Russian hands. The Zeiss refugees were offered employment in the United States and in Great Britain. However, encouraged by Allied interest in their capabilities, they decided to remain in West Germany and organize a new Carl Zeiss Optical works at Oberkochen in the Rhineland. They approached Abs of the Deutsche Bank, who enthusiastically supported their project. He estimated the cost of the project to be 120 million DMs, and shortly thereafter the Deutsche Bank began the funding of the reconstruction project. The only collateral was, in effect, the technical expertise of the 100 technicians and executives; but that proved adequate to pay off the loan. The manufacturing of optical goods and cameras was resumed, invigorated by a big export demand for these scarce goods. Within a few years the reestablished Zeiss Works had a payroll of over 5,000 skilled workers and again its name and products were advertised on the world markets.

Another example of lending money on a plan and a promise and little else involved the postwar rebirth of the Pittler Company of Leipzig, for fifty years an important East German machine tool producer. During the war Herr Abs had been chairman of its *Aufsichträt* while Dr. Hans Pilder of the Dresdner Bank had been vice chairman.

At the end of the war U.S. troops occupied Leipzig briefly and prior to their departure, the Americans offered to transport the senior executives and engineers of the Pittler Company to be resettled in the U.S. occupation zone. Eighteen men and their families moved west in U.S. Army trucks. What remained of the original machine tool plant in Leipzig was confiscated by the Russians as reparations. After currency reform, the Pittler refugees, who had supported themselves by repairing old war-damaged machines, decided to re-create a postwar Pittler Co. in the West. Dr. Wilhelm Fehse, the senior executive, approached Abs for financing. Abs was able to get approval of an initial loan from the Deutsche Bank—though at that time he was not officially connected with the bank—and also helped swing a Marshall Plan grant its way for the construction of a new machine tool plant at Langen, south of Frankfurt. By 1962 this enterprise had expanded to a manufacturing operation employing 17,000 workers, with a gross income of DM 60 million ($15 million). It was another example of risk financing— based on industrial talents and capabilities rather than book assets—that paid off in solid dividends.

In other sectors of the industry, financing was made easier because the central bank, the Bank Deutscher Länder (BDL) was willing to discount much of the short-term paper, thereby freeing that money to return to the banks for new loans. One observer of that period commented:

The eager lenders found eager borrowers. Both were aided by the central banking system *that for a time did not inquire too closely into the quality of the material it was asked to discount*. The rapid expansion and high profits of the period prevented these loans from going bad.* [Italics added.]

In a money-short economy—remember in the first months of currency reform only 6.1 billion deutschemarks of the 10 billion that had been printed were distributed—the circulation of money accelerated. The wage earner spent his income on necessities which had long been denied him; he did not save much in the early days of economic revival. The storekeeper plowed back his sales receipts into building up his slim inventory of goods. The manufacturer sold his growing output of consumer and capital goods at high profits, with which he could pay off his short-term bank loans, and thus be in a position to borrow more money for the repair and expansion of his production facilities. And with these repayments the banks could extend further credit.

Surprisingly, the banks and other financial institutions were able to provide the vast amounts of money required not only for the repair and reconstruction of the war-battered industrial plants and equipment, but also for the expanding operations of the reviving business community. The whole economy existed on revolving credit because there was no other source of financing. No foreign banks were permitted to lend money to Germany; no individual German or corporation could borrow as much as a pfennig from outside the country. The world money markets in New York, London, Zurich, and so on, were closed to them.

However, this temporary isolation, or period of quarantine so to speak, from the global financial scene materially contributed to the renascence and strengthening of the whole German banking system in this crucial phase. For one thing, it was protected from strong foreign competition on its own home grounds. The German business community had to develop long and short credits to keep the economy alive and functioning through their own resources. It was another bootstrap operation. Herbert von der Porten described the early postwar financial system: "In those early days, the German banks, literally and figuratively, operated on a shoestring basis, but *Gott sei Dank*, it proved to be a very elastic piece of string."

Looking back, the Allied plan to dissolve the Big Banks and make them disappear from the German scene, by issuance of a decree of military government, was doomed to failure.

First, the Western Allies had no legal basis, nor any mandate to confiscate or expropriate these *Grossbanken*. Neither did the Russians, but they did not have to live with "a rule of law." In breaking up the Deutsche, Dresdner, and Commerz banks, the Western military governments did not take away, or nullify, the structure of ownership of these institutions for their shareholders. Hence if Hans Schmidt of Essen owned a share of pre-war Dresdner Bank stock, he now was credited with the ownership of a one-tenth share in each of its ten successor banks. The Allied failure to drastically alter the pattern of ownership, either by nationalization of the *Grossbanken* or by expropriation, meant that a return to their prewar policies and practices was inevitable. It would only be a question of time before the shareholders would exercise their rights of management, after the Allied controls had been lifted.

Second, the surviving top executives of the Big Three banks were not about to roll over and play dead at the dictates of the Allied occupation authorities. Herman J. Abs, former chairman of the Deutsche Bank and widely recognized as West Germany's outstanding banker of the postwar era, has provided an insight concerning this resistance of the bankers to the Allied deconcentration program. Abs, who was wartime chairman of the board of managers (*Vorstand*) of the Deutsche Bank, has since re-counted how the board of directors several months before the end of the war, appointed twelve senior officials to be guardians and trustees, even unofficially if necessary, so as to protect the interests of the Deutsche Bank as far as circumstances permitted during the Allied occupation of defeated Germany. As one of the twelve, Abs was sent to Hamburg in April 1945 to set up a sort of underground, or unofficial, management for the remains of the Deutsche Bank until such time as it could resume direction of its own affairs. In Hamburg, where Abs had been firmly instructed by the British not to set foot inside any Deutsche Bank door, he soon had to exercise his unofficial managerial responsibilities. The *Vorstand* of one of the nine successor banks in West Germany was considering cutting com-pletely loose from all ties to the Deutsche Bank and, with its assets in hand, forming a new and independent bank. Abs met quietly with the bank's top officials, informing them that while he had no legal authority over them, they would be wise to desist from carrying out their plans. He pointed out that at some future date, when the Deutsche Bank was freed from outside Allied controls, they could face legal action for working against the in-terests of their former employer. The proposed breakaway was dropped.

Third, and most important, the Allied trustbusters and decartelizers, in their myopic zeal, did not attempt to change or to reform the basic character and operations of German commercial banking, *per se,* while they still had the time and the authority to enforce their demands on the defeated nation. Their big mistake was to believe that they could eliminate the "excessive concentrations of economic power" merely by breaking up the *Grossbanken* into little banks, instead of going to the heart of the matter: the way in which the big banks wielded their great power and influence on the manage-ment and direction of German industry and commerce.

The Allied trustbusters obviously did not perceive, nor did they comprehend, that the close, long-standing, and almost sacrosanct relationship between the German bankers and the industrialists was the true basis for the formation of the "excessive concentrations of economic power" which the financial institutions possessed before the collapse in 1945. In the early days of the Allied military government, the reformers could have effectively curbed the powers of the big commercial banks by removing the main supporting pillars of that special relationship. The following basic reforms would have achieved the aims of General Clay and the Allied deconcentration program:

1. Create a truly free and independent German "money market" by breaking up the monopoly controls of the big banks on the underwriting of industrial stocks and bonds and on the daily trading of securities on the German stock exchanges.
2. Forbid the banks from voting the proxies of shareholders whose securities are deposited with them, as had been common practice in Germany.
3. Ban the practice of officers of commercial banks from serving on the boards of directors of industrial corporations, especially those which are the banks' clients.

Whether such "reforms" would have hindered the economic comeback of West Germany is a debatable point, but if they had been imposed, they would have altered the whole power structure of the West German economy.*

In 1965 the German Companies Law required all joint-stock companies, including the banks, to disclose in their annual reports any holdings of 25 percent or more in another company. This lifted the curtain on another aspect of the wide-ranging operations of the *Grossbanken*. In their annual reports issued June 1966 the Big Three banks disclosed what was long suspected; they had fat portfolios of shares in a variety of industrial and commercial firms, as in smaller banks and credit institutions. For actual investment purposes, banks generally do not hold less than 25 percent of the shares in any company in which they have a long-range interest.

The 1966 reports showed, for example, that the Deutsche Bank held shares in four machinery companies, one shoe and four textile factories, two public utility companies, a major construction firm, one shipping line, 29 percent of Daimler-Benz, one department store chain, one brewery, a sugar and a chocolate factory, and one chinaware plant. In addition, the Deutsche Bank owns shares in twenty-three smaller German banks and credit institutions and in forty-two overseas banks and financial houses.

To a somewhat lesser degree, the Dresdner and Commerz banks also had large portfolios of industrial and commercial shares, participations in German and overseas banks, and so on. Thus these *Grossbanken* are certainly industry-minded and export-minded to the highest degree. Their sensitivity to any changes in the business climate is made more acute by their own direct involvement in a wide variety of industrial and commercial enterprises.

No report about German banking would be complete without information about the newest addition to the ranks of the *Grossbanken*. It is the Bank für Gemeinwirtschaft (bank for social economy), owned by the German trade-union federation and the cooperative movement, with total assets in 1977 of approximately $23 billion.

Karl Marx, the spiritual father of socialism and the trade unions, would be speechless today if he could see his political descendants operating a national banking network along strictly capitalistic lines—and, what's more, making a handsome capitalistic profit.

When the BfG was organized in 1958, Ludwig Rosenberg, who was chairman of the bank as well as chairman of the trade-union federation, set forth the basic policy governing the BfG's operations: "The aim of our enterprises is not to make politics but to make business. A profit is something not to be ashamed of."

The BfG has made good business on an ever-increasing scale. Despite its proletarian background, the trade-union bank has not hesitated to enter into profit-making deals with such arch-capitalists as the Rothschilds of Paris, the Krupps of Essen, Banque Lambert of Brussels, and others. The BfG has just constructed a new 38-story headquarters in Frankfurt, a skyscraper designed to impress the public with the success and solidity of the workers' bank, and, as further proof, if that were needed, that organized labor is fully committed to the support of free enterprise capitalism.

The first bank established by organized labor in Germany, the *Bank der Arbeit* was founded in 1924. But in 1933 the Nazis broke up the trade-union organization, confiscating all its assets and property, including its financial agencies. The Nazi Labor Front established its own Bank der Deutschen Arbeit, which, in turn, was abolished completely after the war by the Allied Control Council in Berlin. However, the postwar West German Federation of Trade Unions (DGB), founded by Hans Boeckler, received whatever assets of the pre-Hitler trade-union movement that were recoverable. Shortly after the currency reform of June 1948 the DGB and the cooperative movement joined forces to found a network of banks that which would be the repository of the funds of the sixteen major trade unions and the income from the various cooperative enterprises, including a nationwide chain of food stores. In 1958 the DGB, as majority partner, consolidated the various trade-union banks into one organization, the Bank für Gemeinwirtschaft. Walter Hesselbach, a professional banker, was named chief executive and he has since emerged on the German financial scene as one of the most astute financiers of the postwar era. However, he was given substantial help by the long periods of strike-free labor-management relations. For the union dues began to pile up in the BfG, as there were virtually no withdrawals for strike funds. Two-thirds of these funds of the trade unions were long-term deposits, which gave the BfG a growing pool of liquidity in a money-short economy. These funds were in great demand for normal commercial and industrial financing. In fact, the BfG became a serious competitor of the Big Three banks. Accusations were made that the trade-union bank was guilty of "sharp" practices, allegedly lending its funds at a small percentage below the interest rates of the *Grossbanken*. Whether true or not, the trade-union bank was in the money market, competing vigorously with the old-line and long-established commercial banks.

The Bank für Gemeinwirtschaft became less of a special-interest financial institution and more of a Big Three-type of bank with every passing day. By 1964 trade-union and cooperative funds accounted for only 18 percent of its deposits and 15 percent of its loans. Assets had grown to almost $1 billion, and the BfG had suddenly emerged as the fourth largest banking institution in Germany.

However, the BfG has shown certain social characteristics in its support of measures to maintain full employment. For example, in the early 1960s the trade union purchased several companies that had been left insolvent with the collapse of the industrial conglomerates of Hugo Stinnes, Jr. The BfG kept these companies afloat, and their workers employed, until they could be resold. The bank also put up DM 8 million to keep a large photo-supply manufacturer in business when its owner was arrested on suspicion of tax fraud. This gesture saved the jobs of thousands of workers and earned the bank much good will in business circles.

In the early 1960s an American banker noted the amazing advance that Walter Hesselbach and the Bank für Gemeinwirtschaft were registering in German financial circles under his direction: "He may well be the most astute and foresighted banker that West Germany possesses today, considering what he has been able to accomplish at the BfG."

Asked if Hesselbach was "even superior to Hermann Abs?," the American replied: "That could be. Bear in mind that Abs has been a leader of the German banking world, and he enjoys all the advantages and opportunities that accrue to the head of the financial establishment in this country. Whereas Hesselbach has been making it 'on his own,' so to speak; he is a one-man operation and therefore his success is all the more remarkable."

By the end of the 1960s, Hesselbach was able to turn his attention to his pet project of coordinating all the varied commercial enterprises of the trade-union movement, such as the proliferating consumer cooperatives, the BfG, the stores and factories, and so on, into one master holding company. In 1974 he organized the Beteiligungsgesellschaft für Gemeinwirtschaft A. G., and by 1978, BGAG had become the largest business group under one corporate roof in West Germany, with assets of $25 billion. Hesselbach is managing director of BGAG, heading a conglomeration of economic power that even Abs, now in retirement, never equaled. Hesselbach has made a unique contribution to this thriving, eco-political West Germany. He has been the marriage broker who brought about the union between organized labor and its traditional adversary, the world of big business. Now both parties have a stake in the survival of this marriage.

14

When it comes to social progress and political efficiency, the modern state and the modern entrepreneur should not be antagonists, but instead should be spiritual relatives.

—CHANCELLOR WILLY BRANDT (*Social Democrat*) *addressing the German Chambers of Commerce, Bonn, February, 1971*

As Darwin discovered the law of evolution in organic nature, so Marx discovered the law of evolution in human history; the simple fact previously hidden under ideological growths: that human beings must first of all eat, drink, shelter and clothe themselves before they can turn their attention to politics, science, art and religion. . . .

—FRIEDRICH ENGELS *delivering the funeral oration at the burial of Karl Marx in London's Highgate Cemetery, March 17, 1883.*

COALITION POLITICS

THE GERMAN CENTRE GETS CROWDED

THIS was the headline for a long article in the *Financial Times,* September 1, 1976, concerning the political situation in West Germany on the eve of its eighth national election. The headline and accompanying article pointed an editorial finger at a singular aspect of postwar West Germany: from the first days of the Federal Republic's existence down to the present, the German voters have shown a distinct and steadfast preference for coalition politics. This is characterized by judicious blending of conservative orthodoxy with sufficient consumer socialism to be palatable to the middle and working classes of the population. The Germans who survived World War II and its traumatic aftermath were successfully immunized by their recent turbulent history against being susceptible to extremist programs, either leftist or rightist, that promised solutions to their collective and individual problems and miseries. A sustained majority of the people have made it plain to the politicians that economic security and political stability came first in their order of priorities. They cast their votes for parties and politicians who seemed most likely to accomplish these objectives. Hence, as a result, the two major political

238

parties have found it expedient, as well as necessary, to hold to a middle-of-the-road line in formulating their policies and actions. There is more centripetal force, pushing them closer to the center, than centrifugal force driving them further apart toward the two extremes of the political spectrum. It is this tendency toward "polarization" that has created the unique eco-political character of postwar West Germany.

In the eight national elections of the postwar period, 1949–1976 inclusive, the averages of the voting strength of the leading political parties have been:

CDU–CSU bloc (conservative and just right of center)	44.8%
Social Democrats (Socialist in origin and just left of center)	37.0%
Free Democrats (liberal and centrist)	9.1%

No one party dominates. Under normal circumstances, no single party can form a government without a minority partner. Seven of the eight postwar administrations that held office in Bonn have been coalition governments. Only once did a major party capture an absolute majority of the votes and take office for four years without a minority partner. That occurred in 1957 when the CDU got 50.2 percent of the total vote. That marked the high point in the conservative rule by Adenauer and his CDU–CSU bloc.

From that point on, the Social Democrats, under the leadership of the dynamic Willy Brandt, mayor of West Berlin, slowly began to increase their popular support while the CDU–CSU started on a slow decline. At some point in 1966 it became apparent to the leaders of the two political parties that, as far as their respective popularity with the voters was concerned, they had reached a stalemate: the Christian Democrats were weary of and inept at carrying the burden of government; the Socialists were hungry for power; and the first serious recession of the postwar period had slowed down the booming economy. These factors combined to make the idea of a "grand coalition" seem very practical and suitable in this set of circumstances. So on December 1, 1966 a government composed of leaders of the CDU–CSU bloc and the SPD took office in Bonn. The Free Democrats, who had garnered 12.8 percent of the total vote, became the opposition party, ironically occupying the very center of the political spectrum, between the conservatives and the Social Democrats. For all practical purposes, the extremists on the left and on the right had disappeared from the political scene, for the time being.

This temporary coalition of traditional political foes was greeted with a great deal of skepticism and some ridicule as a new type of government composed of "Christo-Sozis." The *Economist* caught a relevant note with its pointed question: "It's magnificent, but is it a government?"

As could be expected, the grand coalition began to come apart at the seams, due to the inherent conflicts of interests between the cabinet ministers. The summer election of 1969 provided the German voters with a diverting spectacle: members of the coalition governing the country in a collective fashion, but quarreling and squabbling with each other on the election platforms about why the government was not performing as was originally promised. However, the SPD had less to be blamed for, because it had not been in office for as many years as the CDU–CSU bloc, now headed by Chancellor Kurt Kiesinger. With the momentum built up by the SPD, Willy Brandt was elected chancellor in a new coalition government, this time with the Free Democrats (FDP). But after being reelected in 1972 with even a bigger coalition majority, Brandt was forced to resign suddenly in May 1974, because of the shocking disclosure that his personal assistant, Günther Guillaume, alleged to be an East German anti-Communist refugee, was actually an undercover agent of the Communist intelligence network. Helmut Schmidt, defense minister and number two man in the SPD, took over as chancellor on May 16, 1974 and won reelection on his own record in the *Bundestag* on December 16, 1976. Brandt became chairman of the party.

With the SPD finally installed in power as the senior and dominant member of the coalition government, with the FDP as the junior partner, the metamorphosis of the Socialist party was just about complete. The evolutionary change from Marxian ideology and outlook had been going on for several years. The process of transformation had begun at the history-making SPD conference in Bad Godesberg in 1959. The membership of the party was in a state of frustration, as they failed to win public office at the national level in successive elections. The SPD leaders had confidently expected that they would govern postwar Germany, because they alone were free of the taint of nazism. They expected the defeated Germans to rally behind the SPD banners in overwhelming numbers; but this was not to be. To their surprise the SPD lost the crucial first election in 1949 to Konrad Adenauer and his conservative bloc. Again in 1953, Adenauer was victorious at the polls. In 1957 the CDU–CSU forces were again reelected, this time with an absolute majority of 50.2 percent of the total vote. This last election finally convinced the leaders of the SPD that they must change the public image and ideology of their party if they were ever to take over the government in Bonn. The SPD leaders were painfully aware that *Magenpolitik*—the stomach politics of increasing employment, food and housing, improved standards of living, new social-security benefits, and so on—were winning the elections for Dr. Adenauer and his political allies. The basic lesson to be learned was simple and pragmatic; in postwar West Germany, economic affairs and considerations govern political policies and actions. Up to this point in time, the SPD had held to the dogma that political ideology takes priority over economic affairs and not vice versa, as was the practice of the winning team of Adenauer, Erhard, and Company. Now recognition and grudging acceptance by the SPD leaders of the dominance of economic affairs in the life and development of the Federal Republic of Germany marked the beginning of the era of eco-politics. This new order of priorities has set the *Bundesrepublik* apart from its European neighbors and allies.

At the Bad Godesberg SPD congress in 1959, the craving of the party leadership to win public office triumphed over traditional ideology. The SPD acknowledged that a major job of facial, as well as brain, surgery was involved. No longer would the SPD be the party of just the workers; it would also be the champion of the middle classes. Waldemar von Knoeringen of the party's executive board, told the press: "One thing is abundantly clear, the Social Democrats are moving out of the realm of ideological thinking. They realize that only practical programs will win votes today. And to help make a better German community, they must win political power."

The modern and revised economic philosophy was neatly captured by a line in the SPD declaration of principles agreed upon at Bad Godesberg as follows: "Competition so far as possible; planning so far as necessary!" (*"Wettbewerb soweit wie möglich, Planung soweit wie nötig!"*)

Bad Godesberg, a pleasant, middle-class, residential suburb of Bonn hugging the west bank of the busy Rhine River, was the scene of this history-making transformation of the SPD some eighty-four years after the party was founded at Gotha. It seemed as though the party leaders were undergoing a collective political menopause, as they loosened their ideological bonds with Karl Marx, the German-born father of the international Socialist movement. The SPD jettisoned the ancient and tattered anticapitalistic dogmas and slogans which, in any event, had long ceased to frighten the rich and middle-class sectors of society. The old bogey of Socialist revolution was quietly interred at Bad Godesberg, as were the other stage props of German socialism such as the red flag and the clenched fist of the "embattled workers." The workers themselves were in the process of moving out of their stereotyped backgrounds and into the middle class, or at least into its lower echelons. The Volkswagen had supplanted the worker's bicycle and was symbolic of his new upward social mobility. The Social Democrats of West Germany, who above all other socialists in the world were most closely related to Marx, no longer thought in the Marxian terminology of creating a new society, but rather of improving the society they had to live with just outside their front doors.

It was at this juncture that Willy Brandt took over the leadership of the party from the ailing Erich Ollenhauer, who succeeded the late Schumacher. Brandt was the antithesis of the fanatical, irascible, and puritanical Schumacher, who lived on a diet of Socialist ideology. By contrast, Brandt was intensely human and not without his own personal weaknesses. For sustained periods he had been a heavy drinker; after he resigned in 1974, two magazines, *Der Spiegel* and *Stern,* reported that his male secretary had procured women for him during trips. Brandt publicly denied this but later sent a letter to all SPD members explaining ambiguously, "I am no saint and I have never pretended to be free from human weakness."

Perhaps because of these human failings, he was all the more attuned to the importance of the SPD thinking and acting in terms of the needs and desires of the masses of Germans, the workers and middle-class citizens. Some years later he introduced a new motif in SPD propaganda: the dedication to the improvement of the *Qualität des Lebens,* the quality of life, which meant more than just a better standard of living. It entailed an all-around improvement in the daily existence of the Germans, physically and materially, culturally and socially. This had a strange and hedonistic ring to the ears of old-line socialists, Brandt was persistent in promoting the new "consumer socialism," as the press characterized the post-Bad Godesberg policy line.

Brandt first used the expression, the "new center," on the eve of the 1972 election, which he won by an even larger margin than his victory in 1969. In the months ahead he pushed hard to persuade the public that the SPD had slipped its moorings to the left and moved its ideology and outlook to the new center. This tactic was the open sesame to winning elections. As Brandt told the SPD party conference in Hannover in April 1973: "Our party must not abandon the 'new center' because if you do lose the center position, then you are incapable of governing."

To Willy Brandt, as well as to Helmut Schmidt, his successor, the new *Realpolitik* was simple and logical; if the SPD could capture and hold the middle classes, as well as the workers, it could stay in power as the government for an indefinite period.

The commitment of Brandt and the SPD to open support of the free-market economy originally introduced by Professor Erhard in 1948 was reaffirmed with emphasis by the first SPD economics minister, Prof. Karl Schiller. A right-wing Social Democrat and a disciple of John Maynard Keynes, Schiller was a cautious and conservative steward of West Germany's economic policies for a period of five and a half years. To the pleasant surprise of the German business world, if not to many of his SPD colleagues, he proved to be a staunch champion and defender of the free-market economy. In fact, when Schiller broke with the Brandt administration in 1972 in a sharp disagreement over monetary policies, the government spokesman was quick to issue a press release that Schiller's resignation would not mean "an end to the free market economic order in Germany."

In December 1966, when the Conservative-Socialist grand coalition took office, Schiller, a virtually unknown economist and academician, was installed as minister of economics. He came to Bonn from the University of Hamburg, where he had been the president and head of the economics department and the university's Institute of Foreign Trade. Schiller's first task was to cure the 1966–67 recession which the SPD had inherited from the previous CDU–CSU administration. Erhard had succeeded Adenauer and had proved to be singularly inept as chancellor of the Federal Republic; he had somehow lost his magic touch in the field of economics. His regime ended with the first postwar German recession of 1966–67. As new economics minister, Schiller followed the Keynesian formula, including pump-priming spending to stimulate the stagnant economy, generous tax write-offs to encourage fresh capital investment, and balancing the federal budget. The recession was halted; a new surge of business activity followed. By 1968, Schiller's accomplishments had become a positive political asset for the SPD. The 1969 federal election was won by the SPD, thanks in great part to the professor's successful turnaround of the economy, which was booming along. The orthodox fiscal and economic measures Schiller practiced were reassuring, not only to the general public, but also to industrial, commercial, and financial circles.

In retrospect, Professor Schiller's major contribution to the eco-political development of postwar West Germany rests on his five and a half years of intense and intelligent defense and strengthening of the free-market system, after the Social Democrats came to power. Schiller never permitted Socialist tampering with the *Soziale Marktwirtschaft,* the free-market economy inherited from Adenauer, Erhard, and Company. So West German businessmen benefited from being able to pursue an uninterrupted economic expansion free from governmental interference and direction from 1949 down to the present, despite changes of governments with differing economic philosophies. Again the public's hunger for security and stability was recognized and served.

One of the key factors affecting the postwar political scene after 1945 was the general inability, or unwillingness, of politicians from left to right to recognize that the traditional German nationalism had expired with the suicide of the Nazi *Führer* in his Berlin bunker in the closing days of the war. The *Deutschland über Alles* syndrome that motivated the *Kaiserreich* of Wilhelm II and the *Dritte Reich* of Hitler was a casualty of the lost war. What was left to believe in? Germany was no longer a geographical entity. It had been drawn and quartered by its victorious conquerors, then separated down its north–south axis by the Iron Curtain. Out of this division came two separate states with their respective governments: the Federal Republic of Germany in the west and the Communist-controlled German Democratic Republic in the east. If the West Germans, who could freely express their views, displayed little interest in these developments, they showed even less concern for a return to the Germany of their history books. Their political instincts and reactions were numbed by defeat.

For example, what was believed to be a major political issue of the postwar era—the reunification of defeated Germany—instead proved to be a mirage. When the West Germans first began to plan for their future, no politician could envision the possibility that a division of the *Vaterland* into two separate states would be acceptable to the general public. The politicians could not contemplate the idea that reuniting Germany was not one of the basic aspirations of the postwar Germans. So the government, the opposition, as well as the leading civic personalities paid lip service to *Wiedervereinigung* (reunification), as one might genuflect in a church out of respect to the religious beliefs of its congregation, even if one does not accept its articles of faith. The CDU on the right, the FDP in the middle, and the SPD on the left were all on record strongly favoring *Wiederverinigung* as one of the eternal verities of German existence. Yet in the final analysis, and as successive elections demonstrated conclusively, the West Germans were only reacting to the bread-and-butter issues that affected their daily lives. The fever of Teutonic nationalism had definitely subsided in the immediate postwar years.

Just as there were no deep-seated or irreconcilable political conflicts in postwar West Germany—certainly nothing comparable to the street warfare waged between the Communists and the Nazis in the days of the Weimar Republic—in like manner, there were no unmanageable or insoluble economic controversies that set one segment of society against another. The prewar establishment, a heterogeneous mix of fading aristocracy, the industrial rich, and the *parvenus* of nazidom, had disintegrated. The *Wunderkinder,* who were to be the pillars of the postwar jet-set society, were too busy making their first millions to devote much time or energy to politics, economics, or social affairs. The workers, as a distinct sector of society, were thrown on their own resources as far as survival was concerned. They were virtually powerless in the early days of the *Bundesrepublik* to effectively fight for their own demands. There was nothing to be gained by striking or picketing a bombed-out factory, or by demanding jobs or a living wage. But the millions of workers were a potentially explosive force if they could not provide the necessities of life for themselves and their families.

However, the good fortune of the *Bundesrepublik* and the prime cause of its unprecedented economic comeback and overall political stability can be attributed to Erhard's socially responsive free-market system, which not only stimulated the acquisitive instincts of the storekeepers and industrialists to repair and reconstruct their war-battered business enterprises and thereby give impetus to economic revival, but also launched the postwar social-security system that was to be a firm foundation for the years of political stability that followed.

In a comparatively short time, this social-security program was able to satisfy the demands of the masses who came out of the war empty-handed, and whose prime concern was to be protected against poverty and want, especially in their old age. It would give unemployment compensation to the worker when he lost his job, provide free medical and hospital care for him and his family if they became sick, extra funds (*Kindergeld*) for parents with large families, and liberal pensions for those unable to work any longer due to age or disability.

With the passage of time it would burgeon into the world's most expensive and perhaps most elaborate social-security program. In 1949, when social security began in the postwar era, the total annual expenditure was DM 9.9 billion. ($2.3 billion). In the years ahead it would escalate to astronomical heights. By 1977–78 the total yearly payout for social-security benefits was approximately DM 300 billion ($125 billion at the current rate of DM 2.4 to $1). This is almost 30 percent of the GNP, a figure unmatched by any other country, including such noted welfare states as Great Britain and Sweden. West Germany has a population of just under 62 million; the annual payout for social-security benefits amounts to DM 4,838 ($2,015) per person.

Social security has a long history and tradition in Germany.* Bismarck pushed three historic pieces of social legislation through the *Reichstag*: the Health-Insurance Act of 1883, the Accident-Insurance Act of 1884, and the Old-Age Pension Act of 1889. History also tells us that Bismarck may not have been so much a social reformer as a conservative politician trying to woo the workers away from a growing attraction to the new Socialist movement. There have been respectable critics who question whether Bismarck's laws created true democratic social security. Rolf Dahrendorf, who was Germany's representative on the High Authority of the EEC before becoming head of the London School of Economics in 1976, has described the Germany of Bismarck's time as an "industrial feudal society with an authoritarian welfare state." But the Iron Chancellor's motives are beside the point; his three laws laid the groundwork for the world's first social-security system. Social security was revived after World War II when the postwar West German constitution recognized the obligations of the government to provide some measure of social security in Article 20, which declares: "The Federal Republic of Germany is a democratic and *social* federal state." (Italics added.)

In 1949, when Konrad Adenauer and his CDU–CSU team took over the new postwar government in Bonn to remain in office for the next eighteen years, they introduced the initial phases of an overall social-security program. Adenauer, who has been lauded as the "greatest chancellor since Bismarck," acted in the traditions of the man who first introduced modern social legislation to Germany in the 1880s. Adenauer and his lieutenants could argue from a position of strength, with some convincing evidence at hand, that a CDU–CSU government could offer the workers more real and tangible economic benefits than the "pie in the sky" which the rival SPD could only promise to deliver if and when they ever took over the government. The Adenauer–Erhard team claimed credit for the economic recovery to date, improved living conditions, as well as the new social-security program, as proof that the conservative CDU–CSU government was equally concerned for the economic welfare of the millions of workers. By contrast the SPD opposition could only say in effect: "We will do the same, only we will do it better."

Adenauer was reaping all the political benefits he could out of the new social-security program, just as Bismarck did in his time. Publicly the Socialists could not attack social security; privately they could only seethe with frustration at the Adenauer–Erhard tactics of encroaching on the political fief of the Social Democrats, who considered that it was their special responsibility to better the daily existence of the working class men and women.

The eco-political character of the Adenauer–Erhard strategy was attuned to the mood of the voters. For the CDU–CSU won the next three federal elections in 1953, 1957, and 1961—an impressive string of political victories based on successfully servicing the economic needs and aspirations of the German people.

The social-security system was self-supporting; the worker and his employer each shared 50-50 in the payment of social-security taxes. Initially the tax was about 18 percent of a worker's weekly wage, of which the employer was charged half. By the mid-1970s the social-security package amounted to about 28 percent, also split 50-50 between worker and employer.

However, in recent years it has seemed that the whole social-security system has gotten out of control, facing the possible danger of bankruptcy, unless some strong remedial measures are undertaken. For example, at the end of 1976 there were 15.4 million adults who were receiving government pensions for old age, disabilities, and military service. Considering that West Germany's population in 1977 was 61 million, that means virtually one out of every four Germans got a monthly pension check; these checks are regularly adjusted upward to cover cost-of-living increases. It is likely that the pension fund could be saddled with an DM 80 billion deficit over the next four years.

For example, in 1957 a person who retired after 40 years of steady work received a pension of DM 214 a month; by 1962 the same worker was receiving 548 deutschemarks per month. Another development that was not figured in the original actuarial calculations was the increasing longevity of the German people. In 1964 there were more than 10 million men and women over sixty-five years old; by 1979 there will be approximately 14.8 million in this age group. Attempts by Schmidt to eliminate the 9 percent cost-of-living increase in pension payments was repudiated by his own party members in the *Bundestag*.

In the field of health and medical care the social-security system has become self-indulgent and spendthrift. Here are some examples: In the mid-1960s, despite a steady rise in living standards, the West Germans developed a new disease which soon reached epidemic proportions. It is popularly recognized as the *Sechswochenkrankheit,* or "the six weeks' sickness," for which there is no cure in sight. The sickness is the direct and pleasant spinoff of a very liberal and generous health and medical care program. In the *Bundesrepublik,* if a worker becomes ill, he can remain on the sick list for six weeks and draw full pay. All that is required is a statement from his doctor that he will be unfit or unable to work for at least that length of time. The nature of the sickness is immaterial; it can be double pneumonia or a touch of arthritis. The patient stays at home without a pfennig's loss of income. If he is still sick beyond the six-week period, he then draws 75 percent of his regular wage for the duration of his illness.

After a bout of *Sechswochenkrankheit,* a doctor can certify that his patient needs a four-week convalescent leave (*Kurzeit*); this involves taking a "cure" at one of Germany's many spas and health resorts, all expenses paid by health insurance. To this can be added a doctor-certified *Nachkurzeit* of two weeks, to recover from the rigors of the previous four-week cure; this also takes place at a health resort with all expenses paid. The health insurance-program also offers any German adult, even if he is healthy and rugged as an ox, a four-week, all-expense paid cure at a spa or health resort, just to clean the pollution of modern living out of his system and to recharge his batteries every two years. Incidentally, the *Kurindustrie* has prospered mightily, with about 153 spas, 44 climate resorts, and 22 seaside spas now enjoying a gross annual income of $4.5 billion annually.* In fact, anything connected with the health and medical-care program, which has become its own growth industry, has prospered. The manufacturers of pharmaceuticals and patent medicines have seen sales of pills and placebos increase ninefold in the last 15 years. The medical profession comprising 115,000 doctors is now the highest earning group in the West German economy. According to official statistics, the average income of a doctor in private practice was DM 190,000 ($76,000 at the 1977 rate of exchange of DM 2.5 to $1). By comparison, the average annual income of a white-collar employee was DM 24,000 ($9,600.) German hospitals and clinics, public and private, number about 3,500; they are now treating about 10 million patients a year, or one-sixth of the total population. In an article on German medical care, the *International Tribune* of Paris commented on February 23, 1977 that this high incidence of hospital treatment ". . . is either an alarming sign of the state of the nation's health or an indication of its hypochondriac state of mind."

However, there is no disputing one salient development of the last decade: the West Germans have now become the most health-conscious people on the face of the globe.

The broad-beamed social-security system, now a *potpourri* of Conservative and Socialist planning, has been a unique and vital component in the emergence of postwar Germany as a major industrial nation and economic powerhouse in the European community of nations. It has served two basic requirements: it has gone far to satisfy the demands of the individual German for a sense of economic security for himself and his family; it has functioned as a sort of political gyroscope, keeping the nation from veering too far to the left or right in search of solutions to its manifold problems, thus giving it built-in political stability.

The German worker is aware that he cannot suddenly be brought to the brink of poverty through loss of job or serious illness. He also knows that, barring some unforeseen catastrophe, such as a war, his years of retirement will be made secure against want by an adequate pension and free medical care. There will be no pauperization of the worker and middle classes, such as occurred after World War I.

In a more abstract fashion, social security has muted the demands from the extremists to the left and right for social and economic reforms that would involve submitting postwar Germany to another ideological straitjacket. The modern social-security system, coupled with the equalization-of-burdens program—a partial redistribution of wealth between the haves and the have-nots at the end of the war—was a major factor in political stability. These measures possessed visibility and made extremist reforms seem unrealistic in the eyes of the German voter. These measures also fertilized a growing confidence that the Bonn government was trying to be fair to all segments of society. There was also the realization that the government was fully committed to stimulating economic recovery. This meant more employment, higher incomes, and improved living conditions for the masses, which engendered a reluctance to tamper with the basic political character of the government.

As the daily life of the average German changed from the grinding poverty of the immediate postwar era to the relative prosperity of the 1950s and 1960s, he no longer had to spend all his time and energy scrounging for the necessities of life for himself and his family. With improved living conditions, he could look around with greater interest and curiosity at what had happened to his fellow Germans and to this new *Bundesrepublik*. He could begin to distinguish what was essential for his daily existence and for his future and what was not—and he could think about what he had to do to make his life better and more secure. He and his fellow Germans began to grasp the single most important fact of West Germany's postwar existence: its economic power and resources, as measured in terms of industrial production, modern technology, profitable export trade, and so on, would govern and control his life and future more than anything else. West Germany's position and influence on the world scene, the standard of living of its people and their security all were dependent on its economic capabilities and not on a revived *Wehrmacht,* or some other instrument of political power.

The *Bundesrepublik Deutschland* was something new and different— an *eco-political* state. Was it a new imperium? A Fourth Reich?

15

The ability to accumulate wealth is infinitely more important than the possession of wealth; it guarantees not only possessions and an increase in wealth already accumulated, but also ensures the replacement of what is lost. This applies with even greater force to entire nations.

> —*The economist* FRIEDRICH LIST, *writing in 1846, quoted by the* Frankfurter Allgemeine Zeitung, *June 4, 1976*

. . . Curiously it is in Germany that some of the deep thinkers are beginning to work out the Western answer . . . The intimate connection between German trade policy and German aid policy is, in summary, that one finances the other. And like all questions of economics, it is in the end a pocket-book question—the creation of wealth.

> —JAMES P. O'DONNELL, *"Germany, Partner in World Progress,"* Fortune Magazine, *December 1965; an article about West Germany's foreign-aid program*

EMERGENCE OF
AN ECO-POLITICAL
WORLD POWER

IN TWO VITAL AREAS of its international relations—the OPEC bloc of oil-producing states and the Third World of clamoring, undeveloped countries—West Germany has demonstrated the effectiveness and the money-making potential of its eco-political foreign policy that enables it to stay out in front of the other industrial nations.

The first test came after the start of the Arab–Israeli war in October 1973 when OPEC, without any advance warning, imposed an embargo on oil shipments to West Germany and Holland. The *Bundesrepublik* was stunned and unprepared as it faced the gravest crisis of its postwar existence. In recent years imported oil, because it was cheaper and easier to handle, had gradually replaced Germany's abundance of Ruhr coal as the principal source of fuel and energy. Of the 134 million tons of oil consumed in Germany annually, 110 million tons were imported from the OPEC states. At the time of the embargo, West Germany had only a slim reserve of 22 million tons of oil, or about a two month's supply on hand. So when the OPEC bloc unsheathed its oil weapon, West German businessmen, as well as government officials, feared that the *Bundesrepublik* might suffer total collapse and chaos when the wheels of industry stopped turning for lack of fuel and energy.

Subsequently, when the OPEC states resumed oil shipments, but only after quadrupling the price of crude to over $11 a barrel, the pessimism and anxiety deepened. The massive transfusions of dollars for payments of OPEC oil imports raised the fears that Europe and Germany would bleed to death because of the hemorrhaging of their capital wealth into the treasure chests of Araby. The slim hopes of many German businessmen that perhaps the oil crisis would be of short duration, because of a general misunderstanding by both sides, were soon dissipated by the threats of Islamic firebrands, notably Colonel Khaddafi, the ruler of oil-rich Libya, the source of more than 30 percent of Germany's oil imports. On a visit to Paris in November 1973 the pugnacious colonel spoke menacingly in a press interview of the dire consequences for European industry if the Western nations did not come to terms with the Arab world. ". . . like Samson we shall destroy the temple; we shall ruin your industry, just as we shall ruin your trade with the Arab world. Europe should take heed of the catastrophe that faces it," he said.

And he was addressing Germany.

The economic future of the industrial nations looked bleak indeed. Then, as the trade deficits caused by the outflow of petro-dollars to the OPEC bloc began to sprout like weeds in a summer garden, there seemed little possibility of escaping from the clutches of the Arab petroleum monopoly. There was increasing speculation about a dramatic shift of the economic balance of power from Europe to the Middle East.

Yet, as one now looks back at those early days of the oil crisis, there was a solution to the dilemma in sight, at least in the case of West German industry. In the months and years that followed, the West Germans would seize this opportunity with initiative and gusto. This explains why the *Bundesrepublik,* alone of the Western powers, is now the best-situated and equipped to profitably exploit the impending industrialization of the desert.

The successive Bonn governments under chancellors Willy Brandt and Helmut Schmidt were able to take advantage of several developments in the Middle East which had occurred prior to the outbreak of the Arab-Israeli War of 1973. After years of cautious maneuvering, the OPEC countries had ended the oil concessions to the Seven Sisters—British Petroleum, Royal Dutch Shell, Gulf Oil, Texaco, Esso, Standard Oil of California, and France's Compagnie Française des Pétroles—covering the production and sale of oil reserves of the Middle East. When the major foreign oil companies lost their cartel control of the black gold of the Persian Gulf basin, the way was cleared for West Germany to negotiate directly with the individual OPEC governments without the intervention of the Sisters. Bonn had already created a national oil company, Deminex, as the first step to get its petroleum industry back into German control. The second development was the resumption of diplomatic relations between Bonn and the member states of the Arab League, which had been broken off in 1965 when the *Bundesrepublik* and Israel exchanged ambassadors for the first time.

At the outset of the oil embargo West Germany was not on the "list of friends" of the OPEC nations. Late in 1973, when Arab diplomats visited European capitals to explain what OPEC wanted from the Western nations, they pointedly avoided West Germany. However, in a press interview in Paris with *Der Spiegel,* Sheikh Zaki al-Yamani, the Saudi Arabian petroleum minister, stated that the *Bundesrepublik* could acquire the status of a "friend" by supplying arms to the Arabs and boycotting Israel. West Germany could have all the oil it wanted if it actively participated in the industrial development of Saudi Arabia. In January, Sheikh Yamani visited Bonn to repeat his offer in person. But the Bonn government was unequivocal in disclosing that West Germany would take no actions, political or economic, that would be a threat to the state of Israel, as demanded by the Arabs. However, Bonn would provide as much industrial assistance and goods, as well as technology, as Saudi Arabia could handle—at a price, of course.

The West Germans became aware that they were in a stronger bargaining position than they had originally believed. If the OPEC nations were serious in spending their billions of petro-dollars to industrialize their countries—and no other feasible alternative appeared on the horizon—the Arabs needed the Germans as much, if not more, than the West Germans had need of any single OPEC oil producer.

Incidentally, when the Arab oil embargo was imposed, France and Great Britain were quick to respond with pro-Arab, anti-Israeli statements. The governments in London and Paris also hurriedly disassociated themselves from proposals that the European community take collective reprisals against OPEC's economic warfare. Then, to emphasize its claim to be the Arabs' best friend in Europe, France's President Pompidou gave a state welcome to Libya's Colonel Khaddaffi in November 1973. However, neither the British nor the French could provide the goods and services that West Germany could deliver on schedule, especially in certain categories of heavy industrial materials and technology.

The Arabs were becoming aware of some painful and elemental facts of industrial development. Even armed with all the petro-dollars in the world, the Arab couldn't jump off the back of his camel and into the driver's seat of a bulldozer and begin the industrialization of a harsh, waterless wasteland. They could now see that the transformation of the oil-soaked deserts of Araby was complicated by a number of obstacles and deficiencies that would not be eliminated or remedied for years to come. Except for Iran, most of the Middle East oil-rich states are people-poor;

and without adequate numbers of workers with a modicum of skills, no industrialization is possible.

For example, the idea of Saudi Arabia planning a national industrial development program to cost approximately $140 billion, while having a native and nomadic population of only 6–8 million—no exact census has been carried out—almost borders on the ludicrous. The same can be said for Iraq, with 10 million; Syria, 6–7 million; Kuwait, 900,000; Qatar, 100,000; Bahrain, 200,000; United Arab Emirates, 200,000; Oman 700,000; and Libya, 2.5 million. Algeria, with a population of 11.6 million, having been colonized by the French, has some industrial potential, as a result of its rich natural gas fields. Iran, with 32 million people and substantial agriculture production, also has development possibilities.

In short, the Arab oil producers must build up cadres of hundreds of thousands of trained workers, and provide food, shelter, and social amenities for them. There is also a drain on the local native manpower to build up loyal defense forces for the oil-rich states, most of which have no defensible borders. The defense needs of the OPEC nations will increase in direct proportion to their fears that some other nations have designs on their petroleum wealth. The richer they become, the more they attract or invite the aggression of the have-not countries. Militarization does not mesh well with coordinated economic development.

Industrialization and imports of large labor forces will require water, in addition to the staggering amounts that will be needed for the greening of the deserts to produce food. In fact, the shortage of water is such a major and urgent problem, that one imaginative Saudi prince has financed large-scale research on the feasibility of towing mammoth icebergs from the Antarctic to the Persian Gulf. It's one easy way to get rid of the billions of petro-dollars that keep piling up in Saudi Arabia's bank accounts.

By the end of 1974, German industry was still alive and doing fine. The continuing trade boom had pushed the GNP total over the DM 1 trillion mark for the first time in history. Exports to OPEC countries were increasing by leaps and bounds. Germany had been able to cut its oil consumption by 20 percent, to match its reduced import quota from the OPEC bloc. Because of the bullying tactics of Colonel Khaddaffi, Germany cut down its imports from Libya by one-third and began to increase its consumption of oil from Saudi Arabia and Iran.* Both of these nations had made large-scale and long-term commitments to purchase German-made products, such as whole industrial plants, machinery, vast fleets of autos and trucks, construction equipment, electrical and electronics goods, and so on.

West Germany was well out in front as the leading industrial power in Europe, both from a productive and a technological standpoint. Equally important was Germany's impressive record for producing at prices competitive with the world markets and making delivery of its goods on schedule. This was not the case with British and French industries which were plagued by strikes. Hence, West Germany, in the eyes of the Arab planners, was the leading supplier of industrial goods and services. Their only serious competition would come from the U.S. firms, but the Americans were handicapped in getting contracts because of the fluctuation of the dollar against the more stable deutschemark. This upset the cost-accounting schedules of the Arabs.

Then to emphasize the special trading position that the West Germans enjoyed vis-à-vis the Arab oil-producers, in early 1975 a special economic mission from Saudi Arabia visited Bonn. Hassan ben Said, chief of the mission, announced that Saudi Arabia was embarking on a $100-billion, five-year, industrial-development program, which included construction of petro-chemical plants, refineries, steelworks, factories, airports, 12,000 kilometers of highways, power stations, housing estates, factories, and so on. This was later revised upward to a $140-billion development program. Hassan ben Said announced in a Bonn press conference: "Of all the friendly industrial nations, the *Bundesrepublik* is the one state which can fully assist in the industrial and technological development of Saudi Arabia. . . . You Germans pay your money for our oil at the present [quadrupled] prices, and through your technical assistance to us, the opportunity is provided for your oil money to return to you."

This spelling out of a *quid pro quo* in quite understandable and acceptable terms was seized upon by German industry. The rush to the Middle East was on; the business newspaper *Handelsblatt* of Düsseldorf described the mass migration of German businessmen to the Middle East as "The Orient Express." These traveling salesmen found ripe pickings in the Middle East. By 1976, West Germany's sales to OPEC countries had increased five and a half times its 1972 total, the Bundesbank reported. Germany was in the process of cutting down its deficit payments for OPEC oil, at its quadrupled rate, to manageable proportions. For example, in 1972 before the oil crisis, Germany had a trade deficit with the OPEC bloc of DM 2 billion. By 1974, when things for a time got out of control and oil prices had quadrupled, the deficit with the OPEC bloc jumped to DM 10.7 billion. However, Germany could handle this drop because its total world trade turned in a payments surplus of DM 50.8 billion ($20 billion) for 1974. Furthermore, the tide began to turn favorably. The oil deficit dropped to DM 300 million in 1975 and then to DM 900 million for 1976. The trade for the first half of 1977 was in rough balance, as West Germany's exports to the OPEC bloc were increasing at the rate of 26 percent over the previous year's figures. In addition, the OPEC bloc had already invested DM 12 billion in Germany since 1974.

Thus, West Germany alone of the major industrial nations is not running a trade deficit with the Middle East oil producers. By comparison, the United States in 1977 was paying out at the rate of $45 billion (DM 103 billion) a year for oil from the OPEC bloc.

In a long review of the effects the oil crisis has had on West Germany, *Deutsche Zeitung,* in August 1977, concluded: "The sober figures [listed above] are evidence of the profound economic change which has so far been to the benefit of this country's strong economy."

The eternal conflict between the rich and the poor of this world in olden times was considered to be the local welfare problem of each community; today it has expanded to global dimensions. The world is dividing up into blocs: the haves comprising the industrially developed and affluent nations of Western Europe, the United States, Canada, and Japan; and the have-nots, those underdeveloped countries, most of which were former colonies of the European powers, which are now regrouped under the banners of the Third World. The latter mobilize whatever political and economic clout they can muster to get a bigger slice of the world's economic pie. The Third World nations use the forum of the United Nations in New York and other international gatherings and agencies to push through their demands for a massive share-the-wealth program on a global scale at the expense of the affluent and industrial nations. In essence, they demand that the industrial nations finance and actively assist in the industrialization of the Third World countries so that they can exploit their own natural resources and raw materials and eventually join the ranks of the haves.

With the exception of West Germany and Japan, most of the industrial powers, with the United States in the vanguard, seem to have a defensive attitude toward the Third World. They appear to be groping for a political solution, and the plans of the haves—except for Germany and Japan—are conditioned in some instances by their former colonial relationships with Africa and Asia. Not having been a colonial power in the European sense, the U.S. has been branded as a dollar imperialist by the Third World propagandists in an effort to stimulate feelings of guilt and to make the Americans more amenable to their political blackmail.

Not being stigmatized with any derogatory political identification or by any commitment "to take up the white man's burden," West Germany, and to a lesser degree, Japan, has developed a new approach to the Third World in order to cope with its clamorous demands for money and help. In contrast to the attitudes of other industrial nations, West Germany has evolved a policy line that is almost completely economic in character. It has operated on this simple and fundamental premise: foreign aid should assist foreign trade. The conservative and influential *Frankfurter Allgemeine Zeitung* summarized the motivation behind West Germany's foreign-aid policy with these comments in February 1972:

The earlier one helps the developing countries to get started, the quicker they will orient their industrial structures to the world market. *Their importance as customers of the industrial nations will increase.* [Italics added.]

The West German approach has always been governed to a greater extent by profits than by politics. Bonn's first foreign aid began at the end of the 1950s in the form of financial subsidies or investment guarantees to major German firms, so as to permit them to undertake large industrial development projects in Africa and Asia at no basic risk to themselves. Foreign aid only concerned itself with economic-development projects that meant increased sales of German goods and services. The Bonn government, under both CDU and SPD leadership, has consistently divested its foreign-aid programs of any specific political objectives, except for the international public-relations value involved in helping the underdeveloped nations of the Third World. Bonn, the source of foreign-aid grants and financing, sought to avoid any political confrontation between the haves and have-nots of the world. Exemplifying this nonpolitical approach, the Bonn government later created a foreign-aid agency with the relevant title Ministry for Economic Cooperation.

Egon Bahr, the minister for this new agency, called for a "new economic détente" between the rich and poor nations in a speech given in Bombay, India, in 1976. He said: ". . . the problems of the Third World will overshadow all other important political problems in the next decade."

In this sense, "new economic détente" is a euphemism for the hard policy line that "aid is dependent on trade." Otherwise it has no rationale for the West Germans. In fact, the progovernment newspaper *Frankfurter Rundschau* was more explicit when it informed its readers in May 1976 that: ". . . eighty percent of the foreign aid (DM 3.5 billion for 1975) in the form of capital investment goods, has been a profitable spin-off for the West German economy."

This is the confirmation of what every Ruhr industrialist knows but doesn't talk about, that West Germany has a calculated, businesslike approach to the whole range of its relations with the Third World countries. In short, foreign aid is fine, but it must return a dividend.

The concept of international foreign aid is a postwar development that originated with the Americans. When Greece and Turkey seemed in danger of falling under Communist rule in 1947, President Truman created the first foreign-aid program of $400 million in military and economic assistance to strengthen the governments of these two nations. Next came the billions of dollars in Marshall Plan aid to enable Western Europe, including Germany, to repair the ravages of World War II. Then it became apparent that the underdeveloped countries of Asia and Africa also needed assistance in order to survive the transition from colonies to independent nations. The Point IV program to provide "technical assistance to non-European underdeveloped countries" was launched by President Truman in 1949. From that point on, foreign aid became a permanent fixture in the relations between the haves and the have-nots.

America's Point IV program captured the imagination of West German businessmen and industrialists. The Truman doctrine pointed a way whereby private enterprise and national foreign policy could find a common purpose in opening up new business frontiers in the underdeveloped countries of the Third World.

I remember a 1954 luncheon in the Industrie Club in Düsseldorf with a prominent Ruhr banker. Puffing a fine Havana, he offered me his suggestions on how the Point IV program could operate for the political and economic benefit of both the United States and West Germany:

What you Americans should do to save money and still make friends abroad is to let us Germans be your partners in the Point IV program. We have a lot of experience in dealing with these underdeveloped countries. Besides we have the technicians and the goods required for the work to be done. But we can't do anything on our own, we don't have the necessary capital. But with your money and our experience, this would be the most practical way to achieve your political objectives—and it's cheaper too.

The banker was not being facetious or patronizing. On paper his proposal had its own acceptable logic; it represented a point of view held by many Ruhr industrialists. On numerous occasions German businessmen pointed out that the newly independent states of Africa and Asia are trying to make a quantum jump into the twentieth century. They want all the infrastructure of a modern nation: railroads and harbors to provide easy access to their mineral and agricultural resources; bulldozers and construction equipment; dams and power plants; telephones and trucks; and a host of industrial engineering and heavy capital goods to create the foundation for their economic and technological development. The Germans could easily see their goods and services transforming these ex-colonial countries into self-supporting nations. The opportunities on the far horizon sparked German imagination.

In March 1955 top officials of West Germany's leading industrial firm held a press conference to announce that Krupp of Essen had embarked on its own "Point IV½" program to assist in the industrial development of the backward countries of Asia and Africa. This information created quite a bit of attention in the German and world press for several compelling reasons. It was a far cry from the previous and principal activities of this large industrial complex, which had been Europe's leading armaments producer since Bismarck's time until the end of World War II. Even though it has always been a privately owned business enterprise, the House of Krupp—members of the family and firm prefer this dynastic identification—has always been considered something of a national institution in the eyes of the Germans. In the past, the fortunes of Germany seemed to rise and fall with the good and bad times experienced by the House of Krupp. There was a saying in the Ruhr: *"Wenn Krupp blüht, blüht Deutschland"*—"When Krupp prospers, so prospers Germany." After the last of the Hohenzollern Kaisers abdicated in 1918, the Krupps became the first family in Germany. In 1942, Hitler approved a special law, *Lex Krupp,* to permit the family to retain ownership of the great arms producer, by exempting it from normal inheritance laws and taxes.

However, in the bleak and dark days of 1945, Krupps of Essen had the appearance of having been literally and figuratively bombed out of existence. The Allied air forces had mounted fifty-five large bombing raids on the city of Essen and had smashed the sprawling complex of Krupp factories, machine shops, and power plants into piles of broken stone, brick, and twisted girders. Alfried Krupp, the head of the family, had been arrested and was later to be tried and convicted as a war criminal at Nuremberg, and suffer the confiscation of all his properties. The remains of the Ruhr's greatest industrial combine was to be deconcentrated and dismantled for purposes of reparations.

Following the outbreak of the Korean War in 1950, and after serving three years of a twelve-year sentence at Landsberg prison, Krupp was pardoned by U.S. High Commissioner John J. McCloy, and the confiscation of his industrial empire was nullified. Time and changing circumstances also ended the deconcentration of the coal and steel properties. However, the House of Krupp was forced to carry a heavy burden which it could not shake off as it had the deconcentration commitment: The name of Krupp was notorious and infamous outside of Germany for being directly connected with Hitler's wars of aggression, and for direct involvement in the "war crimes" of slave labor, concentration camps, and genocide.* No Allied pardon could erase or cleanse the wartime history of the House of Krupp.

Following his release from Landsberg prison in 1951, Alfried Krupp kept an exceedingly low public profile as he restructured his industrial empire to meet with the changing postwar circumstances. He was aware that Krupps of Essen must carve out a new commercial existence for itself, and this could best be accomplished by helping to develop the raw-material resources and industrial possibilities of the Third World countries. Krupp would provide the initial planning, the industrial and engineering goods and equipment, plus the technicians to carry out these projects. However, he had another string to his bow; he hoped to persuade some of the large U.S. firms to become his partner in some of these development projects. He made a secret trip to Canada to confer with Cyrus Eaton of Cleveland about possible collaboration. He sent his general manager, Berthold Beitz, to Washington to explore the off-chance that Krupps of Essen might be eligible to participate in America's own Point IV development program and thus share in the U.S. financing of these projects. America would be welcome as a partner because of its freedom of action, its superior technology, and its inexhaustible supply of dollars.

In January 1955, Alfried Krupp was vacationing on the small Andros island in the Bahamas with his host, Swedish industrialist and entrepreneur Axel Wenner-Gren. Wenner-Gren's wartime business connections with the Nazi government had often been criticized in the Allied press, but he knew how to take remedial measures. He advised Alfried Krupp to employ a public-relations counselor, preferably an American, as part of a plan to remove the stigma and obloquy attached to the name of Krupp. A few weeks later on his return to Germany, Krupp contacted me through his lawyer, Dr. Otto Kranzbuhler. I had first come to Krupp's attention when, as correspondent for the *New York Herald Tribune,* I had written several articles critical of the U.S. prosecution's case against Alfried Krupp, for their tactics of trying the son for the sins of the father. In February 1955 I was offered the job as public-relations adviser to Krupp of Essen; after some thought concerning the consequences of this assignment, I accepted the post.

Within a few days, I was being thoroughly briefed on the postwar status and industrial operations of the House of Krupp. The city of Essen and the Krupp installations were being tidied up and repaired, as time and money permitted. Krupp was operating at a higher level of capacity than I had thought possible, considering the extensive wartime bombing it had sustained. For example, Krupp was expanding into the processing of titanium, the new space-age metal. The firm was also engaged in a number of large industrial and heavy engineering projects far from its normal European sphere of business interest. These involved the construction of a 1-million-ton steel mill at Rourkela, India, together with the planning and building of a complete new city to house 100,000 workers, with all the needed installations such as power plants, sewage and water, streets, and so on; exploitation of Pakistan's iron ore deposits, together with the construction of another steel mill; development of Greece's nickel mines, plus construction of a smelter to process the metal; a smelting plant for Spain; harbor installations in Iraq, Thailand, and Chile; small industrial plants in Egypt, the Sudan, Pakistan, and Iran; industrial surveys of Ethiopia and Portugal; plus a number of other industrial and engineering projects in the Near and Middle East, such as the first bridge over the strategic Bosphorus, linking Europe with Asia. Krupp was far out in front of every other European or British firm in signing up contracts for postwar development projects in the former colonial countries.

Alfried Krupp sensed the hunger of these new nations for industrial development to give themselves a foundation on which to build their economies. He saw this as a golden opportunity for the House of Krupp to create new markets for its manifold industrial goods and technical services. Krupp had even established a special department, Krupp Industriebau, headed by Paul Hansen, which could handle the complete planning and construction of industrial-development projects. Alfried Krupp saw his new role as *Weltlieferant,* a contractor to the world, even though all this drastic change in objectives and policy was generally unknown.

I proposed a new image of a postwar House of Krupp completely divorced from its past as the armorer of the Reich. We should publicize the newsworthy fact that Krupp was now devoting its time and energies to the industrial development of the backward areas of the world so that their peoples would have a better way of life and be able to support themselves. We should depict Krupp taking a leading role in a field of endeavor normally reserved for sovereign governments—that of foreign aid. However, the key factor of the public relations theme was to identify Krupp's development projects in Asia and Africa with America's foreign-aid program by the association of names and common purpose. That could be accomplished by giving a provocative and attention-attracting label to Krupp's development projects in former colonial countries. The program would be given the label Krupp's Point IV½.*

When the made-in-Essen Point IV½ program was unveiled, it had a surprising impact on both the Ruhr industrial community and on the Bonn government. Krupp's fellow industrialists were impressed because they could readily see the commercial possibilities for them by following Krupp into the Third World countries. Adenauer was quick to grasp the international public-relations value for West Germany in developing its own foreign-aid program along the lines sketched out by Krupp. Heinz Moeller, editor of *Germany International,* commented: "Germany would gain a new and benevolent world image, which would go far to help ease the memories of the past."

In the last half of the 1950s the Bonn government edged its way into the foreign-aid field, and this move served two basic objectives: it was intelligent international public relations, and it opened up new markets for West Germany's capital goods and services in areas of the world that hitherto had been closed to German exports. The new foreign aid would, in effect, be an extension of the government's financial help to make Germany's exports more competitive in conventional world markets. This assistance involved tax rebates and other disguised subsidies in various forms, enabling West German exporters to keep their prices in line with international competitors. Under the new foreign-aid program the Bonn government gave exporters additional financial assistance in the form of loans or guarantees of loans extended by private firms for purchases of West German goods and services by an underdeveloped country.

For example, if the French railway system ordered ten locomotives from Krupp, the Essen firm was eligible for the normal export assistance of tax rebates and so on. However, if the government of Indonesia contracted to buy ten locomotives from Essen, then Fried Krupp qualified for normal export help and it was also eligible for foreign-aid loans or credit guarantees to finance the sale of the railroad engines. This eliminated a large degree of risk for the industrial firms in their dealings with the underdeveloped countries, as well as giving them encouragement to search out new markets for their capital goods and technical services. In the early years, 1955–60, about $400 million had been allocated by Bonn to finance eighteen large industrial development projects in Asia and Africa, and one in Latin America, carried out by large Ruhr firms, including Fried Krupp of Essen. While this sum was not large by comparison with the billions involved in America's Point IV program, this was the first big commitment by the Bonn government to open up new markets for German industry in what had formerly been the protected colonial preserves of other European powers.* The fact that Germany had been the wartime enemy of Britain and France, the two leading colonial powers, automatically identified the Germans as friends in the eyes of many native officials of the new governments of Asia and Africa.

With the passage of time, the Europeans, especially the Germans, became aware of the long-range political and economic importance of the Third World countries, because they are the source of many vital raw materials. From a political standpoint, the new nations of Africa were very volatile, unpredictable, and disruptive, as witness the civil wars in the Congo and Nigeria for mineral and oil riches and the revolutions in Algeria, Libya, Egypt, and others. Bonn took a neutral stance regarding all conflicts between the Africans themselves and between the Africans, Asiatics, and the Europeans. The Bonn government had no brief or responsibility to democratize or stabilize the warring factions in the ex-colonial states. However, what did seriously concern the Bonn government was the ultimate exploitation and disposition of the raw-material wealth of these underdeveloped countries. The Bonn government could neither predict nor control the future of the new Third World countries, but it could better organize its foreign-aid program as the proper vehicle to handle the economic relations between industrial West Germany and the Third World.

The foreign-aid program had grown in a rather haphazard fashion, but more definitive policies and guidelines for its future operations were needed. Snipping off a few departments from the ministries of economics and foreign affairs, Adenauer created the new Ministry for Economic Cooperation in 1961. Headed by a young Düsseldorf banker, Walter Scheel, to plan and administer West Germany's foreign-aid program, Scheel later became president of the *Bundesrepublik*. The new ministry laid down some broad policies to ensure that West German foreign aid funds would be spent judiciously and in a businesslike manner. Henceforth there would be no outright grants for development projects; but recipient nations could qualify for "soft" loans. No major development projects would be undertaken without cosponsorship of the recipient nation, so as to share in responsibility for the project. No money would be advanced to cover any balance-of-payments deficits of the recipient country, or be diverted for any purpose, such as to cover budgetary expenditures or deficits of the receiving nation. No strings or commitments could tie foreign-aid funds to any German firm; West German aid would be given without advance political commitments or demands. Finally, foreign-aid funding, including grants to be spent by the United Nations agencies in Third World countries, would approximate about 1 percent of the West German gross national product.

Walter Scheel was an enthusiastic convert to the doctrine that trade follows aid, a broad policy line that was never publicly confirmed in such blunt terms, but, nevertheless, was adhered to in practice. Scheel recognized from the outset that a coordinated government-plus-private-industry-foreign-aid program, while contributing to the economic development of the new nations of Asia and Africa, could at the same time increase the exports of West German goods and services. The magazine *German International* quoted him:

From an economic standpoint, the development policy is of vital importance to us because the country's economic growth will in the future be even more dependent on development of foreign trade . . . and because our overseas partners can become better and more stable partners only if they themselves achieve economic growth. I emphasize that in the future we should be more courageous in *our economic exploitation of development aid.* [Italics added.]

During the Scheel period, which ended in 1969, Bonn's foreign-aid program did wonders to stimulate the growth of West German exports to new postwar markets. This in turn was soon to make West Germany the number two trading nation in the world, after the U.S., as well as invigorating the national economy to the point where Germany was the strongest economic power in Europe.

West Germany's foreign aid was different from the programs of the United States, Britain and other countries: it was tailored to serve the economic interests of the *Bundesrepublik* and then, secondarily, to assist the industrial development of the new African and Asian nations.* Bonn put two major objectives in the forefront of its program:

First, foreign aid must increase West Germany's exports of goods and services and help to secure a continuous flow of the necessary raw materials from the developing countries as far as possible. In short, a development project was judged on how well it could contribute to the achievement of the two objectives, singly or collectively.

Second, a foreign-aid loan or credit guarantee was considered on the same basis as any investment: could it pay a dividend? If not, the funds were allocated to some other project with better prospects of earning a return for the German economy.

An example of the type of large-scale foreign-aid project which incorporated the policy objectives laid down by the Bonn government was the Bong Mountain iron ore development in Liberia. The Ruhr has always had to import its iron ore from abroad, and Sweden has been the main source of supply. But the Swedish ore deposits would be exhausted within the foreseeable future, so the German technicians and geologists began looking elsewhere for new sources of supply. After World War II a German survey team returned to the Ruhr to report the discovery of a massive deposit of high-grade iron ore located in the Bong Mountain range about seventy-five miles inland from the seaport of Monrovia. As a result, four of the Ruhr's major steel producers (Thyssenhütte, Dortmunder-Hörde, Rheinstahl, and Bochumer-Verein—in which Krupp is now the majority shareholder) formed a consortium to develop Liberia's major raw-material resource in a 50–50 partnership arrangement with the Liberian government. This $100-million project was the largest single foreign-aid project financially supported by the Bonn government.

In reality, it is a highly profitable commercial project, because the Bong Mountain is today the biggest exporter of iron ore and sells its raw material to the Ruhr as well as to the American steel industry. German firms supplied all the infrastructure, such as building the railway from the ore deposit to the seaport, and supplying the rolling stock, the ore-processing and all the loading and unloading equipment. Finally, though it is 4,000 miles distant, Liberian iron ore makes West Germany much less dependent on the foreign-controlled sources of the vital metal needed to keep the Ruhr's giant steel mills in operation.

This Liberian project is an illustration of the eco-political character of Bonn's foreign policy; a field of international political endeavor, foreign aid is governed or controlled by economic considerations. *Fortune* magazine, December 1965, pointed to this dichotomy of classifying overseas development projects, which are essentially commercial in their character, as foreign aid:

It is when one happens upon a venture of this size, which is a hard-nosed commercial proposition in the bargain, that the whole question of the future role of private enterprise in the developing areas poses itself. The Germans for whom the free market economy is an article of faith, entered Africa like missionaries. But conversion [of the Africans] to capitalism first involves the creation of capital, and infrastructure and some money, for nascent capitalists to learn to play with.

The Bonn government had a long-range objective which it hoped to accomplish through its foreign-aid program: to cultivate strong and lasting economic ties with the present and future generations of the people of the developing countries. Bonn wanted to create new and permanent markets for West Germany's exports to these countries. The most effective way to hold and to expand these business bridgeheads in the Third World countries would be to impress on their recently liberated populations the overall superiority of German goods and services. With this in view, the Ministry for Economic Cooperation invested substantial sums in bringing thousands of young Africans and Asiatics to Germany for high-school and college educations, as well as vocational training. By 1970 more than twenty thousand scholarships had been provided to Africans and Asiatics, mainly in technical universities (Technische Hochschulen), where they studied chemistry, engineering, electronics, machinery and machine tools production, car manufacturing, and other related subjects, bearing on modern industry and technology. The ministry also organized a special program to educate two thousand vocational-training teachers from the Third World in the latest of Germany's industrial operations and techniques. These cadres of vocational teachers were to return to their native lands to seed their knowledge of modern German production technology in new generations of skilled workers, who would probably never visit a modern industrial state. Out of this large-scale educational program for African and Asiatic students would come the future sales representatives and maintenance personnel to staff the local offices of German firms in their respective countries. However, the ultimate value of this program to West Germany would lie in the fact that education and experience passed on to the thousands of students would cause them to "think German" when faced with economic problems arising out of their own nation's industrial development.

One of the basic reasons for the success of foreign aid in stimulating West Germany's exports to the developing countries is that leaders of the German business community "stayed on top of the program," as one executive said. The heads of the great banks and industrial corporations gave much of their personal attention to the industrial development of Third World countries. They did not depend on the men in charge of their international divisions for the information they needed, but frequently traveled to these areas to see for themselves. Group tours of leading West German bankers and Ruhr industrialists would be organized to visit the most important of the Third World countries, such as Saudi Arabia, Iran, Egypt, India, Red China and some of the new African nations.* They were determined to convince the leaders of these countries that their economic betterment was the serious concern of the German firms. These teams of executives served as powerful and persuasive goodwill ambassadors. They could and did negotiate on-the-spot business deals with the heads of governments, such as the Shah of Iran, President Sadat of Egypt, the late Premier Chou En-lai of Red China, King Faisal of Saudi Arabia, Indira Gandhi of India, and others.

The 1973 oil crisis, with the subsequent quadrupling of crude-oil prices by the OPEC bloc, forced Bonn to put its foreign-aid program on even a more businesslike basis. A second-generation policy line was developed which included the following main points:*

1. The developing nations in possession of the vital raw materials that German industry needs (except for oil) will have to enter into "active partnership" with German firms for the extraction and processing of these commodities or risk the loss of West German foreign aid.

2. West Germany's participation in the industrial development of Third World countries will be concentrated in those new nations that have "good future prospects," that is, a growing market for German exports.
3. Bonn will make financial commitments of loans and export rebates only where there is "mutual trust" and "long-term legal protection" for the German partner.
4. Transfers of capital will be made only to areas with prospects for good economic growth.
5. West Germany will not agree to any demands of the Third World nations that their raw-materials prices be tied to the ups and downs of industrial indices in Germany.

In short, stripped of the polite euphemisms used to describe it to the United Nations Assembly in New York, Bonn's second-generation foreign-aid policy is based on a *quid pro quo* arrangement: no foreign aid unless there are assurances that it will pay economic dividends to the *Bundesrepublik*. Behind this pragmatism is the conviction that foreign aid is essentially an investment which should produce benefits for the recipient as well as the investor. And only good investments ever nourish a growing industry and repay the donor.

A further example of the hard-nose pragmatism that governs Bonn's approach to the Third World countries is an innovation introduced by the Ministry for Economic Cooperation. The MEC is now in the business of marketing German technology and know-how to the underdeveloped nations for hard cash. A government corporation, Gesellschaft für Technische Zusammenarbeit (GTZ, Association for Technical Cooperation), was formed to offer Germany's technical, economic, and organizational expertise and assistance to Third World countries for a reasonable fee. This aid is specifically designed to break the bottlenecks that occur when industrial development gets underway and then stalls. German know-how, as well as the managerial and specialist talents that are required, will be available on a contract basis. In turn, the GTZ will probably subcontract the orders for its technical assistance to private German firms.

However, when the maps of the Third World countries, now pinpointed with numerous industrial-development projects and new export markets for German goods and services, are put back on their shelves, the biggest prize of them all, the map of Red China, remains virtually a blank, devoid of any symbols of Germany's postwar economic penetration. Red China, the colossus of 800 million people, which overshadows the Third World of the have-not countries, occupies a special niche in West Germany's eco-political future. With a confidence tinged with possessiveness, the Ruhr industrialists since the first days of recovery have concluded that West Germany is the ideal economic partner for Red China. In the years to come, the

Germans envision a close collaboration to provide the Chinese with the tools, machinery, and technology that will transform China into a true world power. When examining the background of this optimism, there is some surprising logic to support the projected special relationship between Bonn and Peking. And the Chinese Communists, since the end of World War II, have given the West Germans encouraging signals from their side.

Not long after World War I, Bolshevik Russia and the Weimar Republic of Germany were outcasts in the eyes of the victorious powers. Both the defeated nations looked for allies and fulfilled that need in each other, culminating in the Treaty of Rapallo of April 22, 1922. Besides, Lenin wanted to industrialize the great brooding hulk of the European-Asiatic land mass, so as to give the Soviet Union the power and resources to protect the "motherland of world revolution."

The Germans saw in this their big chance. To assist in the industrialization of a predominantly agricultural country the size of Russia was to open up an unlimited market for Germany's capital and consumer goods. So German engineers and technicians, by the hundreds, moved to the Soviet Union to begin its industrialization. More than any other country, Weimar Germany laid the foundations of Russia's present industrial and military power.*

Since the 1950s the more foresighted of the West German industrialists and bankers have seen the opportunity to repeat this performance—this time in Red China. The China that the Communists took over was roughly in the same state of industrial development as was the Bolshevik Russia of Lenin's day. China has been firmly in the grip of the Communists for three decades, but its industrialization has been disrupted, and at times retrogressed, due to the violent political and ideological conflicts within the Communist leadership, verging on the brink of overt civil war. It was the struggle between the hard-line Marxist ideologues and the pragmatists, which now seems to have been settled in favor of the latter, with the arrest and overthrow of the "Gang of Four," headed by Madame Mao.

What gives substance to these visions of large-scale industrial development projects, coupled with the exports of German goods and services, are the overtures that have been made by the Peking government. Years before post-Mao government opened its doors to Western businessmen, Peking had invited German bankers and industrialists to exploratory talks in Peking concerning major industrial-development projects, as well as trade deals, a courtesy not extended to other nationalities at that time. For example, shortly after World War II, Hans Stahmer, who had been Nazi Germany's ambassador to China and Japan, was sought out and quietly invited to Peking. He returned to Germany with the message that the Chinese would welcome possible German assistance in the postwar industrial development of Red China. But the time was not ripe, for in those early days of economic recovery, German businessmen had their hands full repairing and reconstructing their own industry.

In 1963 the first of a series of visits by groups of top-ranking German industrialists to Communist China took place. The tour was organized by the *Ostausschuss,* the East Committee of the Federation of German Industries, formed to explore the realities of east–west trade for West Germany. For example, the Ruhr firm of Demag, Europe's largest producer of heavy capital goods—one-third of the world's rolled steel is turned out on Demag-made mills—was anxious to survey the export market in China for its steel-making, coal-mining, and earth-moving equipment. It sent Alfred Schulz, head of its international division, to open up discussions with the Chinese in Peking. Schulz returned, fervidly believing that Red China was the big new export market for Germany's goods and services. He told the press that "China is like a dry sponge ready to soak up our goods."

As a result of these encouraging prospects for German exports, the Bonn government took immediate steps to open up diplomatic relations with Communist China and to negotiate a trade treaty with Peking. Secret talks were held in Berne, Switzerland, but the war in Vietnam intervened. News of the secret negotiations reached Washington, and President Johnson made it clear that West Germany would sacrifice its special relationship with Washington if it persisted in doing business with Red China, the ally of America's enemy in Vietnam. Chancellor Erhard broke off talks with the Chinese. Schulz and other Ruhr industrialists were angered by this turn of events. Schulz told the U.S. consular officials in Düsseldorf: "Your government is forcing us to ignore one-quarter of the human race. Without a trade agreement and the government-backed export credits, we can't do any worthwhile business with the Chinese."

The Bonn government had to wait until 1972, after President Nixon's surprise visit to Peking, to establish diplomatic relations with Red China; but Schulz and his Ruhr colleagues did not do too badly in the interim period. By 1965, West Germany's exports to China doubled. In the following year Erhard agreed to a federal guarantee of credit for $87.5 million to an industrial consortium headed by Demag, to build a new steel mill with a capacity of 2 million tons, the biggest industrial installation ever to be constructed in China by foreigners.

By the mid-1970s, German–Chinese economic relations were warming noticeably. In June 1975, China opened up the first and biggest trade fair ever organized outside its own frontiers—in Cologne. The fair was a showcase of what China had to offer in exchange for Germany's and Europe's goods and services. Later that year, the West Germans opened a special industrial trade fair in Peking, called Techno-Germa. The two-week fair, featuring the latest products and the technology of 358 of West Germany's largest industrial firms, was the biggest foreign exposition ever staged in Red China, and was the first mass display of capitalist goods ever permitted inside Communist China. The Chinese officials informed Hans Friderichs, the economics minister who opened Techno-Germa, that they had arranged for practically every Chinese technological expert, engineer, and scientist, as well as selected cadres of skilled workers, to visit the exposition, so that each could acquire a working knowledge of Germany's most modern industrial products and technology. It was a blue-ribbon audience of China's industrial elite, numbering over 220,000. These are the men who would be placing the orders for China's imports of industrial products in the years ahead.

The Ruhr industrialists who participated in the Peking Techno-Germa fair do not expect an early flood of orders from Peking for heavy industrial goods and services. Red China still has too many internal political and economic problems that have to be ironed out. Some years will elapse before West Germany's exports to Red China will reach the levels commensurate with China's needs and with its capacity to develop industrially. As the *Financial Times* commented in October 1975:

China could be the *next growth market* . . . The West German approach is typical of the *very long range view* that German industry has taken of its eastern trade. At the heart of the approach lies the *cultivation of a market,* even if the short-term results are not over-encouraging. [Italics added.]

But the Peking correspondent of *Die Welt* was closer to German thinking and planning of its export drive in the Far East. As he wrote at the time:

The image which Germany is trying to project in the largest and most populous developing country in the world, *is not that of a major political power, but rather of the most important industrial country in Europe, a country whose toolmaking and mechanical engineering can compete successfully on the world market.* [Italics added.]

The growing economic *rapprochement* between Bonn and Peking received an added emphasis with the state visit to China of Chancellor Helmut Schmidt in November 1975. He was accorded an extraordinarily long meeting with ailing Chairman Mao Tse-tung of one hour and forty minutes, in which the two discussed, among other things, the social-Darwinist views of the relatively unknown German philosopher, Ernst Haeckle, and the military strategy of Karl von Clausewitz. But the meat and potatoes of future economic relations between West Germany and China were thoroughly explored in five hours of talks between Schmidt and Vice Premier Teng Hsiao-ping. Teng, leader of the pragmatists, had been up and down and up again in the ferocious behind-the-scenes political fighting in Peking, because he had long been demanding that China must be made industrially strong, even if this means diluting its Communist ideology.

The prospects of expanding Germany's exports to Red China are regarded as favorable as long as Teng and the pragmatists control economic planning. Schmidt came away with the solid impression that the Chinese looked on the Germans as the most successful of the postwar Europeans in handling their economic problems. After his long sessions with the Chinese officials, Schmidt met with German journalists at the Peking Embassy. In a somewhat wry vein, he commented: "I really do have the impression that these good people here regard me as sort of an oracle on the problems facing the world economy."*

Be that as it may, the chancellor's visit opened the way for early German–Chinese collaboration in the important spheres of coal research, steel and mining experiments, petroleum, natural-gas and offshore drilling technology, and the two-way exchange of German and Chinese students.

What is the basis for the confidence of the German industrialists that they are in a better position to obtain a lion's share of China's orders for capital goods and technology than other nations, notably Japan and the United States?

Geographically, Japan is the closest nation to China and is its number one trading partner. But at this stage of China's arrested industrial development, Japan's competitive situation is subject to change. This may happen because Japan does not have the broad range of mechanical engineering and heavy-duty equipment needed in any industrialization program; these are Germany's specialties. The Japanese have concentrated on steel production, shipbuilding, electronics (radios, TV sets, business machines, and so on), small cars, motorcycles, and other consumer goods.

The United States equals and exceeds Germany in the variety and range of its production of capital and consumer goods, but they are all designed for sophisticated industrial markets. In addition, the Americans do not have the background and experience or the current market research on China that the Germans can claim. Finally, the United States exports more to China in dollar volume than Germany, but 80 percent of this trade consists of agricultural products, principally grains and cotton.

Incidentally, the British possess a long history of trading with China and would be a touch competitor for Germany, but the constant labor strife on their home front has hobbled Britain's trade in the Far East in capital goods, as far as prices and delivery times are concerned.

If Red China embarks on a major industrialization program, it must do business with the country best able to provide goods and services that are competitive in terms of price, quality, and delivery standards. West Germany seems to be in the best position for this.* Another determining factor is that Germany has been in the front ranks concerning the quality and progress of its technological research and development. A 1975 survey by the Organization of Economic Cooperation and Development found that West Germany has maintained the highest overall rate of R&D expenditures for a twenty-year period of all the industrial nations, including the United States.

In company with the German business community, Schmidt is aware that the global export markets for German goods and services may change in the coming years. It may see a shift of industrial production to these new countries, attracted by the prospect of cheaper labor costs for the years ahead. However, in one area the West Germans are determined not to lose their competitive advantages: that is in the field of industrial technology and its related disciplines. For that is the export market of the future. In a July 1975 press interview, Schmidt called the attention of the journalists to an expected development:

On the horizon of the year 2,000 A.D., we can perceive an era in which national economies like our own, will largely be concerned with the export of patents, technologies and blue prints. But a national economy can support itself on that type of exports.*

In short, possession of natural resources may help, but the true national wealth lies in competitive skills and brain-power, in know-how and know-why. Germany's future is in the hands and in the heads of its educated elite and its aggressive and experienced industrial entrepreneurs.

Under the *Zweite Reich* of Kaiser Wilhelm II and the *Dritte Reich* of Adolf Hitler, the Germans sought for *Lebensraum* in colonies and the conquest of other lands. Under this new *Vierte Reich,* put together by eco-political and centrist-minded governments, postwar Germans have found a new economic *Lebensraum,* global in scale, to absorb their exports and their energies. As *Fortune* magazine commented on the wonderful, business-producing aspects of Germany's foreign-aid program of industrial development of the Third World countries: ". . . the Germans are cashing in on the prestige that comes from having rebuilt Germany from the rubble and ashes of 1945."

Epilogue

When James Callaghan, the British prime minister, visited Bonn in the summer of 1976, Chancellor Helmut Schmidt suggested to him that whenever the heads of government met together in a summit conference of the European Economic Community their respective delegations should be expanded to include a few industrialists, bankers, and labor leaders. This proposal came as something of a shock to the British diplomats who have always considered that the conduct of Britain's foreign affairs should remain in the hands of the educated elite and "off limits" to those "in trade." However Schmidt hastened to explain that in West Germany, Ruhr industrialists, Frankfurt financiers, and Düsseldorf's trade-union bosses have a share in the nation's decision-making processes. Thus, they could make a helpful contribution to improving the official contacts between EEC member states.

The idea that representatives of management and labor can play a quasi-official role in the field of international relations is thoroughly in keeping with the character and outlook of the chancellor of the *Bundesrepublik*. Schmidt is the first of the new postwar breed of eco-political statesmen; men who have grasped the reality of postwar Europe: that economic power is the decisive factor in international relations. Hence, to the West German chancellor, an export-minded banker, industrialist, or trade unionist can be equated with the professional diplomat in serving the nation's self-interests on the global scene.

Schmidt shed the Socialist coloration of his university days to become a right-wing Social Democrat. He is a pragmatic politician who has seen the force and influence of economic ideas and developments in postwar Germany push party politics to the sidelines. He has a touch of the reformer in his makeup; indeed, he has been described as a "modern Luther." In this context, it can be said that his "Reformation" is the acceptance of the new doctrine of eco-politics: that the true measure of a nation's power and influence is to be found in its industrial and technological capacities, in its monetary reserves, and, finally, in its freedom to trade on the world markets. It is true that Schmidt does not use the expression "eco-politics" in connection with his policies and actions; but he is the epitome of the eco-political statesmen. His words and his priorities clearly outline where he stands and what he considers important. For example, while addressing the European council of the EEC in April 1976, a body that he has constantly criticized for its lack of fiscal reality, he stated: "I am not a Marxist, but I understand one thing; you can't get your politics in order, if your economics are not in order."

Again, listing his priorities when speaking to the international energy conference in Washington in February 1974, he said: "I have always experienced myself and have emphasized the need to find joint solutions to the problems of security, trade, money and energy . . . these four complex problems are interrelated and the well-being of all of us depends on finding constructive and realistic answers to them."

Schmidt thinks, talks, and acts in eco-political terms. His view of international relations was spelled out in the prestigious U.S. journal *Foreign Affairs,* in its April 1974 issue:

The world economy has entered upon a phase of extraordinary instability and its future course is absolutely uncertain. What we are witnessing today in the field of international economic relations—in the monetary field and now in the field of oil and raw material prices—is virtually the same as what is going on between trade unions and the employers' associations on a national level. It is the struggle for the distribution and use of the national product and now internationally, *a struggle for the world product*. [Italics added.]

Schmidt's article is noteworthy because he identifies the "struggle for the world product"—oil, the most important source of fuel and energy—as the prime cause for the "extraordinary instability" and tension that grips the non-Communist world today, rather than the atomic bomb competition between the superpowers and their allies. The West German chancellor is fully convinced that economic forces dictate the political climate, with its alternating periods of stormy and fair weather, not vice versa. That has been his experience in the postwar years, and it has been unique. By comparison with the postwar heads of governments of other industrial nations, Schmidt and his predecessors in the chancellory have encountered few, if any, major and unmanageable political problems or issues, at home or internationally. The postwar West German scene has been extremely placid by contrast to postwar Britain, with its domestic labor–management troubles and the disintegration of its empire; to the United States and the bitter controversy over the Vietnam War; to France, with its covert civil strife caused by the loss of Indochina and Algeria; and to Italy, with the constant threat of Communist takeover. In West Germany there has been the normal politicking at election time, but it has not erupted into conflicts that might sharply divide the voters into angry and militant factions. The majority and minority parties, which have studiously followed a middle-of-the-road course, have largely eliminated the vinegar and vitriol from West German election-time politics.*

For example, in the 1976 national election the slogans of the political parties were complacent, unprovocative, and hardly nerve-tingling in their rhetoric. The SPD reminded the voters to reelect Schmidt with the slogan: "The better man must stay on as Chancellor." The junior coalition partner, the FDP, had a slogan that was ambiguous at best: "Vote for service." The CDU–CSU opposition slogan was a hackneyed attempt to arouse the voters with: "Freedom or Socialism."

The CDU–CSU bloc was further handicapped by an internal struggle for the leadership of the conservative opposition, which has locked the CDU into an abrasive relationship with its CSU wing, which dominates Bavaria. The glaring lack of clear lines of demarcation in current West German politics was again demonstrated when the local FDP leadership partially broke away from the SPD alliance, to form a coalition government with the CDU in the state of Lower Saxony. Such acts of opportunism denigrate political slogans and platforms in the eyes of the German voters.

Despite its closeness—the Schmidt government was reelected with a slim ten-vote majority in the *Bundestag*—the last federal election in 1976 was a lackadaisical affair. In fact, there were no demonstrations during the election campaign that could match in intensity and numbers the mass protest marches and meetings against the construction of two large nuclear power plants, one at Brokdorf near Hamburg and the other at Whyl near Freiburg in the Rhineland. In fact, tens of thousands of German civilians were so belligerent in their rioting and protest activities that police had to use tear gas and water cannons to break up the demonstrations, which were spaced over a six-month period. The controversy, which still rages, involves the question of the physical safety of the people living in the areas where the atomic power plants are to be operating. It is not a political issue, and this mass protest movement caught all the politicians by surprise, unprepared to cope with it. But it did involve the personal security of thousands of Germans and, as such, this deep-seated concern generated more heat and public reaction than any political issue of recent times. Whatever the merits of the case, for or against atomic power plants, the mass protests and agitation brought West Germany's nuclear-energy program to a standstill. So it has been left to the courts to decide on the relative safety of a neighborhood nuclear power plant.

Schmidt's policies and outlook are shaped by the priorities of the majority of his countrymen, whose values are orthodox: full employment, a balanced budget, conserving fuel and energy, and money in the bank. These they consider to provide the only true freedom and liberty for the average man. While he is highly respected, Schmidt is not a man who enjoys the affection or popularity of the masses, as does Willy Brandt, now chairman of the SPD, or even the late Konrad Adenauer, the revered and even idolized father figure of the postwar era. Schmidt has none of the gregarious or back-slapping qualities of the average politician. He is remote and somewhat austere, with few close friends and intimates. But he is not hesitant to take action when he feels it is imperative. He knows his own mind and goes after what he wants.

Schmidt first attracted serious attention in West German political circles in 1962 when he took command of the relief work in the catastrophic springtime floods caused by the North Sea's record high tides and stormy weather, all of which caused the Elbe River to inundate Hamburg. Schmidt was a city senator responsible for police supervision. He took over the job of coordinating all flood-relief work from Hamburg's Lord Mayor Paul Nevermann, informing the latter: "Herr Oberburgermeister, you are in the way."*

During the war Schmidt served in the air force as a lieutenant, and ended it as a prisoner of the British. On being released he returned to Hamburg to get his degree in economics at the university. One of his teachers was Professor Schiller, the defender of the free-market economy during the postwar monetary crises. In 1969, Schmidt was named to his first big job as defense minister in the new Brandt government. As soon as he took office, Schmidt began to overhaul and tighten up the whole administration and procurement for the army, naval, and air forces. He wanted to introduce the latest administrative techniques of big business, so he drafted Ernst Wolf Mommsen, a leading Ruhr steel producer, to take on this task as a "dollar-a-year man." The U.S. embassy, which has always had close personal contacts with the ministry, has privately testified that Schmidt was "the best defense minister" in the postwar period. Schmidt next took over the finance ministry and here again he was positive and progressive. After he had been in this post for some weeks, the *Economist,* on February 23, 1974, gave this evaluation of his vigorous administration:

Helmut Schmidt could be the re-maker of Europe. In the ten weeks since early December, the Finance Minister of West Germany has taken his adversaries and partners in Europe by the scruff of the neck . . . has wrought a one-man revolution in Europe. . . . (1) He has put Germany and all its common market partners, bar France, eight-square behind the United States in an Atlantic approach to the problems raised by more expensive oil. (2) He has led the way—again with the Americans—in demanding a rollback of Middle Eastern oil prices and in questioning the usefulness of the oil-consuming nations in selling cowrie shells to the oil producers in return for their oil. (3) He has, in the process of all this, and for almost the first time in the history of the EEC, told France the brutal truth: that the rest of Europe will not feel bound to do foolish things in the name of solidarity, with a partner who says foolish things are wise.

In another issue, the *Economist* further described the German chancellor: "Herr Schmidt has much about him of a modern Bismarck."

Since 1969 when the Social Democrats came to power, the party leadership has been shouldering a burden which they cannot get rid of. It has been the emergence of a militant radical group of young Socialists better known as "Jusos" (from *Jungsozialisten*), a sort of auxiliary youth movement of the SPD for party members under the age of thirty-five. There is some question as to the numerical strength of the hard-core radicals within the movement, but the Jusos total membership is about 250,000.

The leaders of the Jusos are avowed Marxists—but not Communists—and they advocate the traditional Socialist creed of nationalization of heavy industry, big banks, and insurance companies. This militant group was a source of embarrassment to Willy Brandt when he was chancellor, and it now continues to be a burden for Helmut Schmidt, whose view of them is little short of contempt. In a face-to-face confrontation in Hamburg recently, he told them: "Your preaching is about to empty the church."

But angry rejoinders do not silence the Jusos because they hammer away at their central theme: the SPD traces its origins back to Marx and has identified itself in the past with Socialist theory and dogma; today it should return to the "faith of its father."

However, at the 1959 Bad Godesberg party congress, the SPD made a 180-degree turn away from Marxist ideology, in a fresh bid to attract the votes of the middle classes, and thereby to win a national election. Since that *crise d'identité,* the SPD leaders have repudiated the Jusos' demands by outvoting them in successive party congresses. But the radical character of this group has served to frighten the middle classes by raising the specter —however dim and remote it may be—of a Marxist-minded government at some future date. In the 1972 election in the two SPD strongholds of Frankfurt and Munich, there was a sizable shift of voters to the CDU–CSU, because their respective SPD city governments had been dominated by radical Jusos. The radical wing has been gaining in strength and Wolfgang Roth, a prominent Juso, has been predicting: "We are the SPD of the 1980s."

However, the real importance of the Jusos seems to lie in the fact that they are part of a growing chorus of voices questioning the continuing emphasis on economic growth and prosperity being achieved at the expense of neglecting political, social, and cultural values. For some time now, since the late 1960s, there has been concern about the increasing materialistic outlook of German society. The weekly *Simplicissimus* of Munich, which has satirized the foibles of the Germans since the Kaiser's day, has described the mass pursuit of the deutschemark as the "postwar worship of the Golden

Calf." In recent months the Germans have openly began to wonder about the *Wirtschaftswunder*: is it worth the price to be paid? This self-criticism was highlighted by a best-selling book, *Germany's Future* by the veteran philosopher Karl Jaspers. Professor Jaspers, who has taken on the role as a sort of gadfly to stimulate the consciences of his compatriots, sees this new postwar Germany as being "morally adrift" in prosperity, as it was in the chaotic and poverty-stricken days of the 1931 Great Depression. The veteran philosopher and sociologist has diagnosed the Germans as suffering from an "immoderate desire for security." This causes them to engage in a ceaseless search for the unattainable perfect economic and political systems. But this is chasing into the desert after a mirage, Professor Jaspers argues:

We still have neither the roots, nor an ideal in politics; no sense of where we came from and no sense of where we are going. . . . Neither in the operations of our business, nor in our passing, swiftly-forgotten excitements, is there a faith or an ethos.

It is a harsh verdict, but it is echoed by Prof. Ralf Dahrendorf, one of the respected postwar intellects—formerly state secretary of the West German Foreign Ministry in the Brandt government, now director of the London School of Economics. He had this to say in *The New York Times* (October 20, 1977) concerning the spiritual and political emptiness of contemporary German life:

The great slogans of Willy Brandt's government (in which I, as did some of its members, believed as much as most Germans)—"internal reforms," "daring more democracy"—remained slogans, paper promises and never became serious social objectives. There is not only no major position to agree with; there is not even one to disagree with—unless one wants to disagree with everything, with "the system," which is, of course, exactly the sentiments which the terrorists are trying to exploit.

There are many thoughtful Germans who are troubled by a lack of signposts pointing to some recognizable and acceptable goal for themselves and for the *Bundesrepublik*. In their own lives, they are economically secure, with their medical care and old-age pensions. But what is the future role of the *Bundesrepublik?*

Professor Dahrendorf captures this mood in his recent article:

Yes, Germany has become democratic. Yes, German society has become liberal. Yes, the free market economy has served the people well. But what is it all about? That may not be a very sensible question: one may wonder whether societies are about anything; yet the question is asked quite often and answered rarely. . . . Germany is neither a Switzerland that is content with the safe prosperity of its citizens, nor a United States that is responsible for the security and prospects of many others—but what is it? What is the *raison d'état* of the Federal Republic of Germany?

Other questions come to mind: did the economic recovery of West Germany come too fast? Did it come too easily? Those of Schmidt's or Dahrendorf's generation have a good grip on reality. They have experienced war, defeat, and the hunger, poverty, and misery of the immediate postwar years. They have a proper perspective, which explains in part why the economic recovery of West Germany was such an unparalleled accomplishment.

But the succeeding generations who came to adulthood in the mid-1950s and later are quite separated from the grim past. They had no part of it, except as young children, and are quite unaffected by it. They have only known the Germany of the *Wirtschaftswunder*. But in a sense, these succeeding generations are the disinherited. They share no common patrimony with their elders; they did not have to make the laborious climb out of the abyss of defeat. A gap of shared experience separates them from their parents and from the traditions and history of the Germanies of the past. They have no point of reference, they lack a compass to guide them across the uncharted seas into the future. So it is that *Angst*—fear—prevails throughout the land when the present and the future are "viewed through the glass darkly." This mood is compounded of uncertainty, doubts about the economic character of the *Bundesrepublik,* and fears that the West Germans are too far out in front of their European partners and allies in terms of economic resources and power, and thereby being shunned and isolated. Schmidt admits to being baffled by this pervasive attitude, which he describes as a "psychological illness" for which no cure seems available.

Finally, the big questions come to the fore: do the West Germans realize what has happened to them and to their truncated country? Do they understand the nature and mechanics of this eco-political state which they have created for themselves? What about its implications for the lives of their children? For example, does Helmut Schmidt, the leading eco-politician on the European scene, comprehend the character and instincts of this postwar nation which is both a political dwarf mentally and an economic giant physically? At this writing, there can only be intelligent speculation about Germany's future development; no hard and definitive answers can yet be offered.

Karl von Clausewitz (1780–1831), one of the profound theorists of war, made a major contribution to modern Germany's rise to world-power status. His classical study, *Vom Kriege (On War)*, provided a philosophic rationale for aggressive warfare, which greatly influenced the thinking and strategy of Germany's military leaders from the time of Bismarck's empire-building campaigns until Hitler's *blitzkrieg* conquest of Europe skidded to a halt in the snowdrifts outside Moscow almost a century later. Von Clausewitz formulated the master thesis that war itself is an integral part in the life and growth of a state.

In times of peace and equilibrium, the state attempts to serve its national self-interests by exploiting its power and influence in its political relations with other nations. However, when these avenues of expansion and aggrandizement are blocked or strewn with obstacles, then the state must resort to military force to accomplish its objectives. From this line of reasoning, Karl von Clausewitz drew his famous conclusion that "war is the continuation of [foreign] policy by other means."

In the decades that followed, his military philosophy provided Bismarck, Kaiser Wilhelm II, and Adolf Hitler—and their respective general staffs—with a geo-political legitimacy for their aggressive war making, which in turn encompassed the rise and fall of both the Second and Third Reichs.

In seeking the key to West Germany's amazing and unprecedented comeback out of the ashes of World War II to a position of global power and influence—without a threat being voiced or a shot fired—the question comes to mind: what doctrine or philosophy motivates and explains this new postwar Germany?

Schmidt provided the answer in words that have a somewhat Clausewitzian ring, when he outlined to a Swiss journalist the basic reason for this "success story": "For some years now our economic policy has simultaneously been our foreign policy."

In other words, eco-politics has replaced geo-politics. In short, West Germany's civilian-directed economic strength and assets are its ultimate source of power and influence on the international scene. Economic muscle has replaced armies and weapons as the final arbiter of the destiny of this youthful and affluent Federal Republic of Germany.

This is a triumph, not of the traditional school of geo-politics as practiced by Bismarck, Kaiser Wilhelm, and the Nazi *Führer,* but of the evolutionary school of eco-politics fathered by Dr. Adenauer and Professor Erhard and further refined by Helmut Schmidt and his de-Marxized Social Democrats in this last decade.

Is it not a strange and unforeseen end to a phase in the life of a country, which began with a master plan to erase all vestiges of the "thousand-year-Reich" and to reduce defeated Germany to the status and level of a Balkan state; only to conclude with the Fourth and Richest Reich, firmly and securely established as Europe's dominant power, now leading the way into the dawning era of international eco-politics? As the philosopher and historian have discovered, nothing lasts longer than a makeshift arrangement.

Notes

Prologue "WIRTSCHAFT ÜBER ALLES!"

Page 4 *West Germany's gold and dollar reserves, which have been steadily increasing every year since it became an independent state, topped the $50-billion mark in the late 1970s, far outstripping the monetary reserves of every other industrial nation, including the United States.*

Page 5 ". . . the first modern *eco-political* state . . ." *Ever since the Arab oil embargo of 1973 there is a growing awareness that economic power—as expressed in terms of industrial capacity; modern technology; and possession of vital raw materials such as oil, coal, feed grains and so on—can become a more effective instrument to further a nation's self-interests than an arsenal of modern weaponry. U.S. Senator Abraham Ribicoff caught the spirit of the time when he spoke to a seminar of international economists in Budapest in June 1971. He said: "I am convinced that during the last quarter of this century,* eco-politics *will replace* geo-politics *as the prime mover in the affairs of nations."*

Page 9 "This capitalist cell . . ." *Professor Röpke was later employed as an economic consultant by the Bonn government and his advice from the wings helped to buttress Erhard's position as economics minister when his policies came under attack in the Bonn parliament (Bundestag). The University of Freiburg's wartime free-enterprise resistance group has survived in part, as the inspiration of a loose international association of economists known as the Mont Pelerin Society. The members meet at intervals on the heights of Mont Pelerin, above Lake Geneva in Switzerland. The father figure of the group is Prof. Friedrich A. Hayek, Nobel prize-winning economist of Vienna. America has been represented in the past by Milton Friedman, also a Nobel Prize winner; Paul Samuelson; and the late W. H. Grimes, editor of the* Wall Street Journal.

Page 9 ". . . close personal contact with Karl Goerdler . . ." Financial Times, *September 18, 1957.*

Page 10 "The rapid transformation . . ." G. P. GOOCH, Germany (*London: Ernest Benn Ltd., 1926*).

Page 12 "Germany's GNP was increasing . . ." W. O. HENDERSON, The Rise of German Industrial Power (*London: Temple Smith Ltd., 1975*).

Page 15 "The Prussian aristocracy . . ." *Prussia, under Frederick the Great, had become a major continental military power, despite being a country with very limited resources. After visiting Berlin in 1788, the Comte de Mirabeau noted in his journal: "Prussia is not a country that has an army but an army that has a country. War is the national industry of Prussia."* (La Prusse n'est pas un pays qui a une armée; c'est une armée qui a un pays. La guerre est l'industrie nationale de la Prusse.)

Page 15 "All vestiges of the . . ." *A few hours before the arrival of the Soviet advance forces in the closing days of the war in East Prussia, the aged Countess von Bismarck, daughter-in-law of the "Iron Chancellor" Otto von Bismarck, committed suicide at the family ancestral home at Varzin, rather than face a hostile existence under Communist rule.*

Page 16 ". . . most of the surviving Junker officers . . ." *"In Germany . . . before the war, the best brains from the best families went into the army general staff, or at least brought themselves up with what might be called the general staff mentality. Since 1945, the general staff hasn't been quite respectable and these people have swarmed into the top ranks of German business instead."* The Economist, *October 15, 1966.*

Page 18 ". . . guidelines for the Allied occupation. . . ." Handbook for Military

Government in Germany, *issued by Supreme Headquarters Allied Expeditionary Force, December 1944, signed by Lt. Gen. W. Bedell Smith, U.S. Army Chief of Staff.*

Page 20 "Ludwig Erhard was given a complete free hand . . ." TERENCE PRITTIE, Adenauer, a Study in Fortitude (Chicago: *Cowles Book Co., Inc., 1971*).

BOOK 1   THE ALLIED OCCUPATION

Chapter 1   THE DARKEST HOUR

Page 27 ". . . the Germans suffered such losses . . ." *It is impossible to get an accurate body count of the total casualties suffered by Nazi Germany in World War II. However reputable agencies such as the Hilfswerk of the Evangelical Churches (Lutheran), have made surveys which report that Germany suffered between 6 and 7 million killed in action or in bombing raids. Also about 1.5 million of the surviving war veterans were severely disabled. No accurate estimate of civilian disabled was obtainable. According to historians, the Thirty Years War of the seventeenth century reduced Germany's population from 20 million to 13.5 million, or 6.5 million casualties.*

Page 28 ". . . it was not what Adolf Hitler . . ." GOLO MANN, The History of Germany Since 1789 (*New York: Frederick A. Praeger, 1968*).

Page 30 ". . . it was their turn to pay back . . ." *With its soldiers scattered around the globe, the British government was trying to stitch back together some remnants of the empire and hence was reluctant to release the German prisoners at work in England. It was announced in the House of Lords that the government was seeking a "middle course between the requirements of the Geneva Convention and the demands of the British economy," and that speeding up the repatriation of German POWs would 'imperil the harvesting" of the 1946 crops.*

Page 30 "Out of this came the *Gehlenorganisation* . . ." *Gen. Reinhard Gehlen, who had been chief of* Fremde Heere Ost, *the German Army intelligence agency covering the Russian front in the last years of the war, was among those interned at Oberursel. Because of his wide-ranging knowledge and background concerning the Red Army, he became the nucleus around which the CIA built its master intelligence network which penetrated throughout the Soviet-controlled bloc. The* Gehlenorganisation *later was transformed into the official intelligence agency of the Bonn government and is still operating out of a heavily guarded compound in the Munich suburb of Pullach.*

Page 31 ". . . the good ones have been killed." ALBERT SPEER, Inside the Third Reich (*New York: Macmillan, 1970*).

Page 31 "Speer later listed . . ." ALBERT SPEER, Inside the Third Reich (*New York: Macmillan, 1970*).

Page 32 "[Albert Speer] read from these daily reports . . ." *In writing these lines, I think back to the summer of 1940, the high tide of Nazi conquest, when I was living in Berlin at the Hotel Adlon. My room faced onto a small courtyard, and from my windows I could see across the way into a large room which I learned later was Speer's studio. He was not a big name at the time, just identified as Hitler's favorite architect. This spacious studio seemed mainly occupied by large tables, on which rested a variety of white plaster-of-paris models of buildings—massive in style and concept. These were to be the architectural centerpieces of New Berlin, the capital of the "thousand-year Reich," that would be constructed when Hitler had won his wars and was master of Europe. Included in these architectural fantasies was a domed building far larger than St. Peters basilica in Rome, with a capacity for seating 150,000, a giant 400-foot high arch of triumph, and new palaces for Hitler and his paladin, Reichsmarshal Herman Goering, that had the aesthetic quality and body of a large railway station. All these artifacts of the "thousand-year Reich" went up in smoke along with the rest of Berlin in the large-scale Allied air raids of 1944–45.*

Page 32 "The urban . . . centers . . . were reduced . . ." *In 1951, when the repair and reconstruction of West Germany's cities were well underway, it was officially proposed in the city council that two square blocks of downtown Frankfurt, adjacent to the historic Paulskirche, be preserved just as they were left when World War II ended: two square blocks of completely gutted buildings that would serve as a macabre war memorial and a constant reminder to the surviving Germans what it cost to wage and lose a total war. However, the proposal was rejected, and today new shops and buildings have wiped out all evidence of Frankfurt's heavy wartime damage.*

Page 32 ". . . between 30 and 40 percent of all industrial plants . . ." *Reported by the Institute of World Economy and Lindlay Fraser.*

Page 34 "Quite naturally the officers were allotted . . ." *For several years I had wondered why an elegant mansion on Düsseldorf's swank Cecilienallee, next door to the U.S. Consulate, had not been requisitioned and was still the residence of its owner, Wilhelm Zangen, a leading Ruhr steel producer. Then in 1949 I was invited to dinner at the Zangens and discovered that the rear half of the mansion had been neatly sheared off by an Allied bomb, though this damage was not visible from the street. Zangen told me that he would not repair his house until the Allied troops had decamped and the threat of future requisitioning had been removed.*

Page 37 ". . . such items were not for sale . . ." *Exemplifying the scarcity of consumer goods, the* New York Herald Tribune *reported that in February 1947 the total sales of rationed clothing in Düsseldorf, a city of 430,000 people, were: 26 men's suits, 15 boy's suits, 33 adult coats, and 2 towels. Similar scarcities were reported elsewhere in West Germany.*

Page 39 ". . . Lucky Strikes as the universally accepted . . ." *In a detailed survey of the "German Economy" in October 1952, the* Economist *made this acute observation of the cigarette economy in action:*

There was a strange reluctance among both the Allied officials and the German Socialists to admit that before 1948 (when the Deutschemark replaced the Reichsmark), Germany had been on the Lucky Strike standard, with the American PX stores and the displaced persons camps as the central banks of issue.

For some unexplained reason, the U.S. Army PX always seemed to handle a greater volume of Lucky Strikes than other popular brand of cigarettes. It will be recalled that the home-side advertising slogan, "Lucky Strike green has gone to war" was no idle boast. "Lucky Strike green" stayed on to dominate the occupation black market.

Page 40 "For black market wages . . ." LEWIS H. BROWN, *chairman of the Johns-Manville Corp.,* A Report on Germany, *a survey of the postwar German economy in 1947 prepared at the request of U.S. Military Government Headquarters in Berlin.*

Page 42 "The past lost its meaning . . ." *From* A. J. RYDER, Twentieth-Century Germany: Bismarck to Brandt *(New York: Columbia University Press, 1973). Prof. A. J. Ryder, a veteran observer of the West German scene and a senior officer in the British military government, made this pertinent comment concerning the immediate postwar attitude of the German civilians: "Hitler's mystique did not, for most people, survive his defeat, even if he was more discredited by his failure than by his crimes. The majority of the Germans just wanted to forget the recent past and their part in it. The Allied fears of a resistance movement against them proved unfounded."*

Chapter 2   "WE COME AS CONQUERORS"

Page 46 "Never before had a nation at war . . ." *In fact, the U.S. is a pioneer in this specialized field of military government of defeated civilian populations. During the American Civil War, a significant landmark was the state paper, "Instruction for the Government of the Armies of the United States in the Field," prepared by Francis Lieber and issued by the War Department in 1863. The Lieber Code, as it became known, was, in general, an operations manual covering the lines of conduct of the U.S. forces in their relations vis-à-vis the populations in the occupied Confederate states. This manual aroused the interest of Gen. von Moltke of the German general staff. As a direct result, Gen. William Tecumseh Sherman, whose "march through Georgia" was military government with a vengeance, was invited to be the guest of the German Army during its campaign against the French forces in the war of 1870. General Sherman reportedly gave Bismarck and von Moltke his ideas and suggestions about operational aspects of controlling a defeated enemy population. After World War I, the American army participated in the Allied occupation of the Rhineland, virtually untouched by the war, and German governmental and administrative services functioned with only loose supervision from the Americans. Almost from the outset of World War II, the War Department began the recruitment and training of military government personnel at Camp Ritchie, Maryland, and other military posts.*

The German attitude toward the military rule of a defeated enemy country was in sharp contrast to the detailed and long-range advance planning of the Anglo-American forces. In his Official Diary, Joseph Goebbels, the Nazi propaganda minister, penned this admission: "We Germans are not very well fitted for administering occupied territory, as we lack experience. The English who have done nothing else in all their history, are superior to us in this respect." ROGER MANVELL AND HEINRICH FRAENKEL, Dr. Goebbels *(London: Heinemann, 1960).*

Chapter 3   THE DE-TEUTONIZATION OF DEUTSCHLAND

Page 56 ". . . at the end of the war, the demilitarization of Germany . . ." *Of the hundreds of German generals alive at the end of the war, I know of only one who personally "demilitarized" himself, and vowed never to get into uniform again under any circumstances. Maj. Gen. Fritz Bayerlein, Field Marshal Rommel's brilliant chief of staff during the African campaign, was an early "graduate" of the U.S. Army's Oberursel interrogation center, who returned to his native Baden to establish a small garage. While he was held at Oberursel, he asked to be permitted to learn a new trade and soon became a skilled mechanic in the local army motor pool. When I first encountered General Bayerlein, he was lying under a jeep, repairing its transmission. The sight of one of Germany's best military tacticians in grimy, oil-stained dungarees, working alongside and taking orders from an ex-Wehrmacht top sergeant—and seeming to like it too—is one I will not soon forget.*

Page 58 "We have lost Czechoslovakia . . ." *A telecom from General Clay in Berlin to the Pentagon, April 2, 1948.*

Page 59 ". . . the three Allied high commissioners . . ." *The three Allied high commissioners took over the supervisory responsibilities and control functions of the former military governors, whom they replaced when the new West German government took office in September 1949.*

Page 59 ". . . to bring security to Western Europe." *The* New York Times, *May 1950.*

Page 62 ". . . to join the European Defense Community." Welt der Arbeit *(Cologne: Federation of Trade Unions, August 1953).*

Page 62 ". . . nothing attracts enemy bombers . . ." TERENCE PRITTIE, Ad-enauer, a Study in Fortitude *(Chicago: Cowles Book Co., 1971).*

Page 63 "What then was Nation . . ." GOLO MANN, The History of Germany Since 1789 *(New York: Frederick A. Praeger, 1968).*

Page 64 "The Russians and their East German Communist allies . . ." *Report Number 34 of U.S. military government commented as follows on the denazification carried out in East Germany: ". . . a large scale program of removing Nazis from important positions was undertaken in the Soviet Zone. Particular emphasis was placed on the owners of businesses, public officials and persons in important private positions." The report further stated that the confiscation of the assets of businessmen and industrialists cut off the possibility of any financial support from these circles for any anti-Communist political movements in East Germany.*

Page 64 "As we Russians . . ." J. P. NETTL, The Eastern Zone and Soviet Policy in Germany, 1945–50 *(London: Oxford University Press, 1953).*

Page 66 "There were severe penalties . . ." *Article I of Ordinance 1 of the U.S. Military Government Code provided the death penalty for any German found guilty of the "willful destruction, removal, or interference with, or concealment of records, archives of any nature, public or private." Article II of the same ordinance authorized any penalty, except the death sentence, for any German found guilty of "knowingly making any false statement, orally or in writing . . . to any member of the Allied forces in a matter of official concern, or in a manner defrauding, or refusing to give information required by the military government."*

Page 67 "That was over 20 percent of the population in the U.S. zone . . ." *The population figures in the chaotic early days after the end of the war for each of the occupation zones of Germany could never be calculated precisely, due to the constant movements of millions of refugees and displaced persons from other countries. It was estimated that the 3.6 million persons indicted for denazification trials constituted between 20 percent and 27 percent of the total population of the U.S. zone.*

Page 67 "It was soon painfully evident that the American . . ." *In a Wiesbaden press conference in 1946, Howard Teitlebaum, U.S. director of denazification for the state of Hesse, stated: "If Bismarck were alive today, I would denazify him."*

Page 68 "Perhaps never before in world history . . ." GEN. LUCIUS D. CLAY, Decision in Germany (*New York: Doubleday & Co., 1950*).

Page 69 ". . . a convoluted bit of OMGUS reasoning . . ." *OMGUS was the acronym for Office of Military Government, United States Zone.*

Page 69 "This legislation continued the denazification program . . ." *Dr. Ludwig Hagenauer, who was appointed minister for liberation, reflected on the difficulties encountered in trying to carry out the denazification law in Bavaria. In a policy declaration two years after its enactment, he stated it was now his revised objective ". . . to liberate our tormented nation from the Law of Liberation as soon as possible."*

Page 69 "This attempt to put former Nazis into economic quarantine. . . ." *The American denazification program often encountered opposition from the military leaders, highlighted by the dismissal of Gen. George S. Patton from his postwar command as military governor of Bavaria. A brilliant strategist and tactician in combat, General Patton was too outspoken in political affairs. He publicly criticized the denazification and imprisonment of certain key bankers in Munich, whose services he considered necessary to keep the local economy functioning. He told a press conference: "I cannot operate these banks with the charwomen, who are about the only non-Nazis I can find."*
As a result of widespread criticism in the U.S. press as being "soft on the Nazis," Patton was relieved of his command by General Eisenhower.

Page 73 "Denazification was a substitute . . ." A. J. RYDER, Twentieth Century Germany: From Bismarck to Brandt (*New York: Columbia University Press, 1973*).

Page 73 "One pays a high price . . ." H. KOHN, The Mind of Germany (*New York: Scribners, 1960*).

Page 77 "But the fight didn't end there. . . ." *One of the strongest critics of JCS 1067 was former U.S. ambassador to Great Britain, Lewis Douglas, who later served as financial adviser to General Clay in Berlin. Douglas was quoted as saying: "This thing [JCS 1067] was assembled by idiots. It makes no sense to forbid the most skilled workers in Europe from producing as much as they can for a continent that is short of everything." This comment is found in the book,* Diplomat Among the Warriors *by the late Robert D. Murphy, who was chief political adviser to General Clay in Berlin.* ROBERT D. MURPHY, Diplomat Among the Warriors (*Greenwood, 1964*).

Page 78 "He recognized the need for controls . . ." GEN. LUCIUS D. CLAY, Decision in Germany (*New York: Doubleday & Co., Inc., 1950*).

Page 79 ". . . our own needs and specifications . . ." *The French government spent much effort and money after World War I to separate the industrial Ruhr from the rest of Germany by trying to mobilize public opinion to support an independent Rhineland; but it was to no avail. After World War II, though reduced in power and influence, the French tried to revive the smouldering embers of a separatism in Bavaria and southwest Germany, again with little success. The French Consulate in Munich, which has always ranked as one of the most important diplomatic posts in the French foreign service, has encouraged these irredentist developments.*

Page 80 "In order to represent the French Republic . . ." ALFRED GROSSER, Germany in Our Time (*New York: Praeger Publishers, 1971*).

Page 83 "By 1948 these Soviet corporations . . ." *In the following decade most of these SAG companies were deeded over to the East German government and continued to operate as nationalized enterprises. In return for this transfer of owner-*

ship, the East German government assigned a fixed and high percentage of their production for delivery to the Soviet Union until the reparations account had been settled.

Page 84 ". . . [the Russians] did not intend to permit . . ." GEN. LUCIUS D. CLAY, Decision in Germany (New York: Doubleday & Co., Inc., 1950).

Page 85 "The Soviet policy of Communist world domination . . ." The German Communist party (KPD) controlled by the Kremlin through the KPD headquarters in East Berlin continued to be a burr under the Bonn government's saddle until it was officially banned in August 1956 as an illegal and politically unqualified organization. This action was taken by the West German Constitutional Court, the nation's highest judicial body.

Page 86 ". . . the reorganization of Ruhr industry suffered from controversy . . ." GEN. LUCIUS D. CLAY, Decision in Germany (New York: Doubleday & Co., Inc., 1950).·

Page 86 ". . . the "merchants-of-death" . . ." In the early days of the occupation as a correspondent for the New York Herald Tribune, I saw at first hand the effect of the "merchants-of-death" syndrome on U.S. policies vis-à-vis the abortive attempts to reform and to reshape the whole structure and operation of the German economy.

Page 87 "Examples of the problems of deconcentration . . ." IBID.

Page 90 "The Americans are good at making things bigger . . ." ANTHONY SAMPSON, the London Observer, "Bayer Looks Beyond Germany," June 4, 1967.

Page 91 ". . . police power again reigned supreme . . ." The local German police forces continued to function in cities and towns, but under the direct supervision and control of the U.S. military police. The larger police stations were usually staffed with German and American policemen under the command of an American officer. The Germans and Americans made their own separate patrols. The American military police gradually phased out their operations.

Page 94 ". . . to enjoy normal social contacts . . ." Stars and Stripes, the official U.S. Army newspaper, September 25, 1945.

Page 95 "Instead of 'Jim Crowism' . . ." New York Herald Tribune, Paris edition.

BOOK II   THE FOURTH AND RICHEST REICH

Chapter 4   THE FOUNDING FATHER

Page 106 ". . . our German policy would develop." These statements were made in a personal conversation with the author.

Page 107 "Every time we go into . . ." Clay was conscious of his exposed position as the dominant voice in American decision-making in Germany. In 1947, on the eve of the Foreign Ministers Conference in Moscow, he assured the New York Times that he did not determine U.S. policy vis-à-vis Germany; that was the responsibility of the State Department. The newspaper considered this comment sufficiently important and newsworthy to give it front-page display.

Page 107 "I have kept in mind the kind of reconstruction . . ." In his second inaugural address of March 4, 1865, President Lincoln outlined his views regarding the treatment of the defeated Confederacy: "With malice towards none, with charity for all, with firmness in the right, as God gives us to see the right, let us strive to finish the work we are in; to bind up the nation's wounds; to care for him who shall have borne the battle, and for his widow and orphan; to do all which may achieve and cherish a just and lasting peace among ourselves and with all nations."

Page 108 ". . . [Clay] came to Germany . . ." From the end of the war in Europe until March 15, 1947, the senior American officer in Germany was four-star Gen. Joseph T. McNarney, U.S. military governor. As his deputy, Lieut. Gen. Clay was the director of the U.S. military government and the executor of policies as set *forth in JCS 1067. Clay succeeded McNarney as military governor and served in that capacity until he retired from the army in 1949.*

Page 110 "However, if agreement cannot be obtained . . ." GEN. LUCIUS D. CLAY, Decision in Germany (*New York: Doubleday & Co., Inc., 1950*).

Page 111 "At the time . . . these were bold words . . ." A. J. RYDER, Twentieth Century Germany: From Bismarck to Brandt (*New York: Columbia University Press, 1973*).

Page 111 ". . . hatred and distrust still set the tone . . ." *Indicative of the changing American mood, the Bavarian, the official U.S. military-government newspaper in Bavaria pointed out in September 1947 the futility of hating the Germans. It stated: ". . . such hatred would make the reconstruction impossible and the military government a farce. It would place the United States in the completely stupid position of trying to hatch the reluctant egg of democracy by hitting it every few minutes with a sledge hammer."*

Chapter 5 BIZONIA TO BONN

Page 115 ". . . Bizonia was an *ad hoc* . . ." *The late Col. "Tony" Biddle, of the Philadelphia Biddles, who was in charge of the Allied liaison missions attached to U.S. Headquarters in Frankfurt, pinned a label on the experts responsible for the creation of Bizonia. Paying tribute to their talents for making political bricks without straw, Tony Biddle described them as "ad hoc-sters."*

Page 119 "When the institutions of the Federal German Republic were . . ." ALFRED GROSSER, Germany in Our Time (*New York: Praeger Publishers, 1971*).

Page 120 "Few colleagues . . . dared to question . . ." *Nobody ever doubted the courage of Schumacher or his incorruptibility and sincerity to the Socialist cause. Schumacher's words were long remembered for their sting, such as the following reply to an attack on the Socialists by Nazi propaganda chief Joseph Goebbels in a May 1932 session of the old Reichstag. "The whole Nazi movement is only a lasting appeal to the schweinhund (scum) in mankind. . . . For the first time in Germany's political history, somebody has succeeded in completely and absolutely mobilizing German stupidity."*

After World War II, Schumacher repulsed all Communist attempts to join forces with the Socialists. Otto Grotewohl, a former prewar Socialist deputy in the Reichstag, who had become a Communist stooge in the East German government, argued with Schumacher for a merger of their respective parties on the ground that the Communists and Socialists were ideological brothers. Schumacher replied: "Yes, they are brothers, just like Cain and Abel."

Schumacher paid dearly for his anti-Nazi invective. In 1945 he emerged from Dachau a physical wreck, partially paralyzed, toothless, with damaged eyesight, and still carrying seventeen pieces of World War I shrapnel in his emaciated body.

Page 123 ". . . make the SPD a bulwark against communism. . . ." TERENCE PRITTIE, Adenauer, a Study in Fortitude (*Chicago: Cowles Book Co., 1971*).

Chapter 6 OPERATION BIRD DOG

Page 128 "A British MP described the Allied currency reform . . ." AIDAN CRAWLEY MP, The Rise of Western Germany, 1945–52 (*London: Collins, 1973*).

Page 130 *Messrs. Joseph Dodge, the Detroit banker, and Treasury economists Dr. Raymond M. Goldsmith and Dr. Gerhardt Colm have earned their niches in the pantheon of international financiers for their successful introduction of the new deutschemark, which in a few years was to become one of the "hardest" currencies on the world exchange.*

Page 132 ". . . [currency reform] transformed the German scene . . ." HENRY WALLICH, The Mainsprings of German Revival (*New Haven: Yale University Press, 1955*).

Page 133 "*Währungsreform* was the first phase . . ." *There were many ob-*

servers of the postwar German scene who saw more good luck and providence than planning and decision-making in the economic revival of West Germany. The Economist, *which was friendly but skeptical of the emerging West German state, ascribed its progress to the fact that ". . . things have gone most right in Germany, although they came about largely by accidents, which were intelligently followed through."*

Chapter 7   THE PROFESSOR'S GREAT GAMBLE

Page 140 "Most notably, the new objective . . ."   ANDREW SHONFIELD, Modern Capitalism (*London: Oxford University Press, 1961*).

Page 140 "A regular job acquired a new dimension . . ."   *Prices were high in relation to wages after currency reform, but in terms of the deutschemark versus the worthless reichsmark, the prices declined substantially. For example, semiskilled workers had a take-home pay of about 250 DMs per month. The following comparative list of prices, in the weeks after currency reform showed what it meant to the standard of living in the period July to August 1948:*

	PREWAR CURRENCY REFORM IN REICHSMARKS	POSTCURRENCY REFORM IN DEUTSCHEMARKS
1 package U.S. cigarettes	250	8
1 kilo of bread	12	9
1 egg	15	1
1 pound of butter	250	6
1 bottle of wine	80	4
1 liter of gasoline	11	0.80
1 pair of leather shoes	2000	40

Page 141 ". . . Erhard reduced the tariffs . . ."   *In the period of 1948–57 Erhard put through four major tariff reductions, as well as a reduction of quotas on imports. The idea was to make available to the workers a variety of attractive foreign goods, which they could not obtain from domestic manufacturers. This was incentive to increase their productivity and, thereby, their personal incomes. It also kept prices down by providing fresh competition to German manufacturers.*

Page 143 "Tax incentives and 'orderly financial housekeeping' . . ."   *The* Wall Street Journal, *on December 10, 1953, pointed to the singular character of Erhard's policies, in comparison with those of west European nations. The newspaper commented that West Germany's comeback was made possible by ". . . ignoring the prescriptions of the 'new economics' and by following some very old and quaintly orthodox economic principles. . . . Instead of trying to manage its inflation, it stopped inflation—the country was given a hard currency, even though at first this hardness hurt. It eliminated wage and price controls. It progressively returned more and more industry to private management and relaxed its foreign trade and exchange controls. The government got a tight grasp on its budget. . . . It's all rather baffling to the prophets of managed economy. But at least the West Germans don't find it a matter of embarrassment."*

Page 143 ". . . in outward appearance . . ."   HENRY WALLICH, The Main springs of German Revival (*New Haven: Yale University Press, 1955*).

Page 145 ". . . housing construction began to climb . . ."   *By the end of 1962 the West Germans had constructed 6.5 million new single-family housing units.*

Page 147 ". . . were sold to foreigners. . . ."   Financial Times, *November 12, 1956.*

Page 149 ". . . the full-time use of a car . . ."   *In the mid-1950s, the Bonn transportation ministry issued a report on the utilization of passenger cars in West Germany. It found that approximately 95 percent of the licensed vehicles, excluding*

American military and foreign-owned cars, were the property of business firms—not individuals. Of this total, the ministry also reported that over 50 percent were chauffeur-driven and assigned to business executives for their official and private use.

Chapter 8 ADENAUER, THE ABSENTEE LANDLORD

Page 152 "Despite his long and close-working relationship . . ." *In May 1949 the Allied military-government rule of defeated Germany officially ended; the working relation between the Allied armies and the Germans was regularized in an "Occupation Statute." Generals Clay and König, the U.S. and French military governors, retired and were succeeded by John J. McCloy and André François-Poncet. Gen. Sir Brian Robertson, the British military governor, changed his title to that of high commissioner. The three Allied powers, however, reserved for their governments the right to intervene in Germany's internal affairs, or to take military action, in order to protect their legitimate national interests. This Occupation Statute became invalid on May 5, 1955 when the Federal Republic of Germany joined NATO and was recognized as fully and unconditionally sovereign in its internal affairs, except for any contractual commitments to NATO.*

Page 157 ". . . social reforms meant . . . a comprehensive, all-purpose . . ." Time *magazine described the West German social-security program as giving "maternity-to-eternity" coverage.*

Page 157 "Nobody ever votes against Santa Claus." *The quadrennially spaced boosts in social-security benefits was such an obvious ploy to win votes on the eve of national elections that the social-welfare program was described as the "people's porkbarrel" in the English language news letter published by the Merck, Finck private banking group of Munich and Düsseldorf.*

Page 159 "A feature of these . . ." TERENCE PRITTIE, Adenauer, a Study in Fortitude (*London: Chaucer Press, 1971*).

Chapter 9 DISCIPLINE PAYS DIVIDENDS

Page 162 ". . . especially the Americans . . ." *As the cold war increased in its intensity, the underlying ambivalent character of the U.S. policy toward the defeated Germans manifested itself. While still adhering to the four-Ds program, a number of top-ranking U.S. Army officers began to have serious reservations about the policy of punishment and reform of the Germans because of their collective Nazi past. There was a change in the moral and critical attitudes towards the Germans to a more pragmatic approach, in some instances to a policy line that was crass opportunism.*

For example, early in February 1949, Maj. Gen. Charles P. Gross, the newly appointed director of U.S. military government in Württemberg-Baden, outlined his views to his staff concerning future relations with the ex-enemy nationals. He stated: "The time has come when we must seek to invite the former Nazis to cooperate with us. . . . They are the only people left in Germany with the ability and the background to take responsibility for the operations of their own governmental and civilian affairs . . ."

General Gross further argued: ". . . ethnically the Germans are the only nation still capable of fighting in Europe. The French are a finished lot; they don't have what it takes in their genes. If it is ever necessary to arm an ethnic group, it will be the Germans."

A member of Gross' staff, who bitterly opposed this policy change, leaked the general's remarks to the U.S. press; they created a short-lived embarrassment. But in the following months, a reversal in U.S. policy and attitude toward the Germans was fully underway, if not officially acknowledged and publicized by the U.S. military government.

Page 162 "For the Germans alone . . ." THEODORE H. WHITE, Fire in the Ashes (*New York: William Sloane, 1953*).

Page 164 ". . . men in London and Paris called for the elimination . . ." *In the succeeding years the deutschemark has been pressured upward through four re-*

valuations, becoming, in passing, one of the most stable and valued of the world currencies, along with the Swiss franc. Despite widespread predictions in exporting circles that the rise in the exchange value of the deutschemark would adversely affect Germany's world trade, this has not happened. In October 1978 the mark reached a record high of 1.76 deutschemarks to $1.

Page 164 "Adenauer had taken the first step . . ." *So reported* Time *magazine in its January 4, 1954 cover story, which featured Konrad Adenauer as the "Man of the Year" for 1953.*

Page 164 ". . . Germany had piled up greater gold and dollar reserves . . ." *As of September 30, 1979, West Germany's foreign exchange and gold reserves stood at $52.7 billion, according to the International Monetary Fund. The gold and foreign exchange holdings of the United States totaled a mere $20 billion.*

Page 165 "Each . . . had seen his family's savings . . ." *Inflation ran wild in Germany after World War I, when the government's presses printed reichsmarks without any controls. In August 1922 for example, there were 252 billion reichsmarks in circulation. When inflation reached its peak in November 1923 the money supply in circulation was 497 quintillion reichsmarks; that is, the figure of 497 followed by 18 zeros. In other words, at that point, the mark was worth about 4 billionths of a dollar.*

Page 168 ". . . [Vocke was] regarded by many economists as one . . ." Financial Times *editorial comment, June 19, 1956.*

Page 168 ". . . stabilization of the new *rentenmark* . . ." *The* rentenmark, *which was introduced to replace the utterly worthless and inflated reichsmark in 1923, was carefully controlled and issued in limited amounts. It was based on land values, real estate, industrial assets and property, etc., with an exchange rate of one* rentenmark *for one billion reichsmarks. The new mark was, in turn, replaced by a new hard reichsmark, based on gold, in August 1924. Then, in June 1948, once again hopelessly inflated and virtually worthless, the reichsmark was taken out of circulation, this time forever; the new deutschemark became the national currency.*

Page 169 ". . . West Germany's central bank had been directed . . ." *Dr. Karl Klasen, who was Dr. Blessing's successor as president of the Bundesbank, came out of the* Vorstand, *the management board of the Deutsche Bank, Germany's biggest and most powerful banking house. Surprisingly, he was a member of the Social Democratic party, and considered himself a right-wing Socialist who has never displayed any Marxist tendencies. He accepted his appointment to the Bundesbank only after demanding and getting the endorsement of both the CDU and the SDP.*

Page 170 ". . . the appeal of this myth . . ." WILHELM RÖPKE, The Freeman *magazine, August 24, 1953.*

Page 171 "The outstanding aspect of the German system . . ." HENRY WALLICH, Mainsprings of German Revival (*New Haven: Yale University Press, 1955*).

Page 173 ". . . To the economist . . ." Progress, *the magazine of the Unilever Co., London; spring, 1954.*

Chapter 10   LABOR LEARNS FROM THE PAST

Page 176 ". . . the greatest production . . ." BARBARA W. TUCHMAN, The Proud Tower (*Macmillan: New York, 1966*).

Page 177 "Hence the British authorities gave full encouragement . . ." *General Clay took note of the close collaboration between the British and Boeckler and his trade-union colleagues. In his book,* Decision in Germany, *Clay commented somewhat wryly: "It was difficult for the U.S. military government to be as popular with the rank and file of the union members as the British military government, which represented the Labor government [in London]."*

However, the American Federation of Labor established an office in Brussels and sent Irving Brown, a tough union organizer, as its representative and liaison with the anti-Communist sectors of the European trade unions. Known as the "man with the little black bag," Brown spent over six years providing moral and financial support of the anti-Communist trade unions throughout Western Europe. He did not seem to wield much influence in West Germany, where the leadership of Hans Boeckler and

August Schmidt, his deputy, could mobilize more first-hand experience in fighting Communists than Brown and the AFL could muster. In light of what is now known of the covert operations of the CIA in Europe, there is reason to suspect that Brown's work was largely financed by the U.S. government.

Page 179 "The Korean War boom . . ." *In 1959 the West German economic recovery had produced a situation of full employment: the total number of jobless was under 2 percent and these were mainly disabled war veterans unfit for work. From 1960 unemployment remained below 1 percent, a state of affairs virtually unknown in other industrial countries. West Germany began the large-scale recruitment of foreign workers from Italy, Yugoslavia, Turkey, Spain, etc., which continued until the mid-1970s.*

Page 179 *Source of figures:* The Manchester Guardian.

Page 180 "As long as the owners kept reinvesting their earnings . . ." *Years later, when the economic recovery was an accomplished fact, some trade unionists would ruefully argue that they showed too much moderation in their wage demands. They had not realized how large was the pie that was then baking in the oven.*

Page 181 *"Mitbestimmungsrecht is my last . . ."* Hans Boeckler interview, New York Herald Tribune, *July 1, 1953.*

Page 181 "The strength of German labor . . ." HENRY WALLICH, Mainsprings of German Revival (*New Haven: Yale University Press, 1955*).

Page 186 ". . . became a member of the *Vorstand* . . ." *In a German corporation, the day-to-day administration of the firm is the responsibility of the* Vorstand, *which is comparable to the executive committee of a U.S. firm or its top management. Its members usually comprise the executives in charge of production, finance, and personnel. Above and senior to the* Vorstand *is the* Aufsichträt, *the board of supervisors, which is roughly comparable to an American board of directors. The plural of* Aufsichträt *is* Aufsichträte.

The title of Herr Direktor *is rather loosely invoked. It applies, not only to the members of the supervisory board, but also to the senior executives of the firm, such as* Finanzdirektor, Arbeitsdirektor, *etc. In fact, it is quite common for the waiter in a good restaurant to greet the individual guests as* Herr Direktor. *It makes them feel good, even if they don't merit the title.*

Page 186 ". . . one-third worker participation on the *Aufsichträt* . . ." *"Worker Participation,"* Economist Intelligence Unit, Ltd. (*London, 1975*).

Page 188 ". . . Dr. Hans Martin Schleyer . . ." *As the representative of German industry, Schleyer was kidnapped in 1977 by the West German Baader-Meinhof gang of terrorists. After months of fruitless intimidation by the kidnappers to force the Bonn government to release imprisoned terrorists, Schleyer was brutally murdered.*

Page 189 ". . . Bank für Gemeinwirtschaft . . ." *Please see Chapter 13, "The Seats of Power," for further details of this extraordinary trade-union financial institution.*

Chapter 11   DER WEG ZURÜCK (THE ROAD BACK)

Page 192 ". . . Creation of these projects would . . ." New York Herald Tribune, *interview with Schacht, Aug. 11, 1949.*

Page 192 "It was her concentration on capital goods industry . . ." HENRY C. WALLICH, Mainsprings of German Revival (*New Haven: Yale University Press, 1955*).

Page 195 ". . . Paulskirche vintage years." *The leaders of the 1848 revolution in Germany gathered in the Paulskirche, a church in the center of Frankfurt, which they transformed into a national assembly. The revolution petered out in 1849 and the forces of "law and order" gradually regained control of the challenged domains. The Paulskirche has been for the Germans the first bridgehead of democracy in modern history.*

Page 195 "This development encouraged the imports of new technology . . ." *By 1960 the DGB began to employ the labor-saving services of the electronic computer in its administrative work. The trade unionists welcomed modern technology as giving*

Germany a greater competitive edge for its goods and services on the world markets, thereby adding to the job security of their individual members.

Page 195 "Also banned were cartels . . ." *As military governor of the U.S. zone, General Clay suffered one of his few defeats at the hands of the Germans in this area of free enterprise. He had issued an order arbitrarily establishing* Gewerbefreiheit, *which invalidated all previous German laws restricting the right of any German to free entry into any trade, profession, or industry. This Clay decree struck at the entrenched and traditional German system of licensing and controlling the number of businesses or individuals which could operate in any trade, etc., stemming back to the medieval guild system. General Clay's decree was quietly but effectively ignored by the Germans and no attempt was made to enforce* Gewerbefreiheit *in the face of such widespread antipathy and opposition. The licensing system, which itself was sort of a cartel, eventually prevailed over the victor's* Diktat.

Page 196 ". . . German industry thought . . ." PROF. ANDREW SHONFIELD, Modern Capitalism (*London: Oxford University Press, 1961*).

Page 196 ". . . too much speculation." *After being defeated in the war of 1870, France had to pay victorious Germany an indemnity of 5 billion gold francs. The German financial system could not handle this massive transfusion of hard money, which in turn triggered a frenzy of industrial and commercial investments. The collapse came in 1873, producing the first economic recession of Germany's industrial revolution and hundreds of bankruptcies.*

Page 196 ". . . 'children of the financial storm' . . ." W. O. HENDERSON, The Rise of German Industrial Power, 1834–1914 (*London: Temple Smith Ltd., 1975*).

Page 198 "The expedient has been of great value . . ." G. P. GOOCH, Germany (*London: Ernest Benn Ltd., 1926*).

Page 198 "The attitude of the leaders . . ." W. O. HENDERSON, The Rise of German Industrial Power, 1834–1914 (*London: Temple Smith Ltd., 1975*).

Page 198 ". . . cartels are a fact in Germany's economic life . . ." New York Times, *March 17, 1954.*

Page 199 ". . . 'excessive concentrations of economic power' . . ." *This phrase was the official military government expression to describe cartel-like industrial combines and associations, whether or not such groups could be shown to be either "excessive" or "concentrations of power."*

Page 201 *Source of the figures:* Business Week, *July 25, 1977.*

Page 204 "(Flick) employed the legal services of H. Struve Hensel . . ." *At one point of my career in postwar public relations, I was sent by Flick to New York and Washington to ascertain what could be done to get him a visa to the U.S., because he was automatically barred entry as a convicted war criminal. In America I discovered that Flick had already engaged the services of several politically connected law firms in the two cities to perform the same job I was sent to do. But the icing on the cake was supplied by a senior vice president of the Chase Manhattan Bank, who informed me bluntly: "Tell your Mr. Flick that if he deposits five million dollars with us, I'll get him his visa in a matter of days."*

Flick, however, decided that he could make better use of his $5 million, and withdrew from his expensive quest for a visa to America. He never made it to the U.S. before he died, but he died a billionaire.

Chapter 12   THE WIRTSCHAFTWUNDERKINDER

Page 207 ". . . the war would be long and costly in men and munitions . . ." *In August 1940, after his blitzkrieg conquest of France and the Dunkirk retreat of the British army from the Continent, Hitler felt confident that the war was just about won. He ordered a major cutback in the production of munitions, which led to unexpected shortages at a later and crucial phase of the war on the Russian front. This weapons gap led to the wholesale restructuring of production and distribution and the creation of Speer's new armaments ministry.*

Page 211 ". . . to carry out his expansion plans for the shipyard." *In the spring of 1961, Schieker faced another shortage of skilled workers, as did all his com-*

petitors. Nor did he have the time or the facilities to provide on-the-job training of imported Turkish, Italian, or Greek workers in the fine arts of ship construction. So he traveled to the Clydebank in Scotland, the shipbuilding capital of Great Britain, which was then in an economic decline. To the surprise of virtually everyone—the British businessmen were amazed at his temerity, while the German shipbuilders were angry because they had not thought of the idea themselves—he recruited 500 experienced Scot welders, fitters, riveters, and boilermakers for work at his Schlieker-werft yard on a six-months basis. Prior to his imaginative coup, nobody had thought of the possibility that workers from Britain, one of the victorious powers, would even consider employment offered to them in defeated Germany.

Page 220 "The firm was producing . . ." *In 1977 the production of the original Volkswagen was phased out after 19 million cars had rolled off the assembly line. This record for the continuous production of a single car model surpassed the 15 million Model-Ts manufactured in Detroit by the late Henry Ford.*

Chapter 13　THE SEATS OF POWER

Page 221 "In 1964 the conservative Bonn government . . ." *From the* Bericht über das Ergebnis einer Untersuchung der Konzentration in der Wirtschaft, *Bundestags-Drucksache IV/2320, June 1964. (A report on the results of a survey of the degree of concentration in the economy, a Bundestag publication, IV/2320, June 1964)*

Page 222 "German businessmen right from the start . . ." ANDREW SCHONFIELD, Modern Capitalism *(London: Oxford University Press, 1965).*

Page 224 "While in his prime as . . ." *The late Fritz Vogel, publisher of the national business daily, the* Handelsblatt, *commented to me on the power and prestige enjoyed by the bankers in postwar Germany. He said: "In Germany the leading bankers are shown the deference normally given to bishops. However, as for Hermann Abs, he is a special case: he is der Papst (the Pope)."*

Page 225 "Although the initiative . . ." RONDO CAMERON, Banking in the Early Stages of Industrialization, *1967.*

Page 226 ". . . in his study of imperial Germany . . ." G. P. GOOCH, Germany *(London: Ernest Benn Ltd., 1926).*

Page 228 "Their functions and power far exceeded . . ." GEN. LUCIUS D. CLAY, Decision in Germany *(New York: Doubleday, 1950).*

Page 232 "The eager lenders found eager borrowers . . ." HENRY WALLICH, Mainsprings of German Revival *(New Haven: Yale University Press, 1955).*

Page 234 "Whether such reforms . . ." *The powerful and influential German commercial banks have successfully fended off all attempts to "reform" them in recent years. Finally yielding to criticisms in the* Bundestag *that the banks had become too powerful and protected, the Bonn government appointed a commission to study their dominant role in the German economy and to recommend any measures to curb abuses of their fiscal and financial operations. The commission revealed its finding in May 1979 and the comment of the* Economist *indicates that the banks again successfully defended their citadels of economic power: "After pondering the question of reform for nearly five years, the commission has decided to endorse West Germany's universal banking system, which allows the banks to do just about anything and everything, instead of having to confine themselves to certain specialist functions like making loans as, for example, their American counterparts do."*

Finally, the only reform which this commission recommended was a limitation on the individual holdings of banks in industrial firms to a maximum of 25 percent plus one share, which gives them the legal right under German law, to block any major decision by the individual Aufsichträt.

Chapter 14　COALITION POLITICS

Page 245 "Social security has a long history . . ." *In 1971 the city of Augsburg in Bavaria celebrated the 450th anniversary of the founding of the* Fuggerei, *which was probably the world's first, or at least the best remembered, social-housing project.*

In 1521, Jacob Fugger, the leading German banker of his day, established a settle-
ment of 116 small houses to accommodate the "industrious but poor citizens of Augs-
burg." The residents paid a token rent, including daily prayers for their benefactor
and his descendants. Today there are 148 housing units in the Fuggerei, *which con-*
tinues to be supported by lands and forests given by Fugger to finance this social-
housing development in perpetuity.

Page 247 ". . . the *Kurindustrie* has prospered mightily . . ." *The* New York
Times, *July 17, 1975.*

Chapter 15   EMERGENCE OF AN ECO-POLITICAL WORLD POWER

Page 252 "Because of the bullying tactics . . ." *In the intervening years*
Colonel Khaddafi has apparently learned that threats do not frighten Chancellor
Schmidt; the Libyan ruler lifted the restrictions he had imposed on the amount of oil
to be exported to West Germany. In June 1979, Schmidt received further personal
assurances from Colonel Khaddafi that Libya was prepared to increase its oil exports
to Germany over the present volume which covers about 18 percent of West Ger-
many's current consumption.

Page 257 "The name of Krupp was notorious . . ." *Gustav Krupp von Bohlen*
und Halbach, father of Alfried Krupp, had been the chief executive of the firm before
and during World War II. He was then indicted and was to be tried by the Interna-
tional Military Tribunal at Nuremberg with other Nazi leaders. However he was
medically and mentally unfit to stand trial. Thereupon the American and Russian
prosecutors proposed that Alfried Krupp take his father's place in the dock. At this
point, Chief Justice Lawrence, the British member of the tribunal, objected. He
caustically reminded his fellow judges and prosecutors in a public session: "This is
not a football game where another man can be substituted for an injured player."

However, this did not save Alfried Krupp from also being indicted and convicted
as a war criminal in a subsequent Nuremberg trial, together with fellow directors of
the Krupp firm.

Page 259 "The program would be given . . ." *I had originally proposed call-*
ing it "Krupp's Point IV" program. However, we changed this to "Krupp's Point IV½"
program at the intelligent suggestion of H. Struve Hensel, the noted American lawyer.
It added a more personal touch to this bit of political plagiarism.

Page 260 "While this sum was not large by comparison . . ." *The* Kreditanstalt
für Wiederaufbau *(The Bank for Reconstruction), which was established in 1949 to*
channel Marshall Plan funds throughout West Germany to revive the economy, be-
came the new foreign-aid bank. This government-owned institution decides on who
should get the loans and credit guarantees for foreign-aid projects. Its background
and experience in financing the repair and reconstruction of West Germany is now
put to comparable use on a global scale. West Germany's postwar approach and
conversion to the idea of providing foreign aid by applying Marshall Plan operating
procedures is indicative of the political and economic influence of Washington on
German deep thinking.

Page 261 "West Germany's foreign aid was different . . ." *There has been a*
certain parallelism between the German and French foreign-aid programs. After
World War II, France's colonial empire was broken up, as the various colonies in
Africa became liberated countries. Except for Guinea and later Algeria, these new
African nations entered into a special, almost familial, economic and political rela-
tionship with metropolitan France. In short, a Franco-African economic community
was created, giving the new nations preferential entry into the French market as well
as easy access to French financing, in return for special trading and other economic
privileges for the French.

Page 263 "Group tours of leading West German bankers . . ." *For example,*
to assemble a group of U.S. executive talent for a tour of the Third World coun-
tries, comparable to what the Germans put together, one would have to include
the chairmen or presidents of Bank of America, Citibank, Chase Manhattan Bank,
General Motors, Ford Motor Co., I.B.M., I.T.T., DuPont, U.S. Steel, Bethlehem
Steel, General Electric Co., International Harvester, Westinghouse, Dow Chemical,

*etc. etc. In short, the chief executives of the leading U.S. banks and industrial cor-
porations—no less.*

Page 263 "A second-generation policy line . . ."   *This second-generation foreign-
aid policy was spelled out in detail by Bonn's foreign affairs minister Hans-Dietrich
Genscher in a speech to the United Nations Assembly in New York in September
1975.*

Page 265 ". . . Weimar Germany laid . . ."   *The Americans, led by engineer
Hugh Cooper, who built the great Dneiperstroy dam, came later.*

Page 268 "I really do have the impression . . ."   *The predominantly eco-
political character of the Schmidt government in the eyes of the Chinese Communists
was no doubt reinforced by the fact that accompanying the chancellor on this official
visit were two prominent industrialists and two trade-union leaders. In a follow-up
visit to Peking, Foreign Minister Genscher also brought along a small delegation of
industrialists and labor leaders.*

Page 268 "West Germany seems to be in the best position for this."   *According
to a report in the* New York Times, *October 22, 1979, West Germany is now China's
largest trading partner in Western Europe, with exports having risen by 72 percent in
1978, and going up another 42 percent during the first seven months of 1979. West
Germany has concluded a series of contracts for the construction of large industrial
projects with China, including a massive new steel production complex to cost $14
billion, and a $4-billion coal-mining development program. However, work has not
yet started on these projects.*

Page 269 ". . . On the horizon . . ."   *The Economic Reports issued by the
German Information Office, New York, N.Y.*

Epilogue

Page 272 ". . . from West German election-time politics."   *It is symptomatic
of the centrist nature of postwar West Germany that the latest political party to
make an appearance aims its appeal to the middle-of-the-road voters who are disen-
chanted with both the conservative Christian Democrats and the right-wing Social
Democrats. The Citizens party, which made its debut in May 1979, set forth its
political guidelines as follows: "We are patriots but not nationalists. We support
liberalism but not license. We have a social conscience but we do not want socialism.
We may be Christians, but we don't like political Catholicism or Protestantism." The
political "center" is indeed getting crowded these days.*

Page 273 "Herr Oberburgermeister, you are in the way."   *The* New York Times,
October 4, 1976.

INDEX

NORTH SEA

NETHERLANDS

RHINE RIVER

Hamburg

BRITISH
ZONE

JOINT
AMERICAN
SOVIET-
BRITISH

Berlin

RUSSIAN
ZONE

THE RUHR

■ *Essen*

Leipzig

BELGIUM

■ *Cologne*

Bonn ●

LUX.

FRENCH
ZONE

● *Frankfurt*

FRANCE

AMERICAN
ZONE

FRENCH
ZONE

Munich

SWITZERLAND